Theory of Mind and Literature

Theory of Mind and Literature

EDITED BY

Paula Leverage, Howard Mancing,
Richard Schweickert, and Jennifer Marston William

Purdue University Press
West Lafayette, Indiana

Copyright 2011 by Purdue University. All rights reserved.

Printed in the United States of America.

Library of Congress Cataloging-in-Publication Data

Theory of mind and literature / edited by Paula Leverage ... [et al.].
p. cm.
Includes bibliographical references and index.
ISBN 978-1-55753-570-2
1. Literature--History and criticism--Theory, etc. 2. Philosophy of mind in literature. I. Leverage, Paula, 1970-
PN441.T45 2010
801'.92--dc22
2010009895

To our loving families.

Contents

// Acknowledgments //

As most books do, *Theory of Mind and Literature* has accumulated a significant number of debts in the course of its development, not least because it has been a collaborative enterprise on several levels since its inception. The book emerges from the exciting interdisciplinary exchanges that took place at a conference of the same name at Purdue University at the end of 2007. Our first debt of gratitude is to the seventy participants in the conference who met over the course of four days to explore intently the importance of Theory of Mind in reading and understanding literature. The conversations, both formal and informal, were exciting, original, and always productive. Many of the essays submitted for consideration in this volume were reworked in light of insights culled from the conference.

Neither the conference, nor this book would have been possible without the unstinting moral and financial support of Purdue University, especially the College of Liberal Arts, under the direction of former Dean John Contreni; the Department of Foreign Languages and Literatures, under the direction of former Head Paul Dixon; and the Department of Psychological Sciences, under the direction of former Head Howard Weiss. We would also like to thank the following programs and departments for additional generous support: Classics, Film Studies, Jewish Studies, the Department of English, Comparative Literature, and Medieval and Renaissance Studies. We are extremely grateful to Howard Weiss and Christopher Agnew (former and current Head of the Department of Psychological Sciences, respectively) for subsidizing the preparation of the index, and to Tom Berndt (interim Head of the Department of Foreign Languages and Literatures) for additional support.

For permission to reprint the essays by Mark Turner and Lisa Zunshine, we are grateful to Oxford University Press and the British Academy, to Ohio State University Press, and especially to Ilona Roth for her assistance in reprinting Mark Turner's essay. For careful reading and astute suggestions for revision, we are grateful to the reviewers of the individual essays and the book as a whole. Finally, we would like to thank Charles Watkinson, the Director of Purdue University Press, and the staff of Purdue University Press, especially Katherine Purple and Becki Corbin, for guiding this book patiently and expertly to publication.

Introduction

Theory of Mind (ToM) is what enables us to "put ourselves in another's shoes." It is mind reading, empathy, creative imagination of another's perspective: in short, it is simultaneously a highly sophisticated ability, and a very basic necessity for human communication. ToM is central to such commercial endeavors as market research and product development, but it is also just as important in maintaining human relations over a cup of coffee. Not surprisingly, it is a critical tool in reading and understanding literature, which abounds with characters, situations, and "other people's shoes." Furthermore, it is becoming increasingly apparent that reading literature also hones these critical mind reading skills (Oatley 2009; Mar, Djikic, Oatley 2008; Zunshine 2006).

In her popular book *Mindreading: An Investigation into How We Learn to Love and Lie* (1997), the primatologist-journalist Sanjida O'Connell defines ToM as:

> the mechanism we use to understand what is going on in other people's heads. How we react to one another socially is the most important aspect of our lives. Without an understanding of what people think, what they want and what they believe about the world, it is impossible to operate in any society. Theory of Mind is the name given to this understanding of others. It is the basic necessity of humanity and is understood the same way the world over. (2)

O'Connell's use of vocabulary here reflects terms we use frequently in everything we say and write: understand, think, want, believe. She suggests that these verbs have "become invisible" and that "We interpret people's actions using words that describe their mental states so often that we cease to think about what it is we are actually doing" (3). ToM is the core tenet of what is often called *folk psychology* (or belief-desire psychology): the default understanding that other people are (largely) autonomous agents, that they have mental states commonly called beliefs and desires, and that they are motivated by these mental states. When we rely on our folk psychology, we tend to understand, define, and describe people on the basis of their perceived (or understood) beliefs, desires, feelings, values, experiences, and intentions. It is because we understand people's actions in terms of these mental states that we explain to ourselves and to each other why people have done certain things, and predict what they might do in certain contexts.

When we read a work of literature, we treat characters as if they were real people, and we ascribe to them a ToM. We could not understand a novel or a poem if we did not do this:

> Without our ability to form a theory of mind, human culture would not be possible. Much of the world of literature, drama, and humor relies on the supreme ability of humans not only to create theories about each character's mind but also to imagine simultaneously how each of these imaginary minds might view the minds of other characters. The tragic nature of Shakespeare's *Romeo and Juliet*, for instance, comes from a series of misconceptions among the characters that only the audience is aware of. Romeo's suicide is the result of his thinking that Juliet has died, and the audience is aware that if Romeo knew what they knew, this suicide would not have to have happened. To an audience of monkeys, however, Romeo's actions would make no sense, because they wouldn't be able to distinguish between their own beliefs and his.

In this way William F. Allman lays out the basic premise that ToM is as essential for understanding a literary work as it is for understanding a verbal utterance or another human being's motives (68-69).

Psychologist and anthropologist Robin Dunbar attributes to the human ToM the "crucial ability to step back from ourselves and look at the rest of the world with an element of disinterest" (101). Dunbar describes three levels of ToM: 1) the ability to be aware of our own thoughts; 2) the ability to understand other people's feelings; and 3) the ability "to imagine how someone who does not actually exist might respond to particular situations" (101-2). Elaborating on this third level of ToM, Dunbar states its obvious implication: "we can begin to create literature, to write stories that go beyond a simple description of events as they occurred to delve more and more deeply into why the hero should behave in the way he does, into the feelings that drive him ever onwards in his quest" (102).

While psychologists and anthropologists have long recognized the importance of ToM to literature, it was not until very recently, with the publication of the first monograph on the subject, that literary scholars began to take seriously the implications of ToM. Lisa Zunshine's seminal *Why We Read Fiction: Theory of Mind and the Novel* (2006) argues forcefully and eloquently that ToM "makes literature as we know it possible" (10). The title of this work announces the author's basic premise that ToM is not only an essential prerequisite of the reading experience, but also a motivation for reading. Zunshine argues that reading engages and improves mind reading abilities. This presents an argument for an evolutionary bias of the aesthetic experience, which situates literature squarely within the parameters of the essential human experience and not on the periphery as a distraction for people of leisure and means.

However, the history of scientific inquiry into ToM does not start with human beings, much less with the supremely human creation that is literature. The term itself was coined to describe the inferences and predictions made by chimpanzees. In their classic paper, "Does the chimpanzee have a theory of mind?" Premack and Woodruff say, "An individual has a theory of mind if he imputes mental states to himself and others. A system of inferences of this kind is properly viewed as a theory because such states are not directly observable, and the system can be used to make predictions about the behavior of others" (115). Their subject, Sarah, was a fourteen-year-old chimpanzee. Sarah was highly trained and famous for earlier work in which she learned to communicate with plastic shapes placed in order. When Sarah was shown videos of a human confronting a problem, her responses indicated she was imputing knowledge and intentions to the human. Premack and Woodruff concluded that the chimpanzee Sarah had a ToM. If questions about ToM were confined to animals, the topic would be of interest only to specialists. But before long, investigators began to ask whether a human necessarily has a ToM. Wimmer and Perner found that a child less than six years old typically seems to believe that if he or she knows something, then everyone else knows it too. Very young children seem not to have developed a ToM, and it also appears that ToM is underdeveloped in autistic people, who often have impaired socialization, imagination, and communication. Baron-Cohen, Leslie, and Frith found that most autistic children are unable to impute beliefs to others, perhaps a source of difficulties in predicting behavior of others.

Investigators suspect that something in the brain changes when ToM develops. In a recent review, Gallagher and Frith conclude that ToM ability is mediated by the anterior paracingulate cortex, with activity of the superior temporal sulcus and temporal poles in a supportive role. Details remain to be settled, but it is remarkable that we are close to discovering how brain activity differs depending on whether or not mental states must be imputed to others.

Complex stimuli are needed for learning how people apprehend the mental world of others. In experiments on ToM, stories are told, videos are shown, and people act out skits. These materials, richer than usual for cognitive scientists, are minimal compared with what literary theorists study, but on the verge. Cognitive scientists notice this, of course, but are reluctant to follow up on their own. As Premack and Woodruff say in their study of mental states, "there are other, more exotic ones [mental states], belonging to the novelist; we will not be concerned with them in this paper" (515).

As we have seen above, the "exotic" mental states Premack and Woodruff impute to the novelist are beginning to be investigated, along with the mental states of the readers who make sense of the novels. For example, Alan Palmer's *Fictional Minds* proposes that readers construct an embedded narrative for characters from references scattered throughout novels that then permit readers to enter their story world and minds.

Studies in ToM and literature belong to a relatively new area of investigation that brings an understanding of cognitive scientific studies and neuroscience to the reading and interpretation of literature. This "cognitive turn" in literary theory started during the 1980s and was influenced by work in cognitive linguistics (Lakoff and Johnson). In very recent years the field has expanded rapidly, as more scholars seek new perspectives beyond post-structuralist and social constructionist models of literature.

Theory of Mind and Literature is a timely contribution to the field in advancing current research on reading mental states in fictional characters. However, it is important to recognize that while mental states in novels may appear "exotic" in comparison to any mental states imputed to or by chimpanzees, there is, in fact, nothing even vaguely exotic about mind reading in literature. As Mark Turner has so convincingly argued in *The Literary Mind*, the cognitive mechanisms for understanding literature are precisely those we employ in quotidian tasks. Lakoff and Johnson's work on metaphors likewise demonstrated before Turner that human thought processes are largely metaphorical. Literature, as observed above, does not belong to the category of decorative vanities with which we populate our world, but is germane to our human condition. As such, perhaps it may be considered to be a form of distributed cognition, or an agent of what Alan Palmer calls "intermental thought."

It was in order to explore the implications of ToM for literature and literary theory that the international conference on "Theory of Mind and Literature" was held at Purdue University in November 2007. The idea for this conference emerged during the Literature and Cognitive Science Conference at the University of Connecticut in spring 2006, which was the first North American conference to offer a forum to scholars working at the intersection of two disciplines with increasingly good reason to communicate across disciplinary boundaries. The two most popular areas of research at the Literature and Cognitive Science conference were conceptual blending (a general theory of cognition proposed by Mark Turner and Gilles Fauconnier to describe the "blending" that underlies thought and language) and ToM. The aim in bringing a conference on Theory of Mind and Literature to Purdue University was to maintain the momentum of the first conference's intellectual stimulation, while offering opportunities to explore more deeply one particular subdomain of cognitive literary theory through a tightly focused theme.

The academic collaboration and discussion that set in motion a cascade of ideas and exciting research at the first conference on cognitive literary studies at the University of Connecticut, and the first conference on Theory of Mind and Literature at Purdue, illuminate the essays presented within this volume, which hopefully conveys the excitement of pioneering work in a new area of research.

Theory of Mind and Literature is a collection of nineteen essays by prominent scholars working in the field of cognitive literary studies. The essays, by literary scholars, linguists, cognitive scientists, and philosophers, range widely across national literatures (Spanish, French, German, British, American), genres (theatre, poetry, science fiction, novel), and historical periods (from the Middle Ages to the functional brain imaging of the twenty-first century), illuminating the central, enduring importance of ToM to our human condition.

Theory of Mind and Literature aims to explore the functionality of ToM as a concept in literary studies, and the scope of its usefulness across a wide range of contexts. Among our interests in assembling this collection of essays are the following objectives: to introduce readers to the myriad ways in which ToM can illuminate critical readings of literature; to present models of how to approach literary texts from a cognitive perspective; to extend the scope of the Theory of Mind and Literature Conference beyond the four days of the conference itself by sharing the insights and perspectives of the new research presented there with a wider audience; and to promote cognitive literary studies in general.

The book is structured thematically, with the nineteen essays organized into five sections. The first section, "Theory of Mind Now and Then: Evolutionary and Historical Perspectives," features essays by four of the leading scholars currently working in the field: Keith Oatley, Alan Palmer, Mark Turner, and Lisa Zunshine. The following four sections each contain four essays (with the exception of the section on Theory of Mind and Literary / Linguistic Structure with three essays), which cohere thematically under the following headings: "Mind Reading and Literary Characterization"; "Theory of Mind and Literary / Linguistic Structure"; "Alternate States of Mind"; and "Theoretical, Philosophical, Political Approaches."

The opening section, "Theory of Mind Now and Then: Evolutionary and Historical Perspectives," introduces some of the central concerns in current discussions about ToM and literature, and in cognitive literary studies in general: evolution (Oatley, Turner, and Zunshine), embodied cognition (Zunshine), distributed cognition (Palmer), and blending theory (Turner). Keith Oatley's "Theory of Mind and Theory of Minds in Literature" reviews work on evolution, narrative, and ToM. Despite the advantages to having a ToM, data show that humans are "good at theory of mind, but not that good." For millennia, humans have supplemented meager facts about thoughts and feelings of others with knowledge gained from experience in worlds of narrative. Fiction simulates an entire social world, presenting a "theory of minds," not only a "Theory of Mind." It is natural to claim that social understanding benefits from reading fiction, and recent data support this.

Alan Palmer's "Social Minds in *Little Dorrit*" continues Oatley's emphasis on pluralities of mind within fictional social worlds by exploring the workings of social or public minds and intermental thought in the story world of Charles Dickens's *Little Dorrit*. Alan Palmer contends that while traditional narrative theory privileges an "internalist" perspective on fiction, it is important to recognize that novels are largely invested in social minds, and that an "externalist" perspective, which studies the aspects of the mind that are "outer, active, public, social, behavioral, evident, embodied, and engaged," uncovers much unrecognized subtlety. Through careful, close readings, he demonstrates how characters form intermental units that are capable of communicating through facial expressions, looks, and signs, and how Dickens's prose represents socially distributed cognition. He also draws attention to Dickens's awareness of *physically* distributed cognition. In conclusion, he theorizes that eventually, after many more analyses of minds in novels, it may be possible to identify differences among novels, novelists, and literary periods in their emphasis on inner, passive, introspective, individual thought on the one hand, and outer, social, intermental thought on the other, and to attribute these differences to historical, cultural factors.

The essays by Mark Turner and Lisa Zunshine both emphasize cognitive processes integral to everyday living that are manifest in the ways in which we read and construct literature and art: in Turner's essay, "conceptual, and double-scope, integration"; in Zunshine's, the physical body's relation, and perceived relation, to the mind and mental states. In "The Way We Imagine," Mark Turner describes the mental operation of "conceptual integration," a cognitive procedure by which conceptual arrays are combined to produce new mental spaces. Particularly important is "double-scope" integration, a hallmark characteristic of human beings. Turner proposes that this ability arose some fifty thousand years ago in the Upper Paleolithic age, and discusses how these double-scope blendings are constructed, and the implications of recognizing this process.

Zunshine's essay, "Theory of Mind and Fictions of Embodied Transparency," elucidates how the human body functions as a text to be read by others through brief moments of "embodied transparency"—unintentional, physical indications of emotion. Zunshine provides a short overview of ToM before outlining the double perspective that embodied transparency implies: the body might appear to be the window to the mind, but it does not always provide accurate information regarding mental states. Through a variety of examples from literature, painting, and film, Zunshine situates representations of context-dependent embodied transparencies within our cognitive evolutionary heritage. She concludes the essay by suggesting that the double view of the body may be used to productively interpret how other cultural media, such as the disembodied but extremely social network of the Internet, are shaped.

Following the essays by Keith Oatley, Alan Palmer, Mark Turner, and Lisa Zunshine, the section on "Mind Reading and Literary Characterization" illustrates how bringing ToM to literary studies can augment our understanding of the traditional terms of literary analysis such as characterization. This section thus bridges the divide between more traditional forms of literary criticism and a cognitive theoretical approach. Diana Calderazzo's essay on the 2005 Broadway production of *Sweeney Todd*, "Theory of the Murderous Mind: Understanding the Emotional Intensity of John Doyle's Interpretation of Sondheim's *Sweeney Todd*," analyzes the processes of mirroring and empathy, which bring the minds of the audience unconsciously into an intense relationship with those of the production's macabre characters. Her introduction affords a useful overview of the legend of the murderous barber from the nineteenth to the twenty-first centuries, demonstrating the ageless, universal appeal of the grizzly tale, which she attributes to the biological basis of primary emotional response. Drawing on Antonio Damasio's insights into the body as a theater of the emotions, and Bruce McConachie's cognitive analysis of theatrical reception, she addresses aspects of storytelling, concepts of obsession and compulsion, and the function of laughter as a foil to fear within Doyle's production.

Natalie Phillips's essay on "Distraction as Liveliness of Mind: A Cognitive Approach to Characterization in Jane Austen" continues the discussion of the reception of characters, but in relation to characterization in the nineteenth-century novel. She contrasts the distractible and flexible Elizabeth Bennet in *Pride and Prejudice* with her focused and concentrated sister Mary. She argues that the reader's ToM is stimulated unequally by the two characters, and that Jane Austen uses this imbalance to impress upon the reader the relative complexity of the mind of Elizabeth. Phillips's analysis shows that understanding a major character in literature requires extending a comparative ToM to minor characters.

The last two essays in this section by Howard Mancing and Paula Leverage continue to investigate ToM in relation to characterization, but focus less on the reader's use of ToM in constituting the characters, than on the ToM of the characters themselves. Both of these essays analyze literature from a much earlier period: from the early seventeenth and late twelfth centuries, respectively. In "Sancho Panza's Theory of Mind," Howard Mancing examines a scene from early in the second part of Cervantes's *Don Quixote* (1615) in which Sancho uses his chivalric ToM developed throughout the earlier parts of the novel to deceive Don Quixote and make him believe that a peasant woman is the incomparable (and imaginary) beauty Dulcinea. Mancing further argues that the subtlety and sophistication of this scene (and others from Renaissance Spanish literature) refute the claim that the presentation of such subtle mind reading did not appear before the time of Jane Austen.

In "Is Perceval Autistic?: Theory of Mind in the *Conte del Graal*," Paula Leverage reexamines the characterization of Perceval in Chrétien de Troyes's twelfth-century *Conte du Graal* and in the romance's reception from the Middle Ages to the present. She argues that the dominant perceptions in the Arthurian tradition of Perceval as a naïve, ignorant young man are constructions from later works, which misinterpret the first literary incarnation of Perceval, who, in Chrétien's romance, displays the behavioral characteristics of an autistic individual. Leverage's analysis of Perceval as autistic affords a critical perspective that is relevant to many scenes of the romance, which in the past have been interpreted separately, using in each case quite different models to explain Perceval's behavior. She further argues that ToM is an important concern of the romance as a whole, which explores communication and its failures.

The third section "Theory of Mind and Literary / Linguistic Structure" continues to probe the relationship between traditional literary criticism and that informed by cognitive science by considering how stylistic elements of written texts such as Free Indirect Discourse (FID) and attributive style mediate the minds of characters, their narrators, and the minds of readers. Jennifer Marston William's essay "Whose Mind's Eye? Free Indirect Discourse and the Covert Narrator in Marlene Streeruwitz's *Nachwelt*" argues for a reframing of the narrative phenomenon of FID within the context of the cognitive "mind's eye" metaphor. Through the example of Marlene Streeruwitz's 1999 novel *Nachwelt*, which is written primarily in the mode of FID, William illustrates how FID shifts the deictic center and renders the third-person narrator temporarily covert while representing the mind's-eye view of the protagonist. The unmediated thoughts, motivations, and emotions of the character conveyed by FID prompt the reader's mind reading processes. At the same time, particularly in a strongly autobiographical text such as *Nachwelt*, FID allows the author to convey his or her own perspective while maintaining a certain distance from his or her narrator, so that the reader is not encouraged to equate the two positions completely.

In "Attractors, Trajectors, and Agents in Racine's 'Récit de Théramène,'" Allen G. Wood provides a close reading of Théramène's famous *récit* passage in Racine's tragedy

Phèdre. By applying the cognitive poetic concepts of textual attractors, trajectors, and agents, Wood demonstrates how Racine foregrounds certain aspects to elicit an emotional response in the spectator or reader. Wood contends that the *récit* functions for Théramène, the guardian of the young prince Hippolyte, as a mind reading device by which he aims to "update" the beliefs of Thésée, Hippolyte's father, who believes his son to be in love with stepmother Phèdre. At the same time, the passage becomes a mental conduit between the play's cast and its audience members, who receive insights into the mind of the character Théramène, the first-person narrator for the *récit*.

The third and final essay in this section, by Ineke Bockting, "The Importance of Deixis and Attributive Style for the study of Theory of Mind: The Example of William Faulkner's Disturbed Characters," is a linguistically informed analysis that elucidates how deixis and attributive clauses work to present a fictional character's ToM. Through a consideration of Faulkner's characters with cognitive problems, such as the autistic Benjy or the apparently schizophrenic Quentin in *The Sound and the Fury*, Bockting examines how an unanchored or absent deictic projection can result in a challenging narrative style, but one that reflects the confusion and communicative obstacles faced by these literary figures. Bockting also discusses the significance of attributive verb clauses, which directly reveal characters' mental experiences, raw sensations, and temporal perspectives.

The fourth section of the book, "Alternate States of Mind," introduces robots, ghosts, and dream personae, thus expanding the limits of ToM. Orley Marron proposes that we consider what she calls a Theory of Artificial Mind (ToAM) in "Alternative Theory of Mind for Artificial Brains: A Logical Approach to Interpreting Alien Minds." She bases this ToAM on the stories about human-robot interactions in Isaac Asimov's *I Robot* and on the adventures of Alice in the books by Lewis Carroll. We use our ToM in natural, nonconscious ways when dealing with other people, but this is not adequate for understanding the cognitive processes of nonstandard human minds. When dealing with robots or the fantasy inhabitants of Carroll's worlds, Marron suggests, we must more consciously be aware of the types of logical, deductive steps one must go through in our mind reading processes.

Mikko Keskinen's essay "Reading Phantom Minds: Marie Darrieussecq's *Naissance des fantômes* and Ghosts' Body Language" introduces the concept of mind reading in relation to ghosts, which is taken up again in the fourth essay of this section by Klarina Priborkin, who writes about the ghost in Toni Morrison's *Beloved* Keskinen is exploring the limits of mind reading in a situation in which body language has been silenced. In Marie Darrieussecq's novel *Naissance des fantômes* (1999), the female narrator's husband has disappeared. It is unclear whether he has died or simply disappeared. This ambiguity is the premise of the novel as the wife tries to impute intention and emotion to her absent, ghostly husband through ToM. The novel recounts the narrator's efforts to read her husband's mind, basing her inferences on memories, since in her husband's corporeal absence, she cannot read his body language. Keskinen draws a comparison between the narrator's reading of the paranormal with reading fictional characters in general, since in both cases "Theory of Phantom Mind" equals "Practice of Absent Body," and suggests that we supplement Fludernik's "natural narratives" and Richardson's "unnatural narration" with the supernatural aspects of narrative fiction.

Continuing the exploration of alternative Theories of Mind in ephemeral beings such as ghosts, psychologists Richard Schweickert and Zhuangzhuang Xi present their research on ToM in dreams. Their contribution, "Theory of Mind and Metamorphoses in Dreams, *Jekyll & Hyde*, and *The Metamorphosis*," looks at metamorphoses in dreams and in two works informed by dreams, *Dr. Jekyll and Mr. Hyde*, by Stevenson, and *The Metamorphosis*, by Kafka. When a metamorphosis occurs, presumably the inner state of one character is replaced by that of another. But is this noted by the dreamer or author? Schweickert and Xi ask whether an increase in ToM attributions accompanies a metamorphosis.

Klarina Priborkin's "Mother / Daughter Mind Reading and Ghostly Intervention in Toni Morrison's *Beloved*" returns to ghosts, as she shows how Beloved, the ghost of the murdered child in Morrison's novel, enables the character Denver to acquire the mind reading skills necessary to understand the perspective of her mother, Sethe. Priborkin first traces how intermental thinking shapes the environment in which Denver is raised, contributing to a repression of past black slavery as well as to silence about the infanticide committed by Sethe. Priborkin then analyzes the interactions of Beloved and Denver in the context of ToM, illuminating how Denver's empathy for her mother did not materialize suddenly and without explanation, but can be interpreted rather as a result of Beloved's mediation.

The final section of *Theory of Mind and Literature*, "Theoretical, Philosophical, Political Approaches," proposes working models for ToM-based analysis developed through functional brain imaging or philosophical inquiry. This section also extends the discussion beyond literature to consider ToM in the political arena, where its role in propagandist agendas is a serious concern. The first essay, Seth Knox's "Changing Minds: Theory of Mind and Propaganda in Egon Erwin Kisch's *Asien gründlich verändert*," discusses literary propaganda through analysis of the travel book *Asien gründlich verändert* (*Changing Asia*), by German writer Egon Erwin Kisch. Specifically, Knox studies the way in which Kisch employs two mind reading techniques: 1) "anchoring" strategies that resonate with the sympathetic reader's values; and 2) a blurring of the reader's "source-tracking" ability. With reference to these techniques, Knox adapts Simon Baron-Cohen's concept of a "Shared Attention Mechanism" to construct a graphic model of propagandist-propagandee relationships. In the three essays that follow, the authors propose further models for investigating ToM, which focus particularly on the relationship between narration, empathy, and mind reading. In "Functional Brain Imaging and the Problem of Other Minds," Dan Lloyd and his co-authors Vince Calhoun, Godfrey Pearlson, and Robert Astur point out that subjectivity would not be noticed were it not for differences between individuals. This presents a problem for many contemporary attempts to learn about subjective experiences with neuroimaging, because the typical method of averaging over subjects eliminates differences. They discuss an approach in their neuroimaging work in which similar brain images from the same subject at different times are clustered into categories. The passage of the brain from one category to another over time becomes the object of study, and they propose that techniques from narratology may become useful for further development of this approach. Fritz Breithaupt's "How is it Possible to have Empathy? Four Models" compares sources of empathy using evidence arising in narrative fiction. He notes that three commonly proposed sources are not contradictory, namely (a) empathy from similarity of oneself to others, (b) expectation that empathy extended will be reciprocated, and (c) empathy as a basis for understanding the emotions or predicting the behavior of another. He proposes combining the three in a fourth, (d) empathy arising in a narrative scene. With this proposal, narration enables layers of empathy.

José Barroso Castro's "Theory of Mind and the Conscience in *El casamiento engañoso*" opens with a statement by Cervantes from the prologue to his 1613 collection of short fictions, *Novelas ejemplares* (*Exemplary Stories*). Cervantes claims to have metaphorically placed a billiard table in the public square so that all readers might entertain themselves as they choose with his tales. The author then proceeds to study the mental processes of the two main characters in the story *El casamiento engañoso* (*The Deceitful Marriage*), Peralta and Campuzano. Taking a historical perspective, Barroso Castro places his inquiry within the Scholastic and Spanish Golden Age contexts by examining the implications of theologians such as Augustine and Thomas as well as writers contemporary to Cervantes.

The editors of this collection are four Purdue University faculty members who organized the Theory of Mind and Literature Conference at Purdue in November 2007. Paula Leverage, Howard Mancing, and Jennifer Marston William are from the Department of Foreign Languages and Literatures, and Richard Schweickert is from the Department of Psychological Sciences. The editors are the founding members of Purdue University's Center for Cognitive Literary Studies.

WORKS CITED

Allman, William F. *The Stone Age Present: How Evolution Has Shaped Modern Life—From Sex, Violence, and Language to Emotions, Morals, and Communities.* New York: Simon and Schuster, 1994. Print.

Baron-Cohen, Simon, Alan M. Leslie, and Uta Frith. "Does the Autistic Child Have a 'Theory of Mind'?" *Cognition* 21 (1985): 37-46. Print.

Dunbar, Robin. *Grooming, Gossip, and the Evolution of Language.* Cambridge: Harvard University Press, 1996. Print.

Fauconnier, Gilles, and Mark Turner. *The Way We Think: Conceptual Blending and the Mind's Hidden Complexities.* New York: Basic Books, 2002. Print.

Gallagher, Helen L., and Christopher D. Frith. "Functional Imaging of 'Theory of Mind.'" *Trends in Cognitive Sciences* 7 (2003): 77-83. Print.

Holland, Norman N. *The Brain of Robert Frost: A Cognitive Approach to Literature.* New York: Routledge, 1988. Print.

Lakoff, George, and Mark Johnson. *Metaphors We Live By.* Chicago: University of Chicago Press, 1980. Print.

Mar, Raymond, Maja Djikic, and Keith Oatley. "Effects of Reading on Knowledge, Social Abilities, and Selfhood." In *Directions in Empirical Literary Studies: In Honor of Willie van Peer*. Eds. Sonia Zyngier, Marisa Bortolussi, Anna Chesnokova, and Jan Auracher. Amsterdam: Benjamins, 2008. 127-37. Print.

Oatley, Keith. "Changing our minds." *Greater Good* 5 (2009). Print.

Palmer, Alan. *Fictional Minds*. Frontiers of Narrative. Lincoln: University of Nebraska Press, 2004. Print.

Premack, David and Guy Woodruff. "Does the Chimpanzee have a Theory of Mind?" *Behavioral and Brain Sciences* 4 (1978): 515-26. Print.

Turner, Mark. *The Literary Mind*. New York: Oxford University Press, 1996. Print.

Wimmer, Heinz, and Josef Perner. "Beliefs About Beliefs: Representation and Constraining Function of Wrong Beliefs in Young Children's Understanding of Deception." *Cognition* 13 (1983): 103-28. Print.

Zunshine, Lisa. *Why We Read Fiction: Theory of Mind and the Novel*. Columbus: The Ohio State University Press, 2006. Print.

Theory of Mind and Theory of Minds in Literature

Keith Oatley

Part 1. Theory of mind

Not far into *The Way by Swann's* (the title of the rather good new translation by Lydia Davis of the first book of Proust's *À la recherche du temps perdu*) readers find this:

> A real human being, however profoundly we sympathize with him, in large part is perceived through our senses, that is to say remains opaque to us, offers a dead weight that our sensibilities cannot lift. If a calamity should strike him, it is only in a small part of the total notion that we have of him that we will be able to be moved by this. (87)

Because of the opacity of others, human beings need a theory or model, or simulation, or *image* (Proust's term) of mind to infer what a real human being might be thinking and feeling. Theory of Mind, in this sense, has become an important topic in developmental psychology. Thus psychologists have discovered that the soul enters the body not at conception or at birth, but at age four. It is at this age that a child can start to experience herself or himself as a thinking and feeling being who is separate from others. It is at this age that the child can begin to peer through the opacity of others, to infer what they might be thinking and feeling. The same applies to the child's own self: it is at this age that a child begins to know that what she or he thinks and feels now can be different from what she or he had thought and felt in the past (see, for instance, Gopnik and Astington 1988).

Proust was also onto the comparison with other versions of oneself that Gopnik and Astington described. He says: "Even more, it is only in a part of the total notion he has of himself that he will be able to be moved by himself" (*The Way by Swann's* 87).

So, being able to know others and oneself requires imagination. The response of psychologists to these issues has been to conduct many experiments to find out what kinds of inferences children make about others, and at what ages they can make them.

There has been considerable progress. But we might think that in literature, progress has been yet greater, for as Proust says:

> The novelist's happy discovery was to have the idea of replacing these parts [of the real human being], impenetrable to the soul, by an equal quantity of immaterial parts, that is to say parts which our soul can assimilate . . . [the novelist] sets loose in us all possible happinesses and all possible unhappinesses, just a few of which we would spend years of our lives coming to know. (*The Way by Swann's* 87)

Having a Theory of Mind is like having a watch or a clock. These devices are models of the rotation of the earth. The positions of sun and stars are indications of time, but they are difficult to judge accurately, and heavenly bodies are not always visible. A model—a watch or clock—is much better. It allows us to synchronize our activities with each other, as in the following passage from Simenon's *Les vacances de Maigret,* in which the Commissioner has gone on holiday with his wife to the seaside town of Sables-d'Olonne. Recovering from an emergency operation for appendicitis, Mme Maigret is in a clinic run by a strict order of nuns. Maigret is allowed to visit her each day for just half an hour, at three in the afternoon.

> Before putting his foot on the door-step, Maigret took his watch from his pocket: it said three o'clock. At the same moment he heard a bell call lightly from the chapel, then, above the roofs of the little houses of the town, another one, more serious, from Notre Dame. (trans. K. Oatley. *Les vacances de Maigret* 5-6)

After his visit to his wife, Maigret returns to the *brasserie,* where he takes his meals. There he sits, smoking his pipe, sipping a glass of white wine. There, every afternoon, toward the back of the restaurant, some of the town's wealthy men—the old money—who include a ship-owner, a property developer, and an eminent doctor, gather to play bridge. Just as the position of the sun can be difficult to judge, so can facial expression.

> The doctor was not a man to shock anyone. Not a trace of anything on his face. He glanced at his hand and said:
>
> "Two clubs."
>
> Then, as the game progressed, for the first time he began to examine Maigret, mentally undressing him. It was scarcely noticeable. His inspections were so brief, he made them as he glanced casually around . . .
>
> Rarely had Maigret seen eyes that were at the same time so eager and so dry, a man who was master of his nerves, capable of completely concealing his feelings. (trans. K. Oatley. *Les vacances de Maigret* 24-25)

THE REQUIREMENT HYPOTHESIS

Without a Theory of Mind—which psychologists now often call "mind-reading" (see, for example, Ickes 2003)—one would scarcely know what this passage from Simenon was about. With a Theory of Mind, the game of bridge primes us for inferences about what others may know, and for possibilities of deception. The juxtaposition of bridge with Maigret's and the doctor's attempts at mind reading is a metonymic figure in the sense of Jakobson (1988). Maigret and the doctor both have reasons for hiding their thoughts and feelings as they try to comprehend each other. Each tries to assess the other man's character, to know what he is up to.

We can call the relation of mind reading to literature the *Requirement Hypothesis.* Theory of Mind is a *requirement* to understand this kind of narrative. As Lisa Zunshine (2006) has further proposed, we seem to enjoy being able to exercise this skill. So that may account, at least partly, for our enjoyment of detective stories: working out what others keep hidden.

Simenon is a rather good example here, because in the two kinds of books for which he is most famous—Maigrets and psychological novels—the focus is on a particular person. Although in each story in which he appears Maigret seems to set out to solve a crime, really he is making a mental model of another person's character in a circumstance in which this person has, as it were, gone beyond his or her usual limits. So when Maigret works to understand each clue, it is, as in *Les vacances de Maigret*, a clue to character, to the mind of the person who is being analyzed, to some matter that the person prefers to keep private. If such a clue also helps solve the crime, so much the better, but for Maigret (and for Simenon) that aspect is almost secondary.

What about the opacity of which Proust wrote, and with which Maigret and the doctor struggle? What has been made of that empirically? Stinson and Ickes (1992) invited to their laboratory pairs of male participants who were either friends or strangers. Paired participants sat together in a waiting room where they chatted and were covertly video-recorded. Subsequently they were told about the recording. They then watched the tape of themselves, stopped it when they remembered having a specific thought or feeling, and wrote what it was. They also watched the recording of the other man and guessed what he was thinking or feeling at the points where he had stopped the tape. The mean content accuracy between friends was 48%, and this was 50% higher than accuracy between strangers. In a different kind of study, Oatley and Larocque (1995) asked people to record in structured diaries errors that occurred in plans that they had explicitly arranged with another person in their everyday lives. The researchers also asked the other person to recall the error and the emotions surrounding it. Participants were quite good at knowing, after the error, what the other person was feeling when that feeling was anger (73% correct), but they were less good at knowing when the other person felt happiness (27% correct), fear (24% correct), sadness (43% correct), shame (10% correct), or guilt (42% correct).

So, in the quotidian world we adults are good at Theory of Mind, but not that good. Alan Palmer (2004) proposes that fiction offers a fuller disclosure than we can obtain elsewhere of the contents of human minds. Although we are not conscious in our everyday lives of everything in the minds of others or even in our own minds, we can become more completely conscious of the minds of Emma Woodhouse or Emma Bovary . . . or of the people investigated by Commissioner Maigret.

Often the idea of Theory of Mind refers to knowing what another person may be thinking or feeling in the moment, but with people whom we are likely to interact with on future occasions, we gather information to build mental models of them over the long term, from their utterances, from their behavior, and from what other people say about them. Such sources of information are exactly those that a detective uses in a mystery novel. From them we can make a mental model of the person, including socially unacceptable aspects (the criminal, the unconscionable, the unconscious). And, as the study by Stinson and Ickes (1992) implies, the better our mental model of people over the long term (as in friendship), the better we can know what they are thinking and feeling on a particular occasion.

Overall, Theory of Mind has a projective quality: we cast a model onto another person in ordinary life, or onto a character in fiction. The model can be good, but as we interact more with the person or character, we sometimes find our model to be mistaken in some important respect: an opportunity to improve it, engaging in fiction but usually painful in real life.

Evolutionary origins of mental models of others

What do we know about the origins and neurological basis of this model-making function? The first clue was discovered by Robin Dunbar (1992) who recognized that primates—an order that includes lemurs, monkeys, apes, and humans—not only tend to live in social groups (an adaptation against predation), but that the size of these groups varies among different species. Dunbar surveyed group size and brain size across the whole order of primates: for example the maximum size of the social group for lemurs is about 9, for cebus monkeys about 18, for chimpanzees about 50, and for humans about 150. (This number in humans is of individuals with whom personal relationships are maintained, not just people who can be recognized by sight.) Dunbar found a close correlation between size of the social group and the size of the cortex, so for example in lemurs the cortex is about 1.2 times the size of the rest of the brain, in cebus monkeys about 2.4 times, in chimpanzees about 3.2 times, and in humans about 4.1 times.

The primate system of maintaining trust in relationships is by means of grooming: sitting quietly with another individual, stroking, and picking through their fur for insects and twigs. In chimpanzees this activity takes about 20% of each individual's waking time. Dunbar (1993, 2003) has proposed that as group size kept increasing in our forebears, a problem was reached when the amount of grooming time needed to maintain an increasing number of relationships reached about 30%. The problem was that to devote any more time to grooming would not allow enough time to forage and do the other things that primates need to do. In the line that led to humans, the problem was solved by language emerging to replace grooming. So, contrary to what one might have thought, it was not to talk about where to find food or how to make flint tools that language came into being. It emerged in order to converse, and the primary function of conversation is to maintain relationships. Conversation is verbal grooming. Though we never lose the influence of touch, of cuddling, and other such ways of expressing affectionate emotions that our cousins the chimpanzees have, language emerged to supplement them. By means of conversation, we humans can maintain many more relationships than chimpanzees could. One can converse in groups, one can converse when foraging, or when working. Dunbar's hypothesis is known as the social brain hypothesis. It is that the progressive enlargement of the cortex, which has occurred in the evolution of lemurs, monkeys, apes, and humans, has taken place because the brain needs to house the neural machinery to contain mental models of progressively more individuals in the social group, and that language has taken over from grooming as the primary means for maintaining relationships in the group. Although the social brain hypothesis was at first greeted skeptically, it is now regarded as the best hypothesis we have about the origins of language.

And with the new, more efficient, relationship-maintaining method of conversation, one can see in the graphs of hominid evolution that the straight line relating brain-cortex size to group size changed direction about 500,000 years ago. It became steeper than that for other primates. This is the point, argues Dunbar (1993, 2003), at which language-based conversation took over from grooming as the primary way—the more efficient way—of maintaining a large number of relationships.

So what do people converse about? Dunbar has found that some 70% of conversation in a university refectory is about the social lives and plans of ourselves and those we know, the trusted and the less trustworthy. We can pass little fragments of mental models to each other verbally: "She always does what she says she will" or "You wouldn't tell him anything you didn't want everyone else to know." Dunbar has proposed that music and laughter similarly function to promote social bonding: music, when it is shared, is cohesive. Later in human evolution music and laughter get taken, along with language, to a new level in art (the emergence of which I discuss below).

There is another contributor to human brain size. It is Theory of Mind. In terms of models, we can make mental models of others, and recursively, mental models of others' mental models. Chimpanzees are only on the edge of being able to do this (Tomasello 1999; Herrmann et al. 2007). For instance, although chimpanzees follow the line of another individual's sight, they are not good at knowing what the other is looking at. Even quite young children can do this. Chimpanzees do not have the Theory of Mind abilities that four-year-old human children possess. Tomasello and his group have proposed the cultural intelligence hypothesis. It is not so much that we have more general intelligence than our primate cousins. Rather, we are more socially intelligent, and this already shows in young children. So as well as the number of people of whom we maintain mental models, yet more neural capacity has become necessary to allow Theory of Mind (models of other people's models). In fact we humans can maintain several layers of models—of what philosophers call "intentional states" for different other people. (An intentional state is a mental state that is about something: believing something, wanting something, feeling something, etc.)

What does this have to do with literature? First, it is from conversation that literature developed (Oatley 2004). Conversation is the principal kind of event depicted in three of the most important kinds of literature: plays, novels, and short stories, although it is usually less important in three others: action in epic poetry, inward thought in lyric poetry, action and scenic juxtaposition in films. Second, Dunbar has enumerated the layers of intentional states required for certain kinds of literature. Thus, for *Othello,* Shakespeare "*intended* [1] that his audience *realize* [2] that the eponymous moor *believed* [3] that his servant Iago was being honest when he claimed to *know* [4] that his beloved Desdemona *loved* [5] Cassio" (Dunbar 2003, 162).

In terms of the *Requirement Hypothesis:* to understand *Othello,* the audience is required to maintain four layers of intentional states in their models, and to write the play Shakespeare required five layers. Following Dunbar's typographical conventions for these layers, we can say that Theory of Mind or mind reading is *guessing* [1] what another person might be *thinking* or *feeling* [2]. It reaches just the second of these layers. Ability to maintain a third layer may have been reached in our hominid ancestors at about the same time that conversational language emerged. Certainly for us modern humans this third layer is easy. So in conversation we might *think* [1] and say: "You wouldn't tell him anything you didn't *want* [2] everyone else to *know* [3]." Chimpanzees can manage about one and a half layers.

The Social-Improvement Hypothesis

Almost since the invention of written fiction there have been claims that reading it is good for you. We call this the *Social-Improvement Hypothesis.* Important versions of it have been stated by Adam Smith (1759), George Eliot (1883), and Martha Nussbaum (1995), who have proposed that reading improves our social abilities, especially in such realms as social justice, because it gives us practice in projecting ourselves into the minds of others, sympathizing with them, empathizing with them, understanding the world from their point of view. At least two versions of this idea have been tested empirically.

One version involves shifts of attitude: people exposed to fictional characters who exhibit a certain kind of behavior—a child being stoical about separation from parents, a resistance fighter during an enemy occupation, a member of a minority standing up for equality—will shift their attitudes positively toward such behavior although it is not the norm. There have been a number of experimental studies that show this kind of effect. For instance, Flerx, Fidler, and Rogers (1976) found that five-year-olds shifted their views toward more egalitarian norms for women's roles when they were read stories in which such egalitarian roles were portrayed by a protagonist, as compared with stories in which more traditional sex roles were portrayed.

Hakemulder (2000) had European participants read either a chapter of a novel about the difficult life of an Algerian woman or an essay on women's rights in Algeria. As compared with those who read the essay, those who read the fictional piece said they would be less likely to accept current Algerian norms for relationships between men and women. Hakemulder's hypothesis was that by depicting individuals in the fictional portrayal (note the parallel to making mental models of others we know) as compared with discussing generalities in the essay, readers are encouraged to project themselves into the role of a character. This made the readers of the fictional story more empathetic to people in the ordinary world whose roles were comparable to those of the fictional character. In addition, Batson et al. (2002) showed that empathy for a drug addict was shown by participants who listened to a recorded interview with him, and these participants were more likely to allocate funds to an agency to help addicts. A similar though smaller effect was found when people heard the same interview but were told it was fiction based on the lives of addicts. (See also Lamm, Batson, and Decety [2007] for the neural basis of empathetic abilities.)

In a second version of the idea, we can hypothesize that reading fiction in general strengthens abilities of accurate empathy and other social skills. It rests on the parallel between comprehending the minds of characters in a Theory of Mind kind of way and comprehending the minds of people who make up our ordinary social world. This parallel was tested by Mar, Oatley, Hirsh, dela Paz, and Peterson (2006) by examining exposure to fiction and non-fictional texts as measured by Keith Stanovich and Richard West's Author Recognition Tests (see, for example, Stanovich, West, and Harrison 1995) and investigating whether exposure predominantly to fiction as compared with non-fiction would predict performance on measures of social acumen, including empathy. It did. Mar et al. found that the more fiction people read, the more accurate they were in a test of empathy, and the better they were at being able to understand what was going on socially in fifteen video-recorded scenes.

Part 2. Theory of Minds

Theory of Minds is different from Theory of Mind: it is the idea that narrative fiction is a model or simulation of the social world (Oatley 1999)—as William Shakespeare, Samuel Taylor Coleridge, and Robert Louis Stevenson called it, a dream; the dream is of unfolding events among several characters in interaction.

As has been understood since the work of Kenneth Craik (1943), what the mind does is to make models. Language is well endowed with words for this function: allegory, analogy, hypothesis, metaphor, model, schema, simile, theory, and so on. The more recent research of Dunbar, Tomasello, et al. (reviewed above) is that for us humans, who are very social beings, although we can and do make models of the physical world, and although we make models of other individuals, we also make models of the complex social world. As Bruner (1986) put it, narrative is a distinct mode of thought about human intentions and their vicissitudes. Narrative is based on a process of modeling how intentions unfold over time, and the repercussions of these intentions with those of other people. And, as Mark Turner (1996) has argued, because we can assimilate so much of human life to a set of narrative schemas, to understand narrative in this way is to understand mind at a deep level.

To approach an understanding of narrative, let us first think about art in general. To make art is to make something that is both itself and something else. For instance, I can make marks on paper and these are also something else: a story. Art can be thought of as the more or less conscious externalization of models or metaphors. In prehistory, it emerged, as Mithen (1996) showed, between 50,000 and 30,000 years ago. Mithen argues that, before this, domains of knowledge were separate in the mind-brain: the social world / plants and foods / finding one's way about / tool-making / and so on. Then these domains began to overlap. Metaphor became possible: a certain herb is a friend.

From 43,000 years ago in Slovenia comes the world's earliest known musical instrument (Huron 2003): both a piece of hollow wood and a flute. Then from around 30,000 years ago, there have been found ornamentation (both stones and a necklace); human burial (with presumed stories of people who were both dead and living in some other place); and cave paintings (both marks on a wall and animals). One of the earliest cave paintings is from Chauvet, 150 kilometers northwest of Marseille, a rhinoceros, painted 31,000 years ago (Chauvet, Deschamps, and Hillaire 1996). Also, about 50,000 years ago, there was an enormous elaboration in the kinds of tools that were made, not just flint scrapers, but knives, harpoons, needles, and arrows. So in round numbers, language emerged as conversation 500,000 years ago; elaborate tool making, stories, and other art about 50,000 years ago; writing about 5,000 years ago; print about 500 years ago. We can take it that by 30,000 years ago the modern mind was in place with metaphors, stories, and cave paintings, and that later, by means of the technologies of writing and printing, it enhanced itself, with papyrus and paper as externalized memory and a new possibility for communication at a distance. And, as Herman (2003) argues, stories become tools for thinking about the social world.

Shakespeare was a member of the first generations to be educated in writing during the age of print. For seven years from 1571, he is thought to have attended the grammar school in Stratford, modeled after specifications created by Erasmus around 1520.

In or about December 1594, Shakespeare is thought to have read or re-read *Praise of Folly* by Erasmus, and I have proposed (Oatley 2001) that, at this time, he conceived the idea of theater as a model of the social world. He then not only used the idea for his subsequent plays from *A Midsummer Night's Dream* onward (dream = simulation-model), but embedded the idea recursively in some of his plays to explain it to the audience, for instance in the play within the play in *Hamlet,* the transposition to the Forest of Arden in *As You Like It,* Iago's improvised play-simulation to deceive Othello, and Prospero's speech:

> . . . These our actors,
> As I foretold you, were all spirits and
> Are melted into air, into thin air.
> And, like the baseless fabric of this vision,
> The cloud capped towers, the gorgeous palaces,
> The solemn temples, the great globe itself,
> Yea, all which it inherit, shall dissolve,
> And like this insubstantial pageant faded,
> Leave not a rack behind. We are such stuff
> As dreams are made on, and our little life
> Is rounded with a sleep. (*The Tempest* 4, 1, 148-58)

This—I think we can agree—is literary art, in which both creator and reader share in an "insubstantial vision" a "dream." And in a further metaphorical shift, theater becomes a metaphor for life, which closes at the end of the performance.

Now back to the chimpanzees for a few moments. Part of Jane Goodall's (1986) genius in her work with the chimpanzees of Gombe was to realize that in order to understand them she had to recognize them individually, make mental models of each one (as they do themselves), and give them names. Understanding them became partly ethology with particular chimpanzees—for example, following an individual for many days and counting instances of inter-individual aggression in which it was involved—but partly the recounting of narratives about their lives with each other. Recounting a narrative is what Frans de Waal does in *Chimpanzee Politics* (1982) for instance, in the power struggle in which over a period of two months Luit displaces Yeroen from his alpha status. The narrative genre is not too different from that of ancient epics, or even from of that in which Prospero is displaced from his dukedom. The story of Luit and Yeroen went something like this (my version):

> Once, in a group of two-dozen chimpanzees who lived in Arnheim, there was an alpha male whose name was Yeroen. From time to time he would run full tilt at other chimpanzees as they sat quietly: his hair erect, stamping his feet, bearing his teeth. He made a terrible noise. Mothers picked up their youngsters, and everyone would scatter. Then as suddenly as it had been interrupted, peace would return. Yeroen would sit. Everyone would come up to him to make deferential greetings. Then, one day, the younger male, Luit, who shared sleeping quarters with Yeroen, stopped offering him these deferential greetings . . .

Though the chimpanzees knew what went on, and knew the other individuals in their group, only we can understand such events as a narrative. As John Donne put it in his remark about Theory of Mind in one of his sermons given at the beginning of the seventeenth century: "The beast does but know, but the man knows that he knows" (225).

Plays, films, short stories, and novels are about people with intentions who interact with each other. People are good at understanding processes one step at a time, but less good at understanding interactions of such processes. In thinking about the weather, for instance, we can understand that winds blow from areas of high atmospheric pressure to areas of low pressure, but what happens when other factors operate at the same time? Does the simple understanding hold in the same way when a warm air mass is blown toward a cold mass? Does it operate in the same way over land and over water? To give a weather forecast, we need to enter into a computer simulation both the wind-producing effects of different atmospheric pressures and also many other processes that interact with them. When you look at a weather forecast on the television or in the newspaper, you are looking at the output of a computer simulation. A narrative is also a kind of simulation, one that runs on minds (Oatley 1999). It binds a complex of intentions, outcomes, and emotions together into a comprehensible whole. If Alice thwarts Beatrice in an intention, we know that Beatrice is likely to be angry. But what happens when Beatrice is Alice's mother? What if she is Alice's employer? What if she is Alice's lover? What happens when the interactions of Alice and Beatrice unfold over time? It is for such matters that we need not just a Theory of Mind, but a Theory of Minds. It is for such matters that we need narrative simulations.

THE SELF-IMPROVEMENT HYPOTHESIS

Just as there have been claims that reading is good for people, there have been claims that it can promote personal change: see for instance the title of Alain de Botton's (1997) book, *How Proust Can Change Your Life* (see also Schutte and Malouff 2006). We can call this the *Self-Improvement Hypothesis.*

Whereas Theory of Mind has a projective quality, we can think of Theory of Minds (and self-improvement) as reciprocating: we project our self into a story, and the self comes back to us somewhat changed. "Improvement" here should be taken very provisionally: when a person changes the improvement is according to the person's own criteria, not necessarily according to anyone else's. As with the Social-Improvement Hypothesis, until recently empirical evidence for changes of selfhood has been meager.

Consider a short story, a simulation that runs on minds: Anton Chekhov's "The Lady with the Little Dog" (1899), thought of as one of the world's best short stories. The story starts with a casual holiday romance between Anna Sergeevna and Gurov in the Russian seaside town of Yalta. In a hotel room, they make love for the first time.

> "It's not good," she said. "You'll be the first one not to respect me now."
>
> There was a watermelon on the table in the hotel room. Gurov cut himself a slice and unhurriedly began to eat it.

Anna is appalled at what she has done. Gurov is bored by her protestations, but speaks softly to her.... On the next page, they take a cab to Oreanda, where the weather is not just a metaphor for the simulations of literature. It enters the story.

> In Oreanda they sat on a bench not far from the church, looked down on the sea, and were silent. Yalta was barely visible through the morning mist, white clouds stood motionless on the mountain tops. The leaves of the trees did not stir, cicadas called, and the monotonous dull sound of the sea, coming from below, spoke of the peace, of the eternal sleep that awaits us. So it had sounded below when neither Yalta or Oreanda were there, so it sounded now, and would go on sounding with the same dull indifference when we are no longer here. (trans. R. Pevear and L. Volokhonsky 365-66)

At Oreanda the weather and sea are weather and sea. But as in other art, they are also something else. Different levels in literature have been recognized from very early times in Hebrew interpretations of scripture, and they were recognized by Dante (for instance in the *Convivio,* written in the early years of the fourteenth century). Dante proposed there are four levels: the literal, the allegorical, the moral, and the anagogical (having to do with the relationship to God).

In this passage about Oreanda, the weather and the sea are themselves (the literal). At the same time they are reminders that concerns that are almost overwhelming to us humans are ephemeral (the allegorical). Matters that are of great importance in human society (the moral) are of no concern to the physical world but, with the church not far from the bench on which Anna and Gurov sit, these matters may be of concern in the eyes of God (the anagogical).

In a story such as Chekhov's "The Lady with the Little Dog," we imagine ourselves into other lives, we identify with—that is to say empathize with—the characters in their plans, their interactions, their predicaments. As we run characters' plans on our own planning processors in the story-simulation, we experience emotions: our own emotions. Thus the extended version of our self in the simulated world can experience things, and feel things, that in the everyday world it would not. We project ourselves into the simulated world, and we may come back changed.

One of Proust's ideas was that by understanding the faults of others we can recognize them in ourselves, and thus be in a better position to correct them. Can we see in Gurov anything of ourselves, when a companion is in mental turmoil, and we do not use our Theory of Mind to enter into their mental state? So the Theory of Minds includes our own mind.

Djikic, Oatley, Zoeterman, and Peterson (in press) found that people who read the Chekhov story, with its weather and sea-sounds, experienced more changes in emotions and personality traits as a result of reading the story than those who read a control text: an account based on a set of (supposed) divorce proceedings from a courtroom that contained exactly the same information as the Chekhov story, which was exactly the same length and reading difficulty, and which people found just as interesting. So, as a result of such experiences in art, everyday selves can change.

Let us end, as we started, with Proust:

> In reality each reader, when he is reading, is uniquely reading himself. The writer's work is only a kind of optical instrument which he offers the reader to enable him to discern what without this book he might not have seen in himself. (*Finding Time Again* 219-20)

Acknowledgments

I am warmly grateful to my collaborators, Laurette Larocque, Maja Djikic, and Raymond Mar. For grant support I thank the Social Science and Humanities Research Council of Canada.

Works Cited

Batson, C. Daniel, et al. "Empathy, Attitudes and Action: Can Feeling for a Member of a Stigmatized Group Motivate One to Help the Group?" *Personality and Social Psychology Bulletin* 28 (2002): 1656-66. Print.

Bruner, Jerome. *Actual Minds, Possible Worlds*. Cambridge, MA: Harvard University Press, 1986. Print.

Chauvet, Jean-Marie, Eliette Deschamps, and Christian Hillaire. *Dawn of Art: The Chauvet Cave*. New York: Abrams, 1996. Print.

Chekhov, Anton. *Stories*. Trans. Richard Pevear and Larissa Volokhonsky. New York: Bantam, 2000. Print.

Craik, Kenneth J. W. *The Nature of Explanation*. Cambridge: Cambridge University Press, 1943. Print.

Dante Alighieri. *Dante's Il Convivio (the Banquet)*. Trans. Richard Lansing. New York: Garland, 1990. Print.

De Botton, Alain. *How Proust Can Change Your Life*. New York: Random House, 1997. Print.

De Waal, Frans. *Chimpanzee Politics*. New York: Harper and Row, 1982. Print.

Djikic, Maja, Keith Oatley, Sara Zoeterman, and Jordan B. Peterson. "On Being Moved by Art: How Fiction Transforms the Self." *Creativity Research Journal*, in press.

Donne, John. *The Sermons of John Donne*. Ed. G. R. Potter and E. M. Simpson. Volume 8. Berkeley: University of California Press, 1960. Print.

Dunbar, Robin I. M. "Neocortex Size as a Constraint on Group Size in Primates." *Journal of Human Evolution* 20 (1992): 469-93. Print.

---. "Coevolution of Neocortical Size, Group Size, and Language in Humans." *Behavioral and Brain Sciences* 16 (1993): 681-735. Print.

---. "The Social Brain: Mind, Language, and Society in Evolutionary Perspective." *Annual Review of Anthropology* 32 (2003): 163-81. Print.

Eliot, George. "The Natural History of German Life: Riehl." *The Works of George Eliot. Standard Edition: Essays.* Edinburgh: Blackwood, 1883. 188-235. Print.

Erasmus. *Praise of Folly.* Ed. and Trans. R. M. Adams. New York: Norton, 1989. Print.

Flerx, Vicki C., Dorothy S. Fidler, and Ronald W. Rogers. "Sex Role Stereotypes: Developmental Aspects and Early Intervention." *Child Development* 47 (1976): 998-1007. Print.

Goodall, Jane. *The Chimpanzees of Gombe: Patterns of Behavior*. Cambridge, MA: Harvard University Press, 1986. Print.

Gopnik, Alison, and Janet Astington. "Children's Understanding of Representational Change and Its Relation to Their Understanding of False Belief and the Appearance-Reality Distinction." *Child Development* 58 (1988): 26-37. Print.

Hakemulder, Frank. *The Moral Laboratory: Experiments Examining the Effects of Reading Literature on Social Perception and Moral Self-Concept*. Amsterdam: Benjamins, 2000. Print.

Herman, David. "Stories as Tools for Thinking." *Narrative Theory and the Cognitive Sciences*. Ed. David Herman. Stanford, CA: Center for the Study of Language and Information, 2003. 163-92. Print.

Herrmann, Esther, et al. "Humans Have Evolved Specialized Skills of Social Cognition: The Cultural Intelligence Hypothesis." *Science* 317 (2007): 1360-66. Print.

Huron, David. "Is Music an Evolutionary Adaptation?" *The Cognitive Neuroscience of Music*. Ed. I. Peretz and R. Zatorre. Oxford: Oxford University Press, 2003. 57-75. Print.

Ickes, William. *Everyday Mind Reading: Understanding What Other People Feel and Think*. Amherst, NY: Prometheus, 2003. Print.

Jakobson, Roman. "The Metaphoric and Metonymic Poles." *Modern Criticism and Theory: A Reader*. Ed. D. Lodge. Longman: London, 1988. 31-61. Print.

Lamm, Claus, C. Daniel Batson, and Joan Decety. "The Neural Substrate of Human Empathy: Effects of Perspective-Taking and Cognitive Appraisal." *Journal of Cognitive Neuroscience* 19 (2007): 42-58. Print.

Mar, Raymond A., Keith Oatley, Jacob Hirsh, Jennifer dela Paz, and Jordan B. Peterson. "Bookworms versus Nerds: The Social Abilities of Fiction and Non-fiction Readers." *Journal of Research in Personality* 40 (2006): 694-712. Print.

Mithen, Steven. *The Prehistory of the Mind: The Cognitive Origins of Art and Science*. London: Thames and Hudson, 1996. Print.

Nussbaum, Martha C. *Poetic Justice: The Literary Imagination and Public Life*. Boston: Beacon, 1995. Print.

Oatley, Keith. "Why Fiction May Be Twice as True as Fact: Fiction as Cognitive and Emotional Simulation." *Review of General Psychology* 3 (1999): 101-17. Print.

---. "Shakepeare's Invention of Theater as Simulation That Runs on Minds." *Empirical Studies of the Arts* 19 (2001): 29-45. Print.

---. "From the Emotions of Conversation to the Passions of Fiction." *Feelings and Emotions: The Amsterdam Symposium*. Eds. N. H. Frijda, A. S. R. Manstead and A. Fischer. New York: Cambridge University Press, 2004. 98-115. Print.

---, and Laurette Larocque. "Everyday Concepts of Emotions Following Every-Other-Day Errors in Joint Plans." *Everyday Conceptions of Emotions: An Introduction to the Psychology, Anthropology, and Linguistics of Emotion. Nato Asi Series D 81*. Eds. J. Russell, et al. Dordrecht: Kluwer, 1995. 145-65. Print.

Palmer, Alan. *Fictional Minds*. Lincoln: University of Nebraska Press, 2004. Print.

Proust, Marcel. *In Search of Lost Time, 1. The Way by Swann's*. Trans. L. Davis. London: Penguin, 2003. Print.

---. *In Search of Lost Time, 6. Finding Time Again*. Trans. I. Patterson. London: Penguin 2003. Print.

Schutte, Nicola S., and John M. Malouff. *Why We Read and How Reading Transforms Us: The Psychology of Engagement with Text*. Lewiston, NY: Mellen, 2006. Print.

Shakespeare, William. *The Norton Shakespeare*. Ed. S. Greenblatt. New York: Norton, 1997. Print.

Simenon, Georges. *Les Vacances de Maigret*. Paris: Presses de la Cité, 1951. Print.

Smith, Adam. *The Theory of Moral Sentiments*. Oxford: Oxford University Press, 1976. Print.

Stanovich, Keith E., Richard F. West, and Michele R. Harrison. "Knowledge Growth and Maintenance across the Life Span: The Role of Print Exposure." *Developmental Psychology* 31 (1995): 811-26. Print.

Stinson, Linda, and William Ickes. "Empathetic Accuracy in the Interactions of Male Friends Versus Male Strangers." *Journal of Personality and Social Psychology* 62 (1992): 787-97. Print.

Tomasello, Michael. *The Cultural Origins of Human Cognition*. Cambridge, MA: Harvard University Press, 1999. Print.

Turner, Mark. *The Literary Mind: The Origins of Thought and Language*. New York: Oxford University Press, 1996. Print.

Zunshine, Lisa. *Why We Read Fiction: Theory of Mind and the Novel.* Columbus: The Ohio State University Press, 2006. Print.

Social Minds in *Little Dorrit*

ALAN PALMER

THEORETICAL CONTEXT

This essay will consider the subject of Theory of Mind in the novel in terms of the notion of *social minds.* After explaining what is meant by this phrase, I will attempt to illustrate the importance of social minds in the novel by analyzing their functioning in an example text, Charles Dickens's *Little Dorrit.* I hope to show that it is not possible to understand this novel without an awareness of these minds as they operate within its storyworld. They are the chief means by which the plot is advanced. If you were to take all of the social thought out of *Little Dorrit*, very little, I would argue, would be left. So, given the importance of this subject to the study of the novel, it seems to me that it is necessary to find room for it at the centre of narrative theory.

Speaking very broadly, there are two perspectives on the mind: the internalist and the externalist. These two perspectives form more of a continuum than an either/or dichotomy, but the distinction is, in general, a valid one.

> An internalist perspective on the mind stresses those aspects that are inner, introspective, private, solitary, individual, psychological, mysterious, and detached.
>
> An externalist perspective on the mind stresses those aspects that are outer, active, public, social, behavioral, evident, embodied, and engaged.

The *social mind* and the *public mind* are the synonyms that I will use to describe those aspects of the whole mind that are revealed through the externalist perspective.

It seems to me that the traditional narratological approach to the representation of fictional consciousness is an internalist one that stresses those aspects that are inner, passive, introspective, and individual. This undue emphasis on private, solitary, and highly verbalized thought at the expense of all the other types of mental functioning has resulted in a preoccupation with such concepts as free indirect discourse, stream of consciousness, and interior monologue. As a result, the *social* nature of fictional thought has been neglected. But, as the neuroscientist Antonio Damasio suggests, "the study of human consciousness requires both internal and external views" (2000, 82), and so an externalist perspective is required as well, one that stresses the public, social, concrete, and located aspects of mental life in the novel.

An important part of the social mind is our capacity for *intermental thought* (Palmer 2005), which is joint, group, shared, or collective thought, as opposed to *intramental*, or individual or private thought. It is also known as *socially distributed, situated*, or *extended cognition*, and also as *intersubjectivity*. Intermental thought is a crucially important component of fictional narrative because much of the mental functioning that occurs in novels is done by large organizations, small groups, work colleagues, friends, families, couples, and other intermental units. It could plausibly be argued that a large amount of the subject matter of novels is the formation, development, and breakdown of these intermental systems. Much of the mental functioning that goes on within these units may be termed *Intermental Theory of Mind*. *Little Dorrit*, in common with many other novels, contains a number of general or universal statements about the typical behavior of intermental units. For example, when Blandois arrives one evening at a French inn, "There had been that momentary interruption of the talk about the stove, and that temporary inattention to and distraction from one another, which is usually inseparable in such a company from the arrival of a stranger" (167-68). These sorts of statements, though taken little account of in narrative theory because of its preference for the internalist perspective, are quite common in fictional discourse. (For work by postclassical narrative theorists on distributed cognition, see Margolin [1996 and 2000] and Herman [2003a and 2003b].)

Within the real-mind disciplines of psychology and philosophy there is a good deal of interest in *the mind beyond the skin*: the realization that mental functioning cannot be understood merely by analyzing what goes on inside the skull but can only be fully comprehended once it has been seen in its social and physical context. For example, social psychologists routinely use the terms *mind* and *mental action* not only about individuals, but also about groups of people working as intermental units. So, it is appropriate to say of groups that they think or that they remember. As the psychologist James Wertsch puts it, a *dyad* (that is, two people working as a cognitive system) can carry out such functions as problem solving on an intermental plane (1991, 27). You may be asking what is achieved by talking in this way, instead of simply referring to individuals pooling their resources and working in cooperation together. The advocates of the concept of distributed cognition such as the theoretical anthropologists Gregory Bateson (1972) and Clifford Geertz (1993), the philosophers Andy Clark and David Chalmers (1998) and Daniel Dennett (1996), and the psychologists Edwin Hutchins (1995) and James Wertsch all stress that the purpose of the concept is increased explanatory power. They argue that the way to delineate a cognitive system is to draw the limiting line so that you do not cut out anything which leaves things inexplicable (Bateson 1972, 465). For example, Wertsch tells the story of how his daughter lost her shoes and he helped her to remember where she had left them. Wertsch asks: Who is doing the remembering here? He is not, because he had no prior knowledge of where they were, and she is not, because she had forgotten where they were. It was the intermental unit formed by the two of them that remembered (Sperber and Hirschfeld 1999, cxxiv).

The basis of this essay is *attribution theory* (Palmer 2007): how narrators, characters, and readers attribute states of mind such as emotions, dispositions, and reasons for action to characters and, where appropriate, also to themselves. How do heterodiegetic narrators attribute states of mind to their characters? By what means do homodiegetic narrators attribute states of mind to themselves and also to other characters? And, with regard to the issue of characterization, how does an attribution of a mental state by a narrator help to build up in the reader a sense of the whole personality of the character who is the subject of that attribution? Attribution theory rests on the concept of *Theory of Mind*, the term used by philosophers and psychologists to describe our awareness of the existence of other minds, our knowledge of how to interpret our own and other people's thought processes, our mind reading abilities in the real world. Readers of novels have to use their Theory of Mind in order to try to follow the workings of characters' minds. Otherwise, they will lose the plot. The only way in which the reader can understand a novel is by trying to follow the workings of characters' minds and thereby by attributing states of minds to them. (For more on Theory of Mind and the novel, see Zunshine 2006.) Of particular importance to the concept of the social mind is the fact that this mind reading also involves readers trying to follow characters' attempts to read other characters' minds. A basic level of minimal mind reading is required for characters to understand each other in order to make life possible. At the next level up, characters who know each other well form intermental pairs and small groups. To put the point simply, they are more likely to know what the other is thinking than total strangers will. These small groups will obviously vary greatly in the quantity and quality of their intermental thought. In addition, individuals may be part of larger groups that will also have a tendency to think together on certain issues. In all of these units, large and small, the individuals that belong to them will, of course, frequently think separately as well. It is this balance between public and private thought, intermental and intramental functioning, social and individual minds, that novels are preoccupied with, and *Little Dorrit* is no exception.

It is common, when reading discussions of the sustained inside views of characters' private minds in the novels of, say, George Eliot or Henry James, to be told that, by contrast, characters in novels by Charles Dickens are really only ever seen from the outside. We only see their surface. The effect is often to sound rather patronizing about Dickens's achievement. "Brilliant novelist in his way, of course, but without the *depth* of Eliot or James!" I would like to reverse that perspective. In cognitive terms, nearly all of your life is spent on the surface, on the outside, in the sense that all of the minds with which you are involved (with the admittedly rather important exception of your own) are only ever experienced on the surface, and from the outside. From this point of view, it is not surprising that Oscar Wilde said that "It is only shallow people who do not judge by appearances. The true mystery of the world is the visible, not the invisible." Dickens is the novelist of appearances, and of the visible, and his achievement can only be fully appreciated from the externalist perspective.

An emphasis on social minds will inevitably question these twin assumptions: first, that the workings of our minds are not accessible to others; and second, that the workings of our own minds are unproblematically accessible to ourselves. This essay will question the first assumption but will make almost no reference to the equally questionable second.

Private thought

There are very few extended passages of inside views of intramental or private thought in *Little Dorrit*. One such is a long passage of Clennam's inner speech regarding his love for Minnie and his concern about growing old: "And he had plenty of unsettled subjects to meditate upon.... First, there was the subject seldom absent from his mind, the question, what he was to do henceforth in life" (231). In addition, there is a good deal of *contextual thought report* (Palmer 2004, 209): short, unobtrusive sentences, phrases, or even single words that describe characters' mental functioning. Much of the contextual thought report in the novel is related to private thinking. For example, when Fanny cries with Little Dorrit after she tells her that she is engaged, "It was the last time Fanny ever showed that there was any hidden, suppressed, or conquered feeling in her on the matter" (654). From that time onward, Fanny's feelings will be hidden from others.

This intramental thought benefits from an externalist perspective, though, just as intermental thought does. To illustrate, I will draw attention to three features of intramental thought that are undervalued by the internalist perspective. First, it is worth questioning for a moment the apparent inaccessibility of private thought to others. How much mental functioning is there in the novel that at least one other character is not aware of, albeit in general terms? The answer that I would suggest is: not much. Regarding the two passages referred to just now, Little Dorrit for one is aware of Clennam's feelings. She knows immediately that something is wrong with Clennam after he gives up thoughts of Minnie and she knows about his anxieties about growing old: "He never thought that she saw in him what no one else could see" (432). Little Dorrit would also have known of Fanny's subsequently concealed feelings, having been shown them once. When going through the characters one by one asking this question ("Does another character know about their minds?"), I am struck by how public the thought in the novel tends to be. Miss Wade is an obvious exception. Mrs. Clennam, possibly? Flintwinch, perhaps? But there are few others, it seems to me.

Second, as Bakhtin (1984) has shown, intramental thought is intensely dialogic. In a splendidly Bakhtinian phrase that the narrator uses of Mrs. Clennam, "It was curious how she seized the occasion to argue with some invisible opponent" (407). In a phrase that brings to mind Daniel Dennett's notion of "mind-ruts" (1991, 300), Mrs. General is described as having "a little circular set of mental grooves or rails on which she started little trains of other people's opinions" (503). The important point to note here is that it is *other people's* opinions that are running along her mind-grooves. The private thoughts of Mrs. Clennam and Mrs. General, in common with all the characters in the novel, are filled with the thoughts of others.

Third, the presence of intermental thought is often concealed within descriptions of intramental functioning: "From the days of their honeymoon, Minnie Gowan felt sensible of being usually regarded as the wife of a man who had made a descent in marrying her" (541). At first reading, this sounds like a simple example of intramental contextual thought report. However, Minnie's dialogic anticipation of the feelings of others contains an intermental component that is disguised within the passive construction ("regarded as"). It may be decoded as follows: the group of people who know her regard her (Minnie thinks) as that sort of wife. (For more on the use of the passive voice to construct intermental functioning, see Palmer 2005.) When Miss Wade is part of the quarantine party at the beginning of the novel, the narrator makes this remark: "And yet it would have been as difficult as ever to say, positively, whether she avoided the rest, or was avoided" (62). Although this is a statement about Miss Wade's disposition to be unsociable, it is also a statement about the intermental functioning of "the rest": their awareness of her disposition and their resulting behavior in avoiding her. Similarly, it is said of Little Dorrit that "She passed to and fro in it shrinkingly now, with a womanly consciousness that she was pointed out to every one" (118). This is a description of her state of mind, but it also refers to the thinking of the prison population who consider Little Dorrit as the Child of the Marshalsea. The externalist perspective is required in order to tease out the intermental element in sentences that appear to be simply presentations of private thought.

Before discussing in detail the readability of fictional minds, I will briefly refer here to unreadability, or, at the very least, the possibility of incomplete, inaccurate, or otherwise defective reading of other minds. As I have said, some characters tend to be difficult to read. Much is made of Flintwinch's impassivity and impenetrability. Despite being physically pushed about by Blandois, he "brought himself up with a face completely unchanged in its stolidity" (602). When Mr. Casby is questioned by Clennam about Miss Wade, being determined to tell him nothing of what he knows about her, he "knew his strength lay in silence" (594). When Miss Wade herself is similarly intent on revealing nothing of her mind, she "stood by the table so perfectly composed and still after this acknowledgement of his remark that Mr. Meagles stared at her under a sort of fascination, and could not even look to Clennam to make another move" (376). This is a vivid illustration of the importance of publicly available cues when reading other minds. When those cues are missing, as when Miss Wade deliberately reduces them to order to keep the workings of her mind hidden, then Meagles is at a loss. Miss Wade herself thinks that she is able to read other minds accurately: "From a very early age I have detected what those about me thought they hid from me" (725). However, it is clear from the context that she was frequently wrong, simply misinterpreting genuine kindness. On a more amusing level, the workings of Mr. F.'s Aunt's mind are, mercifully perhaps, completely opaque: "Mr. F.'s Aunt may have thrown in these observations on some system of her own, and it may have been ingenious, or even subtle: but the key to it was wanted" (199).

THE EXTERNALIST PERSPECTIVE

Notwithstanding the caveat in the previous paragraph, there are copious examples in this novel of the fact that much of the thought of its characters is public and easily available to others. Even a very solipsistic character like Mr. Dorrit is able to notice when, for example, Merdle is out of sorts (674). The fairly unobservant Young John Chivery knows that Little Dorrit is in love with Clennam, and can make a remark to Clennam such as: "'I *see* you recollect the room, Mr. Clennam?'" (791, my emphasis). Also, the reserved characters referred to earlier such as Miss Wade are not always able to conceal all of their thoughts. During a discussion with Clennam, "She heard him with evident surprise, and with more marks of suppressed interest than he had *seen* in her" (719, my emphasis). This is a novel in which the visibility of thought is frequently and pointedly emphasized. When Pancks gives a glass of wine to Blandois, it is "not without a *visible* conflict of feeling on the question of throwing it at his head" (814, my emphasis). The narrator mocks the efforts made by Merdle and Lord Decimus to keep their thoughts secret. They move about at their dinner party, "each with an absurd pretence of not having the other on his mind, which could not have been more transparently ridiculous though his real mind had been chalked on his back" (624).

In addition to the specific mental events that occur in the minds of others, Theory of Mind also relates to dispositions that persist over time and that form part of another's character or personality. I stress this point because the hugely important area of characters' dispositions has been neglected by traditional narrative theory. For example, Blandois's selfishness is clear from the way he moves around a room soiling the furniture (402). In a particularly vivid image, when Clennam watches Gowan when he is unawares, "There was something in his way of spurning [stones] out of their places with his heel, and getting them into the required position, that Clennam thought had an air of cruelty in it" (245). There are a large number of examples of characters passing judgments, often spiteful but accurate, on other characters' personalities. Fanny says of her loved one, Sparkler, "'If it's possible—and it generally is—to do a foolish thing, he is sure to do it'" (664). Fanny is again perceptive, this time about Mrs. General: "'*I* know her sly manner of feeling her way with those gloves of hers'" (666). Flintwinch is another character whose disposition is to be unsparing about the failings of others. He says of Clennam's father, "'He was an undecided, irresolute chap, who had everything but his orphan life scared out of him when he was young'" (224). At the end of the novel, he shouts to Mrs. Clennam: "'But that's the way you cheat yourself'" (851). The importance of the concept of dispositions is that it links specific mental events and actions (doing foolish, sly, irresolute, or dishonest things) with those characters' stable, long-lasting personalities (being a foolish, sly, irresolute, or dishonest person). Occasionally, the insight that one character has into another extends beyond the aspects of their personality that I have labeled dispositions and encompasses their whole mind. A character may feel that another person knows them completely, all about how their mind works. Miss Wade says of Gowan that "He understood the state of things at a glance, and he understood me. He was the first person I had ever seen in my life who had understood me. . . . He accompanied every movement of my mind" (732).

I will now discuss three specific ways in which the social minds in the novel communicate with each other: the face, sign language, and the look.

The face

One of the obvious ways in which thought is made public is by means of the face. As we do in real life, characters pick up cues about the mental functioning of others by reading facial expressions. Of course, this is only one means amongst others. At one point, Blandois knows what Clennam is thinking simply by watching the back of his head, as when,

> Though Clennam's back was turned while [Blandois] spoke . . . he kept those glittering eyes of his . . . upon him, and evidently saw in the very carriage of the head . . . that he was saying nothing which Clennam did not already know. (819)

Nevertheless, the face is a particularly important source of knowledge about the minds of others and there is a continual stream of references in the novel to the face and its role in the public nature of thought. Some relate to individual mental events. Mrs. Clennam says to Little Dorrit: "'You love Arthur. (I can see the blush upon your face.)'" (859). Clennam "saw a shade of disappointment on [Mrs. Plornish's] face, as she checked a sigh, and looked at the low fire" (178). "There was an expression in his face [Blandois] as he released his grip of his friend's [Cavalletto] jaw, from which his friend inferred that . . . [etc]" (174). "'My God!' said Bar, starting back, and clapping his hand upon the other's breast. '. . . I see it in your face'" (773). On other occasions, the face is seen as an indicator of long-term dispositions. When Clennam was a child, Mrs. Clennam could see him looking at her "with his mother's face" (859) and therefore knows that he will, as she thinks, take after her. "Little Dorrit stopped. For there was neither happiness nor health in the face that turned to her" (857). The narrator comments of Mr. Chivery that "As to any key to his inner knowledge being to be found in his face, the Marshalsea key was as legible as an index to the individual characters and histories upon which it was turned" (346). Changes in the flow of events can be signaled by changes in characters' faces. In the climax of the novel, Mrs. Clennam's face is, at first, as inscrutable as ever: "Her face neither acquiesced or demurred" (837), and "Her face was ever frowning, attentive, and settled" (839). However, as events unravel and get beyond her control, "Mrs. Clennam's face had changed. There was a remarkable darkness of color on it, and the brow was more contracted" (841).

Many of the most powerful moments in the novel involve descriptions of facial expressions. In the scene in which Little Dorrit is meditating on London Bridge and is caught unawares by Young John Chivery,

> She started and fell back from him, with an expression in her face of fright and something like dislike that caused him unutterable dismay. . . . It was but a momentary look, inasmuch as she checked it. . . . But she felt what it had been, as he felt what it had been; and they stood looking at one another equally confused. (260)

Here, her facial expression inadvertently reveals her true feelings, and both she and Young John are shocked as a result. In marked contrast, facial expressions can also serve a dramaturgical function. Characters self-consciously use them to present to the world the sort of self that they want the world to see.

> With these words, and with a face expressive of many uneasy doubts and much anxious guardianship, he [Mr. Dorrit] turned his regards upon the assembled company in the Lodge; so plainly indicating that his brother was to be pitied for not being under lock and key. (269)

However, these efforts can be unsuccessful: "Do what he could to compose his face, he could not convey so much of an ordinary expression into it, but that the moment she saw it, she dropped her work and cried, 'Mr. Clennam! What's the matter?'" (465). Characters are continually attempting to read faces as cues to action. Clennam "suffered a few people to pass him in whose face there was no encouragement to make the inquiry" (118). This face-reading may be only partially successful. A character may find out something of what another is thinking, but not the whole story. For instance, "As she [Little Dorrit] looked at him [Clennam] silently, there was something in her affectionate face that he did not quite comprehend: something that could have broken into tears in a moment, and yet that was happy and proud" (885). Sometimes, the facial expression serves almost as a kind of sign language, as discussed in the next section. Clennam has difficulty following Mrs. Plornish's train of thought because she is rather inarticulate: "He was at a loss to understand what she meant; and by expressing as much in his looks, elicited her explanation" (178).

SIGN LANGUAGE

In addition to the face, another way in which social minds are made publicly available to each other is sign language. There is a surprisingly large amount of this type of communication in the novel. It generally occurs between characters who know each other well and who therefore form an intermental unit. An example is the Dorrit family. Little Dorrit "looked in amazement at her sister and would have asked a question, but that Fanny with a warning frown pointed to a curtained doorway of communication with another room" (284). Tip gives Fanny "a slight nod and a slight wink; in acknowledgement of which, Miss Fanny looked surprised, and laughed and reddened" (536). Within such a unit, nonverbal communication is an efficient supplement to speech. "In answer to Cavalletto's look of inquiry, Clennam made him a sign to go; but he added aloud, 'unless you are afraid of him.' Cavalletto replied with a very emphatic finger-negative, 'No, master'" (821). This is a cooperative, beneficial unit. Fanny and Mrs. General form a conflicted, competitive unit but the sign language is just as efficacious. When "Miss Fanny coughed, as much as to say, 'You are right'" (661), Mrs. General knows exactly what she means.

The choreography of the sign language in the novel is beautifully judged and often extremely subtle. So much so that the absence of any sign can sometimes be sign language enough. Within people of the same social class, who understand each other well, the significance of doing nothing can be well understood. "Ferdinand Barnacle looked knowingly at Bar as he strolled upstairs and gave him no answer at all. 'Just so, just so,' said Bar, nodding his head" (614). In contrast, a refusal to admit to an understanding of sign language is highly significant. Plornish, "having intimated that he wished to speak to her [Little Dorrit] privately, in a series of coughs so very noticeable" (326) that Mr. Dorrit must be aware of their significance, Mr. Dorrit nevertheless refuses to admit that he understands Plornish's sign language. To do so would be an admission that he knows that Little Dorrit works to support him. At the end of the novel, Mrs. Clennam is reduced to a cruel parody of communication in her use of sign language: "Except that she could move her eyes and faintly express a negative and affirmative with her head, she lived and died a statue" (863).

One example of the absence of a sign is worth dwelling on because it raises interesting issues relating to the concept of action. Meagles tactlessly praises Gowan's connections with the Barnacles in Doyce's presence and so "Clennam looked at Doyce, but Doyce knew all about it beforehand, and looked at his plate, and made no sign, and said no word" (248). It is clear from the rhythm of the prose, the emphasis of each clause, that there is a conscious decision by Doyce to do nothing and take no action. But this decision differs very little, in cognitive terms, from a decision to perform a physical action. In addition, this is a social situation in which certain actions are expected such as showing interest by nodding, smiling, and agreeing, and so Doyce's refusal to do any of these things is a non-action that has a dramaturgical function. He is demonstrating that he is unhappy with Meagles's remarks. But who is he demonstrating this disapproval to? Clennam, who is looking at him and will presumably be expecting disapproval-action? Or, less likely perhaps, Meagles himself, who will perhaps insensitively be expecting approval-action? Is he doing nothing because of these conflicting expectations? In any case, the non-action performs the same function as an action. What these questions suggest is that the boundary between actions and non-actions is certainly very blurred and that the refusal to engage in expected social action *is* perhaps an action after all.

It will be illuminating, I think, to consider the role of sign language within a single intermental unit, the one comprising Clennam and Pancks. At first, these two appear to be a distinctly unlikely pair for such a possibility. I referred above to characters with inscrutable faces and Pancks is one.

> With his former doubt whether this dry hard personage were quite in earnest, Clennam again turned his eyes attentively upon his face. It was as scrubby and dingy as ever, and as eager and quick as ever, and he could see nothing lurking in it that was at all expressive of a latent mockery that had seemed to strike upon his ear in the voice. (322)

When Pancks speaks highly of Casby, "Arthur for his life could not have said with confidence whether Pancks really thought so or not" (462). The difficulty that Clennam has in reading Pancks's mind becomes particularly important when Clennam does not know if Pancks's interest in the Dorrit family is well meant or not. His activities "caused Arthur Clennam much uneasiness at this period" (367), and "awakened many wondering speculations in his mind" (323). However, over time, Clennam comes to know Pancks's mind better.

> Between this eccentric personage and Clennam, a tacit understanding and accord had been always improving. . . . Though he had never before made any profession or protestation to Clennam, and though what he had just said was little enough as to the words in which it was expressed, Clennam had long had a growing belief that Mr. Pancks, in his own odd way, was becoming attached to him. (637)

It is important to note the emphasis in this passage on the fact that their relationship does not rely on words. Indeed, during the conversation in which Pancks tempts Clennam to speculate (638-43), much is understood, or partly understood, between the two men, but very little is actually said. Indeed, it is not even explicitly stated that Pancks has been successful in persuading Clennam to speculate.

Over time, the understanding between Clennam and Pancks becomes sufficiently intermental for them to be able to communicate by signs.

> Mr. Pancks in shaking hands merely scratched his eyebrow with his left forefinger and snorted once, but Clennam, who understood him better now than of old, comprehended that he had almost done for the evening and wished to say a word to him outside. (594)

When outside, "Arthur thought he received his cue to speak to him as one who knew pretty well what had just now passed" (595). However, the resulting conversation demonstrates that the efficiency of intermental thought should not be overestimated. Misreadings can occur. When Pancks says that he wants to take a razor to Casby (in fact, to cut his hair), Clennam thinks that he wants to cut his throat!

THE LOOK

The importance of the look is continually stressed in the text. Clearly, for minds to be public and available, it is necessary for characters to look attentively at each other in order to pick up the sorts of cues that I have been describing. This may even require staring at the other person. In fact, there is a noticeable preponderance in the text of those three words—*attentive*, *look*, and *stare*. The word *attention* is used in *Little Dorrit* 60 times, *attentive* 21 times, and *attentively* 11 times (total: 92). As a control, the comparable numbers for *Middlemarch* (about the same length text) are these: 42, 4, and 0 (total: 46), and for *The Ambassadors* (about half the length): 19, 4, and 1 (total: 24). The occurrences in *Little Dorrit* of the words *look*, *looks*, *looked*, and *looking* total 995 (766 in *Middlemarch* and 291 in *The Ambassadors*). The comparable totals for the words *stare*, *stares*, *stared*, and *staring* are 64, 22, and 27, respectively. Clearly, the difference in the usage of these words is significant. However, whilst it may be tempting to ascribe the variation to Dickens's interest in social thought as compared to the more internalist perspective of George Eliot and, in particular, Henry James, further research on the issue is required before any claims of this sort can be made with confidence.

In *Little Dorrit*, the act of looking fulfils a number of very different functions. The list that follows is a selection. Some of the quotations from the text that are used elsewhere in this essay reveal other uses of the look.

> *Information-seeking*: "Monsieur Rigaud's eyes . . . were so drawn in that direction that [Cavalletto] more than once followed them to and back from the pavement in some surprise" (46).
>
> *Information-giving*: When Mrs. Clennam talks to Clennam, "Her emphasis had been derived from her eyes quite as much as from the stress she laid on her words" (747). "Their looks met. Something thoughtfully apprehensive in [Minnie's] large, soft eyes, had checked Little Dorrit in an instant" (544).
>
> *Warning*: "To Arthur's increased surprise, Mistress Affery, stretching her eyes wide at himself, as if in warning that this [Blandois] was not a gentleman for him to interfere with" (599).
>
> *Thanking*: "Mother, with a look which thanked Clennam in a manner agreeable to him" (581).
>
> *Expressing curiosity*: Blandois and Mrs. Clennam "looked very closely at one another. That was but natural curiosity" (403).
>
> *Bonding*: "There was a silent understanding between them [Little Dorrit and Minnie] . . . She looked at Mrs. Gowan with keen and unabated interest" (544).
>
> *Intimidating*: Flintwinch says to Mrs. Clennam: "'Now, I know what you mean by opening your eyes so wide at me'" (850).
>
> *Controlling*: "As Mrs. Clennam never removed her eyes from Blandois . . . so Jeremiah never removed his from Arthur" (602).

The use of the look can be an important element in a character's personality. Little Dorrit looks at Clennam "with all the earnestness of her soul looking steadily out of her eyes" (214). The look is often expressive of the attitude of the looker towards the "lookee." For example, "The visitor [Miss Wade] stood looking at her [Tattycoram] with a strange attentive smile. It was wonderful to see the fury of the contest in the girl, and the bodily struggle she made as if she were rent by the Demons of old" (65); "Mrs. Clennam and Jeremiah had exchanged a look; and had then looked, and looked still, at Affery" (834). However, it can sometimes be that the accusation of staring is more informative about the uneasy state of mind of the "staree" than it is about the alleged starer. Fanny unfairly reproaches Little Dorrit for staring at her (665), and Mr. Dorrit thinks that the Chief Butler looks at him "in a manner that Mr. Dorrit considered questionable" (678). When Mr. Dorrit's mind is collapsing and "his daughter had been observant of him with something more than her usual interest," he demands peevishly,

"'Amy, what are you looking at?'" (701). Miss Wade refers to someone in her past who "had a serious way with her eyes of watching me" (727).

The mechanics of the look are interesting. It may be combined with the sign language discussed above: Clennam, "more with his eyes than by the slight impulsive motion of his hand, entreated her [Little Dorrit] to be reassured and to trust him" (121). Characters sometimes see significance in an exchange of looks by others: When Pancks comes to break the news of the Dorrit wealth, "The excitement of this strange creature was fast communicating itself to Clennam. Little Dorrit with amazement, saw this, and observed that they exchanged quick looks" (437). Characters are frequently uncomfortably aware of being the subject of a stare. When Mr. Dorrit goes to see Mrs. Clennam, "he felt that the eyes of Mr. Flintwinch and of Mrs. Clennam were on him. He found, when he looked up, that this sensation was not a fanciful one" (686). Mrs. Clennam (perhaps the major starer in the novel) "sat looking at her until she attracted her attention. Little Dorrit colored under such a gaze, and looked down" (390). Flintwinch comments dryly to Clennam: "'You'll be able to take my likeness, the next time you call, Arthur, I should think'" (744). Clennam is comically uncomfortable with a look from Flora: "In his ridiculous distress, Clennam received another of the old glances without in the least knowing what to do with it" (194). Occasionally, a look can be so compelling that the lookee has to return it: "Throughout he [Blandois] looked at her [Little Dorrit]. Once attracted by his peculiar eyes, she could not remove her own, and they had looked at each other all the time" (546). Mr. F.'s Aunt "looked at Clennam with an expression of such intense severity that he felt obliged to look at her in return, against his personal inclinations" (590). "'None of your eyes at me,'" she scolds him.

CONCLUSION

I stressed at the beginning of this essay that both perspectives on fictional minds, the internalist and the externalist, are required. The narrator of *Little Dorrit* recognizes this truth. Employing the internalist perspective on those aspects of the mind that are inner, introspective, solitary, private, individual, psychological, mysterious, and detached, the narrator remarks of Mr. Dorrit that "Only the wisdom that holds the clue to all hearts and all mysteries, can surely know to what extent a man, especially a man brought down as this man had been, can impose upon himself" (275). Employing the externalist perspective that stresses those aspects of the mind that are outer, active, public, social, behavioral, evident, embodied, and engaged, the narrator comments of Mr. Chivery (as quoted above in the section on the face) that "As to any key to his inner knowledge being to be found in his face, the Marshalsea key was as legible as an index to the individual characters and histories upon which it was turned" (346).

Nevertheless, within this balance, I have emphasized social minds for two reasons. One is that they have been neglected by traditional narrative theory. The other is that, in my view, the social minds in this particular novel are more important than the solitary or private minds. It is not possible to understand *Little Dorrit* without an understanding of the public minds that operate within its storyworld. It is difficult to think of any important aspect of the novel that is left out of an externalist analysis of it. A good deal of the significance of the thought in the novel is lost if only the internalist perspective is employed. My intention in quoting so frequently from the novel was to show that these social minds are woven into the fabric of its discourse. As to whether or not the conclusions reached here regarding the social minds in this novel can also be applied to other novels, more research is required.

WORKS CITED

Bakhtin, Mikhail. *Problems of Dostoevsky's Poetics*. Trans. Caryl Emerson. Manchester: Manchester University Press, 1984. Print.

Bateson, Gregory. *Steps to an Ecology of Mind: A Revolutionary Approach to Man's Understanding of Himself*. New York: Ballantine, 1972. Print.

Clark, Andy and David J. Chalmers. "The Extended Mind." *Analysis* 58 (1998): 7-19. Print.

Damasio, Antonio. *The Feeling of What Happens: Body, Emotion and the Making of Consciousness*. London: Heinemann, 2000. Print.

Dennett, Daniel C. *Consciousness Explained*. Harmondsworth: Penguin, 1991.

---. *Kinds of Minds: Towards an Understanding of Consciousness*. London: Weidenfeld and Nicholson, 1996. Print.

Dickens, Charles. *Little Dorrit*. Ed. John Holloway. Harmondsworth: Penguin, 1857 [1967]. Print.

Geertz, Clifford. *The Interpretation of Cultures: Selected Essays*. London: Fontana, 1993. Print.

Herman, David. "Stories as a Tool for Thinking." *Narrative Theory and the Cognitive Sciences*. Ed David Herman. Stanford: CSLI, 2003a. 163-92. Print.

---. "Regrounding Narratology: The Study of Narratively Organized Systems for Thinking." *What is Narratology: Questions and Answers Regarding the Status of a Theory*. Eds. Tom Kindt and Hans-Harald Muller. Berlin: de Gruyter, 2003b. 303-32. Print.

Hutchins, Edwin. *Cognition in the Wild*. Cambridge, MA: MIT Press, 1995. Print.

Margolin, Uri. "Telling Our Story: On 'We' Literary Narratives." *Language and Literature* 5.2 (1996): 115-33. Print.

---. "Telling in the Plural: From Grammar to Ideology." *Poetics Today* 21.3 (2000): 591-618. Print.

Palmer, Alan. "Attribution Theory." *Contemporary Stylistics*. Ed. by Marina Lambrou and Peter Stockwell. London: Continuum, 2007. Print.

---. *Fictional Minds*. Lincoln: University of Nebraska Press, 2004. Print.

---. "Intermental Thought in the Novel: The Middlemarch Mind." *Style* 39.4 (2005): 427-39. Print.

Sperber, Dan and Lawrence Hirschfeld. "Culture, Cognition, and Evolution." *The MIT Encyclopedia of the Cognitive Sciences*. Eds. Robert Wilson and Frank Keil. Cambridge, MA: MIT Press, 1999. cxi-cxxxii. Print.

Wertsch, James V. *Voices of the Mind: A Sociocultural Approach to Mediated Action*. Cambridge, MA: Harvard University Press, 1991. Print.

Zunshine, Lisa. *Why We Read Fiction: Theory of Mind and the Novel.* Columbus: The Ohio State University Press, 2006. Print.

The Way We Imagine[1]

Mark Turner

Blending and the human mind

Fifty thousand years ago, more or less, during the Upper Paleolithic, unmistakable archaeological evidence began to accumulate of a remarkable set of human singularities: art, science, religion, refined tool use, advanced music and dance, fashions of dress, language, and mathematics. Human beings began to demonstrate an unprecedented ability to be imaginative in whatever they encountered. Cognitively modern human beings throughout the world since that time have demonstrated this remarkable ability, as a routine part of what it means to be human.

In *The Way We Think*, Gilles Fauconnier and I proposed that this change happened in the following way (Fauconnier and Turner 2002). The basic mental operation of conceptual integration, also known as "blending," has been present and evolving in various species for a long time. Modern human beings evolved not an entirely different kind of mind, but instead the capacity for the strongest form of conceptual integration, known as "double-scope" blending. It is the engine of the human imagination.

What is blending and why is it so important?[2] Let us begin with an example. A man is participating in a wedding. He is consciously enacting a familiar mental story, with roles, participants, a plot, and a goal. But while he is fulfilling his role in the wedding story, he is remembering a different story, which took place a month before off the Cycladic island of Despotico, where he and his girlfriend, who is not present at the wedding, went diving in the hopes of retrieving sunken archaeological treasures from the newly discovered Temple of Apollo and Artemis. Why, cognitively, should he be able mentally to activate and interweave these two stories? There are rich possibilities for confusion, but in all the central ways, he remains unconfused. He does not mistake the bride for his girlfriend, for the treasure, for the fish, for the temple, or even for Artemis. He does not swim down the aisle, or speak as if through a snorkel.

Human beings go beyond merely imagining stories or concepts that run counter to the present environment. We can also connect them and blend them to make a third mental array. The man at the wedding can make analogical connections between his girlfriend and the bride and between himself and the groom, and blend these counterparts into a daydream in which it is he and his girlfriend who are being married at this particular ceremony. This blended story is manifestly false, and he should not make the mistake, as he obediently discharges his duties at the real wedding, of thinking that he is in the process of marrying his girlfriend. But he can realize that he likes the blended story, and so formulate a plan of action to make it real. Or, in the blended story, when the bride is invited to say "I do," she might say, "I would never marry you!" Her response might reveal to him a truth he had sensed intuitively but not recognized.

DOUBLE-SCOPE BLENDING

The most imaginative blending networks are double-scope networks. In a double-scope network, the two inputs have different (and often clashing) organizing frames, and the blend has an organizing frame that receives projections from each of those organizing frames. The blend also has emergent structure of its own that cannot be found in any of the inputs. Sharp differences between the organizing frames of the inputs offer the possibility of rich clashes. Far from blocking the construction of the network, such clashes offer challenges to the imagination. The resulting blends can turn out to be highly imaginative.

The imagination is not arbitrary or accidental. It has elaborate constitutive principles and governing principles (Fauconnier and Turner 2002). It cannot be explained as the sparks of crossed wires, the mere loss of separation between supposedly modular capacities. It is much too systematic for such an explanation to be plausible. In addition, imaginative blending operates with as much systematicity within individual conceptual domains as it does across domains.

The ability for highly imaginative double-scope blending seems to be available to children very early. For example, in Crockett Johnson's (1983) *Harold and the Purple Crayon,* written for three-year-olds, Harold uses his purple crayon to draw, and whatever he draws is real, although the result is clearly a child's sketch.

His world is a blend of spatial reality and its representation. In the blend, the representation is fused with what it represents. When Harold wants light to go for a walk, he draws the moon, and so he has moonlight. The moon stays with him as he moves. This blend has two inputs. One input has elements of the real spatial world as we experience it and perceive it. One of those elements is the moon. The other input to the blend has conventional knowledge about drawing. In the input with the real moon, the moon cannot be created by drawing and it does not come into existence at someone's will. In the input with drawing, a drawn moon cannot emit moonlight, or float along in the sky as the artist's companion. But in the blend, there is a special blended moon with special emergent properties.

The mechanisms of blending that give us this special blended moon work generally throughout *Harold and the Purple Crayon.* When he needs to walk, he draws a path, and then sets off on his walk. When Harold wants to return home, he draws a window around the moon, positioning the moon where it would appear in his window if he were in his bedroom, and so he is automatically in fact in his bedroom and can go to sleep (Figure 8.1).

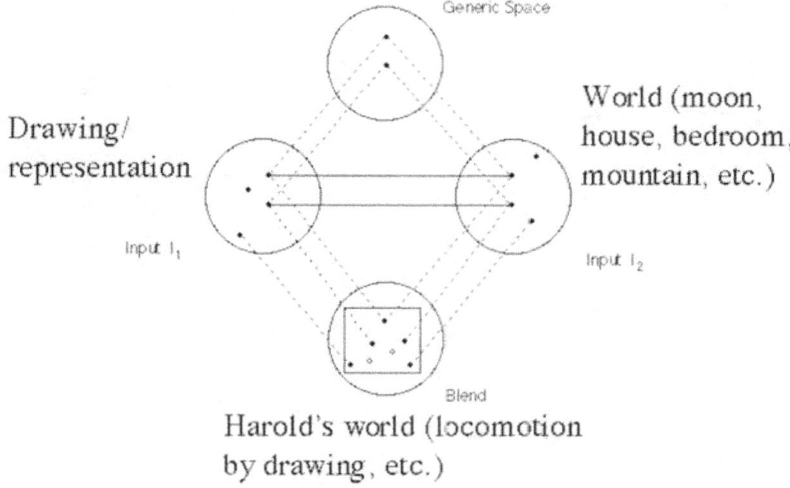

Figure 8.1. Blending network for Harold and the Purple Crayon.

Child Harold's blended world has new kinds of causality and event shape that are unavailable from either the domain of drawing or the domain of spatial living. Blends of this sort are found widely throughout art and literature.

DOUBLE-SCOPE BLENDING AND ATTRIBUTIONS OF MIND

Imaginative double-scope blending is equally the mainstay of everyday thought and understanding. Consider, as an example of routine blending, our perception of a seal. The eyes of a seal are remarkably like the eyes of a human being. When we see a seal at the seashore, it is impossible to resist the conclusion that we and the seal share a category. Compelling and evident analogies leap out at us, between the seal's appearance and ours, between the seal's motion and ours. Our human eyes align toward an object as our limbs propel our bodies toward it, and it seems to be no different for the seal.

We immediately forge a mental blend of ourselves and the seal. The result is a conception of a seal that has not only all of the seal's appearance and motion, but additionally a feature we know only of ourselves—the possession of a mind (Figure 8.2).

In the mental blend, we conceive of a seal as having a mind something like ours, lying behind its appearance and motion. In the mental blend, the seal's eyes are not merely open, round, clear, and active, but also alert, intelligent, inquisitive, and perceptive. It *inspects* us with wide-eyed, penetrating *attention*. It *intends* to *pursue* an object. It has perception, appetite, and memory. We believe in this blend completely, long before we have any refined scientific evidence for it.

This is the sort of blend we assemble unconsciously, from early childhood, for any other human being. In the standard blend that we use for conceiving of another hu-

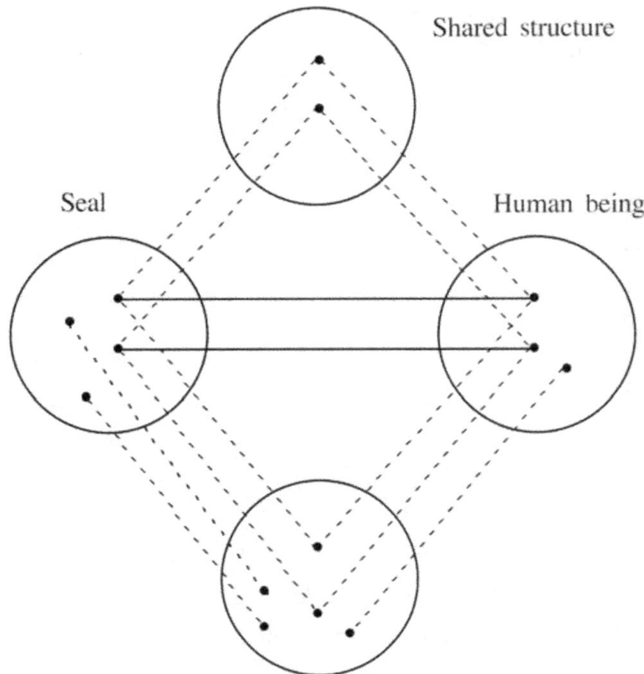

Figure 8.2. Blending network for seal with a mind.

man being, the human being has not only all the organismic appearance and movement that we routinely perceive when we pay attention to the person, but also something we project to it of ourselves—the possession of a mind. It has perception, sensation, and intention behind its appearance and movements, just as we have perception, sensation, and intention behind ours. In the blend, the person whom we watch has mental states that accord with what we see.

We are adept at varying the conceptual structure that we project to the blend. When we perceive that someone is in a situation or condition that is not identical to ours, we can project their situation or condition to the blend, giving their perspective to the blend, with consequences for the thoughts we imagine them to have. When we see that someone's behavior is unlike our own even in identical conditions, we adjust the projection to the blend accordingly.

The projection of mind to the seal automatically gives the seal some viewpoint, but we can vary the specific details. We can choose specific details that belong to the conditions of the seal. Alternatively, we can mix in elements that belong to our own condition. At the one extreme, the seal has a viewpoint very different from ours in both location and disposition, and we apprehend the blended seal-with-a-mind from a distance, as a strange and foreign species. At the other extreme, the blend can be given our own first-person viewpoint, and we can see, in the blend, through the seal's eyes. (Try it: in imagination, be the seal looking at you, the human being, watching the seal from the seashore. Do you suddenly feel a little wet? Do you feel yourself trying to keep yourself afloat?) The nature of the mind possessed by the seal in the blend can also be varied: we can imagine what it is like to be a seal with seal-like abilities and preferences, or we can imagine what it is like to be something like us clothed in seal form. Such blending apparently outstrips by a vast distance anything a non-human species can perform.

Children routinely perform such acts of blending in conceiving of other human beings, and perhaps equally routinely in conceiving of animals, with the result that talking animals are the mainstay of the human nursery. Other species show no disposition to make dolls of other species and then attribute to them their own vocalizations, but the creative projection done by the human child can easily produce a seal who talks, who makes friends with us, who invites us to come swimming for his birthday party, and who winks at us collusively as we engage in adventures.

These are again "double-scope" blending networks, with inputs to the blend that have different (and often clashing) organizing frames and an organizing frame for the blend that includes parts of each of those organizing frames and has emergent structure of its own. *The Way We Think* presents the details of double-scope blending in examples drawn from mathematics, science, grammar, counterfactual reasoning, causal reasoning, humor, the construction of identity, category extension, artifacts, and so on.

In all such cases, there is emergent structure in the blend. In the case of the talking seal, the creature in the blend has specific properties that belong to neither the human being nor the seal, that is, to neither of the two mental concepts that feed the blend. Consider the speech of the talking seal. It might have a sound system for its language that includes barks and growls, and a grammar bizarre for a human being. No human being has such speech, and of course no seal has speech at all, but the talking seal has just this emergent style of speech.

It is an open cognitive scientific question how the modern human being, from infant to adult, activates these conceptions of other minds, and how these blended conceptions differ. One of the most important variations is whether the blend has a counterpart in our conception of our reality. The seal that we see at the beach has an immediate counterpart in our notion of our reality, while Donald Duck does not. We are not deluded, and the difference is strong.

Similarly, there is the question of how the human mind evolved so as to be able to make immediate recognition of other minds. Consider a range of hypotheses:

- Possibility 1: Human beings have "Swiss Army Knife" minds, whose different capacities are like different tools, unrelated in their mechanisms and evolution, and operating separately but with some coordination in the brain. On this view, a separate module evolved to recognize other human beings as having minds, and that module has no particular computational relation to any other.

- Possibility 2: Human beings have the operation of double-scope blending, and put the notion of another mind together from scratch through blending every time they encounter a person or invent an imaginary being.

These are surely straw-man possibilities. Possibility 1 seems implausible because human beings do double-scope blending across many different and perhaps all conceptual domains, and do it for non-human beings. Possibility 2 seems implausible because it offers no place for efficiency and entrenchment. But there are two plausible possibilities:

> • Possibility 3: People have double-scope blending that can achieve attributions of mind for non-human beings, but extremely early in life put together blending templates that serve them thereafter for dealing with people. These templates are quickly entrenched, and people "live in the blend," never aware of the work that went into the template, but able to open it back up actively and on-line when they want to do new work. We never need to construct these templates afresh again. Instead, we activate the blend directly, just like that. This possibility allows for adjustment, so that the newborn who regards the voice-activated mobile as an intentional agent could refine its reactions later.
>
> • Possibility 4: Genetic assimilation has picked up some of the work of double-scope blending in the case of human beings, so that human beings now have a head start in achieving the blending templates for other minds.

Possibilities 3 and 4 could combine: double-scope blending is responsible for our evolution of concepts of robust other minds and accordingly for our outstanding abilities for social cognition. Indeed, the adaptiveness of social cognition contributes to the much greater overall adaptiveness of double-scope blending. Modern human beings continue to do active double-scope blending with robust on-line construction when we assemble imaginary beings such as intelligent robots, or a river that rises up in a Japanese animated film to express, in exotic ways, its pain at being polluted. But the basic human reaction to another human being does not need to be assembled from scratch.

Imaginative blends: The selkie

Let us consider a remarkable blend that has no counterpart in our conception of reality: a blend of *seal* and *human being*. This is the concept of a *selkie*. Selkies have new properties. In the folklore of the Orkney Islands, they are shape-shifting beings. When in seal form, a selkie can shed its coat to become a human being, or rather, something deceptively like a human being. When in human form, it can converse and mate with a human being. Selkies shed their coats in the moonlight and dance on the level shore. A prudent selkie hides its coat carefully before cavorting. Here we see a case where the emergent meaning in the blend includes not new properties for a seal but in fact a new species that falls into the category of neither human being nor seal.

In the selective projection to the blend, the selkie when out of its coat has the anatomical parts and proportions of a human being but the sleek and lithe movements of the seal. Accordingly, when out of their coats, selkies are sexually irresistible to human beings. In the Orkney legends, a man sometimes steals the coat of a female selkie to compel her to agree to marry him if she ever wants to regain her coat.

But male selkies also shed their coats and slip into villages to mate with deliriously grateful women. Selkies have a relation to their coats that is a blend of a seal's relation to its skin and a human being's relation to clothes. Selkies take off their clothes to have fun, and are vulnerable when thus "naked."

BLENDS OF BLENDS

It is common in art to work with many blends, and to make blends of blends. A particularly elaborate development of the selkie legend is offered in a well-known modern tale for older children titled "Aunt Charlotte and the NGA Portraits" (Turner, M. W. 1995). NGA is the acronym for "National Gallery of Art," the one in Washington, DC. It sits next to the Capitol Building on the National Mall.

"Aunt Charlotte and the NGA Portraits" presents a character named Olga Weathers. Halfway into the story, the reader discovers that Olga is a selkie lacking her coat. The word "selkie" never occurs in the story, and no prior knowledge of selkies is required to understand the story.

Olga has the mental character of a woman but, understandably, no native taste for the human world. She would prefer a life of swimming in the water. Wearing her coat, she would have something like the body of a seal, naturally. But not quite, since her coat can be removed, and when it is, she becomes a woman. But not quite, since, when she is a woman, she retains her knowledge of the sea and retains, too, the remarkable instinctive capabilities of a marine mammal.

Olga Weathers has features possessed by no seal. Neither seal nor woman can lose its skin, or assume the skin of another species. Neither seal nor woman can be transformed into a member of another species. And it is not only Olga who is different in the world of this story. A real man in our world cannot obtain a wife by stealing the skin of a seal, but in the story, a man can try to get a wife by stealing the coat of a female selkie.

These things are possible in Olga's world. She switches from species to species according to whether she is wearing her coat. She is never either woman or seal, but always something different, and this difference counts in the story as her "magic." A mean man, it turns out, did steal her coat. He hoped she would marry him in order to regain it but she refused to marry him, because she knew he would have kept her coat forever, and she would never have been free. He thought she was helpless and had no choice, but she was not powerless, and she had a few friends who helped her make a home on Ocracoke, a seaside town in North Carolina, where she earned her living by helping the fishermen. Olga can tell where the fish are, and she can foretell the weather, and she has a sense for the conditions of the sea. The fishermen therefore pay her for advice. In Olga's World, it seems, boats have an intentional nature, too, or at least, they can hear a selkie, and they are happy to comply with her requests. She can call the boats home when they are lost. As luck would have it, the man who stole her coat was injured while hunting narwhals. The wound turned septic and he died without telling her where he had hidden her coat. So there is Olga, beached on Ocracoke.

In the blending network that produces this selkie, the shape and movement that are projected from the human being input and from the seal input to Olga do not make her lithe and frisky. On the contrary, her body is massive, like a seal's, and she has relative difficulty moving on land, as a seal might. She is hefty. Her long hair combs out in perfect waves. She is herself a kind of undulation whenever she passes over the sand.

Olga's world, inhabited by selkies, is brushed to that extent by the magic of shape-shifting, the magic of moving from one category to another, of blending incompatible elements such as woman and seal to make not just a mental blend but elements in the world to which the blend refers.

Picture Worlds

There is another magic pattern of blending in Olga's world, and this additional magic is also based on a very familiar pattern of blending, one that concerns our everyday, entirely pedestrian concept of representation. Human beings effortlessly understand the concept of "representation." As a matter of straightforward practice, we routinely put something and its representation into mental correspondence. The representational element is understood as "representing" a world or a scene or an element in a scene (Figure 8.3).

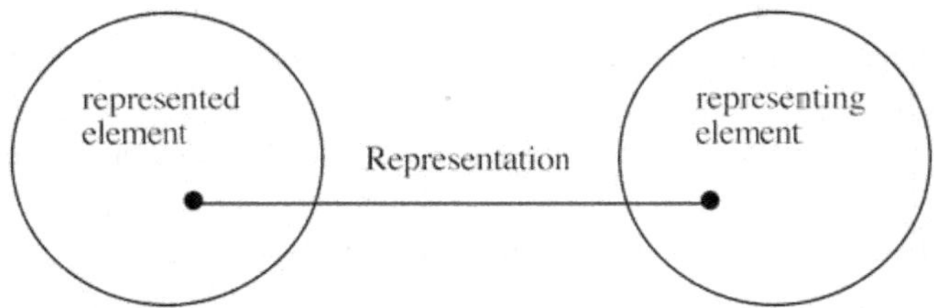

Figure 8.3. A Representation Vital Relation connecting elements in different inputs.

It is extremely common for us to blend these two related spaces and in so doing to compress the "outer-space" relation of *representation* between them into a unique object in the blend, as in Figure 8.4.

For example, a person and a photograph are two quite different things, but we can blend the photographic element and the person. In the blend, the person is fused with the photographic element. We point at the picture and say, "This is John." Of course, we are not deluded in the least: we know that, in the contributing space with the person, John is three-dimensional and moves. We know that the photograph is two-dimensional and does not move. But the conceptual blend in which the representation of John is fused with John is extremely useful. Most blends of this sort, but not all, have outer-space connections not only of representation but also of analogy between the representation and the element represented. That is, the visual image that is the representation of John is visually and topologically analogous to John himself: there are two images of eyes in the representation and two eyes in John's head; the two images of eyes in the representation are above the image of the nose in the representation just as the John's actual two eyes are above John's actual nose; and so on (Figure 8.5).

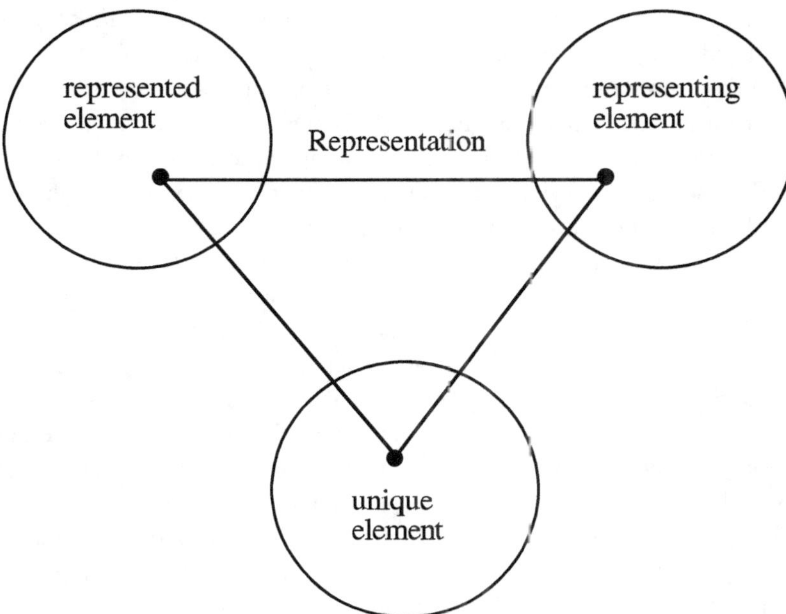

Figure 8.4. Blend of represented element and representing element.

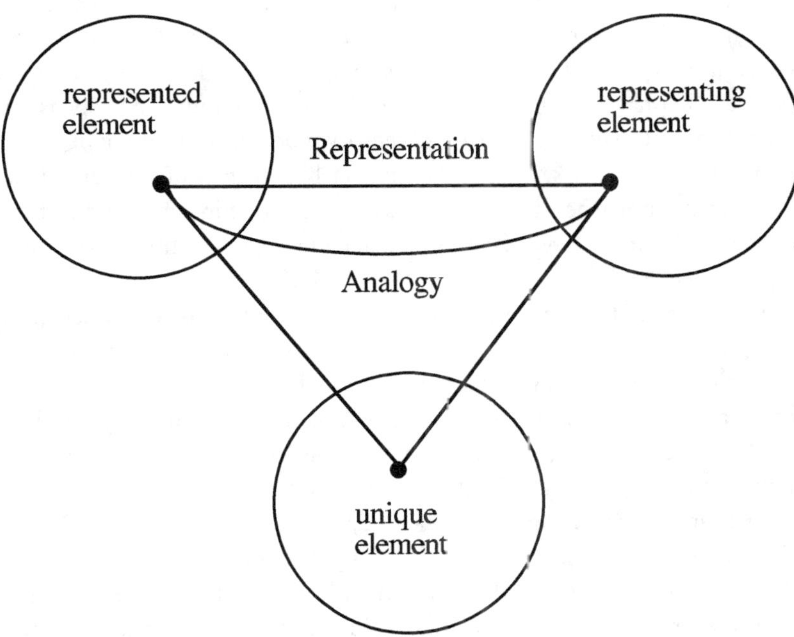

Figure 8.5. Blend of represented element and representing element, with an additional Analogy Vital Relation.

This is, of course, just the kind of blending network we saw in *Harold and the Purple Crayon*. In addition to the contributing mental space that contains the representation and the other contributing mental space that contains what is represented, there is yet another contributing mental space that can be brought into this common "compression of representation" network. A window, or a gap in the curtains or the fence, or a portal of any sort gives us a view. When we catch only a punctual view through a portal, we get a framed glimpse. Many vital conceptual relations create a connection between a framed representation and a framed glimpse. For example, a photograph of a person and a framed glimpse of the same person are strongly analogous not only in the content of what is viewed but also in the fact that there is a viewer of that content. It seems to be conventional to blend the photograph of a person with a framed glimpse of the person, so that, in the blend, the representation of the person is the person while the entire representation is a framed glimpse of the part of the visual field the photograph represents, including the person. (So if you show someone a mug shot against a wall, and ask "what's to the left?" the answer is "the rest of the person," even though the picture does not contain these elements. They are projected instead from our conception of the image as a framed glimpse.) We often say not only that the photograph gives us a "glimpse," but also that a true visual glimpse is a "snapshot."

We project much of what we know about a framed glimpse to the blended space in which the representation is fused with what it represents. Principally, we know that what we see in a framed glimpse is only part of a world that has spatial and temporal extent not directly represented in the framed glimpse. The ability to conceive of a framed glimpse as part of a larger spatial and temporal world may be common across all mammals that have vision, and this tendency to take a limited percept as implying a larger context may extend across all sensory modalities. For example, if we feel something small in the dark, we take it immediately to be part of a larger spatial and temporal world. Human beings, and perhaps dogs and dolphins, are very adept at conceiving of rich dynamic scenes with full spatial and temporal continuity on the basis of very partial perceptions.

When we blend a framed representation such as a photograph with our concept of a framed glimpse, the photograph thereby becomes a spatially and temporally limited part of a rich dynamic world with temporal and spatial continuities and changes that are not directly represented. Our conception of the conditions of photography leads us to project to the blend many elements from the represented scene that have no visible counterpart in the representation itself. If we see a photograph of the middle of a bridge, we routinely and naturally conceive of the bridge as extending beyond the frame. We conceive of the person on the bridge as obscuring elements behind her.

But of course we can do just the same thing with a painting or a sketch. We project to the blend elements that correspond to our understanding of the reality of a framed glimpse even though there is no visible counterpart of them in the representation itself, and we do this even when we know that the representation is fictitious. In the blend, the painted woman on the painted bridge is obscuring something from our view even if the painter invented both her and the bridge.

In the case of Olga, the blend that derives from all three contributing spaces—that is, the representation, what it represents, and a framed glimpse of what it represents—is reified: this blend is "true" in her world, in the following way. Olga's world has paintings, in fact the same paintings that exist in our world. But in Olga's world, those paintings actually are rich dynamic worlds of their own, and the few elite viewers in the world who in fact see properly, that is, with intelligence and open-minded insight, can indeed see the dynamic painted worlds that the paintings present. When they look at paintings, the people move, the sea rolls, the wind blows, vehicles enter and depart from the scene.

This emergent structure in the blend—rich, dynamic worlds inside the paintings—comes in part from projection of what we know about a glimpse through a window or portal. We know that if we prolong the glimpse to a stare, we might, looking through the portal, see change, dynamism, movement. Just so, in Olga's world, if you are talented and trained and you stare at the painting, you might see change, dynamism, movement. Why do you see it? In Olga's world, the answer is straightforward: because it is *there*.

Olga, of course, is one of those who see properly. When she looks at a painting, or at least a certain painting, she can see the people in it move, breathe, and act, because in the blend they in fact do, and in Olga's world, the blend is real. In the reified mental array that blends the painting, what it represents, and a prolonged view of what it represents, the representation of a person is not merely a person but indeed a person who has received very full projections from our notion of staring through a window at a world: the blended painted person can move, converse, think, plan, become hungry, eat, and so on. Yet the projections from the space of the person are not complete: in this blend, these painted people do not age. With a few exceptions, they are unaware of anything outside the world of the particular painting they inhabit.

INTO AND OUT OF THE FRAME

We are all familiar with a basic "Picture World" blending template. We use this template routinely. In it, there is a further set of correspondences between the representation and what it represents, as follows. Suppose that in our real world we have a bridge over a canal. Well, something can literally be part of that scene. If the physics works out right, that thing can literally be put into the scene, or removed from the scene. For example, we can row a real gondola into the real scene. Over in the representation, that is, the picture, there can be individual representations that can be created there; they can be erased, or otherwise made invisible. So, for example, the painter can do something with paint and a paintbrush that results in the existence of a representation of a gondola as part of the represented scene. There is an outer-space correspondence, that is, a correspondence between two of the contributing spaces, that connects two acts: putting something into a real scene, and taking some action that results in a new element in a representation. This correspondence connects two caused changes and their visible results. That outer-space correspondence can be compressed in our routine "Picture World" blending template to yield, in the blend, a blended causality. The blend fuses these two caused changes, so that the performing of actions that result in a representational element in the representation is fused with "putting" what it represents "into" the "scene." We say, "the painter put a gondola into the painting." Of course, we are not at all deluded: while a gondola must exist before it can be rowed into the Grand Canal, the exact flat composition of paint that represents the boat in the representation does not in fact exist as such to be "put" into the picture until the artist is quite finished taking the artistic action. We use such expressions all the time, as when we say that the artist "put some flowers into the sketch" but then "took them out," or "Hey! You forgot to put Grandma into your sketch." The blend that fuses the representation with what it represents gives a very natural way to think and speak about representations at human scale. It lets us recruit for the purpose of talking about representations and their creation the deeply understood logic of manipulating objects. So our notion of the creation of a representation already has some structure that can be projected to the blend to support the idea of "putting" an element "into" the representation. This blend has some remarkable emergent structure: we can for example "put" a "mountain" into the picture. Indeed, we can "put" "the moon" or "the sun" into the picture, even though in the real world we cannot perform the corresponding action.

There is yet further useful structure in what we know of looking through a portal onto a scene. One of the things we know about a window or portal on a real scene is that we can throw things through it or go through it ourselves, and then be part of what we previously only saw. We can project to the blend this action of "entrance," to give, in the blend, the possibility of moving something from our world into the picture world.

Olga's world reifies the "Picture World" blend and additionally provides the possibility of moving an object from our world into the picture world. The man who stole Olga's coat as a means of compelling her to marry him hid it not under a rock, or up a tree, or in any other normal locale in our world, but instead inside a painting, of Venice, by Canaletto. Within the logic of Olga's world, he literally "hid" it "in" Canaletto's painting. The coat is there, in the painting, in the exact sense that it was here, outside the picture, where any actual coat ought to be, but he moved it from here to there, and now it is there and not here. Olga's coat, in accordance with the physics of our world, can be in only one location. But in the hyper-blend that comes of blending Olga's Selkie World network and her Picture World network, this location can literally be inside a painting, and there is a means of moving things from locations outside the painting to locations inside the painting.

Olga's ignorance of the fact that her suitor hid her coat in the Canaletto painting presented her with a difficulty, but she overcame it, partly by studying art history to help her locate its hiding place. When she has located the painting, she faces a far greater challenge. As the suitor-thief had anticipated, it is not so easy for the land-bound selkie to take the coat out of the painting. To get to it, you must first physically enter the painting. But Olga cannot do that; she is too stout to squeeze through the frame. More daunting still, there is nothing but water across the bottom of the frame. Olga, massive and cumbersome, would fall into the water, and, unable to swim in her present unfortunate form, would drown. It is extremely witty to manipulate a selkie through fear of drowning.

Olga's world is a blend of two blending networks. One is the blend in which there are selkies, Selkie World . The other is a Picture World blend in which representation is compressed: in this Picture World network, the outer-space representation link between two separate mental inputs is compressed into uniqueness in the blend, so that the representation and what it represents are fused there into a single element. In this Picture World blend, the painting of the water really is water, for example, even as it is part of the painting. The Picture World blending network in Olga's World has, as mentioned, yet another input to the blend: the concept of a portal, such as a window, on a real scene. Projecting *portal* to the Picture World blend results in a Picture World that is much fuller than our view of it, a Picture World into which we can insert elements from the external world, such as a coat.

In the blend of blends that comes from blending these two blending networks, there is a selkie , and her coat can be hidden inside a painting (Figure 8.6). In Olga's world, although the separate Picture Worlds that correspond to individual pictures are rich, they do not possess anything like the completeness of our world. Someone who enters this world from the outside finds that the world inside the Picture World fades out. If you are in the Canaletto Picture World, and you walk through the marketplace to where the side streets lead deeper into the city, and you open yet one more door, you are then confronted with "impenetrable grey mist." There is not anything there, you see. As a character in the story says, "It's a painting. It only goes so far." There are other ways in which the Picture World in Olga's world is unlike our world, some of them influenced by projections from the representation input. For example, one can enter the Canaletto Picture World and take a chicken away from its marketplace and dine on it. But when you go back, the chicken is still there. "It's a painting," the story explains. "When you go back, everything will be just exactly as it was before you came."

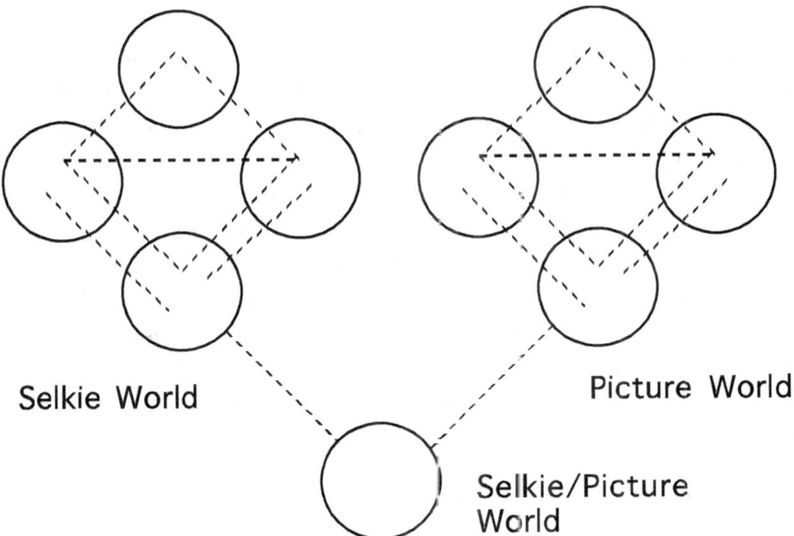

Figure 8.6. Blend of Selkie World and Picture World.

Well, not exactly. Olga recruits a young girl to help her. This girl, Charlotte, is a talented but solitary child, adept at solving puzzles. She is visiting Ocracoke in November with her adequate but bored mother and adequate but distracted father. Through Olga's tacit coaching, Charlotte learns to see the people moving in the Canaletto painting. It is not clear to the reader that even a talented and motivated human child could perceive the Picture World of Canaletto's painting of Venice without both Olga's training and influence: Charlotte encounters the painting in Olga's home, which is perhaps a magical place itself. Olga sings, puts her arm around Charlotte, and unpins her own long hair so its smooth waves brush across Charlotte's bare arm. Charlotte sees, and a few minutes later goes through the frame to retrieve the coat. Charlotte is much smaller than Olga, and she can swim very well.

In general, "Picture World" is a generic double-scope conceptual integration network, which we have at our mental disposal to apply to any picture. It guides the mental act of blending and offers options. It does not dictate all the details of the particular picture world. For example, some picture worlds can be entered by outsiders, others cannot. In some picture worlds, a visitor from outside the picture can be perceived by those who inhabit the picture, but in other cases, the visitor is invisible to the natives.

In Olga's world, the picture worlds can be entered, at least by those who have the knack to see that they are picture worlds. Insight brings new possibilities, a central theme of this story. In Olga's world, the usual blend of understanding and seeing that we all know and deploy ("I *see* what you are saying") undergoes remarkable conceptual development. Charlotte must work on her literal ability to see. She must strive to attain advanced vision. As she looks at the painting, its elements and their movement become clearer and clearer. Seeing better, she understands deeply. She already had, as Olga knew, talent in that direction: solitary and friendless Charlotte spent her time on jigsaw puzzles, looking at each piece, seeing its significance, perceiving its place. After their first meeting, Olga and Charlotte worked together on jigsaw puzzles, and Charlotte improved. The idea that Olga might have superior perceptual abilities is naturally projected to her from our knowledge of a seal: we are familiar with the idea that many animals have perceptual abilities we lack—the ability to hear sounds we cannot hear, to see patterns we cannot. Olga explains to Charlotte why she attends to people: "I like to piece together their actions in order to understand their thoughts." Charlotte has honed the identical knack through inspecting her mother and father. She turns it on Olga, too, and figures her out. She sees. She looks at the Canaletto painting, and she sees.

Charlotte hooks her foot on the frame, which turns out to be as solid as a rock banister (because it is a rock banister), and throws herself over the banister through the frame into the Grand Canal. Most of the rest of the story presents the adventures of the real girl, Charlotte, inside the Picture World that happens to contain the hidden coat of a selkie.

DOUBLE-SCOPE BLENDING AND EVERYDAY LANGUAGE

All of these networks rely on an important power of blending, to compress outer-space relations to inner-space elements in blends. It is a useful virtue of compression that it can result in human-scale elements in the blend that can then be expressed through existing basic human-scale grammatical constructions. While a full integration network, with its network of outer-space relations, might be quite difficult to express without using language that is extensive, discursive, or periphrastic, compression can save the day. The compressed human-scale mental array in the blend can often fit into available grammatical forms. For example, "Mom could make us work" seems entirely prosaic. But the workaday grammar underlying that sentence is readily available for a wonderful blend that is compressed in the right way: "Honey, you could make a blind man see." Here is an example that involves a cascade of blending compressions, but that can be fit into everyday grammatical constructions because the blending compressions result in a conceptual array that suits the grammar:

> A halloween costume that limits sight or movement is an accident lurking in disguise. (National Public Radio warning a few days before Halloween, October 2000)

Let us consider one of these examples in some detail. It is an advertisement broadcast on the radio a few days before a three-day holiday weekend:

> At South Shore Lumber, get no sales tax Friday, Saturday, Sunday, and Monday!

In one mental space, there is a person buying something at South Shore Lumber during Friday, Saturday, Sunday, or Monday. The buyer pays a price. In another mental space that is highly analogous but somewhat disanalogous to the first, the buyer pays the price and an additional amount, namely, sales tax on the price. In the blend, the buyer pays the price. But the blend now contains an element that is available in neither of the inputs; it is a compression of the outer-space disanalogy between the two spaces. That new imaginative element in the blend is an event, a transitive event in which what is transferred to the buyer has a certain property, namely, the property of being the absence of something that is in one of the inputs. The buyer receives both what he buys and something extra, the absence of sales tax. This conceptual structure is very compressed and familiar, and can be expressed in an existing common grammatical construction, a transitive verb phrase whose noun phrase has a quantifier in the determiner sequence: "get no sales tax." One customer "gets a screwdriver"; another "gets a sheet of plywood"; and they both "get no sales tax." This last phrase prompts us to construct an entire blending network in order to understand the disanalogy between the two input spaces, and, motivated by that disanalogy, to go to South Shore Lumber (Figure 8.7).

Now consider a somewhat different example. I overheard someone ask in the Sangre de Cristo Mountains, "At what altitude do the deer turn into elk?" Here, we actually notice a compression pattern that is highly productive but usually unremarked. We notice that the analogy and disanalogy between the two mental spaces is compressed. In the blend, the outer-space analogy has been compressed to an inner-space category (the animals), and the outer-space disanalogy is compressed to a change for that category (the animals turn from deer to elk). Of course, no one is fooled or deluded. We know perfectly well that one species of animal does not change into a different species

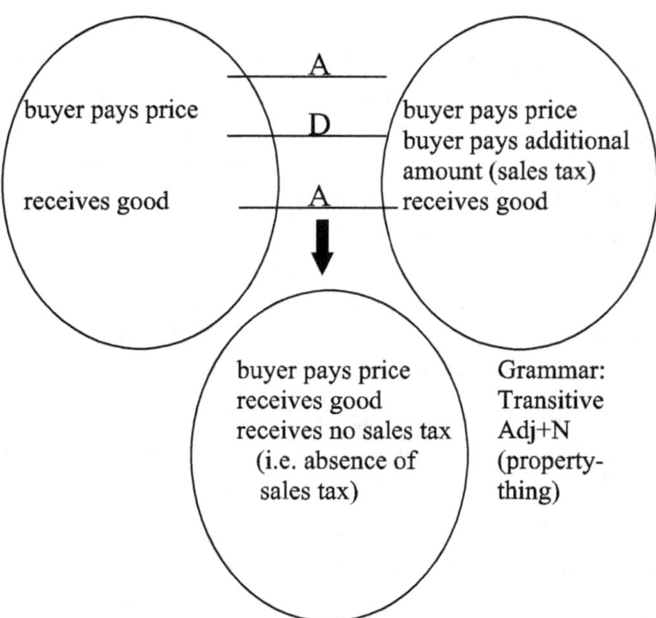

Figure 8.7. Blending network for Get No Sales Tax.

of animal. But the compressed blend has human-scale structure that can be expressed in an existing and relatively simple clausal construction. "At what altitude do the deer turn into elk?" is striking, but the same conceptual and grammatical patterns sound perfectly straightforward in expressions like "The new theory is that dinosaurs turned into birds." In the outer-space, diffuse array of inputs, dinosaurs did not turn into birds. Instead, organisms were born and died over very long stretches of time. None of those organisms itself changed in any of the relevant ways. Instead, there were analogies and disanalogies across these organisms in a long line of descent, and cause–effect connections between ancestors and descendents. Those analogies and disanalogies are compressed into change for a category in the blend: dinosaurs turned into birds. These compressions make it possible to use existing grammatical forms to evoke the blend and hence the integration network. New ideas usually do not require new grammatical constructions. Instead, what they require for their expression is imaginative compression into a blend that fits existing grammatical.

Now consider a third phrase, heard on a National Public Radio broadcast:

> We are eating the food off our children's plates. When we overfish, we eat not only today's fish, but tomorrow's fish, too.

In one mental space, we have a certain amount of fishing. This mental space has reference to present reality. In another mental space, we have a lower level of fishing that would lead causally to an acceptable amount of fish reproduction later in time (Figure 8.8).

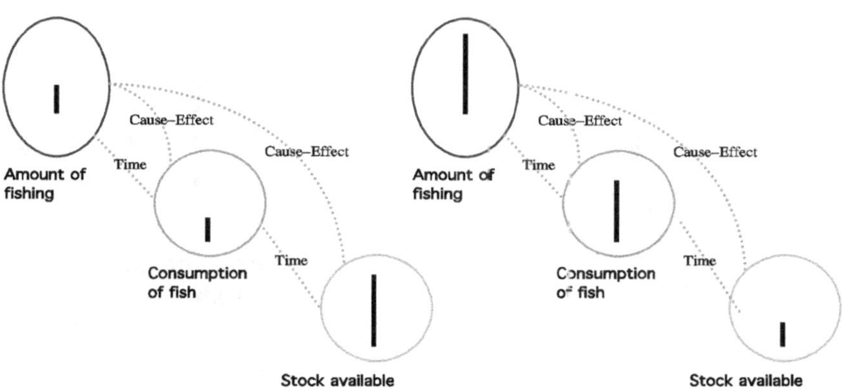

Figure 8.8. Mental space networks for fishing and stock, under two different initial conditions.

The disanalogy between these two amounts of fish is compressed so that, in the blend for the present moment, a portion of present fishing is now "overfishing" (Figure 8.9).

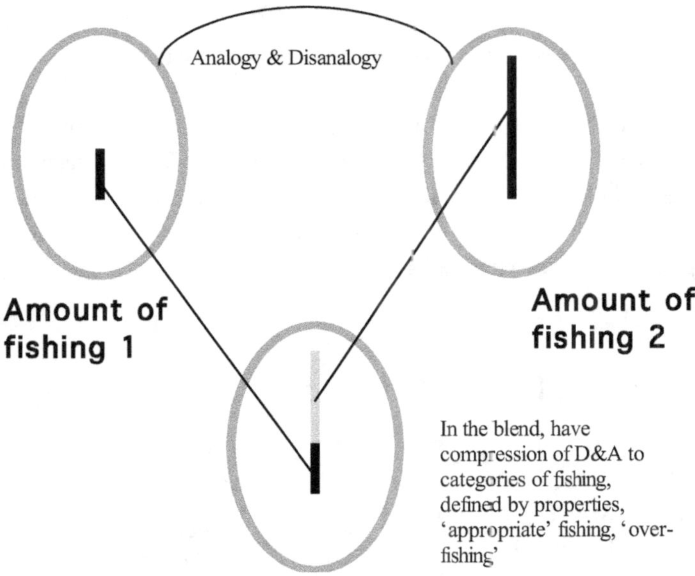

Figure 8.9. Blending network for "overfishing."

Similarly, a portion of present consumption of fish can be thought of as "over-consumption" (Figure 8.10).

There are cause–effect vital relations between the overfishing and the eating of the fish, and there is also a long-range cause–effect vital relation between the overfishing and the smaller amount of fish reproduction and accordingly the smaller number of fish in the future. A blending network is created for a hypothetical future. In it, the disanalogy between the small number of fish that will be available in the future as a consequence

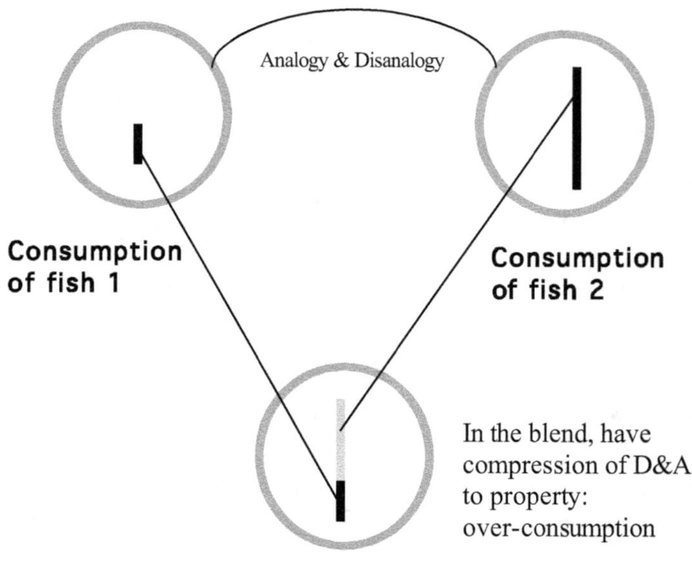

Figure 8.10. Blending network for "over consumption."

of the overfishing and the number of fish that would be there under appropriate fishing is compressed: from both of those future spaces we project the category *fish* to the hypothetical blend for the future, and the outer-space disanalogy between the inputs is compressed to a particular property: *missing*. Now we have *missing fish* in the blend for the hypothetical future (Figure 8.11).

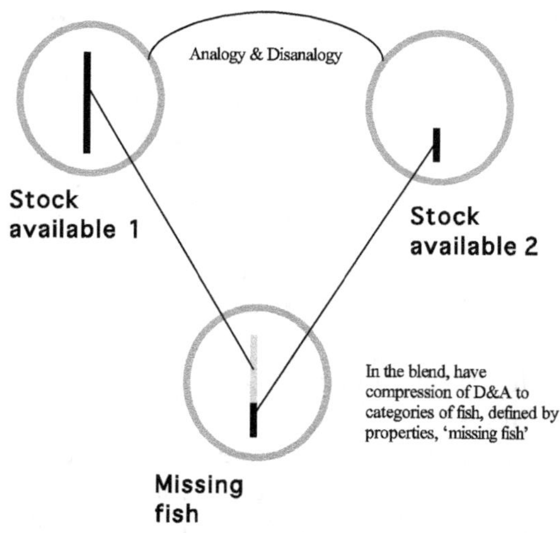

Figure 8.11. Blending network for "missing" fish.

The Time vital relation between now and the future is compressed by scaling it down to a day, so that, in the blend for the hypothetical future, the future is tomorrow. The *missing fish* in the blend for the future are now part of tomorrow's fish, the missing part. Then there is another compression: the cause–effect relations between eating fish now, fishing a lot now, and the missing part of tomorrow's fish are compressed into one scene in which the fish are missing tomorrow because we are eating them now (Figure 8.12).

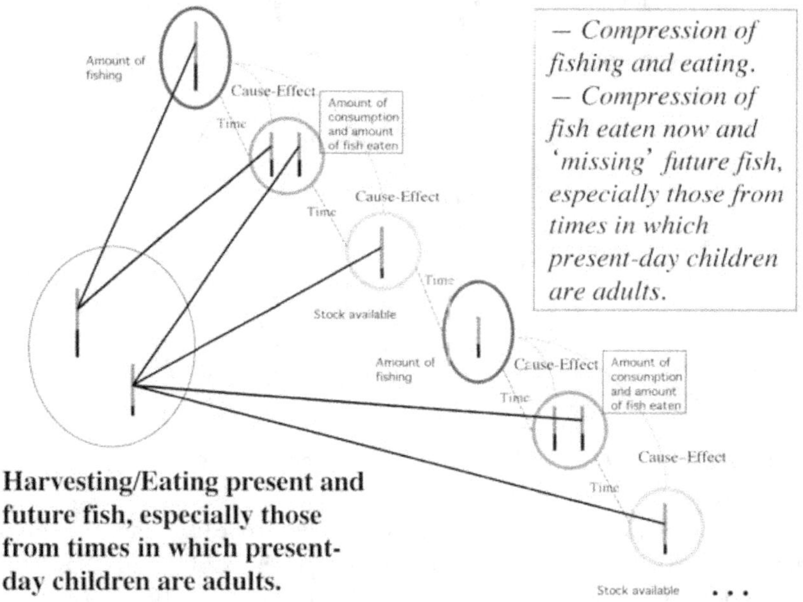

Figure 8.12. Blending network for Harvesting/Eating over time.

This structure fits a standard frame of indulgence. We all know the normative stricture against raiding the icebox and eating up food reserved for tomorrow. Dramatically, there is an additional compression that brings even the one-day lag down to the immediate moment. Those missing fish are not only in the space for tomorrow. Now the future fish are compressed with the food that is on our children's plates. But the food is "missing." Why? Because we are taking it from them and eating it ourselves. We are eating the food off our children's plates. This compression produces a highly human-scale scene, with a strong judgemental framing (Figure 8.13). (Note, incidentally, that we are taking the food off our children's plates, not the fish off their plates, because fish is not, for the relevant audience, the mainstay of child fare. It is also more exhaustive and serious to take their food than their fish.)

Again, no one is fooled by the blend. The fishing that is happening today out in the oceans is completely unlike taking away the food your children are eating today in order to eat it yourself. But the compressed blend, expressible in basic grammatical

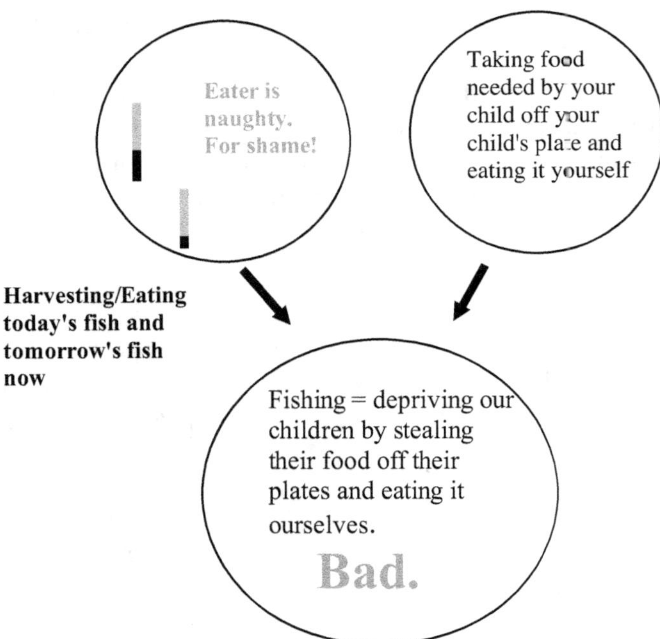

Figure 8.13. Blending network for Fishing/Eating food off our children's plates.

forms, evokes the entire and elaborate integration network, with the appropriate normative inferences.

Human beings, all of them, are geniuses at double-scope blending. They produce imaginative compressions inconceivable to other species. But they do it so routinely that we notice the performance only very rarely, such as when a writer places it explicitly on stage, as it were, drawing attention to it. Even then we miss the extraordinary systematicity of the operation and sophistication of the operation. It is only now that cognitive science is beginning to unearth the real powers of the imagination to show how different from their ancestors human beings really are.

NOTES

1 This essay also appears in *Imaginative Minds*, ed. Ilona Roth (London: British Academy & Oxford University Press, 2007). Reproduced by permission from The British Academy. We are grateful to Ilona Roth for her help in bringing this chapter to fruition. The essay draws on Mark Turner, "The Origin of Selkies," *Journal of Consciousness Studies* 11(5–6) (2004): 90–115.

2 Technical introductions to the nature and mechanisms of blending can be found in Fauconnier 1997; Fauconnier and Turner 1998, 2002; Turner 2001, 2003. See also Goguen.

Works Cited

Fauconnier, Gilles. *Mappings in Thought and Language.* Cambridge: Cambridge University Press, 1997. Print.

---, and Mark Turner. *The Way We Think: Conceptual Blending and the Mind's Hidden Complexities.* New York: Basic, 2002. Print.

---. "Conceptual integration networks." *Cognitive Science*, 22 (2) (April–June 1998): 133–87. Print.

Goguen, Joseph. "An Introduction to Algebraic Semiotics, with Application to User Interface Design." In *Computation for Metaphor, Analogy, and Agents.* C. Nehaniv, ed. Berlin: Springer-Verlag, 1999. 242–91. Print.

Johnson, Crockett. *Harold and the Purple Crayon.* New York: Harper & Row, 1983 [1955]. Print.

Turner, Mark. *Cognitive Dimensions of Social Science: The Way We Think About Politics, Economics, Law, and Society.* New York: Oxford University Press, 2001. Print.

---. The Blending Website. Web. <http://blending.stanford.edu> 1999-2007.

Turner, M. W. "Aunt Charlotte and the NGA Portraits." *Instead of Three Wishes.* New York: Greenwillow Books, 1995. 45-71. Print.

Theory of Mind and Fictions of Embodied Transparency[1]

Lisa Zunshine

1. Upping the agony

It's another day at *The Office*—a British mock documentary about the "boss from hell," David Brent, regional manager of a fictitious paper company. David (played by Ricky Gervais) is about to interview two candidates for the position of secretary, and he has just put his receptionist, Dawn Tinsley (Lucy Davis), in an embarrassing situation, flaunting his own lack of professionalism and making Dawn seem somewhat complicit in his offensive behavior. Used to her boss's ways yet painfully ashamed of his antics in front of the two strangers and the camera, Dawn stands next to him silently, now smoothing her hair nervously, now checking her nails, and trying to avoid any eye contact (see Fig. 1).

The Office cultivates such scenes of recorded unease. The documentary format allows the film crew to focus pitilessly on people's faces just when they would rather not be seen, encouraging the kind of staring that would be considered rude in real life. As Gervais, who co-directed the miniseries with Stephen Merchant, puts it, one "advantage" of having the ever-watchful camera in *The Office* is "that it would up the agony" (Commentary). And although we may share some of that agony as we watch Dawn cringe and squirm, we remain glued to our screens.

Such moments of embodied transparency—we can see what Dawn feels even if she does not want us to see it—appear to arise naturally out of the unique makeup of this particular show: its genre (documentaries have a complex relationship with voyeurism), its setting (offices build strange interfaces between intimacy and bureaucracy), and the peculiar sensibilities of the directors and actors.

However, I want to consider yet another factor behind *The Office's* obvious fascination with putting people into such trying emotional situations that they can't control their behavior and so their feelings are written all over their bodies: a factor grounded in our cognitive evolutionary heritage and, specifically, our Theory of Mind (ToM).

Figure 1. The Office.

Why turn to evolutionary history? We know so much about the immediate cultural history of *The Office* that it is not at all clear why we must also put Dawn's squirming into a hundred-thousand-year perspective. As this essay will argue, however, by cultivating moments of transparency, *The Office* participates in a particular representational tradition that extends well beyond its immediate genre, but to uncover this fascinating pedigree we need that hundred-thousand-year-old evolutionary perspective.

I begin with a brief overview of ToM,[2] drawing on the work of cognitive evolutionary psychologists and cognitive neuroscientists. I then spell out the key assumptions underlying my argument, first, that ToM is a "hungry" adaptation that constantly needs to process thoughts, feelings, and intentions, and, second, that the body occupies a double position in relation to this cognitive hunger, figuring as both the best and the worst source of information about the mind. I show further how this double perspective informs our cultural representations—novels, paintings, and moving images—in which bodies are temporarily forced into functioning as direct conduits to mental states. I conclude by speculating about further applications of this cognitive-evolutionary view of the body to analyses of cultural media, including the Internet. Prompted by *The Office*'s commitment to "agony," my essay thus seeks to explain why our cultural representations repeatedly invent new contexts for making characters reveal their true feelings, often against their will, and why these moments of embodied transparency must be brief to be convincing.

2. Theory of Mind

Theory of Mind, also known as mind reading, is the term used by psychologists and philosophers to describe our ability to explain behavior in terms of underlying thoughts, feelings, desires, and intentions. We attribute states of mind to ourselves and others all the time[3] (e.g., we see somebody reaching for a cup of coffee and assume that he is thirsty). Our attributions are frequently incorrect (the person who we thought was thirsty might have actually wanted to read the name of the manufacturer on the bottom of the cup).[4] Still, making them is the default way by which we construct and navigate our social environment. When ToM is impaired, as it is in varying degrees in the case of autism and schizophrenia, communication breaks down.

Cognitive evolutionary psychologists believe that mind-reading adaptations must have developed during the "massive neurocognitive evolution" that took place during the Pleistocene (1.8 million to 10,000 years ago). The emergence of these adaptations was evolution's answer to the "staggeringly complex" challenge faced by our ancestors, who needed to make sense of the behavior of other people in their group, which could include up to two hundred individuals. As Simon Baron-Cohen points out, "attributing mental states to a complex system (such as a human being) is by far the easiest way of understanding it," that is, of "coming up with an explanation of the complex system's behavior and predicting what it will do next" (21). In other words, mind reading is both predicated on the intensely social nature of our species *and* makes this intense social nature possible. (Lest this argument appear circular, think of our legs: their shape is both predicated upon the evolution of our species's locomotion *and* makes locomotion possible.)

Note that the words *theory* in ToM and *reading* in mind reading are potentially misleading because they seem to imply that we attribute states of mind intentionally and consciously. In fact, it might be difficult for us to appreciate just how much mind reading takes place on a level inaccessible to our consciousness. For it seems that while our perceptual systems "eagerly" register the information about people's bodies and their facial expressions, these systems do not necessarily make all that information available to us for our conscious interpretation. Think of the intriguing functioning of "mirror neurons." Studies of imitation in monkeys and humans have discovered a "neural mirror system that demonstrates an internal correlation between the representations of perceptual and motor functionalities" (Borenstein and Ruppin 229). What this means is that "an action is understood when its observation causes the motor system of the observer to 'resonate.'" So when you observe someone else grasping a cup, the "same population of neurons that control the execution of grasping movements becomes active in [your own] motor areas" (Rizzolatti et al 662). At least on some level, your brain does not seem to distinguish between you doing something and a person that you observe doing it.[5]

In other words, our neural circuits are powerfully attuned to the presence, behavior, and emotional display of other members of our species. This attunement begins early (some form of it is already present in newborn infants), and it takes numerous nuanced forms as we grow into our environment. We are intensely aware of the body language and facial expressions of other people, even if the full extent and significance of such awareness escape us. As cognitive neuroscientists working with ToM speculate,

> [Mirror] neurons provide a neural mechanism that may be a critical component of imitation and our ability to represent the goals and intentions of others.

> Although the early functional imaging studies have mostly focused on understanding how we represent the *simple actions* of others . . . recent articles have proposed that similar mechanisms are involved in understanding the *feelings and sensations* of others. . . . The growing interest in the phenomenon of empathy has led to the recent emergence of imaging studies investigating sympathetic or empathetic reactions in response to others making emotional facial expressions or telling sad versus neutral stories. (Singer et al *xv–xvi*)[6]

Cognitive scientists thus begin to enter the territory that has been extensively charted by philosophers and literary critics exploring mimesis (from Aristotle's *Poetics*, David Hume's "Of Tragedy," and Erich Auerbach's *Mimesis* and Walter Kauffmann's *Tragedy and Philosophy*, to the recent rethinking of mimesis and performativity in cultural studies), phenomenology (such as George Butte's compelling reintroduction of Maurice Merleau-Ponty into literary and film studies, *I Know That You Know That I Know*), and intentionality (such as Martha Nussbaum's critique of the tradition of correlating "an emotion and a discernible physical state" [96]). Although the work on mirror neurons is still in a relatively early stage, one can see exciting possibilities emerging at the intersection of traditionally humanistic research and the inquiry into the neural basis of interpersonal subjectivity.

3. Two underlying assumptions

The first assumption underlying my argument is that cognitive adaptations for mind reading are promiscuous, voracious, and proactive. Their very condition of being is a constant stimulation delivered either by direct interactions with other people or by imaginary approximations of such interactions, which include countless forms of representational art and narrative.

To clarify this assumption, it is useful to compare our adaptations for mind reading with our adaptations for seeing. Because our species evolved to take in so much information about our environment visually, we cannot help seeing once we open our eyes in the morning,[7] and the range of cultural practices grounded in the particularities of our system of visual adaptations is staggering. Similarly, as cognitive evolutionary psychologist Jesse M. Bering observes, after a certain age people "cannot turn off their mind-reading skills even if they want to. All human actions are forevermore perceived to be the products of unobservable mental states, and every behavior, therefore, is subject to intense sociocognitive scrutiny" (12). Hence, although we are far from grasping the full extent to which our lives are structured by adaptations for mind reading, we should be prepared that the cultural effect of those adaptations may prove just as profound and far-ranging as that of being able to see.

The second assumption is a paradox. We perceive people's observable behavior as both a highly informative and at the same time quite unreliable source of information about their minds. This double perspective is fundamental and inescapable, and it informs all of our social life and cultural representations.

To appreciate the power of this double perspective, consider the reason we remain suspicious of each other's body language. When I am speaking to somebody, she counts on my registering information conveyed by her face, movements, and appearance. That is, she cannot know what particular grin or shrug or tattoo I will notice and consider significant at a given moment; indeed, I don't know either. Our evolutionary past ensures, however, that she intuitively expects me to "read" her body as indicative of her thoughts, desires, and intentions. Moreover, the same evolutionary past ensures that I intuitively know that she expects me to read her body in this fashion. This means that I have to constantly negotiate between trusting this or that bodily sign of hers more than another.

Were I to put this negotiation in words—which will sound funny because we do *not* consciously articulate it to ourselves—it might go as follows: "Did she smile because she liked what I said or because she wanted me to think that she liked what I said, or because she was thinking of how well she handled an argument yesterday, or was she thinking of something altogether unrelated?"

Thus, we treat with caution the information about the person's state of mind inferred from her observable behavior precisely because we can't help treating her observable behavior as a highly valuable source of information about her mind—*and we both know it*. Because the body is *the* text that we read throughout our evolution as a social species, we are now stuck with cognitive adaptations that forcefully focus our attention on that particular text.

Nor would we want to completely distrust the body—our quick and far-from-perfect reading of each other is what gets us through the day. Still, as we unreflexively interpret each other's observable behavior in terms of underlying mental states, on some level we keep active the hypothesis that the observable behavior is misleading. (Note, too, that it does not have to be intentionally misleading: If I meet a person whose natural expression is a frown, I may incorrectly assume that he does not like me. The body may misrepresent the mind.)

What all this adds up to is that we are in a bind. We have the hungry ToM that needs constant input in the form of observable behavior indicative of unobservable mental states. And we have the body that our ToM evolved to focus on in order to get that input. And that body, the object of our ToM's obsessive attention, is a privileged and, as such, potentially misleading source of information about the person's mental state.

The research on ToM complements our own discipline's insight about the body as a site of performance. Because we are drawn to each other's bodies in our quest to figure out each other's thoughts and intentions, we end up *performing* our bodies (not always consciously or successfully) to shape other people's perceptions of our mental states. A particular body thus can be viewed only as a time-and-place-specific cultural construction, that is, as an attempt to influence others into perceiving it in a certain way.

Cognitive evolutionary research thus lends strong support to theorists in cultural studies who seek to expand the meaning of performativity, such as Joseph Roach, who argues that performance, "though it frequently makes references to theatricality as the most fecund metaphor for the social dimensions of social production, embraces a much wider range of human behaviors. Such behaviors may include what Michel de Certeau calls 'the practice of everyday life,' in which the role of spectator expands into that of participant" (46). Indeed, work on ToM indicates that our everyday mind reading turns each of us into a performer and a spectator, whether we are aware of it or not.

A closely related implication of the studies on ToM is that they encourage us to think of a broad variety of cultural institutions and social practices as both reflecting our overarching need to attribute minds *and* remaining subject to the instabilities inherent to our mind-reading processes. For example, our social infrastructure seems to be chock-full of devices designed to bypass our fakeable, performable, constructable body in reading the person's mind. We use blood and hair samples, credit and medical histories, fingerprinting and polygraph tests to avoid the situation in which we have to make an important decision based on information provided solely by the person's immediate observable behavior.

Some of these devices succeed better than others and none are perfect. We may not yet be living in the future depicted in *Gattaca* (1997), whose protagonist (played by Ethan Hawke) fakes his blood and hair samples to deceive others about his intentions, but that sci-fi moment does capture an important sociocognitive feature of our world: there is a constant arms race going on between cultural institutions trying to claim some aspects of the body as essential, unfakeable, and intentionality-free, and individuals finding ways to perform even those seemingly unperformable aspects of the body.

Again, compare this cognitive-evolutionary insight with the work done by cultural theorists ranging from Judith Butler to Peggy Phelan, who have written extensively on the body as a constantly receding signified, a perennially contested depository of reliable meanings. Think, for example, of Phelan's observation that whereas "the living performing body is the center of semiotic crossings, which allows one to perceive, interpret and document the performance event," we long to "return to some place where language is not needed," an "Imaginary Paradise" where there are no "linguistic and visual distinctions between who one is and what one sees" (15, 29). Think, too, that some of the resistance to the view of the body as always constructed and always performed can come from our hoping against all hope that it *must* be possible to carve some zones of certainty in the exasperating world where our favorite source of information, the body, is often untrustworthy in direct proportion to the extent to which we trust it.

4. To know and know not

With such a peculiar setup in place, what should we expect from our cultural representations? Or, to put it differently, how will our worldview change if we think about our culture as enmeshed with paradoxes and instabilities of our greedy ToM? Of course, this big question cannot be answered in one essay. But as a starting point, let us consider step-by-step what it means to live in a world in which we know and at the same time don't know what other people are thinking.[8]

First, we *know* that there must be a mental state behind an observable behavior. Say you see somebody jumping up in the middle of a meeting. Try making sense of his action without talking about his presumed mental state; for example, he had an idea; he remembered something suddenly; he wanted to see how high he could jump; he felt something sharp on the seat beneath him; he saw a snake and was terrified; he wanted to check if everybody was awake.

Our belief that there must be a mental state behind a behavior is itself a cognitive artifact that reflects the way we perceive people. The question of whether my colleague over there *truly and really* had some thought, feeling, or emotion that prompted him to jump is relatively irrelevant.[9] What is relevant is that for you and me and every other human being with fully functional ToM, his jump signals an underlying mental state.[10]

Second, even though we know that there must be a mental state behind a behavior, we don't *really* know what that state is. That is, there is always a possibility that something else is going on behind even the most seemingly transparent behavior. We can remember situations when our thoughts did not fit the circumstances, and no observable behavior could reveal them to people around us, or so we hope. On these occasions we say to ourselves, "Thank God, we can't read each other's minds, so that they have no way of knowing what goes through my head."

Third, even though we can't really know what other people are thinking, we conduct our daily lives on the assumption that we do, more or less. To borrow from a related discussion by the cognitive literary critic Ellen Spolsky, our everyday mind-attributions are "good enough."[11] Obviously, I don't know what that man is really thinking as he strides purposively toward that particular weightlifting machine, but it has served me well in the past and is likely to serve me well in the future to assume that he wants to use it right away, which means that for the next five minutes I'd better turn to a different machine. Such rough-and-ready interpretations get us through the day. To quote the cognitive evolutionary anthropologist Dan Sperber, in "our everyday striving to understand others, we make do with partial and speculative interpretations (the more different from us the others, the more speculative the interpretation). For all their incompleteness and uncertainty, these interpretations help us—us individuals, us peoples—to live with one another" (38).

Were we to stop and try to figure out what the people around us are really thinking, we would become socially incapacitated, overwhelmed with possible interpretations, and unable to commit to any course of action. Perhaps the reason that we even notice our moments of "Thank God, we can't read each other's minds!" is because they stand out amid our daily unreflective mind-attribution. They interrupt its course. They force us to juxtapose a *good enough* mind-attribution—that is, what people could be expected to think in such a situation—with an *exact* and unexpected mind-attribution: what I really thought in that situation.

Fourth, because we go around knowing that there must be a mental state behind the behavior, and because we don't really know what that state is, even as we act as if we know, our cultural representations exploit this precarious state of knowing and not knowing. One important distinction between daily life and fiction is that we generally get through the day with our far-from-perfect attributions of intentionality, but authors are less interested in such "good enough" attributions.[12] Works of fiction magnify and vivify various points on the continuum of our imperfect mutual knowledge:

Spectacular feats and failures of mind reading are the hinges on which many a fictional plot turns.

5. EMBODIED TRANSPARENCY

Here is one specific argument we can make approaching cultural representations from the cognitive perspective outlined above. There seems to be a representational tradition, which manifests itself differently in different genres and individual works, of putting protagonists in situations in which their bodies spontaneously reveal their true feelings, sometimes against their wills. Such moments are carefully foregrounded within the rest of the narrative. In each case an author builds up a context in which brief access to a character's mental state via her body language stands out sharply against the relative opacity of other characters or of the same character a moment ago.

Every moment of transparency is thus entirely relative and context-dependent, but the wish to create and behold such moments seems to be perennial, grounded in our evolutionary history as a social species. Representations of embodied transparency regale us with something that we hold at a premium in our everyday lives and never get much of: perfect access to other people's minds via their observable behavior. As such, they must be immensely flattering to our ToM adaptations, which evolved to read minds through bodies but have to constantly contend with the possibility of misreading and the resulting social failure. The pleasure derived from moments of embodied transparency is thus largely a social pleasure—a titillating illusion of superior social discernment and power.

To see what forms such illusions of perfect access may assume, consider the three following examples, which deal respectively with novels, genre paintings, and moving images.

A. ANGRY BODIES AND SADISTIC BENEFACTORS

At first glance, novels seem to be an unlikely setting for cultivating special moments of embodied transparency because they are *already* in the business of revealing their characters' thoughts and feelings. Alan Palmer captures this when he observes in his remarkable *Fictional Minds* that one "of the pleasures of reading novels is the enjoyment of being told what a variety of fictional people are thinking. . . . This is a relief from the business of real life, much of which requires the ability to decode accurately the behavior of others" (10).

Yet there can be an important difference between telling how the character feels using omniscient narration and making the character show his or her true feelings. Thus in the first proposal scene of Austen's *Pride and Prejudice* (1813), we hear of Elizabeth's anger but we *see* Mr. Darcy's anger. Here is Elizabeth's listening to Mr. Darcy's confession that he "struggled . . . in vain" to repress his love for her:

> In spite of her deeply-rooted dislike, she could not be insensible to the compliment of such a man's affections, and though her intentions did not vary for an instant, she was first sorry for the pain he was about to receive; till, roused to resentment by his subsequent language, she lost all compassion in anger.

> She tried, however, to compose herself to answer him with patience, when he should have done. (129)

Elizabeth does not fully succeed in composing herself. Toward the end of Mr. Darcy's speech, "the colour [rises] into her cheeks." Still, heightened color can be indicative of a variety of mental states, some flattering to the suitor, whereas Mr. Darcy's subsequent bodily reaction to Elizabeth's disdainful answer provides direct and unequivocal access to his feelings:

> Mr. Darcy, who was leaning against the mantelpiece with his eyes fixed on her face, seemed to catch her words with no less resentment than surprise. His complexion became pale with anger, and the disturbance of his mind was visible in every feature. He was struggling for the appearance of composure, and would not open his lips, till he believed himself to have attained it." (129)

Note the contrasts that went into constructing Mr. Darcy's transparency. Not only is he now more readable than Elizabeth, but he is also more readable than himself earlier in the novel and a moment before. In the first sentence of the last quoted passage, he is described as *seeming* to catch her words with no less resentment than surprise. That is, there is still some possibility of misinterpreting his body language at that point—he *seems* to be resentful and surprised, but he might not actually be so. Then the next sentence ("His complexion became pale with anger" [ibid.]) leaves no doubt that his body reflects his mind fully and faithfully. These contrasts convey a strong impression that this moment of perfect mental access cannot last long, sharpening our appreciation for the vision of the body caught in spontaneous emotion.[13]

Here is an example from a more recent work, Helen Fielding's *Bridget Jones: The Edge of Reason* (1999). Fielding's treatment of embodied transparency is particularly interesting because, written from the first-person point of view and obsessed with the issue of gender and communication, her novel provides an apparently exhaustive report of Bridget's feelings and those of women surrounding her. Men's minds remain strategically obscured—in the tradition of Austen, whose *Pride and Prejudice* and *Persuasion* inspired "Bridget Jones" duology.

But even in the novel in which transparency (at least for women) seems to be the default narrative mode, moments of embodied transparency are still presented as rare and valuable flashes of insight. For example, there is the scene at a ski resort in which Bridget is talking to her boyfriend, Mark Darcy, and an attractive woman, Rebecca, who is trying to steal Mark from Bridget. Rebecca invites Mark and Bridget to a skiing party, where she would have more opportunities to flirt with Mark, especially if Bridget, a poor skier, could be separated from him:

> "Oh, it's so exhilarating," said Rebecca, putting her goggles on her head and laughing into Mark's face. "Listen, do you both want to have supper with us tonight? We are going to have a fondue up the mountain, then a torchlight ski down—oh sorry, Bridget, but you could come down in the cable car."
>
> "No," said Mark abruptly, "I missed Valentine's Day so I'm taking Bridget for a Valentine's dinner."

> The good thing about Rebecca is there is always a split second when she gives herself away by looking really pissed-off.
>
> "Okey-dokey, whatever, have a fun time," she said, flashed the toothpaste advert smile, then put her goggles on and skied off with a flourish towards the town. (73)

Observe all the careful framing that goes into foregrounding Rebecca's embodied transparency. First, her involuntary giving "herself away by looking really pissed-off" is contrasted with her fake spontaneity one moment earlier, when she appears unable to contain her good spirits buoyed by skiing, and her fake friendliness right after, when she smiles broadly to show that she does not mind Mark's rejection. Second, Rebecca's bodily display of feelings is contrasted with Mark's opacity—his answer is "abrupt," which means that nothing in his body language has prepared the two women for what he is about to say. Third, Fielding has Bridget actively draw our attention to both the value of this revelatory moment ("the good thing about Rebecca . . .") and to its transience: it lasts only a "split second," so one is lucky to catch it.

It may seem, based on my examples from Austen and Fielding, that embodied transparency always finds an appreciative spectator within the story itself (for example, when Mr. Darcy looks angry, Elizabeth is there to observe him and interpret his body language), but the situation is more complex. Many fictional characters remain oblivious of others' momentary transparency. In Henry Fielding's *Tom Jones* (1749), Tom ignores Lawyer Dowling's uncomfortable twitching during their conversation about Tom's parentage. Similarly, Mr. Allworthy remains blind to Doctor Blifil's grimacing attempts to conceal his laughter in response to Allworthy's heartfelt "sermon" about love and marriage (62).[14] Sometimes such obliviousness is gently glossed over by the narrative; sometimes it is strategically foregrounded to illustrate the protagonist's unfortunate lack of awareness or his tactful reluctance to pry into other people's thoughts.

But if characters may notice or miss moments of embodied transparency, we readers are always made to notice them. We may perceive such moments as perceived by characters in the story or as *not* perceived by them, but, either way, they offer us a dazzling possibility of an escape from our double perspective of the body as a highly privileged and yet unreliable source of information about the mind.

This is why Bridget Jones's insight is our gain but so is Mr. Allworthy's blindness. We look at Doctor Blifil and we see what Mr. Allworthy does not see—a body that desperately does not want to be read and thus *is* readable in this desire not to be read. So when I speak of representations of embodied transparency and their effects, I mean primarily their effects on the ToM of *readers*. We are the ultimate appreciative audience for such representations.

Hence a fascinating sub-tradition in the novelistic treatment of embodied transparency, which I call a tradition of sadistic benefaction. Some fictional characters do not seem to be content with serendipitously observing (as Elizabeth and Bridget do) other people's spontaneous reactions. Instead, they want to *script* such reactions, forcing others into revelatory body language and appropriating, in effect, the privileged positions of readers as ultimate observers of moments of embodied transparency. The ethics of these situations are extremely ambiguous. The characters are presented as believing that their actions will ultimately benefit the people whom they are forcing into transparency, but the impression of emotional sadism lingers.[15]

Consider, for example, Sarah Fielding's *The History of Ophelia* (1760), in which a rich man sends a poor man on an emotional rollercoaster to enjoy the spectacle of his feelings against his will. The novel's protagonist, Lord Dorchester, comes across a starving half-pay soldier, Captain Traverse, and decides to help him. Through his connections at the court, he secretly procures Traverse the choice of two jobs and then proceeds to torture the man by telling him first only of the job that he knows the Captain will not be able to take due to family circumstances. The poor Captain, unwilling to appear ungrateful, receives "this News with as much Gratitude as if it had been the very Thing he wished" and turns it down politely. Lord Dorchester then expresses his disappointment in such terms as to drive the Captain to break down in tears when he thinks nobody is watching (1: 252)—when, in fact, everybody is.

Not yet content with this show of emotions, Lord Dorchester then reveals the Captain's family waiting in the next room and urges him again to take the first job. In response, the Captain "faint[s] away instantly," terrifying his wife and making the onlookers fear for his life. When the Captain comes to, Lord Dorchester augments "the general Joy" that his recovery occasions by telling him of the second job, one that is completely acceptable and will save the whole family from starving. The joy now increases "to a great Degree of Extacy," raising to a "Height that must have been painful." The Captain and his wife look upon the "Lord with Adoration, and [give] way to Raptures that would have forced a Heart the most insensible to the Sensations of others, to partake of theirs" (1: 254–55).

Lord Dorchester is a grotesque embodiment of the eighteenth-century obsession with private philanthropy, social class, and sentimental discourse. His privileged social standing allows him to torture such people as Captain Traverse before helping them. Fielding thus draws on recognizable cultural contexts of her day to construct a scene in which the poor man's feelings are rendered transparent against his desires and observed hungrily by the rich benefactor.

Lest we think that the eighteenth-century sentimental novel holds the exclusive right to such scenes, consider Chuck Palahniuk's *Fight Club* (1996), in which Tyler Durden holds a gun to a head of a man he has just met (who turns out to be a twenty-three-year-old college dropout) and extracts from him the promise that he will go back to school to finish his degree in veterinary medicine. Tyler wants to impress on "Raymond Hessel" (the name he reads off his driver's license) an important life lesson: Death can strike any minute, so study hard and follow your dreams.

But before Tyler gets to the salutary follow-your-dreams part, he uses every grisly cliché to convince Raymond of his imminent and terrible demise. He explains to the crying man how he will "cool" down, passing from a "person" to an "object" and how his "Mom and Dad would have to call old doctor whoever and get [their son's] dental records because there wouldn't be much left of [his] face." The scene is so structured that Tyler seems merely to report the images arising in his victim's mind. Raymond is forced into embodied transparency: half-paralyzed with fear, crying harder and harder, following meekly Tyler's orders, thinking of things that Tyler tells him to think of.

When Tyler finally lets Raymond go, his thoughts stay on him as he muses with great satisfaction: "Raymond fucking Hessel, your dinner is going to taste better than any meal you've ever eaten, and tomorrow will be the most beautiful day of your entire life" (155). Like Lord Dorchester, Tyler apparently believes that to intensify somebody's happiness you have to first make him truly miserable. More importantly, like Lord Dorchester, Tyler treasures every moment of transparency he can wring out of his victim. Tyler enjoys knowing exactly what Raymond is thinking now and what he will be thinking tomorrow.

Or does he? Scenes of sadistic benefaction reveal an asymmetry in novels' treatment of embodied transparency. Readers are indeed occasionally allowed to transcend the double position of the body and enjoy the illusion of perfect readability (Mr. Darcy looks angry and he *is* angry; Rebecca looks pissed off, and she *is* pissed off), but when characters themselves try to create contexts of such direct access, the results are often mixed. Subversion lurks. Because there is a potential for a gap between the forced emotion and the actual emotion, the performing body may reassert itself.

Look again at the scene in *Fight Club* in which Tyler reads his victim's body as an open book:

> "You [are] going to cool, the amazing miracle of death. One minute, you're a person, the next minute you're an object, and Mom and Dad would have to call old doctor whoever and get your dental records because there wouldn't be much left of your face, and Mom and Dad, they'd always expected so much more from you and, no, life wasn't fair and now it was come to this." (153)

If we return to this scene after we have finished the novel and found out that Tyler is what we call an unreliable narrator,[16] we may start seeing problems with this assured interpretation of Raymond's body. We may notice, for example, that Tyler's account of Raymond's thoughts draws on conventional images provided by crime dramas. That is, we cannot know exactly what really goes through a person's head when he has a gun pressed to his cheek. After all, he might be thinking that now he will not have to go through his scheduled biopsy to find out what that scary lump is. We do, however, have a visual repertoire of scenes associated with violent deaths, for example: cut to the bereaved family; cut to the corpse in the morgue; cut to the dentist, or some other doctor, confirming the victim's identity; and so forth. This is the repertoire that Tyler dips into for his "report" from Raymond's head.

Similarly, when Tyler confidently foretells what Raymond will be thinking even after he is out of Tyler's clutches ("tomorrow will be the most beautiful day of your entire life"), I see his point. I can certainly imagine how tomorrow Raymond might feel almost unbearably happy to be alive and thankful for every crumb that passes his lips and for every leaf that he sees trembling in the wind. I can also imagine Raymond racing to school, profoundly grateful for the opportunity to "work [his] ass off" (154) on various hard subjects, just as Tyler told him he should. Finally, I can imagine Raymond eventually becoming a successful veterinarian, loved by his family, respected by his neighbors, and remembering now and then with wonder and gratitude that fateful moment when a stranger with a gun forced him to turn his life around and make the most of it.

But then I can also imagine Raymond falling into a profound depression soon after his encounter with Tyler, thinking obsessively that his life depends on the whim of some jerk with a gun, and killing himself one day after school.

In other words, Raymond's body remains transparent and his mind accessible as long as we consider this scene in isolation from the tradition of unreliable narration. For within this tradition, when a first-person narrator reports another character's thoughts, he is almost immediately suspect and his reporting must be scrutinized for signs of inconsistency, vested interests, or even madness. So Palahniuk's readers believe that Tyler really knows what Raymond is thinking only as long as they are not aware that Tyler is an unreliable narrator. Once they are aware of it, they have an option—which, of course, they may choose not to follow—of assuming that they have learned very little about Raymond's actual feelings on the occasion.

But even if we do not consider this episode in relation to the tradition of unreliable narration, something else in it alerts us to the possible gap between Tyler's assured interpretation of Raymond's body and Raymond's actual mental state. The scene's timing is off. Tyler keeps reading Raymond's mind for three straight pages, and somewhere along the way embodied transparency is bound to become a performance. The same applies to the protracted exchange between Lord Dorchester and Captain Traverse. Tyler and Lord Dorchester may convince themselves, egomaniacs that they are, that they can sustain their victims in the state of spontaneous emoting for as long as they choose. The longer they keep it going, however, the more willing we are to entertain the possibility that after a while Raymond and Captain Traverse intuit something about the twisted psychology of their torturers / benefactors and start performing their despair and gratitude at the top of their lungs.

In contrast, think again about Helen Fielding's emphasis on transience as she describes Rebecca's body language: her give-away "pissed off" expression is visible for only a "split second."[17] Think, too, how quickly Austen's Mr. Darcy regains control of his features and ceases to be transparent. True, Austen emphasizes that time slows down for Elizabeth as she watches his internal struggle—"the pause was to Elizabeth's feelings dreadful" (130)—but we know that this pause could not really have lasted very long. To be credible, embodied transparency has to be brief and spontaneous. Brevity makes it ethically defensible, too:[18] we do not want to think that Elizabeth actually enjoys watching Mr. Darcy at his most transparent.[19]

There is yet another side to the issue of spontaneity. It is not enough if a specific moment of embodied transparency in a specific work of fiction is unexpected and short. To be convincing, it also has to look unconventional in the larger context of its genre. I said earlier that there is a constant arms race going on between cultural institutions trying to claim some aspects of the body as performance-free and individuals finding ways to perform even these seemingly "essential" aspects of the body. The history of cultural representations that create contexts of transparency must be viewed in the relation to this larger arms race. Writers, artists, and movie directors have to keep inventing *new* ways of forcing the body into a state of transparency because as soon as one way of doing it emerges as an established convention, it becomes vulnerable to subversion and parody. The mind retreats further, leaving the body as a front going through the expected motions of "revealing" the "true" states of mind. The double perspective of the body returns with vengeance.

As an example of such a subverted context of transparency, consider the eighteenth-century sentimental novel with its loving attention to blushing, crying, panting, fainting bodies. In Samuel Richardson's *Pamela* (1739), such bodily displays still stand for real feelings,[20] but in his next novel, *Clarissa* (1747–48), they are already consciously faked for the benefit of naïve observers.[21] The term "sentimental" itself undergoes a change between 1740 and 1820. Originally neutral, "characterized by sentiment," or positive, "characterized by or exhibiting refined and elevated feeling," it acquires a pejorative meaning of "addicted to indulgence in superficial emotion."[22] In other words, keep looking at the emoting body in hopes that it will keep providing direct access to the person's mental states, and you will soon be treated to "superficial emotion," performed for your viewing pleasure. So when Lord Dorchester tries to script Captain Traverse's embodied transparency in 1760, not only is his script too long, but it is also quickly becoming outdated.

B. Problem pictures and proposal compositions

At first glance, genre paintings seem another unlikely candidate for bracketing off special moments of embodied transparency. Paintings that depict people engaged in everyday activities rely as heavily on our ToM as do novels. To make sense of such scenes we have to attribute intentions to each character, or to a group of characters if the painting encourages us to construct them as sharing a certain attitude. Still, compare two kinds of genre paintings, partially overlapping in time but pointedly different in their treatment of transparency: problem pictures and proposal compositions.

Problem pictures, writes Pamela M. Fletcher in her *Narrating Modernity: The British Problem Picture, 1895–1914*, "were an extraordinarily popular feature of the Edwardian Royal Academy. The term referred to ambiguous, and often slightly risqué, paintings of modern life which invited multiple, equally plausible interpretations" (1). Consider John Collier's *A Confession* (1902), which depicts a "couple engaged in an emotional conversation," in which the woman's face is "in shadow, while the man, leaning forward with his elbows on his knees, brings his face into the light of the fire," staring down and slightly to the viewer's right (62; Fig. 2).

According to Collier, he received "many inquiries" about the picture's subject. In one extant letter, the "writer pleads: '*Oh!* Honourable John, I want to know *very* badly which (*please* tell me) is confessing in your Royal Academy picture—the man or the woman'" (62, original emphasis). In response to such queries, the artist apparently offered "multiple interpretations," cultivating "oracular ambiguity" along the lines of "The woman did it and the man confessed it" (63). In 1913, he revisited the subject

Figure 2. The Confession.

with his *Fallen Idol*, in which a "woman kneels at a man's feet, her upper body resting on his knees and her head bowed in an attitude of grief or shame. The man holds one of her hands in his, and stares directly out of the canvas, his face illuminated by a shaft of light" (129). As Fletcher reports,

> Critical responses in the press were almost equally divided between those who read the story as completely open to interpretation, and those who assumed that the woman had "fallen." The *Daily Mirror*, *Queen*, *Reynolds's*, and the *Daily Sketch* all read the picture as ambiguous, predicting, "Lots of stories will be woven around this picture, and probably none of them the right one." The *Daily Mirror* made the point by "quoting" two visitors: "'Of course, he's just confessed something he's done,' said one woman yesterday confidently. 'She's just been found out' said the next comer with equal assurance." (130–31)

The spatial arrangement of the figures in problem pictures and the pattern of lighting do not consistently single out one gender as more mysterious than the other: the man is just as likely as the woman to be "in the position of the 'problem'" (62). Contrast this with the pattern identified by Stephen Kern in his study *Eyes of Love: The Gaze in English and French Paintings and Novels, 1840–1900*. As Kern puts it, when "French and English artists . . . depicted a man and a woman in the same composition [they] typically rendered the face and eyes of the woman with greater detail and in more light. Most important, the men are in profile, while the women are frontal" (7). These works exemplify what Kern calls a "proposal composition":

> Such a composition highlights the woman's moment of decision after the man has proposed that the relationship move to some higher level of intimacy. At such moments she must respond, whether it be to his searching look or friendly inquiry, or more significantly, to his seductive offer or proposal of marriage. Her eyes convey an impending answer to the question *Will she or won't she*? And because she is thinking about many possible consequences of her answer, her expression is especially intriguing. In contrast, the man has done his thinking and said what is on his mind. He wants to hear a *Yes*, so his face bears a more predictable and less interesting expression. (7)

Kern makes a convincing case against the accepted critical view that visual representations of women—especially beautiful women—always objectify them. He argues that in proposal compositions, such as, for example, William Midwood's *At the Crafter's Wheel* (Fig. 3), women "are not objectified by the male gaze but retain a commanding subjectivity that, in comparison to the man's more erotically focused purpose and expression, conveys a wider range of thoughts and emotions" (228).

More interesting, *less* predictable, *especially* intriguing, conveying a *wider* range of emotions—contrasts and degrees are at the heart of proposal compositions. Of course, any art that appeals to the eye must cultivate gradients. As Ernst Gombrich observed, "even newly hatched chickens classify their impressions according to relationships" (298). Still, what is important for the purpose of the present argument is that using both our interest in contrasts and the familiar social script of courtship, proposal compositions construct the context in which the body of one protagonist is maneuvered into embodied transparency. We know what the man is thinking, his "erotically focused" purpose made even more obvious because it is contrasted with the "intriguing" thought processes of the woman.

In her study, Fletcher demonstrates that interpretations of problem pictures reflected some of the "most pressing issues of the early twentieth century, including the nature of modern marriage and motherhood, the emergence and definition of the new professional classes, and the existence of a specifically feminine morality" (1). No doubt many of the same issues were at play in proposal compositions, but observe the crucial difference between their respective constructions of protagonists' subjectivity.

Whereas a problem picture leaves their feelings largely open to interpretation and only somewhat constrains them within broad categories, such as "distress" or "surprise," the proposal composition constructs one participant as more transparent than another.

Moreover, it turns out that the issue of time, so important in fictional representations of embodied transparency, is just as important in paintings. In a proposal composition, we know what a man is thinking, but this moment of transparency cannot last. For, depending on the woman's reaction, the man will soon adopt a different posture, attempting perhaps to conceal his disappointment if she says *no* or hesitates for too long. The same cultural narrative—the courtship narrative—that makes the instance of transparency convincing ensures that it is but an instance, serendipitously "caught" by the artist.

Figure 3. At the Crafter's Wheel.

Something else might be at work in sustaining this illusion of a serendipitously caught moment of transparency: it steals upon the spectator unexpectedly. After all, "proposal compositions" were not known as such to their contemporaries. Whereas "problem picture" is a recognizable historical term referring to a particular sub-genre associated with a specific style, "proposal composition" is a term introduced by Kern to describe not so much a genre as a recurrent compositional pattern and interpersonal dynamic that can be found across different schools, styles, and representational traditions of the second part of the nineteenth century.

Note too that the titles of such paintings rarely indicate that we are witnessing a scene of romantic inquiry and hesitation (in contrast to the straightforward titles of problem pictures, e.g., *A Confession*). Very few titles are leading (e.g., *The Proposal*, *Pleading*, or *Showing a Preference*); the majority are all over the place, referring to a setting, to a prominent artifact present on the scene, or to the main protagonist (e.g., *A Dance in the Country*, *Nameless and Friendless*, *Waiting for the Ferry*, *Effie Dean*, *A Rest by the Seine*, *Blossom Time*, *The Picnic*, *The Umbrellas*, *At the Crafter's Wheel*[23]). Because there is neither an explicit genre affiliation nor a title that would mark a proposal composition as such, viewers have to infer on their own in the case of each specific painting that it contains a deliberation induced by a proposal of marriage or romantic liaison.

So as contemporary spectators approached a painting, say, Renoir's *A Dance in the*

Country,[24] Osborn's *Nameless and Friendless*,[25] or Horsley's *Blossom Time*,[26] they did not know beforehand that the body of one of its protagonists was supposed to be strikingly readable (even though they could see it right away). Had it been known—that is, had the proposal composition indeed emerged as an established sub-genre with its own set of typical titles—the man's transparency would have eventually become a convention and as such would have required an extra effort to be rendered convincing. (The fate of French eighteenth-century absorptive paintings, as discussed by Michael Fried in *Absorption and Theatricality*, is a vivid example of what conventions and expectations can do to destroy the illusion of immediate access to a represented subject's mental state.[27]) This did not happen, however: the impression of serendipity was not marred by the thought that in this artistic sub-genre serendipity *is* a convention.

I am not making any teleological claims about the history of proposal compositions, such as that late nineteenth-century artists and art critics consciously avoided recognizing a new sub-genre in their midst in order to be able to continue constructing compelling narratives of embodied (male) transparency. Rather it seems that authors of proposal compositions differed widely from each other in their styles and sensibilities and did not give much thought to this particular common denominator, and neither did their audiences. We needed Kern's book to finally see this common denominator, and we need research on ToM to see why we intuitively value so much the moments when bodies reveal minds so vividly.

C. Mock documentaries

Let us now return to the scene of social torment that opened this essay. Observe that what *The Office* does here (and for the purposes of this discussion I am thinking of this mock documentary as representing moving images at large[28]) is similar to what novels and paintings do when they build their moments of transparency.

The Office cultivates contrasts. That is, Gervais and Merchant constantly prod us to gage one character's embodied transparency as contrasted to that of other characters or to her own embodied transparency a moment ago. For example, in the scene in which David makes a fool of himself in front of Dawn and the two job candidates, both interviewees must be unpleasantly surprised by David's behavior. Still, the scene is shot so as to emphasize the contrast between what we may infer about their respective feelings and what we may infer about Dawn's feelings. We can see that Dawn goes through the agony of embarrassment *and* tries to conceal her disapproval of David's actions. Because we can imagine how much mental energy this must take, we conclude that it is highly unlikely that Dawn is capable of thinking of anything else at this moment (e.g., about her fiancé, Lee, her co-worker, Tim, or the book that she was reading earlier). Just now Dawn is strikingly transparent.

Not so Karen and Stuart, the interviewees. Karen smiles a lot, and at one point she also shoots a curious glance at Dawn. We may infer that she is taken aback by David's lack of professionalism but determined to get through the interview. Other than making this tentative inference, however, we have no way of knowing what goes through her head as she listens to David's harangue.

Stuart is even less transparent than Karen. We may guess that he is disappointed and angry, and that he has already given up on this job and is now keeping up the appearance of polite interest because the camera is present. These speculations, however, draw more on the context of the scene than on his body language. For he wears a small, noncommittal smile throughout and otherwise betrays no emotions.

The contrast propels the story. We take in the characters' body language—almost all at once—and then align it along the continuum of transparency. This subconscious process of comparing, contrasting, and aligning builds both on the cues planted by the directors (e.g., the actor playing Stuart must have been told to maintain a poker face) and on the particularities of our information processing (i.e., to make sense of our world we need to construct it in relational terms). As such *The Office* is similar to thousands of other television shows and feature movies—but also to novels and paintings—whose makers intuitively cultivate such hierarchies of transparency to charge their tableaux with inner dynamism.

Then there is also the issue of time. We have seen already how important it is for writers and artists to convince their audiences that the moment of transparency is transient and hence particularly valuable. Did the makers of *The Office* do something special to keep the instances of embodied transparency brief?

It turns out that they did, even if they did not think about it in these terms. In their commentary to *The Office*, Merchant and Gervais explain that they wanted to avoid the feel of "situation comedy" and to keep their material jumpy and raw. To achieve that, they made a point of cutting abruptly from one scene to another. Note, however, one important side effect of this editing technique: it ensures that whenever characters are forced into a state of embodied transparency, we never stay with them long enough for them to seize control of the situation and start performing their feelings.

This really is an effective narrative trick. *The Office* never dwells on the same person for a long time, yet it leaves us under a strong illusion that it does, by making us aware that we stare at the protagonists when they are embarrassed or making fools of themselves for much longer than would be polite in real life. So we are made to feel that we have seen too much when, in fact, we have seen just enough to be convinced that the protagonists were caught off-guard and did not have time to rally their spirits and put on a suitable performance.

With its treatment of embodied transparency, a mock documentary occupies a peculiar position in relation to its grandparent genre of regular documentary and its immediate progenitors, cinéma vérité and direct cinema.[29] Cinéma vérité thrived on the spontaneous embodiment of emotions—indeed actively looked for contexts that would allow for maximum transparency. As Hope Ryden, who wrote, directed, and produced documentary films from 1961 through 1987 and was part of the Drew Associates team that developed cinéma vérité / cinema direct in the early sixties,[30] puts it, "What we were doing was finding an upcoming event in which some character would have a great stake. At that moment they would either win or lose. And it didn't matter whether they win or lose. What mattered was that they cared a whole lot about what they were doing" (*Cinema Vérité*).

And what this caring "a whole lot" meant for a movie is that no matter what a character might do on camera during that make-or-break moment, viewers knew what she or he was really feeling. So if the character showed emotions, such as anxiety, happiness, or disappointment, those emotions could be counted on as being authentic; and if she did not show any, she would still be transparent, because the viewers knew that she was trying hard to conceal her feelings. In the words of Robert Drew, who directed the documentary *Primary* (1960), featuring presidential candidates Hubert Humphrey and John F. Kennedy during the Wisconsin primary elections: "The idea of capturing human emotion spontaneously as it happens was the key idea that made *Primary* work, that made all of our films work, and that is making cinéma vérité work today in many ways across the spectrum of television" (*Cinema Vérité*). As historians of documentary film Jack C. Ellis and Betsy A. McLane put it:

> [In] *Primary*, Humphrey and Kennedy were much more concerned with winning an election than with how they would appear on screen. . . . *Mooney v. Fowle* (1961, also known as *Football*) builds up the climaxes with high school football game in Miami, Florida, between two rival teams. It concentrates on the players, coaches, immediate families—those most completely preoccupied with this contest. *The Chair* (1962) centers on the efforts of a Chicago attorney, Donald Page Moore, to obtain a stay of execution for his client, Paul Crump, five days before it is scheduled to take place. *Jane* (1962) concerns Jane Fonda in the production of a play, from the rehearsal period through the negative reviews following its Broadway opening and the decision to close it. (216)

So, when in *The Chair*, "the attorney breaks into tears and expresses his incredulity after he receives a phone call from a stranger offering support for him in his efforts to save his client's life" (219), we cannot doubt that we see the man at his most transparent, that his body language provides direct access to his mind.

Yet doubt is never far enough given the cognitive underpinnings of the phenomenon that we are dealing with. We cannot escape for long the double view of the body: the promise of direct access is always fraught with the possibility of manipulation and deception. Once a culture becomes aware of a seemingly reliable representational context for embodied transparency in its midst, that context is rendered suspect. (We have seen it happening in the eighteenth-century sentimental novel: in *Clarissa*, Lovelace carefully fakes "spontaneous" body language.)

Thus, on one hand, it was the credo of cinéma vérité that their "subjects would reveal what they really felt and were like when unself-consciously relaxed or deeply involved in some activity" (Ellis and McLane 217). On the other hand, however absorbed the subject may be by what she is doing, it is still possible that the presence of the camera influences her emotional responses, if even ever so slightly. As Jean Rouch, the director who originated the term cinéma vérité, saw it, "the camera acts as a stimulant. It causes people to think about themselves as they may not be used to doing and to express their feelings in ways they ordinarily would not" (Ellis and McLane 217).[31] The double perspective of the body worms its way into "vérité."

So perhaps we should look at certain films made between the late 1960s and now as attempts by filmmakers to reclaim the documentary as a reliable context for embodied transparency.[32] Among such attempts would be documentaries that depict people killed during rock concerts (e.g., *Gimme Shelter* 1970), victims of war in Vietnam (e.g., *Hearts and Minds* 1974), people dying of AIDS (e.g., *The Broadcast Tapes of Dr. Peter* 1994), and people literally growing up on camera (Michael Apted's "Up Series" of 1970, 1977, 1984, 1991, 1998, and 2005). Such a perspective would be both cognitive (that is, acknowledging that we remain ever-seducible by the body's promise of direct access to the mind) and historicist (that is, following specific circumstances that led, but did not *have to* lead, to the creation of each film).

Note how many of these films depict death: the ultimate moment of embodied transparency. Of course, with exception of certain unique circumstances, such as those created by the epidemic of AIDS in the 1980s and 1990s,[33] the directors did not and could not set out expecting to film *that* kind of transparency.[34] It is interesting, then, that the 1970s saw a number of movies appearing to be documentaries shot in cinéma vérité style, such as *No Lies* (1973), a "staged film about rape,"[35] and *Rushes* (1979), a staged film about suicide.[36] Following in the wake of the original cinéma vérité of the 1960s, these fake documentaries indicated the genre's intuitive awareness that a strenuous extra effort might eventually be required to sustain its claims to direct access. And they were right to the extent to which in the years to come the real cinéma vérité did turn to death and other unfakeable physiological experiences, such as growing up.

Where would *The Office* and other recent mock documentaries fit our hypothetical narrative of the twentieth-century documentary filmmakers' intuitive quest for reliable contexts of embodied transparency? They are the direct descendants of the fake cinéma vérité films of the 1970s. (Note that not all of those films dealt with injury and death. There were others, for example, ones in which the camera filmed everyday life of families and of women in the workplace.[37]) *The Office* takes the original cinéma vérité promise of transparency as its absolute raison d'être. Whereas cinéma vérité *hoped* to catch at least some moments of embodied transparency and looked for situations that were likely to produce such moments, a mock documentary *transforms* every situation into an occasion for embodied transparency.

As one brief illustration of how this transformation happens, consider Gervais's commentary on the "talking heads" of *The Office*. He refers to the scenes in which the protagonists are interviewed individually and thus can presumably put on any attitude or personality:

> I really love the talking heads in the show. Because we shot it like a documentary, we couldn't do things people wouldn't do in front of the camera. They can't shut the door and take a line of coke. Or they can't blurt out things they're thinking.
>
> But, ironically, when they're by themselves and they're just being filmed, they're a little bit more honest. People do let their guard down because it's flattering. When a camera's pointed at someone, they think, "This is my chance, this is my

> platform. I can tell the world my all great philosophies on life." And of course, they open their mouth and they blow it and can't take it back.

Note what just happened here. The least likely moment for revealing one's true thoughts is turned into its opposite. It is one thing to be *caught* on camera as Dawn is in the scene with David and the two job candidates; it is quite another to be invited into a separate room to be filmed during a formal interview. In the latter case, you have all the opportunities in the world to prepare well and to act out your better self. After all, many early cinéma vérité directors prided themselves on *never* interviewing their subjects. Interviews were the mainstay of stodgy traditional documentaries—they spelled out performance. But in *The Office* this context of performance par excellence becomes yet another context for transparency. The protagonists "blow it and can't take it back."

6. Suggestions for further interpretations

I wrote this essay because I wanted to understand why our cultural representations repeatedly invent new contexts for making characters betray their true feelings and why these moments of embodied transparency are generally short-lived and unstable. To think through these issues, I developed a four-level model, going from the broadest question to the most specific. I first asked how our worldview will change if we begin thinking about our culture as enmeshed with our hungry ToM (Level One). More specifically, I wondered how our cultural representations engage with our double view of the body as both a highly informative and at the same time quite unreliable source of information about the mind (Level Two). Even more specifically, I wanted to see how our novels, paintings, and moving images construct the contexts of forced transparency, when the double view of the body is temporarily transcended and the observable behavior serves as the reliable index to the underlying mental state (Level Three). And, most specifically, I wanted to know if certain features of these fictional moments of mental transparency are actually defined by the impossibility of reliable and lasting escape from the double perspective of the body, itself grounded in our cognitive evolutionary history (Level Four). Thus I suggested that artists and writers might actively look for pointedly short-lived social situations—such as the moment between the man's proposal and woman's answer (in proposal compositions) or a moment of acute social embarrassment (in mock documentaries)—to construct more *plausible* contexts for complete mental access.

To what extent is this four-tier model applicable to further literary and cultural analysis? It seems to me that whereas my fourth question is geared toward a very specific set of problems, the first three can be used to approach a variety of cultural representations. Of particular interest here might be cognitive-historicist interpretations that place our flawed need to read bodies for states of mind within specific historical and socioeconomic environments. One may ask, for example (staying on the first level), what happens when a mind-reading species, such as ours, enters a capitalist economy. How do the laws of supply and demand operate when you have a mind that wants to process representations of other minds and a marketplace geared toward offering an increasingly broad range of such representations? A student of late seventeenth- and eighteenth-century literature and culture may speculate here about the proliferation of hybrid genres and publication outlets and ask how the economics of publishing drove the readers' cognitive appetites and vice versa. A student of contemporary culture may similarly think of how the rapid fragmentation of cultural production and consumption caters to and cultivates new mind-reading interfaces.

To quote Nick Gillespie, when "everywhere we look, the cultural marketplace is open and ready for business," when "in economic terms, the opportunity costs of both making and enjoying culture have dropped through the floor; [and when] it keeps getting cheaper and cheaper to produce and to consume culture under increasingly diverse circumstances," one result is "more and more of everything" (48–49). And "more of everything" means, in the words of Charles Paul Freund, that in a consumerist society, people can "grab the first opportunity to escape the traditionalist boundaries of selfhood" by experimenting "with different modes of self-presentation" (29).[38] To put this in terms of second-level inquiry, people can now engage in endlessly diverse experimentation with our double view of the body as a privileged yet unreliable source of information about the mind.

Moreover (to continue with this example, but coming to the third level) new cultural forms and niches generate new attempts to carve zones of certainty in our perception of the body. Think of the Internet today—a powerful cultural institution that thrives because it offers us yet another way of figuring out what is happening in other people's minds. Yet if you ask yourself which feature of the Internet has been causing us the most anxiety since its inception, the answer will be the absence of the body behind the message. The "disembodied" nature of electronic communication leaves its users strikingly vulnerable to deception. As Peter Steiner's cartoon in *The New Yorker* has it, "On the Internet, nobody knows you're a dog." The physical body thus gets implicitly re-valorized as the source of "true" information about our correspondent. If only we could see the actual man or woman typing in his or her message—if only for a second!—oh, we would surely know what he or she is really about!

As a matter of fact we would not. To be reminded just how informative the sighting of the actual body is, we have Web sites such as dontdatehimgirl.com, which features letters from women who have been deceived by flesh-and-blood men and now want to warn other women who may unknowingly come in contact with those cheaters. Ironically, the disembodied medium thus re-alerts readers to the unlimited lying potential of the body. Some aspects of this situation are captured by yet another *New Yorker* cartoon, by Liza Donnelly, in which a street vendor with a laptop offers to passersby a service called "Vet your date." (Although, of course, there is no way of knowing if anonymous reports posted on dontdatehimgirl.com are actually written by women, just as there is no way to gage the trustworthiness of those posts.[39]) The double view of the body thus continues to shape our representations. Whereas we cannot predict the exact forms that the construction of embodied transparency will yet take on the Internet, we know that the arms race between rendering some aspects of observable behavior transparent and subverting that transparency will go on.

NOTES

1 This essay also appears in the journal *Narrative* 16 (2008): 56-92. Reproduced by permission from The Ohio State University Press.

2 For discussions of applications of research on ToM to literature, see Palmer, *Fictional Minds*; Vermeule, "God Novels"; Zunshine, *Why We Read Fiction.*

3 As Goldman puts it, in his account of simulation theory of mind-reading, "people routinely track the mental states of others in their immediate environment" (301).

4 I am referring here to the scene from Bryan Singe's *The Usual Suspects* (1995), in which, we assume, Roger "Verbal" Kint uses the name of the cup manufacturer to corroborate his yarn.

5 See Goldman for a discussion of the relationship between mirror neurons and ToM.

6 See also Ramachandran for a discussion of anosognosia (38) and autism (119) as possibly associated with damage in the system of mirror neurons.

7 Unless, of course, our visual system is severely damaged.

8 And what you yourself are thinking, too. For discussion, see Palmer.

9 Compare to Baron-Cohen's description of Daniel Dennett's view of the Intentional Stance: "Dennett is not committed either way on the question of whether there really are such things as mental states inside the heads of organisms. We ascribe these simply because doing so allows us to treat other organisms as rational agents" (*Mindblindness* 24).

10 I concede that in a sci-fi movie, his jump may mean that there was a magnet planted in his body and he was pulled up by aliens who use such magnets to reel in earthlings to their ship. Note two things, though. To counterbalance our immediate tendency to read a mental state into his behavior, I had to come up with a truly outlandish scenario. ToM-less explanations apparently require quite a bit of work. And, furthermore, my explanation is not really completely ToM-less. I did not manage to get rid of intentionality altogether. Only instead of ascribing an intention to the man, I ascribed it to the aliens. See if you can do any better.

11 Spolsky, *Satisfying Skepticism* (7); "Darwin and Derrida" (52).

12 For a related discussion, see Spolsky's "Purposes Mistook."

13 Note that in this context I use the word *emotion* interchangeably with *mental state*. For a discussion of the relationship between emotion and cognition, see Hogan, Keen, and Palmer.

14 For a discussion, see Zunshine, "Lying Bodies."

15 Compare to physical torture as another attempt to render the body the direct index of the mind. As Michaels puts it in his discussion of *American Psycho*, "You can be confident that the girl screaming when you shoot her with a nail gun is not performing (in the sense of faking) her pain" (70). See also Scarry, *The Body in Pain* (35–38).

16 Using James Phelan's categorization of unreliable narrators, we can say that Tyler underreports and underreads (219) Raymond's mental states.

17 Compare to Alan Richardson's analysis of Johanna Baillie's tragedy *Count Basil* (1798), in which Victoria, the main heroine, "ends up resorting to all but nonstop simulation of emotion, allowing her genuine feelings to become manifest only obliquely, largely against her conscious wishes, and in the briefest of flashes" ("Facial Expression").

18 Compare to Cohn's discussion of E.T.A. Hoffmann's *Master Flea* in *Transparent Minds*. She writes that in Hoffmann's story, "the microscopic magician of the title gives to his human friend Peregrinus Tuss a tiny magic lens, that, when inserted in the pupil of his eye, enables him to peer through the skulls of all fellow human beings he encounters, and to discern their hidden thoughts. Peregrinus soon curses this 'indestructible glass' for giving him an intelligence that rightfully belongs only to the 'eternal being who sees through to man's innermost self because he rules it'" (3). Peregrinus thus forces "all fellow human beings" into a state of embodied transparency *which can last infinitely*—an ethically indefensible situation that is resolved to the extent to which Peregrinus is rendered unhappy by his privileged access.

19 For a related argument, see Spolsky, "Elaborated Knowledge."

20 See Mullan (61).

21 See Zunshine, "Richardson's *Clarissa*."

22 *OED*; second online edition, 1989.

23 I am using the titles of paintings from Kern's lavishly illustrated study.

24 For discussion, see Kern (71).

25 For discussion, see Kern (93).

26 For discussion, see Kern (65). Note that I am purposely choosing proposal compositions of very different styles.

27 For discussion, see Zunshine, "Theory of Mind and Michael Fried's *Absorption and Theatricality*."

28 For a useful broader perspective on ToM and cinema, see Per Persson's brilliant *Understanding Cinema*.

29 Here I use the terms cinéma vérité and direct cinema interchangeably, but there are important differences between the two. For an overview of these differences, see Ellis and McLane (216–18).

30 Quoted verbatim from Hope Ryden's official Web site, http://www.hoperyden.com/disc.htm, as accessed on August 18, 2007.

31 And the other side of this issue is that such revelatory moments were carefully staged and edited. As Frederick Wiseman, a pioneer of direct cinema, puts it, "It's all manipulation. Everything about that kind of movies is a distortion" (*Cinema Vérité: Defining the Moment*).

32 Compare to Michael Fried's argument in *Absorption and Theatricality* (61), and my analysis of it in "Theory of Mind and Michael Fried's *Absorption and Theatricality*."

33 *The Broadcast Tapes of Dr. Peter* (1994) and *Silver Lake Life: The View from Here* (1990) were made by filmmakers diagnosed with AIDS, who chronicled their fight with the disease until they died. For a discussion of these movies, see Ellis and McLane (284–87).

34 Albert and David Maysles and Charlotte Zwerin (*Gimme Shelter*) could not know that a person would be killed on camera during a Rolling Stones performance. For a discussion of the history of that moment, see Ellis and McLane (290–91).

35 Ellis and McLane (236).

36 For a discussion, see Ellis and McLane (237).

37 For a discussion, see Ellis and McLane (235–36).

38 Compare to Dick Hebdidge's earlier argument about "the articulation of commodity consumption, personal identity and desire which characterizes life under hypercapitalism" (*Hiding* 168) and his yet earlier analysis of subcultures' movement through "commercial and cultural matrices" (*Subculture* 130).

39 For a discussion, see Alvarez and Jones.

Acknowledgments

I am deeply grateful to James Phelan for his thoughtful response to an earlier draft of this essay, to Stephen Kern for his detailed corrections and suggestions, and to Anna Laura Bennett for her superb editing skills.

Works Cited

Auerbach, Erich. *Mimesis.* Princeton University Press, 1991. Print.

Austen, Jane. *Pride and Prejudice.* New York: Dover Publications, 1995. Print.

Baron-Cohen, Simon. *Mindblindness: An Essay on Autism and Theory of Mind.* Cambridge: The MIT Press, 1995. Print.

Bering, Jesse M. "The Existential Theory of Mind." *Review of General Psychology* 6.1 (2002): 3–24. Print.

Alvarez, Lizette. "(Name Here) Is a Liar and a Cheat." *The New York Times.* February 16 (2006). Web. http://www.nytimes.com/2006/02/16/fashion/thursdaystyles/16WEB.html.

Borenstein, Elhanan, and Eytan Ruppin. "The Evolution of Imitation and Mirror Neurons in Adaptive Agents." *Cognitive Systems Research* 6.3 (2005): 229-42. Print.

Butte, George. *I Know That You Know That I Know: Narrating Subjects from Moll Flanders to Marnie.* Columbus: The Ohio State University Press, 2004. Print.

Cohn, Dorrit. *Transparent Minds: Narrative Modes for Presenting Consciousness in Fiction.* Princeton: Princeton University Press, 1978. Print.

Ellis, Jack C., and Betsy A. McLane. *A New History of Documentary Film.* New York: Continuum, 2005. Print.

Fielding, Helen. *Bridget Jones: The Edge of Reason.* New York: Penguin, 1999. Print.

Fielding, Henry. *Tom Jones.* [1749] Ed. John Bender and Simon Stern. Oxford University Press, 1996. Print.

Fielding, Sarah. *The History of Ophelia*. London: Printed for R. Baldwin, 1760. Print.

Fletcher, Pamela M. *Narrating Modernity: The British Problem Picture, 1895–1914*. Aldershot: Ashgate, 2003. Print.

Freund, Charles Paul. "In Praise of Vulgarity." *Choice. The Best of Reason*. Ed. Nick Gillespie. Dallas: Benbella, 2004. 11–33. Print.

Fried, Michael. *Absorption and Theatricality: Painting and Beholder in the Age of Diderot*. Berkeley: University of California Press, 1980. Print.

Gervais, Ricky, and Stephen Merchant. *The Office. The Complete First Series*. BBC Worldwide Americas, Inc., 2003. Warner Home Video. 2 disks. Film.

Gillespie, Nick. "All Culture, All the Time. *Choice: The Best of Reason*. Ed. Nick Gillespie. Dallas: Benbella, 2004. 47–60. Print.

Goldman, Alvin I. *Simulating Minds: The Philosophy, Psychology, and Neuroscience of Mindreading*. New York: Oxford University Press, 2006. Print.

Gombrich, E. H. *Art and Illusion: A Study in the Psychology of Pictorial Representation*. Third edition. New York: Princeton University Press, 1969. Print.

Hebdige, Dick. *Hiding in the Light*. London: Routledge. Comedia, 1988. Print.

---. *Subculture: The Meaning of Style*. London: Methuen, 1979. Print.

Jones, Carl. "Scorned Attorney Sues Kiss-and-Tell Web Site." *Daily Business Review*. July 5 (2006). Web. http://www.law.com/jsp/article.jsp?id=1151658319991.

Kaufmann, Walter. *Tragedy and Philosophy*. New York: Doubleday, 1968. Print.

Keen, Suzanne. "A Theory of Narrative Empathy." *Narrative* 14.3 (October 2006): 207–36. Print.

Kern, Stephen. *Eyes of Love: The Gaze in English and French Paintings and Novels, 1840–1900*. London: Reaktion Books, 1996. Print.

Merleau-Ponty, Maurice. *Phenomenology of Perception*. Translated by Colin Smith. London: Routledge & Kegan Paul, 1962. Print.

Michaels, Walter Benn. *The Shape of the Signifier: 1967 to the End of History*. Princeton: Princeton University Press, 2004. Print.

Mullan, John. *Sentiment and Sociability: The Language of Feeling in the Eighteenth Century*. Oxford: Clarendon Press, 1988. Print.

Nussbaum, Martha C. *Upheavals of Thought: The Intelligence of Emotions*. Cambridge: Cambridge University Press, 2001. Print.

Palahniuk, Chuck. *Fight Club*. New York: Henry Holt and Company, 1996. Print.

Palmer, Alan. *Fictional Minds*. Lincoln: University of Nebraska Press, 2004. Print.

Persson, Per. *Understanding Cinema: A Psychological Theory of Moving Imagery*. Cambridge: Cambridge University Press, 2003. Print.

Phelan, Peggy. "Reciting the Citation of Others, or, A Second Introduction." *Acting Out: Feminist Performances*. Ed. Lynda Hart and Peggy Phelan. Ann Arbor: The University of Michigan Press, 1993. 13–31. Print.

Ramachandran, V. S. *A Brief Tour of Human Consciousness: From Impostor Poodles to Purple Numbers*. New York: Pi Press, 2004. Print.

Richardson, Alan. "Studies in Literature and Cognition: A Field Map." *The Work of Fiction: Cognition, Culture, and Complexity*. Ed. Alan Richardson and Ellen Spolsky. Aldershot: Ashgate, 2004. 1–30. Print.

---. "Facial Expression Theory from Romanticism to the Present." *Introduction to Cognitive Cultural Studies*. Ed. Lisa Zunshine. Baltimore: The Johns Hopkins University Press, 2010. 65-83. Print.

Richardson, Samuel. *Clarissa or The History of a Young Lady*. Ed. Angus Ross. New York: Penguin, 1985. Print.

Rizzolatti, Giacomo, Leonardo Fogassi, and Vittorio Gallese. "Neuropsychological Mechanisms Underlying the Understanding and Imitation of Action." *Nature Reviews. Neuroscience* 2.9 (2001): 661–70. Print.

Roach, Joseph. "Culture and Performance in the Circum-Atlantic World." *Performativity and Performance*. Ed. Andrew Parker and Eve Kosofsky Sedgwick. New York: Routledge, 1995. 45–63. Print.

Scarry, Elaine. *The Body in Pain: The Making and Unmaking of the World*. New York: Oxford University Press, 1985. Print.

Singer, Tania, Daniel Wolpert, and Christopher D. Frith. "Introduction: the Study of Social Interactions." *The Neuroscience of Social Interaction: Decoding, Imitating, and Influencing the Actions of Others*. Ed. Christopher D. Frith and Daniel Wolpert. Oxford: Oxford University Press, 2004. xiii–xxvii. Print.

Sperber, Dan. *Explaining Culture: A Naturalistic Approach*. Oxford: Blackwell, 1997. Print.

Spolsky, Ellen. "Cognitive Literary Historicism: A Response to Adler and Gross." *Poetics Today* 24:2 (2003): 161–83. Print.

---. "Darwin and Derrida: Cognitive Literary Theory As a Species of Poststructuralism." *Poetics Today* 23.1 (2002): 43–62. Print.

---. "Elaborated Knowledge: Reading Kinesis in Pictures." *Poetics Today* 17. 2 (Summer 1996): 157–80. Print.

---. "Purposes Mistook: Failures are More Tellable." Talk delivered at the panel on "Cognitive Approaches to Narrative" at the annual meeting of the Society for the Study of Narrative, Burlington, Vermont, 2004. Print.

---. *Satisfying Skepticism: Embodied Knowledge in the Early Modern World*. Aldershot: Ashgate, 2001. Print.

---. *Word vs Image: Cognitive Hunger in Shakespeare's England*. Basingstoke: Palgrave Macmillan, 2007. Print.

Wintonick, Peter (director). *Cinema Vérité: Defining the Moment*. Montreal: National Film Board of Canada, 1999. Film.

Woloch, Alex. *The One Vs. The Many: Minor Characters and the Space of the Protagonist in the Novel*. Princeton: Princeton University Press, 2003. Print.

Vermeule, Blakey. "God Novels." *The Work of Fiction: Cognition, Culture, and Complexity*. Ed. Alan Richardson and Ellen Spolsky. Aldershot: Ashgate, 2004. 147–66. Print.

Zunshine, Lisa. *Why We Read Fiction: Theory of Mind and the Novel*. Columbus: The Ohio State University Press, 2006. Print.

---. "Theory of Mind and Michael Fried's *Absorption and Theatricality*: Notes Toward Cognitive Historicism." *Toward a Theory of Narrative Acts*. Ed. Frederick Aldama. Austin: University of Texas Press, 2010. 179-203. Print.

---. "Lying Bodies of the Enlightenment: Theory of Mind and Eighteenth-Century Studies." *Introduction to Cognitive Cultural Studies*. Ed. Lisa Zunshine. Baltimore: Johns Hopkins University Press, 2010. 115-33. Print.

Theory of the Murderous Mind: Understanding the Emotional Intensity of John Doyle's Interpretation of Sondheim's *Sweeney Todd*

DIANA CALDERAZZO

Through the experience of engaging in the theatrical event, audiences take part in a process of storytelling on a visceral level—one that appeals to sensory reception and often elicits evidence of emotional response in audience members who relate on some level to the contents of the characters' minds. This path from sensory reception to emotional response with regard to theatrical storytelling, from a cognitive perspective, is the topic of this article; I will explore its function in defining stated audience emotional reactions to a specific theatrical production—Stephen Sondheim's *Sweeney Todd*, debuting on Broadway in 2005 with direction by John Doyle. In the fall 2007 issue of *The Sondheim Review*, I explored emotional intensity in Doyle's production based in cognitive mirroring, conceptual blending, and the link between gesture and speech; here, I retain the cognitive approach but build a more in-depth analysis of mirroring and empathy. In addition, I offer an exploration of the aspects of storytelling and concepts of obsession and compulsion as these elements serve to link the minds of characters and audiences within the production. Finally, I will address the function of laughter as audience reaction to the macabre characters in Doyle's *Sweeney*.

Doyle's production of Sondheim's musical lends itself to such a study for several reasons. First, Sondheim composed the piece, which he wrote in 1979, with the intent of emphasizing its visceral appeal to its audiences. In 1980, the composer stated that "the theatre is the one place where you can create larger than life . . . " and melodrama, the stuff of *Sweeney Todd*, is "high theatre" (Sondheim 4). Significantly, the story itself is based upon an ancient European legend that has served to inspire images of the macabre for nearly two hundred years: that of a mad barber who murders his clients with his razor only to have their bodies baked into meat pies and fed to a ravenous nineteenth-century London public. Sondheim has expressed his fascination with this legend, further asserting that "the true terror of melodrama comes from its revelations about the frightening power of what is inside human beings. . . . [That is] exactly what this show is" (6). *Sweeney Todd*, then, is a prime manifestation of Sondheim's own dedication to this traditionally heightened form.

The fact that Sondheim proposed to appeal to his audiences on a basic human level through his vision of melodrama in *Sweeney Todd* is appropriate, considering the nearly two-hundred-year history of the Todd legend and the popular allure of its interpretation on the melodramatic stage and in literature, visual art, and cinema. In his 1980 book on melodrama, Daniel Gerould carefully relates much of this history, enumerating and briefly describing seventeen artistic and literary interpretations of the London-based Todd legend (believed to have previously originated in France) between the years 1825 and 1970 (43-47).[1] Many of these interpretations no doubt elicited further public intrigue and the suggestion of historical veracity through their eerie resemblance to the Jack the Ripper murders in Whitechapel, during which prostitutes in the poor areas of 1880s and 1890s London became the victims of an infamous string of throat slittings. The legend made its way to Broadway for the first time in 1924 (a version written by George Dibdin-Pitt), followed in 1979 by the debut of Sondheim's version, which received two revivals, in 1989 and 2005. Simultaneously, literary and popular culture has displayed sustained interest in the Todd legend, spurred by folklore historian Peter Haining's controversial 1997 book, *Sweeney Todd: The Real Story of the Demon Barber of Fleet Street*, in which Haining claims to have obtained access to documents proving the existence of a very Todd-like murderous barber in London around the turn of the eighteenth century. This book and others like it,[2] as well as the Broadway revivals of Sondheim's musical, sustained popular interest in the Todd legend and led to the much-anticipated and hailed 2007 American movie version of *Sweeney*, based on Sondheim's musical and starring Johnny Depp.[3]

It was a 1970 version of the legend, written by British playwright and actor Christopher Bond, however, that most inspired Sondheim. Expressing his attraction to Bond's version over others he had experienced, Sondheim asserted that "Christopher Bond humanized all the characters and gave the story motivation which had never existed before in the earlier versions of *Sweeney Todd*. Yet while enlarging the human dimensions of the play, Bond remained true to the melodramatic tradition" (5). It was Bond's version, then, that offered the combination of the traditional, larger-than-life feel of the Grand Guignol and an emphasis on humanity ("the frightening power of what is inside human beings") that Sondheim admired and strived to feature in his 1979 musical.

Twenty-six years later, Doyle's production, it seems, fulfilled Sondheim's goal more effectively than previous productions, as Sondheim himself noted. "Of all the productions I've seen," the composer told Charles Isherwood of *The New York Times*, "this is the one that comes closest to Grand Guignol, closest to what I originally wanted to do. I characterize all the major productions I've seen in terms of a single adjective. Hal's [Prince, 1979 on Broadway] was epic. Declan Donnellan's [1993 in London] production was exactly the reverse, it was very intimate. John's [Doyle], for me, is the most intense" (qtd. in Isherwood 1). The emotional intensity Sondheim observed and commended was also noted by critics. For example, Celia Wren, writing for *Commonweal*, observed that in general "director Doyle ratchets up the emotional voltage" (18-19); while Elysa Gardner of *USA Today* stated that the show "rel[ies] almost entirely on emotional expression and interpersonal contact ..." (3E). Ben Brantley of the *New York Times* described the characters as follows: "Empty-eyed and defeated-looking in their German Expressionist makeup and thrift-shop clothes, they nonetheless vibrate with the energetic anger of folks done wrong" (1). Robert Brustein (*New Republic*) noted a similar parallel with the emotionally heightened genre of German Expressionism, stating that "Michael Cerveris's bald-pated, pasty-faced, hollow-eyed Sweeney [was] skulking, slinking, stalking, like the somnambulist in *The Cabinet of Doctor Caligari*" (25). Other visceral adjectives found in the reviews described either the characters or the production as a whole as "smarmy," "mournful," "sinister," and "sulfurous," suggesting through their onomatopoeic nature the show's visceral appeal—the element that lent the production its "capacity to freeze your vertebrae" (25), in the words of Brustein. Given these observations, it is no wonder Sondheim applauded the "intensity" of Doyle's production.

In commending such intensity within a story that has for centuries fascinated its audiences through its eerie appeal, Sondheim emphasizes the importance of communicating to audience members on an emotional level. Referencing *Sweeney Todd*, he states that "most people can understand and identify with any emotion; the writer simply must draw the audience into the feelings of the characters that he has created on the stage" (10). His interest in his spectators' emotional engagement, in fact, lies behind Sondheim's decision to subtitle the piece a "musical thriller," rather than a musical melodrama. Aware that the use of word "melodrama" would conjure audience expectations of a more traditional style, Sondheim stated, "If we had called *Sweeney Todd* a musical melodrama, it would have unfailingly suggested making fun of the genre, with villains galloping across the stage, the heroine tied to the railroad tracks, and the audience cheering and clapping" (7). Though Sondheim expresses personal fascination with melodrama (the form arguably considered to feature the most exaggerated interpretation of humanity found on the stage), he argues for the maintenance of a presentation style that does not become so over-the-top that it loses its capacity to engage its audiences on more complex emotional levels. The retention of the "human dimensions" that Sondheim applauded in Christopher Bond's adaptation of the Todd legend is indeed critical, even within a piece that is "larger than life as a story and larger than life in technique" (Sondheim 5). His concept of the "musical thriller," then, serves to illustrate Sondheim's brand of melodrama, featuring many of the exaggerated elements of Grand Guignol while preserving the piece's ability to "draw in" audiences through engagement in genuine human emotions. To begin to understand how the suggestion of "the frightening power of what is inside human beings" onstage may elicit emotionally intense reactions in audience members of a musical as engaging as *Sweeney Todd*, we turn to cognitive conceptualizations of audience engagement in thematic threads and presentational elements as well as music and lyrics. My ongoing research focuses on cognitive science's growing contributions to the study of music and lyrics as these contributions relate to the work of Sondheim, while the present analysis addresses cognitive audience reception of thematic and presentational elements within the context of Theory of Mind. I begin by referencing the concept of mirroring, a cognitive procedure often said to be linked to the development of Theory of Mind.[4] In a recent short article in *Psychiatric Times*, John Medina described in basic terms the tendency of the human brain to mimic, or mirror, functions occurring in other human brains to which it is exposed. This includes the mimicking of and response to affect, a process known as empathy, defined by Medina as "the capacity to comprehend and react to the distinct affective experiences of another person" (14). Based upon a number of studies conducted by neuroscientists, this mirroring concept and the resulting emotional contagion describes a process of receiving sensory images, such as those presented by actors on the stage; mimicking the brain functions suggested by those images, and manifesting that mimicry in empathetic comprehension and response—perhaps in the form of cathartic laughter or tears in theatrical audiences.[5] Thus, mirroring appears to describe an essential aspect of the theatrical experience, and its resulting empathy may account for much of the emotional response we detect in audiences—an emotional response, which, as noted above, was apparently particularly "intense" among audiences of *Sweeney Todd* in 2005.

In applying a cognitive approach, then, it will be necessary to first understand the process of the formation of emotions as described by cognitive neuroscientist Antonio Damasio. Damasio states that emotions develop within six basic categories (and their subsets)—happiness, sadness, fear, anger, surprise, and disgust—and are stimulated either internally by a modification in chemical patterns within the body, or externally by sensory perception that is visual, aural, topical, etc (35-81). For the purposes of analyzing emotional reaction to a theatrical event such as *Sweeney Todd*, I will assume that the stimulants discussed here are external, received by the senses (predominantly the eyes and ears) and emanating from the staged performance. Damasio finds five characteristics common to all emotions, quoted as follows:

> (1) Emotions are complicated collections of chemical and neural responses. . . . Their role is to assist the organism in maintaining life.
> (2) Notwithstanding the reality that learning and culture alter the expression of emotions and give emotions new meanings, emotions are biologically determined processes, depending on innately set brain devices, laid down by a long evolutionary history.
> (3) The devices which produce emotions occupy a fairly restricted ensemble of subcortical regions. . . .
> (4) All the devices can be engaged automatically, without conscious deliberation. . . .
> (5) All emotions use the body as their theater . . . (51).

I will not expand upon numbers 1 and 3, which address the chemistry and regions of the brain from a solely scientific approach; however, number 2 is relevant to this analysis in its statement that emotions are "biologically determined." In other words, the human ability to emote is fairly universal, although the causes and behavioral manifestations of emotions vary among individuals. This may shed light on the cause of the multi-century popular interest in a tradition such as melodrama, and more specifically on the legendary nature of a narrative such as that of Sweeney Todd. Since emotions tend to formulate under the six simple headings listed above and appear to be natural human responses to stimuli presented, it is not surprising that the Sweeney legend has, as described above, resonated with audiences in similar manners throughout the past two hundred years and within multiple countries and cultures. Thus, on a simple cognitive level, the nature of emotion supports Sondheim's goal of appealing to the emotions as demonstrations of "the frightening power of what is inside human beings." Indeed, biologically, emotions are "inside human beings" and they form in response to the human experience.

Further, Damasio's fourth stipulation regarding emotion is relevant to this analysis because it posits that much of the brain activity that contributes to the formation of emotions may occur on a subconscious level. Emotions appear to have the ability to affect us cognitively long before we become aware of them and long before we form conscious reactions to them. According to Damasio, we become aware of emotions only after we begin to "feel" them: "Feeling an emotion is a simple matter. It consists of having mental images arising from the neural patterns which represent the changes in body and brain that make up an emotion. But knowing that we have that feeling, 'feeling' that feeling, occurs only *after* we build the second-order representations necessary for core consciousness" (280). Subsequently, Damasio states that such awareness of our emotions depends not only upon the development of such representations leading to core consciousness; it also relies upon autobiographical memory, allowing us to experience emotions within the context of our own past experiences.[6] This indicates that we often cannot help experiencing the emotions we experience, even though we may often judge ourselves afterward.[7] Perhaps this relative unavoidability of formulating emotions in specific situations explains what is "frightening," in Sondheim's terms, regarding the power within human beings. It certainly suggests frightening possibilities in terms of the results of emotions often leading to obsessive thoughts and compulsive behavior, an observation that will become relevant as I further analyze *Sweeney Todd*.

Finally, Damasio's fifth characteristic of human emotion, addressing the body as emotional theater, provides the foundation for examples of bodily reflection of emotion, such as audience laughter, to be discussed later.

A second concept functioning on a basic cognitive level to heighten emotional intensity in terms of both Sondheim's piece and Doyle's interpretation is the concept of compulsion. Compulsion as it is represented on stage forms a basic-level concept addressed in some detail by Bruce McConachie, whose recent book, *Engaging Audiences*, examines audience experience from a cognitive perspective. In applying specific cognitive concepts to the audience experience, McConachie quotes scientist Mark Johnson's concept of compulsion as follows:

> In his comments on the embodied nature and gestalt cognitive structure of compulsion, Mark Johnson notes, "Everyone knows the experience of being moved by external forces, such as wind, water, physical forces, and other people.

> When a crowd starts pushing, you are moved along a path you may not have chosen, by a force you seem unable to resist." (McConachie 201)

Compulsion, then, describes the type of repeated behavior that typically drives tragic heroes to their downfall. From Oedipus to Willy Loman, tragic heroes have succumbed to their own compulsive behavior resulting from pressure exerted by external forces; and Sweeney appears to follow this pattern exactly. When Sondheim's *Sweeney Todd* begins, the audience sees a main character who is acted upon by external forces—his unjust imprisonment at the hands of Judge Turpin, the Judge's lecherous behavior toward Todd's wife, and the evident social imbalance created by Victorian London society's treatment of those less fortunate than others. When Todd narrowly misses an opportunity to kill the judge, irrationality takes hold of him, compelling him to attain revenge not only on Judge Turpin in particular, but on society as a whole, making it his goal to murder every person who possesses the misfortune to enter his shop. His compulsion, if it has not been irresistible until this point, certainly becomes so now. Exhibiting the blindness of Oedipus, and driven by a parallel determination to "set things right," he ultimately kills the Beggar Woman, who was his wife, as he discovers only afterward. Todd, like Oedipus and other tragic heroes throughout history, displays the type of compulsive behavior that drives him to his downfall.

Sondheim's vision for the show confirms this conceptual approach to understanding *Sweeney Todd*:

> For me what the show is really about is obsession. I was using the story as a metaphor for any kind of obsession. Todd is a tragic hero in the classic sense that Oedipus is. He dies in the end because of a certain kind of fatal knowledge: he realizes what he has been doing. I find it terribly satisfying—much more so than any kind of accidental death, which often occurs in flimsy forms of melodrama. (qtd. in Zadan 245)

Sondheim, then, bases his melodrama on the concept of obsession, one that has appealed to human audiences since the time of the ancient Greeks. Obsession, the term Sondheim applies to the driving force behind *Sweeney Todd*, describes a mental "preoccupation or feeling" (*Merriam-Webster's Dictionary*), often leading to compulsion, or the need to act upon obsessive thoughts. Thus, Todd's compulsive behavior and accompanying obsessive thoughts form the concept that drives his own need for revenge as well as Sondheim's excitement in regarding the piece as good melodrama.

In Doyle's production, in which the characters played the orchestral instruments and thus did not leave the stage, audience members were never really allowed relief from Todd's presence and the compulsion associated with his mental world. As a result, reviewer Celia Wren credited the presence of "the ten dynamic performers on stage the entire time" (18-19) with heightening the emotional nature of the show; and Charlotte Headrick noted that audiences may likely find themselves identifying with Sweeney beyond the level of comfort: "Through all the blood and violence, we are on an electric and grueling journey with Sweeney, but we also know that going to the dark side may not bring us release" (478). In witnessing Sweeney's compulsion, it seems, audiences may have on some level entered the world of Todd's mind, feeling themselves compelled to join the deranged barber on his journey despite knowledge of imminent downfall.

In establishing this driving concept of obsession/compulsion in *Sweeney Todd*, Sondheim relies on the assumption that spectators will identify with this concept, and he argues that they will find themselves emotionally engaged with Sweeney's desire for revenge. Indeed, we have seen that at least one reviewer found herself on a "journey" with Sweeney, even though she was consciously aware of the dark nature of such a journey. This process relies once again on the human cognitive tendency of the mind/brain to "mirror" and therefore emotionally empathize with the actors on stage. Indeed, when audiences can be potentially "drawn in" to the minds of the characters through emotional contagion on a subconscious level, as Damasio describes, a piece as visceral as *Sweeney Todd* may be said to possess great affective potential; and both Sondheim and Doyle appear to have made choices designed to heighten this potential. In other words, a key goal of both artists seems to have been to "draw in" audience members on a subconscious level—to "catch" them unaware in the midst of this macabre London world where disconcerting human tendencies such as impulsiveness, vengeance, and, as we have seen, obsession/compulsion reign supreme.

The first line of the opening song, in fact, "Attend the tale of Sweeney Todd," serves to "draw in" the audience in a way that presupposes the allure of childhood storytelling. In addition, throughout the piece, as Sondheim scholar Craig Zadan notes, the composer stimulates audience cognitive interaction with the stage scenario by presenting the story of the Beggar Woman as a puzzle: "The Beggar Woman is in disguise," Sondheim explains. "A few, very alert people caught on right away, though, . . . because when the young wife appears and is raped, the minuet they're playing is the Beggar Woman's theme in a different guise" (qtd. in Zadan 252). Sondheim ingeniously communicates through the language of musical motif that the Beggar Woman and Sweeney's wife are the same character, drawing audiences in on a level meant to appeal to their sense of the allure of mystery. Sondheim offers other, more obvious clues to the Beggar Woman's identity as well, such as her indication early in the show that Todd appears familiar to her. In these ways, he calls upon his audience to participate, and although such participation obviously requires cognition on more than a simple subconscious level, it inevitably returns to the most basic level of emotional engagement culturally associated with storytelling, and the empathetic response likely to result when audiences are "drawn in" to the theatrical event.

In 2005, Doyle sought to further heighten this visceral style of communication between performer and spectator, utilizing a minimal set and focusing on the storytelling aspect of the piece. "It's more poetic than prescriptive. It's playful—almost told in a way that children would tell the story, using what was available to them" (qtd. in Isherwood 1), said Doyle. Sondheim agreed: "When an audience's imagination is engaged they enjoy it even more. . . . The theatre is a poetical medium . . . that's the fun of the theatre" (qtd. in Isherwood 1). Finally, producer Richard Frankel proudly noted what he viewed as the success of this poetic, storytelling approach based upon a nearly tangible tension within the audience: "I think it's great that at previews people are leaning forward in their seats hanging on every word. I stand in the back of the theatre and am delighted by the silence" (qtd. in Isherwood 1). Thus, an observed sense of collective audience suspense during the 2005 production as spectators watched and listened to the piece points to the existence of a heightened intimacy between performers and spectators—evidence of the performance's tendency to engage its audiences cognitively in ways that do not appear to require conscious awareness of engagement. Doyle thus creates the ideal setting for communicating affect in a way that illustrates the formation of emotion, as Damasio states, "without conscious deliberation."

As stated above, the fifth main characteristic of human emotion, according to Damasio, is the utilization of the body as theater for emotions. Damasio notes that the purpose of emotions is to maintain a healthy existence in the organism (either animal or human), and the result is an appropriate manifestation of the emotion within the body: "In an animal, for instance, the reaction may be to run or become immobile or to beat the hell out of the enemy or to engage in pleasurable behavior. In humans, the reactions are essentially the same . . ." (53-54). This type of reaction in response to spectators' theatrical experiences has of course been observed through the ages as what Aristotle termed catharsis, based in the emotions of pity and fear, while cognitively oriented studies such as McConachie's offer a more scientifically-based understanding of the truly beneficial nature of audience cathartic response. Although I cannot detail here the elaborate bodily process leading to physical manifestation of empathy and emotion in spectators, I would like to address the basic emotional precursors to the physical response of laughter, since Sondheim discusses laughter specifically with regard to *Sweeney Todd*. Sondheim has stated that "as Alfred Hitchcock made millions of dollars proving, there is a very thin line between melodrama and comedy, between being scared and laughing. An audience is more vulnerable to laughter—as we are in real life — not just in the theater, when it's most tense. If somebody is tense, you can tickle him; if he's relaxed, you can't" (12). Robert Latta confirms these statements from a cognitive perspective, explaining that in order for laughter to occur, a subject must exist in an "un-relaxed state," only to experience a "cognitive shift" from the un-relaxed state to a relaxed state, resulting, as Sondheim states, in the release of tension. This release of tension consequently leads to laughter (Latta 37-44). This formation and release of tension is similar to what Sondheim notes in spectators who laugh at the Beggar Woman. As Sondheim explains: "there is something creepy about the Beggar Woman, and by laughing at somebody or something, we attempt to ward it off. . . . This is the kind of laughter you can only create in melodrama where an audience will laugh to protect itself from being scared" (12). In this example, spectators' fear of the Beggar Woman and the resulting formation of tension result in the necessary release of such tension through laughter. Tension, fear, melodrama, and laughter—all resonate closely in Sondheim's *Sweeney Todd* and all appear closely related as cognitive stimulants and reactions played out in the theater of the body.

In a parallel vein, Sondheim also posits that his characters in *Sweeney Todd* possess a simplicity in their melodramatic nature that paradoxically allows them to communicate a passionate richness prompting them to become comic:

> In *Sweeney*, Mrs. Lovett's venality can be treated in a comic way because that is what she is: a venal character. . . . She is defined by her practicality combined with her greed. . . . Todd is a man bent on revenge, he thinks of nothing else; that is his dimension. . . . When you have characters like that, you can get laughs quite easily. (12)

Sondheim refers to audience laughter that can result from these characters' exaggerated obsessions, such as the practicality Mrs. Lovett displays when she hits upon the master plan of processing Todd's victims into meat pies. Her actions are larger-than-life, and they evoke tension among spectators—tension that finds its release in laughter. Interestingly, spectators' ability to laugh specifically at this character finds confirmation in the writing of Robert R. Provine, whose book examines laughter from a cognitive perspective. In his description of laughter within the context of theatrical and operatic repertoire, Provine describes the following scenario:

> As the house lights dim and the curtains part, settle into your pricey front-center seat and get ready for a wild ride. Much operatic laughter occurs in a decidedly grim setting. . . . Laughter merges with cannibalism in Stephen Sondheim's *Sweeney Todd*, where the invective Mrs. Lovett recycles the byproduct of Sweeney's homicidal tendencies in her meat pies ("A Little Priest"). (65-66)

Though Provine's example comprises a single sentence within his book, his selection of *Sweeney Todd* illustrates the ease with which Sondheim's work is understood on a cognitive level; and it speaks to the grotesquely comic nature that Sondheim rightly believes to be inherent in these characters.

It is likely the tension and fear created by all that is creepy and abnormal, then, that explains John Lahr's ghoulish delight in observing:

> Patti Lupone is Sweeney's pragmatic and pathological helpmate, Mrs. Lovett. A gargoyle of toughness, with an angular haircut, red lips and nails, a short skirt, and fishnet knee socks, LuPone looks positively Weimar. . . . [She] is never better than when Mrs. Lovett hits on the idea of disposing of one of Sweeney's victims by getting others to swallow the evidence. "Think of it as thrift / As a gift / If you get my drift," she sings. (96)

This is merely one example out of many of the moments in Doyle's *Sweeney* that combined the look of the characters with Sondheim's lyrics to create spectator engagement resulting in laughter as a form of tension release.

Doyle's *Sweeney Todd*, then, as Sondheim has stated, successfully drew out the emotional intensity already implicated within the writing of Sondheim, as evidenced through the beginnings of a cognitive analysis of audience reception of the production. As audiences became drawn emotionally into Todd's mental world despite their understanding of its inherent creepiness, processes of mirroring and empathetic response allowed a nearly firsthand experience of basic concepts, such as compulsion, on a heightened level. Laughter, it seems, offered a form of tension release; but those who wrote about the *Sweeney* experience did not soon forget its emotional intensity, and Sondheim and Doyle appear to have justly reawakened the legend that has gripped audiences for centuries.

NOTES

1 Gerould's study specifically focuses on the Todd legend, and therefore leaves out earlier relatable British narratives such as that of the pie-eating cannibalism in Shakespeare's *Titus Andronicus.*

2 Related books include: (1) *The London Monster: A Sanguinary Tale*, by Jan Bondeson (2000), detailing the history of Jack the Ripper's late eighteenth-century murderous precursor; (2) *The Wonderful and Surprising History of Sweeney Todd: The Life and Times of an Urban Legend*, by Robert L. Mack (2007), discussing the Todd legend itself. Mack's book and a 2007 paperback edition of Haining's book, mentioned above, were both released in time to accompany the debut of Tim Burton's 2007 film version of *Sweeney.*

3 Three British films, debuting in 1936, 1928, and 1926 (the latter two are silent) and based on the Dibdin-Pitt version, preceded the American film.

4 See Roch-Levecq (2006), whose study of a group of congenitally blind children revealed a possible link between these children's underdeveloped empathetic mirroring abilities and their comparatively low scores on Theory of Mind tasks. Also, in her 2005 article, "Finding the Self in Mind: Vermeer and the Reflective Function" (in *Psychodynamic Practice* 11.3, 255-68), Rosemary Rizq analyzes apparent connections between mothers' visible mirroring of their infants' emotional facial expressions and the infants' later development of Theory of Mind.

5 In *Engaging Audiences*, Bruce McConachie draws this connection between mirroring and experiencing the theatrical event in more detail.

6 See Damasio pages 222-26 for descriptions of the role memory plays in an integrated model closely orienting previous descriptions of emotion with elements of consciousness and memory.

7 Patients and clients have been shown to exert some control over their emotional reactions through Aaron T. Beck's cognitive-behavioral therapy process, during which they learn to modify their belief systems in order to consciously create an environment in which more positive emotions and fewer negative emotions will form. However, this process is not spontaneous—it does not allow for the regulation or exchange of emotions as they are forming; instead it seeks through practice to establish mental outlooks conducive to the formation of positive emotions and less conducive to the formation of negative ones.

WORKS CITED

Bondeson, Jan. *The London Monster: A Sanguinary Tale.* Philadelphia: University of Pennsylvania Press, 2000. Print.

Brantley, Ben. "Grand Guignol, Spare and Stark." *New York Times* 4 Nov. 2005: Sec. E, P. T1, Col. 3: 1. Print.

Brustein, Robert. "Making the Familiar Strange." *New Republic* 19 Dec. 2005: 25-27. Print.

Damasio, Antonio. *The Feeling of What Happens: Body and Emotion in the Making of Consciousness*. New York: Harcourt Brace and Co., 1999. Print.

Gardner, Elysa. "Great Musical Returns on a Much Smaller Scale." *USA Today* 4 Nov. 2005: 3E. Print.

Gerould, Daniel, ed. "A Toddography: Sweeney Todd in Literature and the Performing and Visual Arts." *Melodrama*. New York: New York Literary Forum, 1980. Print.

Haining, Peter. *Sweeney Todd: The Real Story of the Demon Barber of Fleet Street*. London: Anova, 2007. Print.

Headrick, Charlotte. "Performance Review of *Sweeney Todd*," ed. Sonja Arsham Kuftinec. *Theatre Journal* 58 (2006): 477-78. Print.

Isherwood, Charles. "Cutting 'Sweeney Todd' to the Bone." *New York Times* 30 Oct. 2005: Sec. 2, P. 1, Col. 3. Print.

Lahr, John. "Music Men." *New Yorker* 81:36, 96-97. Print.

Latta, Robert L. *The Basic Humor Process: A Cognitive Shift Theory and a Case against Incongruity*. Berlin: Mouton de Gruyter, 1999. Print.

Mack, Robert L. *The Wonderful and Surprising History of Sweeney Todd: The Life and Times of an Urban Legend*. New York: Continuum, 2007. Print.

McConachie, Bruce. *Engaging Audiences: A Cognitive Approach to Spectating in the Theatre*. New York: Palgrave MacMillan, 2008. Print.

Medina, John. "Mirroring in the Human Brain." *Psychiatric Times* 24:10 (2007): 14-17. Print.

Provine, Robert R. *Laughter: A Scientific Investigation*. New York: Viking, 2000. Print.

Sondheim, Stephen. "Larger than Life: Reflections on Melodrama and *Sweeney Todd*." *Melodrama*. Ed. Daniel Gerould. New York: New York Literary Forum, 1980. Print.

Wren, Celia. "'Rabbit Hole' and 'Sweeney Todd.'" *Commonweal* 10 Mar. 2006: 18-19. Print.

Zadan, Craig. *Sondheim and Co.* Second Edition. New York: Harper and Row, 1989. Print.

Distraction as Liveliness of Mind: A Cognitive Approach to Characterization in Jane Austen

Natalie Phillips

> "How could you begin?" said she. "I can comprehend your going on charmingly, when you had once made a beginning; but what could set you off in the first place?"
>
> "I cannot fix on the hour, or the spot, or the look, or the words, which laid the foundation. It is too long ago. I was in the middle before I knew that I *had* begun."
>
> —Jane Austen, *Pride and Prejudice*

What should we make of Elizabeth Bennet's liveliness? At the end of *Pride and Prejudice*, she asks Darcy "to account for his having ever fallen in love with her": "'Now be sincere,'" Elizabeth asks, "'did you admire me for my impertinence?'" Darcy replies: "'For the liveliness of your mind, I did'" (378). Frequently, Jane Austen uses three main words to describe a character; for Elizabeth, these are "lively," "playful," and "quick." Liveliness of mind and quickness of thought are, of course, Elizabeth's defining traits in the novel. However, as I will argue, the nuances of her "lively, playful disposition" only fully emerge when Elizabeth's habits of mind are compared with those of the other, minor characters by whom she's surrounded—specifically those within her family (51). It is, then, no accident that when Mr. Bennet introduces Elizabeth into the novel he sets her mind against her siblings': "'They have none of them much to recommend them,' replied he; 'they are all silly and ignorant like other girls; but Lizzy has something more of quickness than her sisters'" (45).

In this early scene, Austen cues the reader to pay close attention to Elizabeth's quickness of mind by having Mr. Bennet describe it explicitly. She also encourages the reader to understand the character in comparative terms: Elizabeth is noteworthy because she possesses a swiftness that Lydia, Mary, Kitty, and Jane lack. Throughout, the novel itself rewards such attention, for Austen strategically modulates her narrative so that implicit comparisons among characters can begin to convey—rather than merely describe—that quick liveliness that makes Elizabeth so vibrant. As Austen works to capture Elizabeth's cognitive agility and intellectual vivacity within what Blakey Vermeule calls the "fragile casing of narrative," however, she also develops a new structure for literary characterization using representations of attention—a paradigm in which distraction can build the fiction of a heroine's liveliness of mind (7). Darcy may say as much about Austen's narrative, then, as he does about love when he says: "'I cannot fix on the hour, or the spot, or the look, or the words, which laid the foundation . . . I was in the middle before I knew that I *had* begun'" (378). Darcy cannot pin down his impression of Elizabeth's impulsive quickness to a single moment because Austen has so finely integrated distraction within the novel's texture; Elizabeth's vivacity—and the techniques that produce it—are embedded almost intangibly within the story and structure.

A number of critics have recognized the rich effects of Austen's structure of characterization without quite being able to identify their cause, to say *how* they give Elizabeth such energy and life. Tony Tanner notes that Elizabeth has a "dimension of complexity, a questing awareness, [and] a mental range and depth" which makes her seem "trapped in a constricting web of . . . simple people" (126). Alex Woloch builds on this, suggesting that this depth is the effect of the "central tendency of the narrator" in *Pride and Prejudice* "to closely link the description of an 'intricate' mind with a counterpoised description of a 'simple' one" (52). Understanding how attention structures the novel's characterization, however, gives such arguments new specificity and texture; for, as I will show, Austen carefully links intricate minds with distraction and simple minds with narrow focus—and it is the *comparative* "reading" of these minds and attention spans on the reader's part that gives Elizabeth's questing awareness the illusion of range and depth.

Pride and Prejudice often brings minor characters into focus so—and only so—we can compare the inferior quality and complexity of their concentration to Elizabeth's. Austen severely limits the complexity of minor characters' attention spans; against them, the intricacy of Elizabeth's mind emerges in relief, and she claims the psychological richness of a central character. This means that Austen's minor characters play anything but a minor role in this drama of attention and characterization. Mary Bennet, for example, is essential to the narrative development of Elizabeth's "quickness." Austen carefully deprives Mary's attention of complexity and sets it against Elizabeth's livelier distraction. As I argue, Austen's process for simulating her heroine's vivacity has two key components: first, she associates Mary's rigid attention with mental stupor and uses this to play up the "something more" of Elizabeth's "quickness"; next, she develops a well-crafted set-piece of distraction that seems able to model—and perhaps actually narrate—the heroine's vibrant mind in action, and places it at the novel's center. Using distraction to convey Elizabeth's creative vibrancy, the novel develops a structure for comparing characters' minds and attention spans—one where Mary's rigid focus defines by contrast the playful flexibility of Elizabeth's mind.

Deep intersubjectivity and comparative Theory of Mind for literature

Many of Austen's novels use such uneven comparisons to develop psychological intricacy for a main character—which gives her famous portrayals of deep intersubjectivity a complex twist. In his book, *I Know that You Know that I Know: Narrating Subjects from Moll Flanders to Marnie* (2004), George Butte defines deep intersubjectivity as

> the web of partially interpenetrating consciousnesses that exists . . . when a self perceives the gestures, either of body or word, of another consciousness, and . . . perceive[s] in those gestures an awareness of his or her own . . . [O]ut of this conversation of symbolic behaviors emerges a web woven from elements of mutually exchanged consciousness. (28)

Lisa Zunshine's pioneering work uses Theory of Mind to discuss such moments, revealing that Austen's "layering of human consciousness" emerges, in part, from her ability to represent increasingly recursive levels of "multiply embedded states of mind" in prose ("Why Jane Austen Was Different" 278). The model of deep intersubjectivity has produced excellent readings of the layered scenes of observation in Austen's novels; however, when we bring it into the larger, messy world of a novel, we need new language. Phrases like "mutually-exchanged consciousness" begin to ring oddly false here, especially in narratological discussions of Austen's characterization. Why?

Butte and Zunshine can use deep intersubjectivity's language of openness and exchange so constructively, I think, because they tend to approach Austen's novels from a micro-level, often analyzing multiple short episodes or passages. When these same moments of multi-character observation are viewed from a macro-level, however, they seem to perform a radically different function. At the level of characterization, the idealized principles behind theories of deep intersubjectivity—its webs of interpenetrating minds, its mutuality of exchange, its reciprocal fashioning of multiple selves—give way to a much more imbalanced system of exchange. And, though many things are negotiated, narratologically speaking, through Austen's webs of fictional consciousness, such exchanges are rarely mutual.[1] Austen creates networks of characters, I argue, not to model the mutuality and reciprocity of multiple subjectivities, but to produce competition for the scarce resources of narrative space and cognitive richness. Scenes of intersubjectivity (and mutual exchanges of observation) from her novels, ironically, support a distinctly anti-reciprocal, *intra*subjective process of characterization.[2]

Analyzing the interplay between Mary and Elizabeth's attention to reading (and recognizing how vital it is to Austen's depiction of their mental states) thus underscores the need for what I call a *comparative Theory of Mind* for discussions of literature, as compared to Theory of Mind proper. Theory of Mind (ToM), or "mind reading," is a model used in cognitive science to describe "our ability to explain people's behavior in terms of their thoughts, feelings, behaviors, and desires" (Zunshine 6). In this essay, I emphasize the importance of distinguishing between ToM and ToM for literature in one specific point: how we manage the presence of "extra people." When we attribute mental states to fictional characters, peripheral figures have an unusually strong influence on literary mind reading. When I walk into a supermarket, ToM engaged, and decide that the person in front of me looks angry and the person behind me bewildered, I may compare them implicitly, but the fact that they are in the same line will have very little to do with the precise mental states I attribute to them.[3] In the novel, however, such a juxtaposition of characters can change everything.

As Zunshine points out, literature relies on "stimulat[ing] our Theory of Mind mechanism":

> On some level, then, works of fiction manage to "cheat" these mechanisms into "believing" that they are in the presence of . . . agents endowed with potential for a rich array of intentional stances.
>
> The very process of making sense of what we read seems to be grounded in our ability to invest the flimsy verbal constructions we generously call "characters" with a potential for a variety of thoughts, feelings, and desires and to look for the "cues" that would allow us to guess at their feeling and thus predict their action. (*Why We Read Fiction* 10)

When certain psycho-narratological cues in *Pride and Prejudice* encourage us to "mind read" Elizabeth as distracted, however, something more happens than "guessing at" Elizabeth's feeling. Such cues urge us to interpret the heroine's distraction as a basic sign of her cognitive complexity—the literary mark of a fictional mind endowed with a rich array of intentional stances, or one worth spending the time "reading."

However, our ability to invest characters like Elizabeth with an imaginary mind worthy of complex mentalizing may not only rely upon but arise from our awareness of other, "simpler" minds, specifically those of surrounding minor characters like Mary. This opens up a crucial difference between the ToM process for real and fictional minds. In the world, whether we believe people to be fascinating or dull, we still automatically assume that the people we see have minds, and that their mental states are worth "reading" for signs of potential threat or benefit. This is not so true of fiction, where the illusion of a character's mind (and a fictional mind with psychological richness) must be built, sentence by sentence. Moreover, unlike a person, a novel can be skimmed, or ignored, without much danger to us. Literature, in this sense, must not only develop narrative strategies that "'cheat' these mechanisms into 'believing' that they are in the presence of . . . [real] agents" (Zunshine, *Why We Read Fiction* 10), they must also give enough realism to a fictional character so that we exercise our ToM extensively on his or her mind. Since narrative space is limited, underdeveloped minor characters that receive less description (and thus provide us with less ToM information to process) must vie with protagonists both for our attention and for our activation of literary ToM. This competition for cognitive richness may be essential to crafting the illusion of psychological depth for main characters in the first place—a narratological mechanism for fooling our ToM into thinking a character made up of typeface and sentences has a mind to read at all.

If so, how can we describe a character's potential for this rich array of intentional stances? The techniques that build this cognitive richness? In the pages that follow, I suggest that the analysis of attention not only offers us new models for understanding Austen's novels, but also reframes discussions of the fictional representation of human minds to better appreciate the intricate variety of thoughts (and habits of thinking) modeled in narrative fiction. Traditional models of characterization, often based on E. M. Forster's classic distinction between the "flat" and the "round" character, tend to rely on a generative but ultimately limited paradigm of psychological "depth" that requires us to measure cognitive richness and realism in terms of volume. Here is Forster: "[A] novel that is at all complex often requires *flat* people as well as *round*, and the outcome of their collisions parallels life more accurately" (108). Looking at how characters' inner lives and minds develop around collisions of attention as I do, however, opens this discussion to descriptors of character far more complex than the flat and the round. Analyzing characters' various modes and habits of focus moves us toward a range of characteristics for fictional minds that explode the simplicity of mental volume—qualities of mind like quickness, endurance, flexibility, capacity, intensity, divisibility, and fluidity. My reading of *Pride and Prejudice* looks at how Elizabeth's "liveliness" interweaves three of these: flexibility, quickness, and fluidity.[4]

Changing theories of attention and distraction

Understanding why distraction, of all things, could work in Austen's novel to convey such mental liveliness, however, requires us to return to its historical moment. For most of the early modern period, distraction was associated with madness, sin, and error. Such interpretations emerged from religious (and thus moral) readings of concentration. Attention and distraction were seen as the product of effort, and consequently were linked to virtue and vice. The basic metaphor for attention was a straight line, with distraction as a divergent angle. Distraction was therefore a sinful mental digression—a wandering from the right way of godliness. Such ideas supported a single-object theory of concentration, where proper focus was seen as maintaining stasis, or fixing the attention—imagined as narrowing the concentration to a single point or path (and keeping it there).[5] This is the basic logic behind the allegorical topography of John Bunyan's *The Pilgrim's Progress* (1678): the sin of the pilgrim, Christian, is allowing himself to be diverted by characters like Mr. Worldly Wiseman, and thus straying from the narrow road of righteousness on his way to the "Celestial City."

In the late seventeenth and early eighteenth century, however, writers began to move away from such conspicuously moralistic descriptions of distraction to develop a more neutral, psychological framework for interpreting attention. By the 1740s, there were at least two competing philosophies of attention at play: a moral one, in which attention and distraction mark the line between virtue and vice; and a psychological one, in which attention and distraction are just two different modes, or states, of mind. Those using this newer psychological model believed that thoughts rarely stand still or follow a straight path, and created new definitions to accommodate the mind's natural movements. John Locke and David Hume, for example, emphasized that the narrowing stretch of intensely focalized attention was an essentially temporary mental posture, only one of the many states the mind shifts through on a daily basis.[6] They were more interested in describing the spontaneous movements—and changing modes—of attention over time than in assessing its success or failure in sticking to a point. Accordingly, philosophers in this tradition began to describe distraction, not as a geometric angling off path, but as an interruption in attention's proper temporal rhythm, a moment (or set of moments) when our moving thoughts do not match up with our intended object of focus. Distraction, for them, was a kind of temporal disjunct, an inequality between the amount of time a task requires and the time the mind devotes to that task. Some began to suggest that this odd mental tempo could have benefits as well as costs—specifically, the ability to bring unusual ideas together, and thus spark creativity.

Denis Diderot articulates this shift in ideas about attention most explicitly, and he voiced the strongest challenge to the perception of distraction as pure vice:

> La distraction a sa source dans une excellente qualité de l'entendement, une extrême facilité dans les idées de se réveiller les unes les autres. C'est l'opposé de la stupidité, qui reste sur une même idée… Un bon esprit doit être capable de distractions, mais ne doit point être distrait.

"Distraction," Diderot argues in the *Encyclopédie* (1754), "stems from an excellent quality of the understanding."[7] It has its source in an "extreme facility" of mind—for distraction, he argues, "allows ideas to trigger, or awaken one another." Diderot believed distraction to be a vital state of mind for generating new thought. He also considered it the creative opposite of compulsive attention, which he described as the over-focused stupor of "remaining, unchanging, on one idea." According to Diderot, a "good mind" was spontaneous enough to accommodate distractions but stable enough to avoid going mad.

If Diderot's redefinition of distraction articulated the wider cultural reorganization around the concept of attention, Austen's *Pride and Prejudice* is its narrative realization.[8] The novel takes up the idea that distraction contains a productive kernel of creative energy (as well as the suggestion that excessive concentration could make one intellectually numb) and turns attention into a literary device for better simulating the complexity of Elizabeth's inner life. In this context, Elizabeth's capacity for distraction (and other characters' lack of it) is just as important as her oft-discussed powers of observation. *Pride and Prejudice* sets up Elizabeth's distraction to signify her liveliness and spontaneity and silhouettes it against a backdrop of obnoxiously over-attentive minor characters. The most noteworthy of these is Elizabeth's sister, Mary. In Austen's careful (and satirical) hands, the girl's unshifting attentiveness becomes the antithesis of creativity.

MARY BENNET: OR, THE PROBLEM OF HYPERFOCUS

Austen's Mary Bennet gives us one of the earliest and clearest descriptions of a character stuck in the heightened state of absorption scientists now call *hyperfocus*. Psychologists like Thomas Brown, who approach distraction from a neuro-cognitive perspective, describe this state of mind as follows:

> Hyperfocus is an intense form of mental concentration that focuses consciousness on a narrow subject. [Those who hyperfocus] are unable to stop focusing on one thing and redirect their focus to another when they need to. They end up "locking on" to some task, sight, or sound—and totally lose track of everything else. (33)

If the cognitive term "hyperfocus" is anachronistic, the concept it refers to is not. John

Locke began looking at the problems of absorption in his 1688 *Essay on Human Understanding*, in which he notes that intense contemplation threatens to shut out other thoughts. When the mind "fixes it self with so much earnestness on the Contemplation of *some* Objects," Locke worries, it will "take no notice of the ordinary Impressions made then on the Senses" (228). Such over-attention, for both Locke and Brown, has distinct costs: a shutting down and a subsequent inability to notice the ordinary impressions of the surrounding world.

Austen experiments with this idea (and its narrative implications) in *Pride and Prejudice*, where she makes Mary Bennet a figure of hyperfocus.[9] For much of the book, the girl remains inflexibly locked in a state of close attention, taking "no notice of the ordinary Impressions made on [her] Senses." Mary focuses stubbornly on two main actions: reading books and playing piano. And, though Austen shows her absorption in these to be deep, earnest, and focused, it is also, importantly, static. Mary seems to attend to all tasks in precisely the same way—with unremitting, relentless concentration. The costs for her in terms of character development are intentionally high. When Elizabeth and Jane return home from Netherfield, "they found Mary, as usual, deep in the study of thorough bass and human nature" (95). The novel implies that Mary's focus has not shifted at all in the meantime: she is still reading as intently as she was when they left a few chapters before. The key is not just that Mary's still reading, but that she is still absorbed—deeply absorbed—in her study.

Fifty years prior, when more traditional religious ideas about attention clearly held sway, depicting a character's absorption in the study of morality could be imagined to reliably convey piety and goodness, as well as the psychological depth of that character's mind and interest. As Michael Fried notes in *Absorption and Theatricality*, French painters of the 1760s intentionally sought to "capture" characters in visible states of heightened attention in their artworks so as

> to arrive in the end at the sort of emotionally charged, highly moralized, and dramatically unified situation that alone was [thought] capable of embodying with sufficient perspicuousness the absorptive states of suspension of activity and fixing of attention that that painter and critic alike regarded as paramount. (56)

However, for absorption to carry such cultural significance and emotional resonance, such moments of intense focus needed an additional quality: they needed to be temporary. With the short iterative "as usual" (and the tedious cycle of repetition it connotes), Austen drains Mary's absorption of the potential for such emotional and narrative charge.

The monotony of this "as usual" holds throughout the novel. Mary is only granted one mode of attention—hyperfocus. This stoic intensity limits her as character, conversationalist, and thinker; for the narrator implies that Mary's clockwork diligence robs her of mental agility. Inflexible-minded from too much study, she cannot even keep up, Austen suggests, with the basic temporal flow of conversations going on around her. We see this most clearly when Mr. Bennet teasingly asks Mary to comment on the etiquette rules for introducing a suitor like Bingley. She fails woefully, producing the following painful exchange: "'What say you, Mary?,' Mr. Bennet asked, 'for you are a young lady of deep reflection I know, and read great books, and make extracts.'" Here the narrator interrupts to note that though "Mary wished to say something very sensible," she "knew not how." "'While Mary is adjusting her ideas,'" Mr. Bennet interjects, tongue-in-cheek, "'let us return to Mr. Bingley'" (47). The joke relies on the sharp contrast between Mary's supposedly "deep reflections" and her shallow—in fact, absent—contribution to the conversation. Mary's habit of absorption seems to slow down her mind, producing such verbal stupor that the conversation moves on before she can adjust her ideas, or get her thoughts flowing so as to speak. Mary thus becomes a figure for the cognitive costs of excessive attention—inflexibility, rigidity, and a deep social awkwardness.

Since Mary cannot loosen her attention, she is also barred from character change. After Lydia's elopement, an event that fuels much character development for Elizabeth, Mary remains unmoved. Unable to cobble together a single new thought in the face of family disaster, Mary recycles undigested maxims she's picked up in her old readings. In this, her longest speech of the novel, she produces four rather frozen gems of morality, culled from her conduct books:

> "that loss of virtue in a female is irretrievable—that one false step involves her in endless ruin—that her reputation is no less brittle than it is beautiful,—and that she cannot be too much guarded in her behaviour towards the undeserving of the other sex." (298)

Mary's focus on morality (much like her blind concentration on piano performance at the Netherfield ball) remains disturbingly undisrupted by any attention to her family's reaction. The problem, as Zunshine might put it, is that Mary is attuned, not to the dynamic "presence, behavior, and emotional display" of people around her, but to an inert set of objects—her books, and to a static memory of the morals they contain ("Why Jane Austen Was Different" 277). Indeed, undismayed by (and perhaps completely oblivious to) Elizabeth's uplifted eyes, Mary continues "to console herself with such kind of moral extractions from the evil before them" (298)

This concentration on studying becomes the novel's "excuse" to keep Mary "indoors," not only excluded from the many walks in *Pride and Prejudice*, but also from any kind of productive mental wandering.[10] Set up only to study and be static, Austen's Mary can "never spare time" from reading, and thus can't indulge in a walk:

> Lydia's intention of walking to Meryton was not forgotten; *every sister except Mary* agreed to go with her. . . .
>
> Mrs. Bennet was not in the habit of walking, *Mary could never spare time,* but the remaining five set off together. (105, 364-65; emphasis added)

Indeed, when Lydia tries to tempt Mary to go outside by describing the joys of travel—coach rides, new ribbons, and cucumber sandwiches—Mary can only respond: "'Far be it from me, my dear sister, to depreciate such pleasures. . . . But I confess they would have no charms for *me*. I should infinitely prefer a book'" (238). No model for Austen's audience, the over-attentive Mary is instead a cautionary figure for the dangers of reading too much. The novel mocks Mary for her habit of reading to the exclusion of all else, and lauds Elizabeth for her ability to stop (and to digress in thought and action). In such a world, when Miss Bingley calls Elizabeth a "great reader" who takes " no pleasure in anything else," Mary's novelistic presence sharpens the insult. And, Austen's caricature of Mary both fuels the outrage (and raises the value) of Elizabeth's famous retort: "I am *not* a great reader, and I have pleasure in many things" (74).

Mary's absorption in books is literalized in her lack of mobility in the novel, and her absorption limits her both in mental (and in narrative) space. Austen now uses Mary's motionlessness to reflect a still deeper inflexibility—that of mind and character. For example, when Elizabeth returns home from Pemberley, stunned and altered by the news of Lydia's decision to run off with Wickham, Jane hurries downstairs to meet her. Mary and Kitty, however, stay upstairs, both too focused on their daily routines to notice their older sister's entrance. The narrator suggests that this habitual self-absorption has left the two girls oddly unmoved by any reaction to Lydia's elopement:

> [They] had been too busily engaged in their separate apartments to make their appearance before. One came from her books, and the other from her toilette. The faces of both, however, were tolerably calm; and no change was visible in either. (297)

Their sister's tragedy, Austen implies, has not influenced them in any way. Their surface calm reflects the shallowness of their respective characters. Mary's calm derives from obliviousness; she is too busy in her books, it seems, to be bothered. A few lines later, Jane accidentally explains Mary's inertia—and why she has not asked Mary to help manage their mother's hypochondriac nerves. The others "'would have shared in every fatigue, I am sure,'" Jane tells Elizabeth, "'but I did not think it right . . . and Mary studies so much, that her hours of repose should not be broken in on'" (301). With her absorption in books seemingly unbroken by any distraction, the ever-attentive Mary is not only compressed but crystallized into a minor figure. She remains a tableau—not character but unshifting caricature—of excessive, and ultimately impoverished, attention.

ELIZABETH BENNET: OR, THE BENEFITS OF DISTRACTION

Elizabeth, swift of thought and quick of tongue, has (distinctly unlike Mary) the capacity for distraction, and thus, I argue, the capacity for change. Playing on the notion that distraction reawakens ideas, Austen mixes in some absentmindedness with Elizabeth's normal attentiveness to establish her difference from flatter characters like Mary and to demonstrate her superior flexibility of mind. Though Elizabeth's powers of observation are unparalleled in the first half of the novel, in the second half, her attention is frequently interrupted—often while reading—and still more often by her conflicting emotions for Darcy. Austen places the most important scene of disrupted focus at the center of *Pride and Prejudice*, when Elizabeth reads Darcy's letter. And it is here—at the novel's turning point, or *volta*—that Austen uses Elizabeth's distraction to cultivate her most detailed, and realistic, descriptions of the heroine's mind.

Distraction, for Diderot, marked a creative mind in movement, though one perhaps not always quite moving at the right tempo. Michael Posner and Raja Parasuraman, two contemporary leaders in the field of attention, both emphasize this aspect of attention's cognitive complexity, and the importance of such movements in time. Each describes attention as a continuous, multilayered process—optimally, the ongoing process of focusing on the right things, at the right time, at the right speed—which allows us to adapt to the shifting conditions and demands of the surrounding world. Attention, for Parasuraman, "is not a single entity but the name given to a finite set of brain processes that can interact, mutually and with other brain processes, in the performance of different perceptual, cognitive, and motor tasks" (3). Posner's *The Cognitive Neuroscience of Attention* explains attentional orienting "as the set of processes by which neural resources are deployed selectively . . . on the basis of changing motivation, expectation, or volition in order to optimize perception and action" (157). Brown, I think, best synchronizes these two theories for a discussion of distraction when he writes:

> The continuous process of attention involves focusing and shifting focus, regulating alertness, sustaining effort, and regulating the mind's processing speed and output . . . Attention, in this sense, is essentially a name for the integrated operation of the executive functions of the brain. Distraction marks the failure to activate and manage these various cognitive functions in the right way at the right time. (11, 21)

In one sense, distraction is still clearly a cognitive failure here—or at least a mark of cognitive inefficiency. The neurochemical networks associated with the executive functions have failed to direct and shift the mind's focus appropriately to concentrate on the "right" object or task at the "right" time. But distraction is not the opposite of attention, Brown makes clear; it simply marks a certain disruption, or pattern of cognitively clustered disruptions, in attention's normal process and rhythm. What Diderot (and I think Austen) emphasize is that such mistimings and disruptions can be oddly useful—at times, essential—for bringing new thoughts together spontaneously to catalyze innovation.[11]

Distraction, in this sense, marks not a deficient but an unpredictable, or sporadic, tempo of focus. The mind bounces loosely and haphazardly at a changing pace, moving between intense concentration and sharp interruption, delving into an idea and then snapping away from it. Austen spends a full chapter describing Elizabeth reading (and re-reading) Darcy's letter in this quick shifting mode of mind, and her description is replete with such spontaneous, playful leaps of attention. This chapter—and the distraction it contains—fleshes out the heroine's otherwise stock characteristic of liveliness by creating a space in which the narrative can model her mind's quickness, flexibility, and fluency, creating a more textured sense of her inner life.

For Elizabeth's reading there is none of Mary's frozen "as usual." Elizabeth's distracted reading habits thus open out into complexity.[12] As her mind moves swiftly and erratically through Darcy's letter at ever-shifting paces, it begins to convey not only the heroine's impulse and emotion, but also the fluency of her ideas and her elasticity of mind. Mind, again, is literalized in motion. Unlike Mary, Elizabeth not only walks, but walks while she reads; and, in truth, reads much like she walks: "crossing field after field at a quick pace, jumping over stiles and springing over puddles with impatient activity" (70). Austen grants this same breathless quickness to Elizabeth's reading of Darcy's letter:

> She read, with an eagerness which hardly left her power of comprehension, and from impatience of knowing what the next sentence might bring, was incapable of attending to the sense of the one before her eyes. (223)

This energetic, distracted reading—a kind of mental jumping and springing through the text—as well as her strong yearning for the next line make Elizabeth unable to focus fully on the sentence before her.

At the end of this first speed-reading of Darcy's missive, Austen is careful to tell us, Elizabeth's mind is left so scattered that she "scarcely know[s] anything of the last page or two." She ends the letter still pacing restlessly in a "perturbed state of mind," with "thoughts that [can] rest on nothing" (223). Though such mental restlessness may keep Elizabeth from fully absorbing the meaning of Darcy's letter at first, her distraction produces what Mary's plodding mind cannot: a rapid burst of thoughts.[13] Pausing only halfway through, Elizabeth "instantly" 1) establishes Darcy's belief of Jane's insensibility to Bingley to be false; 2) assesses the letter's style as "not penitent, but haughty"; and 3) firmly labels him "all pride and insolence" (223). Only thirty seconds later, Elizabeth begins reading the letter again; however, this second time, distracting thoughts and emotions now endlessly interrupt the swift flow of her reading. She must stop and re-read after almost each paragraph, and at times, after each sentence. This makes her reading seem full of motion, if also restless and haphazard. Moreover, these interruptions create narrative, and clearly, it is the back and forth within Elizabeth's mind, and not Darcy's letter, that Austen ultimately seeks to convey.

The narrator, in fact, lingers for an entire chapter over Elizabeth's distraction, using the space created to articulate the new thoughts it produces. Austen here seeks to capture Elizabeth's mind in process within the narrative form itself; the very structure of the novel begins to take on the tempo of Elizabeth's particular liveliness.[14] The illusion of the heroine's cognitive intricacy and vibrancy of mind seems to emerge from within the chapter's montage of leaps, stops, and starts:

> The letter was unfolded *again* . . . she *again* began the mortifying perusal.
> But when she read, and re-read . . . *again* was she forced to hesitate. She put down the letter.
> *Again* she read on.
> After pausing on this point a considerable while, *she once more continued to read* . . .
> From herself to Jane—from Jane to Bingley, her thoughts . . . soon brought to her recollection that Mr. Darcy's explanation *there* had appeared very insufficient; *and she read it again* . . . (223-25, 227; all but the penultimate emphasis added)

Again and again, her returns to Darcy's letter are interspersed with extensive descriptions of her distraction. Some interrupting new thought (often in free-and-indirect discourse) necessitates the "again" of a more attentive reading—and each new close reading again scatters her thoughts. The narrator shuttles between narrative input 1 (Elizabeth's stages of reading) and input 2 (the thoughts that make up her distraction). The more ragged texture of this distracted reading can connote Elizabeth's liveliness, in part, because the caricature of Mary as all-absorbed monotonous reader works as such a fit foil for her sister's energetic mind. Mary's strict mode of study does nothing better than show us what Elizabeth's style of reading is not.

A lively-minded heroine, the novel imagines, must not read in a neat and orderly fashion. Instead, Elizabeth's mind, like the narrative that describes it, refuses linear development. And as the novel layers distraction upon distraction, we seem to get a bundle of insights produced in short, erratic bursts of concentration. This makes the novel, like her mind—or, in fact, her mind, like the novel—dart in and out, back and forth, as it throws light on a variety of fresh ideas and emotions. This switching back and forth creates an eccentric narrative rhythm—one that plays out spontaneously against the steady, calm rhythm of Darcy's carefully written letter itself, embedded in full (and uninterrupted) just a chapter before. It is here, in this narrative simulation of distraction-punctuated thoughts, that I think Austen renders Elizabeth's liveliness of mind most subtly—for she invites her audience not only to "read" the heroine's distraction, but to enact it (and reflect upon it) as readers themselves.

Incorporating distraction within the novel's form, Austen not only finds a way to capture the richness of her heroine's spontaneity; she also turns distraction into a powerful catalyst for narrative movement and character development For example, it is in one of the moments of free-and-indirect discourse that emerge in the distracted spaces between her re-readings that Elizabeth finally realizes: "Mr. Darcy's conduct,"

> which she had believed it impossible that any contrivance could so represent, as to render . . . less than infamous, was *capable of a turn* which must make him entirely blameless throughout the whole. (224, my emphasis)

In the first half of the novel, of course, Elizabeth declares Darcy "'the last man in the world whom I could ever be prevailed on to marry'" (214). Only after her distracted reading of his letter does Elizabeth undergo "so material a change" that her "sentiments" become precisely the opposite (366). The very halts and leaps, slants and errors of the heroine's mind as she reads seem, in fact, to fuel the novel's crucial moment of double transformation: Elizabeth's acknowledgment of her emotions for Darcy and her profound recognition of her prejudices against him. *Pride and Prejudice* imagines that distraction stimulates rapid bursts of thought in a strong mind; it is this production of new, if disordered, thoughts that makes Elizabeth's distraction the novel's vehicle for deep mental change.

Playing on this idea of distraction-as-transformation, the chapter ends with a complex scene that shows Elizabeth's creative mind adrift; distraction, as always, prompts in her an energetic, chaotic awakening of ideas:

> [Elizabeth] wander[ed] along the lane for two hours, giving way to every variety of thought; re-considering events, determining probabilities, and reconciling herself as well as she could, to a change so sudden and so important. (227-28)

Wandering, it seems, is what allows her mind to churn, both giving way to and producing "variety of thought." Elizabeth's final ability to let her mind roam affirms that she has true mobility of mind and is capable not only of rich thought and variety, but of character change both "sudden" and "important." Austen builds the eccentric rhythm of concentration—and its generative power—into the chapter itself.

In a letter to her sister, Cassandra, Jane Austen claims that Elizabeth's playfulness is in fact the novel's, and teasingly suggests that the insertion of some distraction would perfectly offset its liveliness:

> Upon the whole however I am quite . . . well satisfied enough.—The work is rather too light, & bright, & sparkling;—it wants shade;—it wants to be stretched out here & there with a long Chapter—of sense, if it could be had, if not, of solemn specious nonsense—about something unconnected with the story: an Essay on Writing, a critique on Walter Scott, or the history of Buonaparté—or anything that would form a contrast & bring the reader with increased delight to the playfulness & general Epigrammatism of the general style. (203)

Liveliness. Comparison. Distraction. The building blocks are all here: "the playfulness of the general style"; "anything that would form a contrast"; "a long chapter . . . about something unconnected with the story." It is only in these moments—when distraction's playful creativity becomes, in this sense, both its protagonist's main trait and the defining stylistic quality of the novel—that we are able, I think, to read Elizabeth's mind as that of a fully fleshed-out heroine. And if attention has become part of the novel's structure, as I suggest, the modality of distraction is not only vitally tied to Austen's strategies of characterization, but inextricable from the novel's deepest levels of meaning making.

In this sense, it is no surprise that *Pride and Prejudice* encourages us to measure out the spontaneity and vitality not only of novels' styles, but of fictional minds by their ability to accommodate creative distraction. Though descriptions of attention and multilayered observations can provide both readerly challenges and rich narrative texture, they too are enfolded into Austen's comparative, competitive structure of characterization. Elizabeth is invested with the potential Zunshine speaks of, the rich array and variety of thoughts, feelings, and desires; Mary is not. Novels often encourage us to attribute more mental depth and ToM to characters (like Elizabeth) who are given the room to demonstrate mental variation than we do to characters (like Mary) who can only demonstrate one rigid habit of mind, or what Alan Palmer has called a "mind-rut." However, as my discussion of *Pride and Prejudice* also shows, some characters activate readers' ToM more than—or even, perhaps, against—others, and this may need to occur if we are ever to gain a sense of our heroes and heroines as fully-realized psychological entities. Maneuvering the reader's selective attention and attribution, as orchestrated by the novelist, becomes an important and deliberate tactic for developing psychological richness in the closed, structured world of fiction.

If it is only against the unchanging absorption of simple characters like Mary that scenes of Elizabeth's distraction can build the illusion of her cognitive complexity, we need a comparative literary model of ToM to talk about Austen's novels—and perhaps about fiction in general. Using a comparative model to understand how ToM works when we read fiction lets us take the potential distribution of mentalizing into account in a novelistic zero-sum-game of character development. Though all characters may stimulate our ToM, some characters stimulate it more than others. Not all minds (or mind readings) are created equal in narrative fiction; it is only by depriving Mary of mental richness that Austen can give Elizabeth's novelistic mind such subtlety. And it is only by caricaturing Mary's absorption that Austen can use distraction as she does: as a measure of character, as an invitation to mind read "liveliness," and as a literary device for conveying the cognitive richness of an intricate mind.[15]

NOTES

1 The major exception to this point, of course, is Austen's modeling of reciprocity for the central couples of her marriage plot. The chemistry, for example, between Elizabeth and Mr. Darcy, Emma and Mr. Knightley, or Anne and Mr. Wentworth all rely on this narrative principle of mutual exchange. These pairs, however, are still pairs of major characters; and they still claim subjectivity, cognitive complexity, and narrative space at the expense of minor characters like Mr. Collins, Miss Bates, or Mrs. Clay.

2 It is no accident, I think, that our favorite passages modeling intersubjectivity from Austen make main characters—Elizabeth (not Lydia or Mr. Hurst) or Anne Elliot (rather than Louisa or Miss King)—the subject of the sentence. In the famous example from *Persuasion,* "It did not surprise, but it grieved Anne to observe that Elizabeth would not know [Wentworth]. She saw that he saw Elizabeth . . ." (117), there is an intricate hierarchy of observers and observation embedded within the passage's multiple recursivity—with Anne at the top, then Wentworth, then Elizabeth. Butte implicitly acknowledges this privileging of certain characters over others in deep intersubjectivity when he notes that Austen's "favorite observers" are often her heroines, "women . . . finely attuned to the network of perceptions that surround them" (110). And, it is Anne's finely honed skills for "observing observation, even observation of herself," according to Butte, that give this scene's deep intersubjectivity such power (112).

3 These inferences, presumably, are based on the separate sets of physical and verbal cues I have picked up unconsciously from each shopper, not on a comparison of the two based on their accidental position in the same line.

4 Fluidity of thought can be imagined as a combination of what cognitive scientists call ideational fluency, that is, the ability to "generate a certain *quantity* of new and

imaginative responses to a task" and what they call ideational flexibility, that is, the ability to produce novel responses in a wide range of *categories* (Turner 190).

5 *Attention* originally comes from the Latin *ad-tendere* (to stretch toward), implying that the attentive mind consciously elongates and narrows itself in a fine, taut beam toward the thing upon which it wishes to focus. Traditional seventeenth- and early eighteenth-century definitions of attention conventionally describe attention as a voluntary mental stretch. Writers of this period often represented it as an intense gaze, where attention seems to reach along an invisible line from the eye to the object. Similarly, since distraction derives from *dis-trahere* (Latin for to drag away, or apart), distraction originally referred to anything that dragged the mind from the direct line of attention. This idea of attention as line supported religious readings of concentration as a moral good, for if one could only be on the proper path of attention or off of it, the divine consequences of attention could seem equally clear.

6 Locke argued that there were a number of "various *Modes of thinking* which the Mind may observe in itself" (227). He believed that "the Mind employs itself about [its present Ideas] with several Degrees of Attention," and, in a day, necessarily moves through "a great variety of degrees," ranging "between earnest Study & very near minding nothing at all" (227-28). "Men," argued Hume in his *Treatise*, "are nothing but a bundle or collection of different perceptions, which succeed each other with an inconceivable rapidity; and are in a perpetual flux and movement . . . the thought has evidently a very irregular motion in running along its objects, and may leap from the heavens to the earth, from one end of the creation to the other, without any certain method or order. . . . The capacity of our mind is not infinite" (39, 92). By 1757, Hume imagined that the mental stretch required of aesthetic attention necessitated so much self-discipline that, at even the slightest interruption, the Mind, like a spring, would relax: "The least exterior hindrance to such small springs, or the least internal disorder, disturbs their motion," he claimed, "and confounds the operations of the whole machine" ("Taste" 139).

7 Translations in this paragraph are my own.

8 Associations of distraction with spontaneity, innovation, and creativity like those we see in Diderot's article gathered currency throughout the 1760s, 70s, and 80s, and such suggestions appeared in a number of Austen's favorite literary works—including Samuel Johnson's *Rasselas* (1759), Laurence Sterne's *Tristram Shandy* (1759-1767), and William Cowper's *The Task* (1785). However, Austen may well have read Diderot herself. Tutored by her French cousin, Eliza de Feuillide, she "read French with facility" (Holbert 83, citing Leigh 24) and Diderot's *Encyclopédie* was published widely in cheap editions (see Darnton's *The Business of Enlightenment*).

9 For a more detailed reading of Jane Austen's relationship to John Locke—specifically her "dramatization" of Locke's educational tracts in *Northanger Abbey,* see Jocelyn Harris's *Jane Austen's Art of Memory,* 1989, pp. 1-33.

10 For more on this point, see Alex Woloch's *The One vs. The Many.* I base my cognitive work on attention in *Pride and Prejudice* on his brilliant analysis of Austen's structure of characterization.

11 Useful terms for discussing Austen's early association of distraction and creativity may be found in the modern work of cognitive psychologists interested in the conditions for increasing our ability to link seemingly disparate concepts into novel synthesis (Snyder 416). For such increased creativity, researchers like Alice M. Isen and Ellis Paul Torrance emphasize the importance of maintaining a defocused attention, thus having additional cognitive materials available for association, increasing the breadth and range of the elements seen as pertinent, and facilitating cognitive flexibility, all of which raise the chances that unusual, or diverse, cognitive elements will in fact become associated to produce new thought (Isen 1987; Torrance 1974).

12 The contrast Austen sets up here between Mary and Elizabeth's styles of reading resonates with the differentiation of general crystallized intelligence (gC) and general fluid intelligence (gF) in cognitive science. Crystallized intelligence refers to the acquisition and maintenance of culturally specific knowledge (Mary's memorization of specific lines from Francis Burney's *Evelina*, or of Bach's musicological principles for analyzing figured bass). Fluid intelligence applies to the flexibility of mind needed to solve complex and changing problems (Elizabeth's unscripted process of interpreting Darcy's letter).

13 This depiction of Elizabeth's reading as made up of short bursts of attention punctuated by distraction, interestingly, seems to follow the rhythms of what we now call working memory. In his article, "Cognitive Science and the History of Reading," Andrew Elfenbein defines *working memory* as the "mental faculty allowing readers to store, process and manipulate recently read textual input through such operations as comparison with other parts of the text, retrieval of relevant background knowledge, and the creation of forward and backward inferences" (487). As he argues, individual reading span is determined by a reader's "ability to control attention" so that he or she can "maintain information in an active, quickly retrievable state" (Engle 20). For an investigation of how working memory serves as a predictor of reading span, and how reading span tests figure into assessments of general fluid intelligence and ideational fluency, see Engle et al., 1999.

14 This experimental representation of mind in *Pride and Prejudice* foreshadows her later stylistic innovations in *Persuasion*. As A. Walton Litz claims, *Persuasion* moves "away from the Johnsonian norm," developing a "rapid and nervous syntax designed to imitate the bombardment of impressions upon the mind" (228-29). In "Of Heartache and Head Injury: Reading Minds in *Persuasion*," Alan Richardson says further that the stylistic innovations critics have ascribed to the novel result from its prominently including "the gaps and disruptions in the represented flux of consciousness" (11).

15 I am grateful to John Bender, Denise Gigante, Blakey Vermeule, Lauren Caldwell, and the anonymous readers from the *Theory of Mind and Literature* volume for their abundant insights and assistance in the preparation of this essay.

WORKS CITED

Austen, Jane. "Chawton Thursday Feb: 4." 4 Feb. 1813. Letter 80 of *Jane Austen's Letters.* Ed. Deirdre Le Faye. 3rd. ed. Oxford: Oxford University Press, 1995. Print.

---. *Persuasion.* Ed. R. W. Chapman. Oxford: Oxford University Press, 1969. Print.

---. *Pride and Prejudice.* Ed. Robert Irving. Peterborough, Ont.: Broadview, 2002. Print.

Brown, Thomas E. *Attention Deficit Disorder: The Unfocused Mind in Children and Adults.* New Haven: Yale University Press, 2005. Print.

Butte, George. *I Know that You Know that I Know: Narrating Subjects from* Moll Flanders *to* Marnie. Columbus: The Ohio State University Press, 2004. Print.

Devlin, D. D. *Jane Austen and Education.* London: Macmillan, 1975. Print.

Diderot, Denis. *Encyclopédie ou dictionnaire raisonné des sciences, des arts et des métiers.* Ed. Denis Diderot and Jean le Rond D'Alembert, vol. 4 (Paris, 1754), s.v. "Distraction."

Elfenbein, Andrew. "Cognitive Science and the History of Reading." *PMLA* 121.2 (2006): 484-502. Print.

Engle, Randall W. "Working Memory Capacity as Executive Attention." *Current Directions in Psychological Science* 11.1 (2002): 19-23. Print.

Engle, Randall W., et al. "Working memory, short-term memory, and general fluid intelligence: A latent-variable approach." *Journal of Experimental Psychology: General* 128.3 (1999): 309-31. Print.

Forster, E. M. *Aspects of the Novel.* 1927. London: Edward Arnold Publications, 1958. Print.

Fried, Michael. *Absorption and Theatricality: Painting and Beholder in the Age of Diderot.* Chicago: University of Chicago Press, 1980. Print.

Harris, Jocelyn. *Jane Austen's Art of Memory.* New York: Cambridge University Press, 1989. Print.

Hume, David. "Of the Standard of Taste." *Selected Essays.* Ed. Stephen Copley and Andrew Edgar. New York: Oxford University Press, 1993. Print.

---. *Treatise on Human Nature.* Ed. L. A. Selby Bigge. Oxford: Clarendon Press, 1978. Print.

Isen, Alice M., et al. "Positive affect facilitates creative problem solving." *Journal of Personality and Social Psychology* 52.6: 1122-31. Print.

Johnson, Claudia L. *Jane Austen: Women, Politics, and the Novel.* Chicago: University of Chicago Press, 1988. Print.

Litz, A. Walton. "Persuasion: Forms of Estrangement." *Jane Austen: Bicentenary Essays.* Ed. John Halperin. Cambridge: Cambridge University Press, 1975. Print.

Locke, John. *An Essay concerning Human Understanding.* 1688. Oxford: Oxford University Press, 1975. Print.

Parasuraman, Raja, ed. *The Attentive Brain.* Cambridge, MA: The MIT Press, 2000. Print.

Posner, Michael I., ed. *The Cognitive Neuroscience of Attention.* New York: The Guilford Press, 2004. Print.

Richardson, Alan. "Of Heartache and Head Injury: Reading Minds in *Persuasion.*" *Poetics Today* 23.1 (2002): 141-60. Print.

Snyder, Allan, et al. "The Creativity Quotient: An Objective Scoring of Ideational Fluency." *Creativity Research Journal* 16.4 (2004): 415-20. Print.

Tanner, Tony. *Adultery in the Novel: Contract and Transgression.* Baltimore and London: Johns Hopkins University Press, 1979. Print.

Torrance, Ellis Paul. *Torrence Tests of Creative Thinking: Norms and Technical Manual.* Bensenville, IL: Scholastic Testing Service, Inc., 1974. Print.

Tucker, George Holbert. *Jane Austen: The Woman: Some Biographical Insights.* New York: St. Martin's Press, 1994. Print.

Turner, Michelle A. "Generating Novel Ideas: Fluency Performance in High-functioning and Learning Disabled Individuals with Autism." *Journal of Child Psychology and Psychiatry* 40.2 (1999): 189-201. Print.

Vermeule, Blakey. *The Fictional Among Us: Why We Care about Literary Characters.* (forthcoming)

Woloch, Alex. *The One vs. The Many: Minor Characters and the Space of the Protagonist in the Novel.* Princeton: Princeton University Press, 2003. Print.

Zunshine, Lisa. "Why Jane Austen Was Different, And Why We May Need Cognitive Science to See It." *Style* 41.3 (2007): 273-97. Print.

---. *Why We Read Fiction: Theory of Mind and the Novel.* Columbus: The Ohio State University Press, 2006. Print.

Sancho Panza's Theory of Mind

Howard Mancing

Sancho Panza's dilemma

Sancho Panza faces a dilemma. He had previously served as squire to the knight-errant Don Quixote de la Mancha on a chivalric quest (this was the story of the first part of Cervantes's novel, published in 1605), and after a brief interval of just over one month, the two of them have again set out in search of adventure and fame (and this comprises the second and final part of the novel, published in 1615). But rather than wander aimlessly, as before, this time they head directly for the village of El Toboso, supposedly the home of the incomparably beautiful lady named Dulcinea del Toboso. Right now they are located outside the village, and Don Quixote has ordered Sancho to go to Dulcinea's palace and deliver a message of the knight's love and devotion, tell her that he requests an audience, and then bring back her response. The trouble is that Sancho knows full well that Dulcinea does not exist. How is he to carry out his master's orders? How do you deliver a message to, and return with a response from, a figment of someone's imagination?

There is in this scene a subtle and complex interplay between fictional minds as each character employs his Theory of Mind in various ways to achieve his private agenda. Before he sends his squire off on his errand, Don Quixote prepares him for the mission by laying out a probable scenario. His instructions are for Sancho to remember all the details of how Dulcinea receives him: Does her color change as the message is delivered? Does she show agitation upon hearing his name? Does she shift her weight from one foot to another, repeat her answer two or three times, change emotional state from harsh to loving? Does she subconsciously reveal her agitation by smoothing her hair (even though it is not disarranged)? Pay close attention, he says, and report back all these details because

> si tú me los relatares como ellos fueron, sacaré yo lo que ella tiene escondido en lo secreto de su corazón acerca de lo que al fecho de mis amores toca; que has de saber, Sancho, si no lo sabes, que entre los amantes, las acciones y movimientos

> exteriores que muestran, cuando de sus amores se trata, son certísimos correos que traen las nuevas de lo que allá en lo interior del alma pasa. (104)[1]
>
> [if you relate them to me just as they occurred, I shall interpret what she keeps hidden in the secret places of her heart in response to the fact of my love; for you must know, Sancho, if you do not know it already, that with lovers, the external actions and movements, revealed when the topic of their love arises, are reliable messengers bringing the news of what transpires deep in their souls.] (514)[2]

Note here that Don Quixote's Theory of Mind is based less on personal experience in life than on his readings in the romances of chivalry where such scenes between lovers frequently take place. He is providing Sancho with what Roger Shank and Robert Ableson call a "script": a prototypical scenario for a frequently-encountered and highly-structured scene. All Sancho has to do is come back after a while and report: Yes, as you said, when I delivered your message, she blushed; she became agitated when I mentioned your name; she nervously shifted her weight from one foot to the other; and she reached up her hand to smooth her perfect hair. But the only thing Don Quixote does not provide is the lady's answer: will she agree to a meeting with her lover?

Sancho rides off, leaving his master in a state of mind that the narrator reports to the reader thus: "Don Quijote se quedó a caballo, descansando sobre los estribos y sobre el arrimo de su lanza, leno de tristes y confusas imaginaciones" (104) ["Don Quixote remained on horseback, resting in the stirrups and leaning on his lance, full of melancholy and confused imaginings" (514)]. Meanwhile, Sancho rides away "no menos confuso y pensativo" (104) ["no less confused and thoughtful than his master" (514)]. Once he is out of sight, Sancho stops, dismounts, and sits at the foot of a tree to contemplate his situation, to work to clarify his confusion. Speaking out loud, he queries himself about what he is doing (and I am paraphrasing here):

> Well, brother Sancho, where are you going? —To look for a princess.
> Where? —In the village of El Toboso.
> Why are you doing this? —For the sake of the famous knight Don Quixote.
> Fine, and do you know where this princess lives? —My master says it is a royal palace.
> Have you ever seen her? —No, and neither has my master.

Sancho ends this self interview with the conclusion that "¡El diablo, el diablo me ha metido a mí en esto; que otro no!" (106) ["the devil, the devil and nobody else has gotten me into this!" (515)].

But here Sancho shifts gears and brings into play not only his Theory of Mind, but his "Machiavellian intelligence," a term coined by Richard Byrne and Andrew Whiten to describe that practical, pragmatic ability to act in one's own best interests, often in a way that involves deceit of others. He rejects Don Quixote's script and writes his own. First, he acknowledges that his master is crazy (and he adds that he must be just as crazy, since he follows and serves him). Furthermore, he reminds himself, Don Quixote often transforms one thing into another—windmills into giants, flocks of sheep into warring armies—so he, Sancho, ought to be able to deceive him by turning the tables on him and making the transformation for him. So, thinks Sancho:

> [N]o será muy difícil hacerle creer que una labradora, la primera que me topare por aquí, es la señora Dulcinea; y cuando él no lo crea juraré yo, y si él jurare, tornaré yo a jurar, y si porfiare, porfiaré yo más, y de manera que tengo de tener la mía siempre sobre el hito, venga lo que viniere. . . . [y] quizá pensará, como yo imagino, que algún mal encantador de estos que él dice que le quieren mal la habrá mudado la figura por hacerle mal y daño. (106)

> [It won't be very hard to make him believe that a peasant girl, the first one I run into here, is the lady Dulcinea; and if he doesn't believe it, I'll swear it's true; and if he swears it isn't, I'll swear again that it is; and if he insists, I'll insist more; and so I'll always have the last word, no matter what. . . . [and] maybe he'll believe, which is what I think will happen, that one of those evil enchanters he says are his enemies changed her appearance to hurt him and do him harm.] (516)

In fact, the scene plays out exactly as Sancho has scripted it. Just as he returns to where Don Quixote is waiting, three peasant women are coming from El Toboso, riding on three donkeys. Sancho tells Don Quixote that Dulcinea and two of her damsels are coming from the city to meet with him now. Quixote's first reaction is one of disbelief (perhaps because he never really expected to see his nonexistent lady). He says, "¡Santo Dios! ¿Qué es lo que dices, Sancho amigo? Mira no me engañes, ni quieras con falsas alegrías alegrar mis verdaderas tristezas" (107) ["Holy God! What are you saying, Sancho my friend? Do not deceive me, or try to lighten my true sorrows with false joys" (516)]. Sancho maliciously responds with his best Machiavellian deceptiveness, "¿Qué sacaría yo de engañar a vuesa merced?" (107) ["What good would it do me to deceive your grace?" (516)]. When Sancho points to the three peasants and calls them beautiful ladies riding richly adorned palfreys, Don Quixote is confused: "Yo no veo, Sancho, sino a tres labradoras sobre tres borricos" (108) ["Sancho, I do not see anything except three peasant girls on three donkeys" (517)]. Sancho pretends to be stunned and insists that they are beautiful ladies on snow-white palfreys, and all Don Quixote can do is say that he sees nothing but three women riding on some kind of donkeys, adding, "a lo menos, a mí tales me *parecen*" (108; emphasis added) ["at least, that is what they *seem* to be" (517; emphasis added)].

At this point, Sancho knows that his deception has been successful. When Don Quixote admits that they seem to be peasants on donkeys, he opens the door to the possibility that there could be another explanation of what they actually are. I will not go into further detail about how the scene plays out.[3] Don Quixote winds up talking with what he now believes is an enchanted Dulcinea, and much of the remainder of the novel deals with the restoration of his beloved lady to her original form. This is the single most significant episode in the second part of the novel, and it all hinges on the characters' Theory of Mind. If one does not read *Don Quixote* as a constantly evolving, ever more intricate series of scenes involving thoughtful fictional minds interacting with each other in the widest possible variety of ways, both theorizing about how other minds work and simulating the feelings of other minds, the novel simply cannot be understood.

Perhaps the most difficult thing Sancho has had to learn in his service to a knight-errant is how to deal with two kinds of people he cannot even see. The first of these is an evil enchanter (later there are multiple enchanters) who, out of envy, constantly attempts to thwart the knight's achievements. But, even more importantly, he learns that all knights-errant are in love with a beautiful lady, and Don Quixote loves the incomparably beautiful princess Dulcinea, who, furthermore, lives in the nearby village of El Toboso. Throughout the first part of the novel Sancho becomes increasingly familiar with the chivalric mind of Don Quixote and learns how to function in relation to it.[4] By the time we get to the scene I have described in some detail, Sancho has mastered the art of manipulating not only his master, but invisible enchanters and imaginary women as well.

The brilliant combination of Theory of Mind and Machiavellian intelligence employed by Sancho during this episode, how he is increasingly able to take control in his relationship with Don Quixote, and the way in which the events that play out in this scene become the focal point for the remainder of the novel, are some of the subjects that could be explored at length. Sancho's mind at work in episodes such as those involving the duke and duchess who entertain him and Don Quixote for their amusement, his brilliance as governor of the island of Barataria, the clever ruse he invents to "disenchant" Dulcinea, and his genuine grief when a defeated and disillusioned Don Quixote returns home and dies, provide ample material for study. Sancho Panza's emergence as the greatest mind reader of a world full of expert mind readers should be considered one of the best examples ever of a Theory of Mind at work.

What I would like to do in the limited space remaining is to place Sancho's Theory of Mind in context. Recapping: Sancho *knows* [1] that Don Quixote *believes* [2] that evil enchanters *want* [3] to foil his *desire* [4] to gain fame as a knight errant; therefore, he (Sancho) is *sure* [5] that he can make Don Quixote *believe* [6] that a peasant woman is Dulcinea.[5] This is as mature and modern an example of the narrative presentation of the fictional mind as I have ever read. It suggests that the way our minds function to understand the minds of other people has not changed in very many years, nor has the narrative presentation of these minds. Yet it has recently been proposed that such an ability to present complex, multileveled mind reading abilities simply did not exist at the time Cervantes was writing.

THEORY OF MIND IN CERVANTES

George Butte is the author of a book bearing the wonderful title *I Know that You Know that I Know* (2004). Butte discusses what he refers to as "deep intersubjectivity": "the ways human subjects narrate and get themselves narrated" (vii). In effect, deep intersubjectivity is nothing but a sophisticated Theory of Mind. Butte never uses the term Theory of Mind and displays no knowledge of this concept as it has been studied in primatology and cognitive and developmental psychology; rather, he works within what he calls a "poststructuralist phenomenology." Butte begins his book by citing an interesting scene of recognition and understanding from Jane Austen's *Persuasion*. His comments on this scene deserve being cited at length:

> This scene in *Persuasion*, about the observation of observations, gives voice to a profound new way of shaping narrative that takes coherent form, at least in English literature, in the early nineteenth century. When Anne Elliot watches Wentworth and Elizabeth negotiating complex force fields of memory and protocol, the enabling strategy of her story is a new layering of human consciousness, or a new representation of those subjectivities as layered in a specific way. Deep intersubjectivity has made its appearance in storytelling in modern culture, and it has altered our sense of self and community and the discourses that construct and reflect them. To conceptualize credibly this sea change in narrative practices requires a different kind of reading of consciousness, a re-formed phenomenological reading, by means of a poststructuralist phenomenology, or at least a phenomenology attuned to poststructuralist questions that also attends to the situating of reader and text in a gendered world of class, race, and political power. (4)

This is quite a claim: that the narrative tools needed for representing "deep intersubjectivity" were not developed until about the time of, and perhaps specifically by, Jane Austen.

Lisa Zunshine has been the major theorist of Theory of Mind and literature, primarily in her book *Why We Read Fiction: Theory of Mind and the Novel* (2006), a work that is essential to any consideration of the subject. In a recent essay titled "Why Jane Austen Was Different, and Why We May Need Cognitive Science to See It," Zunshine first praises Butte's theory and then demonstrates that in fact his deep intersubjectivity is precisely the concept of Theory of Mind as studied in evolutionary psychology and cognitive psychology, thus providing a much stronger theoretical background for the idea than Butte's so-called "postmodern phenomenology." Next, Zunshine extends the technique studied by Butte back into English sentimental fiction of the eighteenth century and, further still, to one example from the English theater of the late seventeenth century. We can presume that both Butte and Zunshine, like virtually all other professors of English literature, subscribe to the classic theory of Ian Watt (1957) that the novel "rose" for the first time in England in the eighteenth century. Perhaps because of such an assumption, it seems not to occur to them to look much further back than the Enlightenment period or to other countries in search of examples of Theory of Mind (or deep intersubjectivity).[6]

But the scene I have described in *Don Quixote* seems to suggest that the narrative skill required for the multi-leveled presentation of fictional minds existed and was practiced much earlier, at least in Spain. Furthermore, my claim that such presentation of fictional minds is common in Cervantes's novel calls Butte's assertion into question in a very fundamental way. If Cervantes was presenting fictional minds with every bit as much subtlety in 1605 and 1615 as Jane Austen was in her novel published posthumously in 1818, then it becomes more difficult to make Butte's claim for Austen's originality.

But perhaps it is possible to set forth Cervantes as a lone genius, two centuries ahead of his time in his psychology and his narrative technique. Even Butte recognizes that "elements of deep intersubjectivity occur in . . . Cervantes" (37-38). If this were the case, then Butte's argument might still hold for the most part. Unfortunately for Butte's thesis, however, Cervantes was not alone in the fictional presentation of a sophisticated Theory of Mind in fiction. Let us briefly consider the example of the anonymous 1554 picaresque novel *Lazarillo de Tormes*, the story of a street urchin who rises to become town crier of the city of Toledo.

By the end of the short novel, Lázaro, the protagonist and first-person narrator, is married to the servant and mistress of his patron, an archpriest who tells him that everything is perfectly legitimate and that he should pay no attention to what people say but look to his own honor, that is, to what is in his best material interest:

> Lázaro de Tormes, quien ha de mirar a dichos de mala lenguas nunca medrará; digo esto porque no me maravillaría alguno, viendo entrar en mi casa a tu mujer y salir della. Ella entra muy a tu honra y suya. Y esto te lo prometo. Por tanto, no mires a lo que pueden decir, sino a lo que te toca: digo a tu provecho. (133)
>
> [Lázaro de Tormes, anyone who pays attention to what evil tongues have to say will never get ahead in the world. I say this because I wouldn't be at all surprised if someone who sees your wife enter and leave my house would say such a thing. She enters very much to your honor, and hers. And I promise you this. Therefore, pay no attention to what people might say, but to what matters to you: I mean to what is to your advantage.] (translation mine)

Although Lázaro swears that his wife is as virtuous as any woman in Toledo, the reader is left to assume that he is a consenting cuckold, a willing participant in his wife's (and the archpriest's) lies and their illicit sexual affair. He forbids his friends to talk about the matter and ends the book by proclaiming that at that time he was at the height of all good fortune.

But here is Lázaro's dilemma (not, in a way, unlike Sancho's described at the beginning of this essay): a high-ranking church official (identified only as *Vuestra Merced*, "Your Grace") has written to him requesting information about the affair. What to tell him? Lázaro *knows* what is going on. The archpriest and his wife *know* that he *knows*, and he *knows* that they *know* it. But the archpriest, because he *understands* Lázaro's situation, *realizes* that Lázaro doesn't *dare* say or do anything about it because he is *certain* that the archpriest would *withdraw* his support and ruin Lázaro's materially comfortable life. The inquiring church official must have heard the rumors about the affair, and he *knows* (or *assumes*) that Lázaro is *aware* of the situation and can, if he *wants* to, *tell* him the full story about the matter. Your Grace *knows* (or at least *suspects*) what is going on. Lázaro *knows* that Your Grace *knows*, and he *knows* that Your Grace *knows* that he *knows*. And they both *know* what the archpriest and his lover *know*. Furthermore, the reader *knows* all of this and fully *understands* the implications of this web of knowledge and lies. And, best of all, the anonymous author *knows* that the reader *knows* all this.

Or if 1554 is not early enough, then we can go back to 1499 and the publication of Fernando de Rojas's novel in dialogue titled *La Celestina*.[7] The young nobleman Calisto loves the beautiful Melibea but believes that she disdains him. In fact, she secretly loves him but pretends not to. But the old bawd, sorceress, and procuress Celestina knows that she has to deceive Melibea's mother (who knows Celestina's reputation and is suspicious of her) in order to talk with Melibea and get her to reveal her true feelings, so that she, Celestina, can manage a secret love affair between the two youths. The entire work is filled with beliefs, desires, secrets, lies, manipulations, levels of intentionality, Theory of Mind, and Machiavellian intelligence, all as complex and compelling as anything found in any novel written by Jane Austen or anyone else.

In the long passage previously cited from George Butte's book, the author claimed that Austen's deep intersubjectivity was "a profound new way of shaping narrative that takes coherent form, at least in English literature, in the early nineteenth century" (4). I believe that such a statement must be qualified in two important ways: First, it certainly was not anything new in Spanish literature, where, as the examples I have briefly cited, show that it was common in the Renaissance. Second, if Butte is right that there was nothing comparable in the English Renaissance, then apparently he believes that writers like William Shakespeare were not capable of as profound an understanding of human nature as Jane Austen was two centuries later. One does not need to be a Shakespeare scholar to recognize that Butte is guilty of a serious misunderstanding of literature, history, and human psychology.[8]

A failure to make use of human biology and evolution sometimes leads humanists into truly embarrassing errors. George Butte's myopic view that pre-nineteenth-century storytellers were not able to convey a sense of an advanced form of human subjectivity is an example of such an error.[9] Not only has the human mind functioned as he describes it since at least the early modern period, as has been illustrated by the examples I described from Spanish literature, but it has been basically unchanged throughout all of human recorded history and well before that. Daniel Levitin reminds us that, according to best estimates, "it takes a minimum of fifty thousand years for an adaptation to show up in the human genome. This is called evolutionary lag—the time lag between when an adaptation first appears in a small proportion of individuals and when it becomes widely distributed in the population" (250). *Homo sapiens* had virtually the same brain and the same mental capabilities fifty millennia ago that our species has today.[10] To claim that Jane Austen was doing something unprecedented in the history of literature is not convincing. Just ask Sancho Panza.

Notes

1 This and all subsequent citations from *Don Quijote* are from Volume II of the revised Cátedra edition by John J. Allen.

2 This and all subsequent citations from *Don Quixote* in English are from the translation by Edith Grossman.

3 The classic study of this scene is Erich Auerbach's chapter on "The Enchanted

Dulcinea." I have previously studied the comic role of the terms used to describe the three animals in "Dulcinea's Ass"; see also Johnson's response to this article.

4 Roger Schank, an authority in artificial intelligence and human storytelling, points out that our "[e]xplanations of human behavior are always grounded in the beliefs of the person we are trying to understand" (63). It is because Sancho has spent so much time with Don Quixote that he has come to know better than anyone else—perhaps even better than Don Quixote himself—how his master the knight-errant thinks and what he believes about the world.

5 This illustrates what Daniel Dennett calls multiple levels of intentionality. Dennett illustrates the concept of intentionality thus: "I suspect [1] that you wonder [2] whether I realize [3] how hard it is for you to be sure [4] that you understand [5] whether I mean to be saying [6] that you can recognize [7] that I can believe [8] you want me to explain [9] that most of us can keep track of only about five or six orders [of intentionality], under the best of circumstances" (1988, 185-86). As evolutionary psychologist Robin Dunbar has suggested in a recent book on human evolution (46), humans can rarely follow a complicated multi-level expression of intentionality beyond about five levels, and Sancho is working at the upper limit in this scene with Don Quixote.

6 Zunshine's claim is not as extravagant as Butte's, but she, too, suggests that a very sophisticated Theory of Mind is essentially a modern cognitive skill. This is seen, for example, when she doubts that it would have been possible to depict a Theory of Mind as sophisticated as what we see since the eighteenth century in a pre-literate work like *Beowulf* (2006, 73-75). It is worth noting, too that Merlin Donald, whose brilliant work on the evolution of the modern mind is essential reading, falls into the same trap as Butte and Zunshine when he asserts that "[w]ith a few notable exceptions, literature did not plumb consciousness in depth until the last two hundred years or so" (78). My point throughout this essay is that a profound understanding of human consciousness and Theory of Mind has been a characteristic of literature for more than four centuries.

7 Earlier I cited Ian Watt's theory of the "rise of the novel," the idea that what we consider the modern novel appeared for the first time in eighteenth-century English literature. This is the view that is almost universally accepted in Anglo-American critical circles. But a more convincing alternate view is that of M. M. Bakhtin in the essays of *The Dialogic Imagination* and other writings that the novel "emerged" in the Renaissance and was best exemplified in the fictions of Rabelais and Cervantes. It seems clear to me that, by any standard, *Lazarillo de Tormes* "qualifies" as a novel and that works like *Celestina* probably do also. Although I have referred to *Celestina* as a novel in dialogue, others consider it a humanistic comedy; similarly, Rojas's work is considered to be the last great exemplar of Medieval Spanish literature while others consider it one of the first masterpieces of the Renaissance. It is one of the great complex, fascinating, original, influential works of European literature.

8 One example of a perceptive non-literary scholar is Robin Dunbar, who, in his

previously-cited book on human evolution (161-62), cites two examples of fourth- and fifth-orders of intentionality in Shakespeare.

9 To be as clear as possible: Lisa Zunshine does not by any means share Butte's apparent lack of familiarity with biology and evolution. In fact, she has studied with the evolutionary psychologists Leda Cosmides and John Tooby, prominently cites their work, and acknowledges the embodied nature of human cognition.

10 Michael Tomasello has proposed that there has really only been one significant adaptation in the evolution of human beings, one that because of its overarching importance and inclusive ability to be manifest in numerous ways is the basis for all other human cognitive skills: "understanding others as intentional (or mental) agents (like the self)" (15)—essentially, that is, having a Theory of Mind. Gilles Fauconnier and Mark Turner have proposed that what they call "double-scope" blending—a concept intimately related to Theory of Mind—became a characteristic of the human species some 50,000 years ago, that is, about the time of the emergence of *homo sapiens* (183-87; see also the later essay by Turner). Mind reading—together with the imaginative taking of cognitive elements from one input space and projecting them onto another space (conceptual blending)—has been a characteristic of our species much longer than Butte or Zunshine would have it.

ACKNOWLEDGMENTS

I am thankful to my colleagues and friends Catherine Conner, Charles Ganelin, Paula Leverage, Rich Schweickert, and Jen William for their perceptive and helpful comments and suggestions after reading an earlier draft of this essay.

WORKS CITED

Anon. *Lazarillo de Tormes*. Ed. Francisco Rico. Madrid: Cátedra, 1990. Print.

Auerbach, Erich. "The Enchanted Dulcinea." *Mimesis: The Representation of Reality in Western Literature*. Trans. Willard R. Trask. Princeton: Princeton University Press, 1953. 334-58. Print.

Bakhtin, M. M. *The Dialogic Imagination: Four Essays*. Ed. Michael Holquist. Trans. Caryl Emerson and Michael Holquist. Austin: University of Texas Press, 1981. Print.

Butte, George. *I Know that You Know that I Know: Narrating Subjects from* Moll Flanders *to* Marnie. Columbus: The Ohio State University Press, 2004. Print.

Cervantes, Miguel de. *Segunda Parte del Ingenioso Caballero Don Quijote de la Mancha*. Ed. John J. Allen. New ed., rev. Madrid: Cátedra, 2005. Print.

---. *Don Quixote de la Mancha*. Trans. Edith Grossman. New York: Ecco, 2003. Print.

Dennett, Daniel C. "The Intentional Stance in Theory and Practice." *Machiavellian Intelligence: Social Expertise and the Evolution of Intellect in Monkeys, Apes, and Humans*. Ed. Richard W. Byrne and Andrew Whiten. Oxford: Clarendon Press, 1988. 180-202. Print.

Donald, Merlin. *The Origins of the Modern Mind: Three Stages in the Evolution of Culture and Cognition*. Cambridge: Harvard University Press, 1991. Print.

Dunbar, Robin. *The Human Story: A New History of Mankind's Evolution.* London: Faber and Faber, 2004. Print.

Fauconnier, Gilles, and Mark Turner. *The Way We Think: Conceptual Blending and the Mind's Hidden Complexities.* New York: Basic Books, 2002. Print.

Johnson, Carroll B. "A Second Look at Dulcinea's Ass: *Don Quijote*, II, 10." *Hispanic Review* 43 (1975): 191-98. Print.

Levitin, Daniel J. *This Is Your Brain on Music: The Science of a Human Obsession.* New York: Dutton, 2006. Print.

Mancing, Howard. "Dulcinea's Ass: A Note on *Don Quijote*, Part II, Chapter 10." *Hispanic Review* 40 (1972): 73-77. Print.

Rojas, Fernando de. *La Celestina. Comedia o tragicomedia de Calisto y Melibea.* Ed. Peter E. Russell. 3rd ed., corrected and revised. Madrid: Editorial Castalia, 2007. Print.

Schank, Roger C. *Dynamic Memory Revisited.* Cambridge: Cambridge University Press, 1999. Print.

Tomasello, Michael. *The Cultural Origins of Human Cognition.* Cambridge: Harvard University Press, 1999. Print.

Turner, Mark. "Double-Scope Stories." *Narrative Theory and the Cognitive Sciences.* Ed. David Herman. Stanford, CA: CSLI Publications, 2003. 117-42. Print.

Watt, Ian. *The Rise of the Novel: Studies in Defoe, Richardson and Fielding.* Berkeley: University of California Press, 1957. Print.

Zunshine, Lisa. "Why Jane Austen Was Different, and Why We May Need Cognitive Science to See It." *Style* 41.3 (2007): 275-99. Print.

---. *Why We Read Fiction: Theory of Mind and the Novel.* Columbus: The Ohio State University Press, 2006. Print.

Is Perceval Autistic? Theory of Mind in the *Conte del Graal*

Paula Leverage

The character of Perceval as a knight of the Grail quest appears for the first time in the twelfth century in Chrétien de Troyes's *Conte del Graal*, and thereafter in various incarnations throughout history to the films of the twentieth and twenty-first centuries.[1] *Le Conte del Graal* is the last of five romances attributed to Chrétien de Troyes. It was written in the 1180s for Chrétien's patron, Philippe d'Alsace, Count of Flanders, and at 9,234 verses, it is unfinished.[2] In France the story was taken up by four authors who wrote what are commonly referred to as the *Continuations*.[3]

Perceval across the literary and filmic representations of his character is variously described as a "bumbling hero" (Wise 52), "naïve, charming and slightly absurd" (Lacy, Ashe, and Mancoff 344), "socially inept" (McCullough 48), and a "country bumpkin" (Eckhardt 205). Chrétien's romance itself has been called "a story of the blunders of a teenage knight" (Wise 48). In Monty Python's *Holy Grail* Perceval has devolved into Piglet, played by the actress Avril Stewart.[4] This modern and critical reception of the character of Perceval as a less than perfect knightly model is already evident in the selection of material from Chrétien's romance, which is reworked in later medieval narratives, and in the choice of scenes illustrated in the manuscript tradition of the romance (Busby, "The Illustrated Manuscripts" 359-60). Beate Schmolke-Hasselmann has shown that it is material relating to Perceval's "nicetè" (naïveté) that is reworked, while Keith Busby observes that almost all of the miniatures in the illustrated *Perceval* manuscripts depict scenes that belong to the canon of reworked material (360).[5] Given the apparent bias in the reception of the character of Perceval, which is ostensibly stable by 1250 (ibid. 360), it is not surprising that, generally speaking, the characterization of the Perceval of Chrétien's romance is simplified and loses interest within the tradition, until his position as the principal knight of the Grail Quest is finally usurped by Galahad.[6]

Putting aside centuries of insistence on Perceval's *niceté*, and returning to the first literary incarnation of the character, I re-examine here Chrétien de Troyes's presentation of the character, which, I argue, has been misrepresented to the extent of distorting modern critical discourse about the romance as a whole. My principal interest is in the representation of Perceval's mind in Chrétien de Troyes's twelfth-century romance *Le Conte del Graal*, which is not simply naïve, comic, bumbling, or effeminate, but appears to be struggling with a very specific cognitive deficit. At least one modern interpretation of the Perceval character approaches a similar reading. Robert Wilson in his production of *Parzival* cast the autistic actor, Christopher Knowles, as Parzival.[7] In spite of this casting decision, critical insistence on a naïve, foolish Perceval continued to trump any possible suggestion of cognitive difference in the character, as is clear from John Rockwell's review in the *New York Times* (May 8, 1988), which suggests that this casting decision was made "to portray a Parsifal closer to the ideal of a pure fool than any seen or heard before in opera or play."

Chrétien de Troyes, however, is known for his fine psychological portrayals of his characters and their relations, and to that extent we could compare him today to novelists such as David Lodge and Ian McEwan, who consciously explore the workings of their characters' minds.[8] Regardless of how he, or his contemporaries, might have labeled Perceval's behavior, in *Le Conte del Graal* Chrétien de Troyes appears to be exploring what we now call Theory of Mind (ToM). Recognizing Perceval's apparently deficient ToM has important consequences for reading *Le Conte del Graal* and understanding the Grail / Perceval tradition as a whole, as well as for literary ToM studies, specifically in the following three areas of enquiry: a) the influence of the reception of Chrétien's romance on the subsequent tradition; b) the relationship between Perceval and the other characters of the romance; c) transhistorical analysis of cognition and how it is represented.

Starting with the question of the reception of Chrétien's romance, it is clear, as we have seen above, that subsequent literary and filmic treatments of Chrétien's character have extrapolated from the atypical behavior of Perceval to present him as a country bumpkin, a naïf, or an effeminate character. In many works, most notably Mallory's late fifteenth-century *Morte d'Arthur*, under the influence of the Vulgate Cycle, Perceval becomes a secondary character to Galahad, whose purity replaces, or is an extension of, the naïveté of Perceval. Under the considerable influence of works such as the *Morte*, it is easy to read back into Chrétien's romance characterizations, which mask the original depiction of character. By reading Chrétien's text and recognizing ToM in action, it is possible to return to a characterization of Perceval that is not filtered through the common clichés so readily associated with him. Secondly, by considering ToM in connection with Perceval, it becomes clear that the romance also explores the ToM of other characters, who are not usually discussed in criticism of the romance. Thus ToM emerges as a central interest of the romance and demystifies some of the problematics of its textual interpretation. Thirdly, in the context of much current discussion about ToM in literature, theorists have raised the issue of the importance of looking at the fictional mind in a historical perspective, and this single example of a twelfth-century fictional mind begins to extend the discussion of ToM and literature beyond the nineteenth- and twentieth-century novels, which have been its focus in recent books.[9]

ToM is mind reading, or the attribution of mental states and intentions to others that affords us the possibility of adapting our behavior in response, and it has been argued that this evolved ability supports characteristically human activities, such as the use of irony and sarcasm, as well as more basic communicative functions (Baron-Cohen, *Mindblindness* 132).[10] While some researchers would go so far as to suggest that ToM is what makes us human (O'Connell 5), others have argued that TOM activity can be observed in non-human animals. However, it is difficult to ascertain in non-linguistic situations to what extent observed actions in animals are driven by mind reading rather than stimuli.[11] Two groups of individuals notably lack function in mind reading to varying degrees: most notably autistic individuals, and young children who do not begin to develop ToM until around the age of four or five.[12] Simon Baron-Cohen describes autism as "mindblindness," which emphasizes quite graphically the relationship between ToM and autism ("Autism: A Specific Cognitive Disorder of Mindblindness"). Sanjida O'Connell lists three core deficits in autistic people: 1) they cannot communicate; 2) they cannot imagine (and so show no pretend play); 3) they are unable to deal with people socially (*Mindreading* 12). These three deficits must, of course, be assessed on a relative scale, since there are varying degrees of autism. Asperger's syndrome, for example, is often termed "high functioning autism."

Several scenes in Chrétien's *Le Conte du Graal* suggest that Perceval is deficient in reading minds, and perhaps autistic. Naturally, Chrétien de Troyes would not have thought of Perceval either in terms of autism or ToM, since these are modern terms. The term "autism" was coined independently in 1943 and 1944 by Leo Kanner and Hans Asperger, respectively (O'Connell 11), while the term "Theory of Mind" dates from David Premack and Guy Woodruff's 1978 study of chimpanzees, which investigated whether these animals could attribute states of mind to others and then use this information to predict the others' actions. However, in the past, individuals known as idiot savants, noble savages, or holy or "blessed" fools were probably autistic (O'Connell 9-11). The so-called Wild Boy of Aveyron is one such "noble savage" from the late eighteenth century who was discovered at the age of twelve in a forest in France. He could not talk and displayed behavioral characteristics that Uta Frith has identified as being characteristic of autism. Frith further points out that autistic people are relatively well equipped to survive in the wild, since they can better tolerate extremes of temperature, pain, hunger, and discomfort (*Autism and Asperger Syndrome* 95). While these are examples of historical individuals, it is plausible that Perceval is modeled on an autistic individual known to Chrétien de Troyes. However, this hypothesis is not necessary in order to recognize that Chrétien is exploring ToM in his romance.

Le Conte de Graal assigns three kinds of explanations to Perceval's atypical behavior: a) physical; b) social; and c) racial. The first is reflected through the characters who meet Perceval and who describe him in terms that imply that he is cognitively challenged. For example, he is described at various junctures as "sos" (mindless) (v. 200); "fols" (mad) (v. 688); "niches" (simple) (v. 689); "muiaus" (mute) (v. 1863).

The social explanation, which derives from the circumstances of Perceval's upbringing, is very prominent in scholarly analyses of the romance and it is frequently associated with psychoanalytical readings of Perceval's relationship with his mother.[13] He has been raised in isolation by his mother after the death of his father and two brothers in combat. Devastated by this loss, his mother has raised Perceval in the country, far from any contact with knightly culture in the hope that she can prevent him from becoming a knight. Thus when he leaves his mother's home, he is ignorant of the world beyond the one he knows. The author remarks that at the time of this traumatic family event, Perceval is two years old and still nursing. In his mother's account to him of the loss of his father and brothers in childhood, she states:

> Et vos, qui petis estiiez,
> .II. molt biax freres aviiez;
> Petis estïez, alaitans,
> Peu aviiez plus de .ii. ans. (vv. 455-8)
>
> [And you, who were little,
> You had two very handsome brothers;
> You were little and still at the breast,
> You were barely older than two years.]

Chrétien seems to be highlighting the tragedy of such a young child losing his father and siblings to heighten the pathos of the passage. A psychoanalytic reading might point to the traumatic impact on Perceval of this loss, and the consequences for his subsequent development. In the context of reading Perceval through an approach that focuses on ToM, it is relevant to observe that autism is often recognized in children of around the age of two through behavioral patterns.[14] Secondly, the age difference between Perceval and his brothers suggests that he was born to older parents, and studies have recently associated a higher risk of autism with advanced parental age (Croen, Fireman, and Grether 338-39).[15]

The third explanation within the romance of Perceval's atypical behavior relies on a racial explanation, which is tantamount to saying that he is odd because he is Welsh. This explanation surfaces in a conversation between two knights after they have encountered Perceval near his home at the beginning of the romance. The knight who has engaged Perceval in conversation gives the following assessment of Perceval:

> "Il ne set pas totes les lois,"
> Fait li sire, "se Diex m'amant,
> C'a rien nule que li demant
> Ne me respont il onques a droit,
> Ains demande de quanqu'il voit
> Coment a non e c'on en fait."(vv. 236-41)
>
> ["He doesn't know the rules of conduct,"
> Said the lord, "for the love of God,
> Because he does not ever reply to anything
> I ask him properly, but
> He asks the name of everything he sees
> And what it's used for."]

To this, his knight companion offers the following explanation:

> "Sire, sachiez tot entresait
> Que Galois sont tot par nature
> Plus fol que bestes en pasture;
> Cist est ausi come une beste." (vv. 236-45)
>
> ["Lord, know straight up front
> That the Welsh are all, by nature,
> More stupid than a beast in pasture;
> This one is just like a beast."]

These three explanations (stupidity or naïveté, education, and race) spill over into scholarship on the *Conte del Graal*, with the exception of the racial explanation, which is re-interpreted as cultural difference. While all of these perspectives on Perceval's character and behavior have some validity, they do not, either individually, or accumulatively, account fully for Perceval's actions across the romance. This has resulted in readings that explain awkwardly individual scenes in relation to the work as a whole, which might be more straightforwardly interpreted by recognizing Perceval's difficulties with ToM. Before returning to this point, it is important to establish which scenes suggest that Perceval's ToM is deficient. Two scenes especially illustrate Perceval's difficulties in understanding: the scene in which Perceval encounters knights for the very first time (vv. 69-342), and the narration of his experience with the damsel in tent (vv. 635-781). The first scene also includes a brief perspective on the ToM of the knights, as one of their group attributes a state of mind to Perceval, in stark contrast to Perceval, who is apparently incapable of such mind reading.

After the prologue, the romance opens with a description of Perceval riding across his mother's land. He hears the discordant sound of knights in the forest and thinks that these must be the devils his mother had told him about. Then he sees the knights emerging from the forest with their armor shining in the sun and jumps to the immediate conclusion that these are angels, since his mother has told him that angels are the most beautiful creatures of all. He falls to his knees in prayer, whereupon the principal knight of the group, attributing an emotional state to Perceval, advises the others to stay back because a boy has fallen to the ground in fear ("A terre est de paor cheüs" v. 161), and he may die of fear if they approach. The knights approach him since they want to ask him if he has seen five knights and three maidens pass this way. The oddity of the conversation that then ensues between him and one of the knights exemplifies Perceval's social awkwardness and complete lack of communicative skills, which lead the knights to attribute his foolishness to his identity as a Welshman, as we have seen above. Perceval pays no heed to the conversation. He does not answer the knight's questions, and instead, referring to the knight's equipment repeatedly asks him questions of the type: "Ce que est et de coi vos sert?" "What's that? What's it for?" (v. 214).

This inability to engage in conversation resurfaces when his mother, realizing that her son now has knowledge of the knightly culture from which she has successfully shielded him, decides to tell him about his knightly heritage and how his brothers and father were knights and were killed in combat.[16] She also describes her emotional state then and now. However, Perceval is detached, he does not attribute emotion to his mother (i.e., he does not read her mind), and he does not respond appropriately in the context of the conversation. He simply interrupts and demands food:

> Li vallés entent molt petit
> A che que sa mere li dist.
> "A mangier, fait il," me donez (vv. 489-91)
>
> [The young man is hardly listening at all
> To what his mother is saying to him.
> "Give me something to eat," he says]

This indifference, or inability to attribute a mental state to his mother, is re-emphasized in the scene in which Perceval leaves his home and mother in search of knighthood:

> Quant li vallés fu eslongiez
> Le get d'une pierre menue,
> Si se regarde et voit cheüe
> Sa mere al pié del pont arriere,
> Et jut pasmee en tel maniere
> Com s'ele fust cheüe morte. (vv. 620-5)
>
> [When the young man was at a stone's
> throw distance
> he looked and saw his mother back there
> at the foot of the bridge
> and she was lying in a faint in such a way
> that it was as if she had fallen down dead.]

The use of the phrases "en tel maniere" (v. 624 "in such a way") and "com s'ele" (v. 625 "it was as if") preserve a necessary ambiguity that is exploited at the end of the narrative when we learn that Perceval's mother had not just fainted, but had died precisely at this moment and that he is subsequently considered to be guilty of her death because of the emotional pain his departure had caused her to suffer. However, even in circumstances in which his mother is not dead, the total lack of empathy is disturbing. The subsequent verses describe how Perceval whips his horse with a switch and speeds away.

Before he leaves in search of Arthur's court, Perceval's mother gives him advice about how to treat women, how to deal with men he meets, and how to pray. She is clearly concerned about her son, and indicates an awareness of his difficulties in social situations:

> Ce que vos ne feïstes onques,
> Ne autrui nel veïstes faire,
> Coment en sarez a chief traire? (vv. 518-20)
>
> [How will you know how to accomplish
> That which you have never done,
> Nor seen anyone else do?]

Perceval's mother's concern highlights the basic principles of what is known as a simulation ToM, which holds that ordinary people discern the mental states of others by trying to replicate or emulate them. This is in distinction to theory theory, which proposes that people construct or are endowed with a naïve psychological theory that guides their assignment of mental states, or the rationality theory, which suggests that people map others' thoughts by assuming that all follow the same postulate of rationality.[17] The mother is ostensibly referring to knightly conduct, and how her son will ever know how to be a knight when he has never been a knight, nor seen anyone act as a knight. However, her question goes to the very heart of Perceval's problem with ToM. He cannot ever truly fit into the knightly culture because his low level of function in mind reading does not allow him to emulate and replicate the mental states of others by which process he might better understand how to engage with the community to which he aspires. It is thus significant that throughout most of the romance Perceval is wandering alone through the country. He cannot assign a mental state or intention to another because he has difficulty in emulating the mental states of others. Thus to paraphrase his mother, how can he be a knight if he cannot simulate something he has never been and thus understand others by trying on their mental states? Perceval's inability to read minds properly is illustrated in the following scene in which he tries to put into practice what he has misunderstood his mother to mean.

When Perceval comes upon a woman in a tent (vv. 635-781), he tries to follow the advice his mother has given him before his departure on how to treat women (vv. 532-56). The advice and Perceval's literal application of the advice is repeatedly underlined throughout the scene by Perceval's references to his mother: for example, "Si com ma mere le m'aprist" "Just as my mother taught me (v. 683); "que ma mere le m'enseigna" "as my mother taught me" (v. 695). The relationship between the mother's advice and how Perceval applies this advice to real situations illustrates beautifully the role of ToM in communication. As Simon Baron-Cohen, basing his statement on the theorists Grice, Sperber, Wilson, and Austin, explains:

> . . . the key thing we do as we search for the meaning of the words is imagine what the speaker's communicative intention might be. That is, we ask ourselves "What does he mean?" Here the word "mean" essentially boils down to "intend me to understand." (*Mindblindness* 27)

Perceval takes his mother's advice extremely literally, to the point of terrifying a young woman whom he kisses and from whose finger he forcibly takes a ring. While a rape does not occur, the use of phrases such as "volsist ele ou non" "whether she wanted or not" (v. 708) or the phrase "a force" "by force" (v. 718, v. 720) suggests a violent scene in which the woman is stretched out beneath Perceval and kissed forcibly.[18] Then while the woman is crying and wringing her hands (vv. 756-64), he makes a hearty meal of the food and wine in the tent.

Clearly Perceval has not read his mother's mind properly, and has not discerned what she intended him to understand, but he has followed her advice to the letter and kissed the woman he encountered, without going further, and he has taken her ring as a token. Perceval's literalness is a hallmark of autism, and it results from an inability to represent the minds of others, or in other words, from a deficient ToM. Temple Grandin, who is probably the most famous person with Asperger's syndrome, has described in her autobiography how she used to believe that other people were telepathic because they magically understood the meaning behind words and the intentions of others (*Thinking in Pictures*). Not only has Perceval not understood his mother's intention in the advice she gives him, but he is completely oblivious to the mental state of the woman he finds and assaults in the tent.

These scenes suggest persuasively that Perceval's skills in ToM resemble those of an autistic individual, but beyond problems with ToM, there are of course other indicators of autistic spectrum disorder, which should also be considered. Analysis of Perceval's ToM in the scenes reviewed thus far has already yielded several of the diagnostic criteria for autism: a) he is unaware of others' feelings; b) he appears not to hear at times; c) he repeats words or phrases verbatim but does not understand how to use them; d) he cannot easily start a conversation or keep one going; and e) he is unusually sensitive to light, sound, and touch (the thunderous sound of the knights' arrival and the sun reflecting on their armor have such an impact on the young boy that he believes them to be heavenly).[19] Other signs of autism in Perceval, which will emerge from subsequent analysis of scenes in which ToM is important, include: a) a propensity to retreat into a world of one's own; and b) constant movement (in the sense that he never stays in one place for long).

One of the less frequently cited characteristics of autistic spectrum disorder is a difference in visual processing, which is often manifest in a superior grasp of engineering, mathematical, or geometric problems:

> Increasing evidence show an atypical visual processing style in autism. This includes the processing of details in priority, in opposition to controls for whom the global context is most salient. This particular processing style in autism has been named weak central coherence (eg. Frith 1989) and it has been suggested that this capacity to focus on local elements may bring about superior performance in various domains, notably in visual tasks. (Rondan and Deruelle 197)

Autistic individuals will engage in local rather than global processing of facial profiles (Rondan and Deruelle 198). In other words, rather than analyzing a whole impression of a face, it is more likely that they will perform a feature by feature analysis. Perceval demonstrates this tendency toward weak central coherence in response to questions about where he has been and where he is going. Instead of giving a general, functional description, Perceval focuses somewhat obsessively on details.

In the first example, Blanchefleur has just asked Perceval from whence he has traveled that day. Perceval's reply is striking in its emphasis on the architectural structure of the castle where he has stayed, and its lack of generalization either in terms of location, name, or description that would help Blanchefleur identify it:

Damoiselle, fait il, je gui
Chiez un preudome a un chastel
Ou j'oi hostel et bon et bel;
S'i a cinc tors fors et ellites,
Une grant et quatre petites;
Si sai tote l'oevre assomer,
Mais le chastel ne sai nomer;
Et si sai bien que li preudom
Gornemans de Gorhaut a non. (vv. 1884-92)

[Lady, he says, I stayed
With a nobleman in a castle
Where I received great hospitality;
It has five strong, tall towers,
One big one and four small ones;
And I can reckon the whole edifice,
But I can't name the castle;
And I know that the nobleman's
Name is Gornemant of Gorhaut.]

In the second example, Perceval is again trying to describe the location of a castle, but this time with the explicit intention of giving directions to a knight whom he has defeated in combat and whom he is dispatching as a prisoner. Once again the description is more local than global, focusing on detail to such an extent that the narrator comments that a mason could not have described the castle more effectively:

Et lors li dist cil que il aille
A un chastel, chiez un preudome;
Del preudome le non li nome.
En tot le monde n'a maçon
Qui mix devisast la façon
Del chastel qu'il li devisa;
L'eve et le pont molt li prisa,
Et les torneles et la tour
Et les murs fors qui sont entor,
Tant que cil ot tres bien et set
Que en liu ou on plus le het
Ke velt envoier en prison. (vv. 2292-2303)

[And then he told him that he should go to
A castle, the home of a nobleman
And he gave him the name of the nobleman.
There is not a mason anywhere in the world
Who could have outlined better the aspect of the castle
He described to him.
He praised the water and the bridge
And the small towers, and the tower
And the strong surrounding walls,

> To such an extent that that man heard and knew very well
> That he wanted to send him as a prisoner
> To the place where he was most hated.]

This geometrically oriented perspective is rendered exceptionally well by the set of Eric Rohmer's film, which eschews realism for stark shapes and contrasts. While Rohmer is not as explicit as Robert Wilson in making an explicit association with autism, his sets and framing render eerily perspectives of a weak central coherence.

I return now to the issue I raised previously about how the three explanations (physical, social, and racial) for Perceval's odd behavior, given by the text, and adopted to a greater or lesser degree in criticism, do not offer a satisfactory global reading of the romance. The logic of the social explanation demands that we recognize a development in Perceval, and this is precisely what we find in criticism. For example, the romance has been described as "the story of his education" in which the naïve youngster of the *enfances* or childhood episodes of the romance matures (*The Arthurian Handbook* 344). It is generally accepted that Perceval develops during the course of the romance and that he makes progress in knighthood, love, and religion, in this order.[20] Penny Simons who sees Perceval as "naturally curious and disposed to ask questions" (9) attributes his problems to his education:

> Part, at least, of Perceval's difficulty arises from the fact that his education has been sadly deficient. A deficient education will produce a deficient human being as skills do not come naturally, no matter how great natural aptitudes. (8)

We can argue for a degree of development in Perceval. He does leave behind his rustic life in isolation with his mother and is more or less successfully initiated into knightly culture. To some extent this perception is the consequence of the social explanation of Perceval's behavior. In other words, he has to be seen to develop, once he leaves the social isolation that is seemingly responsible for his behavior, and enters society. However, by the middle of the extant romance, he is still exhibiting strange behavior, illustrated clearly in three of the most famous, and frequently analyzed scenes of the romance, which I discuss here in the following order: a) Perceval's contemplation of the three drops of blood on the snow (vv. 4162-236); b) Perceval's encounter with the pilgrims on Good Friday (vv. 6217-314); and c) Perceval's failure to ask the relevant, necessary questions about the Grail procession in the castle of the Fisher King (vv. 3191-311).

In the episode known as the scene of the three drops of blood on the snow, Perceval suddenly becomes obsessively withdrawn. One morning as Perceval is out riding in a snow-covered landscape, he sees a falcon attack one of a flock of wild geese. From the wounded goose's neck three drops of blood fall to the snow and spread out, and upon seeing this, Perceval is reminded of the white and rose complexion of his beloved, Blanchefleur. This causes him to fall into a trance, which the text describes using the Old French verb "s'oblier" (v. 4202), which is translated as "to be carried away" or "to become distracted" but which literally means "to forget oneself." He spends all morning gazing at the drops of blood, and the squires who find him run to tell the king that there is a knight outside dozing on his horse. When Sagremor rides up to Perceval and demands that he come to the king, we are told that Perceval does not move, and appears not to hear him. Perceval does not return to awareness until Sagremor, after challenging him, is charging toward him tilting his lance. Perceval's reverie over the three drops of blood on the snow is usually interpreted as symbolic of his initiation into the world of love, and of chivalry motivated by love (e.g., Poirion 155; Henri Rey-Flaud 23), but when it is considered in the context of the scenes discussed above, it appears to belong to an emerging pattern of behavior.[21] While the progression interpretation would suggest that Perceval's behavior improves as the romance proceeds, and he learns more about the world and knightly culture, in fact his behavior in the scene of the three drops of blood on the snow is markedly more troublesome. In earlier scenes, he is isolated because he is unable to engage in meaningful social exchanges, since he has difficulties in discerning the mental states and intentions of others. Here Perceval is completely withdrawn and absorbed with his own thoughts. This is where the social explanation of his atypical behavior in the opening scenes fails, since in spite of his acculturation, his behavior remains atypical, while an interpretation based on cognitive deficit remains valid for both the earlier and later scenes.

A second example of atypical behavior toward the end of the romance involves Perceval's encounter with a group of pilgrims on Good Friday (vv. 6217-314). Once again the narrator emphasizes a mental decline, and once again Perceval is withdrawn and indifferent. He has lost his memory, he has been wandering for five years, and he doesn't know which day it is. This scene is often juxtaposed to the scene in which Perceval first encounters the knights and believes them to be angels, and underscores a consistency in cognitive deficiency that is first evident in the parallel opening scenes of *Le Conte del Graal*. If Perceval has acquired knowledge between these scenes, it is clear that in the later scenes he is still exhibiting behavior suggestive of a cognitive deficiency.

The most famous scene of Chrétien's romance, and the one that inaugurates the tradition of the Grail quest in literary tradition, is also one of the most informative in an analysis of the behavioral characteristics of a possibly autistic Perceval. In addition to demonstrating further that Perceval's naïveté of the opening scenes is significantly more complex than a temporary lack of *savoir-faire* in the knightly culture, reading this passage in view of the scenes discussed above that suggest cognitive deficiency in Perceval casts new light on an obscure and enigmatic episode of the romance.

At the Grail Castle of the Fisher King, Perceval first glimpses the bleeding lance and grail that pass before him repeatedly in procession. The central issue in this part of the narrative is that Perceval fails to ask the key question about the grail procession, which he must ask if the Fisher King is to be healed. There is a considerable body of scholarship on this issue of the unasked question.[22] Ann McCullough has recently argued that the foregrounding of the question in a ceremonial context brings to mind the ritual questions which are part of the Passover seder: for example, "Why is this night different from other nights?" These questions are posed by the youngest present at the seder, and thus McCullough draws a comparison between the purportedly naïve Perceval and children present at a seder (51-2). Another frequently cited explanation, and one that appears to be supported by the text is that Perceval does not ask the question because he remembers advice given to him by a patron named Gornemant earlier in the text that he should not talk too much (McCullough 53-4). Yet another explanation within the romance itself, and cited often in criticism, is that Perceval's failure to ask the question is a punishment imposed upon him in retribution for his mother's death (McCullough 55). This explanation is given both by the Demoiselle Hideuse whom Perceval meets shortly after the Grail episode, and the hermit who hears Perceval's confession after he meets the pilgrims on Good Friday (vv. 6392-8). Explaining his failure to ask the questions, the Demoiselle Hideuse says:

> Por lo pechié, ce saiches tu,
> De ta mere t'est avenue,
> Qui est morte de doel de toi. (vv. 3593-5)
>
> [Know that this happened to you
> Because of the sin committed against your mother,
> Who died sorrowing for you.]

Jean Frappier's insightful observation that Perceval notices the brightness of the Grail as it passes before him, but yet fails to ask the question that would reflect consciousness of the Fisher King's suffering anticipates Perceval's deficient capabilities in mind reading before the concept of ToM had been named and recognized (*Le Roman breton* 54-5).

The correlation between Gornemant's advice and Perceval's silence, and between his mother's death and his silence, is not as straightforward as the criticism on the romance, or the romance itself, may suggest. In light of the evidence presented here, relating to Perceval's difficulties with ToM and his autistic characteristics, it is possible that Perceval does not ask the question simply because he is heeding advice, but rather because he is taking the advice too literally, in the same way in which he took his mother's advice about how to treat women too literally. He is not struck silent in retribution for his mother's death, but rather the lack of ability to read his mother's gestures and her mental state is the same cognitive deficiency that prevents him from engaging in the social exchange of question and answer, which is so dependent on ToM. Williams, Donley, and Keller have conducted research into question-asking in autistic children, and specifically how to teach autistic children to ask questions about hidden objects. They state:

> Most children with autism fail to engage in typical social interactions. For example, often they are not skilled in asking questions (Charlop & Milstein, 1989). According to Charlop and Milstein, asking questions must often be explicitly taught. Researchers have demonstrated recently that behavioral techniques are effective in teaching children with autism to ask questions. For example, Taylor and Harris (1995) taught young children to ask "What's that?" when presented novel pictures in a classroom, and then when encountering new objects on a walk in the school building. Similarly, Koegel, Camarata, Valdez-Menchaca, and Koegel (1998) taught children to ask "What's that?" in training and non-training settings with novel items as reinforcers. (627)

In light of this study Perceval's failure to ask the question essential to the Fisher King can be understood as yet another instance of a general cognitive deficiency that is so marked in the protagonist throughout the romance.

While we may not be prepared to go as far as identifying an autistic individual in Chrétien de Troyes's Perceval, the analysis of these episodes of the romance, well known by both medieval and modern audiences, suggest an interest on the part of the author in what we now call ToM. One of the advantages of considering Perceval as autistic is that this description is relevant to many scenes that in the past have been interpreted separately, using in each case quite different models to explain Perceval's behavior. In approaching Chrétien de Troyes's story of Perceval from the perspective of ToM, we highlight the importance in this romance of communication between the characters, and, more significantly, the failure of that communication.

NOTES

1 The tradition is rich and too complex to adduce here completely. I refer throughout this article to various versions of the Perceval legend where it is relevant to do so. For an overview of medieval texts relating to the Grail legend, see the comparative table in Mahoney's *The Grail: A Casebook* (101), and the narrative comparison in the introduction of this volume (1-78); for an overview of texts relating specifically to Perceval, see the essays in Groos and Lacy's *Perceval = Parzival: A Casebook*; for a more general, but comprehensive, tabulated chronology of Arthurian literature throughout the centuries, see *The Arthurian Handbook* (eds. Lacy, Ashe, and Mancoff), xviii-xxxv. Examples of modern films that feature the character of Perceval are as follows: *Monty Python and the Holy Grail* (dirs. Terry Gilliam and Terry Jones, 1975); *Perceval le Gallois* (dir. Eric Rohmer, 1978); *Excalibur* (dir. John Boorman, 1981); *The Natural* (dir. Barry Levinson, 1984), an adaptation of Bernard Malamud's novel of the same name, which models a gifted baseball player who plays for the New York Knights (managed by Pop Fisher) on Perceval; and a new film by Christophe Mavroudis, *Perceval*, which is based, like Rohmer's film, on the text of Chrétien's romance, is currently in production. I refer throughout to William Roach's edition of Chrétien's romance. Translations from the Old French are my own.

2 The date of the romance has been the subject of much discussion. While the romance was dated to 1177-81 and 1182-83 by Lejeune and Fourrier, respectively, during the 1950s, more recently Luttrell (30-32) and Diverres (97) have proposed the later dates of 1189-90 and 1188-91, associating the romance with the Third Crusade. In his 1990 edition, Charles Méla dates the poem to 1181-85.

3 There are four *Continuations* of which the Second, signed "Gauchier de Donaing" (c. 1200), the Third by Manessier (c. 1230), and the Fourth by Gerbert de Montreuil (c. 1230) continue the story of Perceval, while the First (c. 1200) follows the story of Gauvain (Lacy, Ashe, and Mancoff,76-7).

4 Piglet accompanies Galahad to Castle Anthrax where in a clever comic take on Perceval's failure to ask the question that will save the Fisher King, Piglet declares "There's no grail here" to Galahad's "I have seen it! I have seen it!"

5 "An zweiter Stelle stehen Motive aus dem *Perceval*: hier jedoch scheint es, als sei nur den Anfangsteil, nämlich Percevals *niceté*, sein Abschied von der Mutter, die Begegnung mit den Rittern und sein erster Besuch am Artushof, als bleibende Eerinnerung in das literarische Bewusstsein des Publikums arthurischer Versromane eingegangen" (161).

6 Although Galahad is foreshadowed in the *Perlesvaus* (1200-10), he is not named until the *Queste del Saint Graal* (1215-35) of the Vulgate Cycle. Thereafter he becomes the prominent knight of the Grail quest, significantly in Sir Thomas Malory's fifteenth-century *Le Morte d'Arthur*. Galahad is the only knight to succeed in the quest for the Holy Grail.

7 I am grateful to Fritz Breithaupt (Indiana University) who told me about Wilson's casting of an autistic actor in the role of Perceval during the course of the Theory of Mind and Literature Conference at Purdue (November 2007). It is intriguing to ask if Eric Rohmer's version of Chrétien's romance also suggests autistic tendencies in the principal character. I return to this below in my discussion of weak central coherence.

8 Much of this reputation rests on the author's nuanced, extended interior monologues, which, for some, earn him the merit of being designated as the first French novelist. Robert Anacker, for example, dubs him "The First French Psychological Novelist." Jody Enders has analyzed memory and the psychology of the interior monologue in another of Chrétien's romances entitled *Cligés*. Robert A. Johnson, a Jungian analyst in private practice, has published a popular book which interprets Perceval and his search for the Grail as the story of a developmental masculine psychology. Barbara Nelson Sargent-Baur takes a more cognitive approach in her article on vision and cognition in the *Conte del Graal*.

9 For example, the books of Alan Richardson, Alan Palmer, and Lisa Zunshine.

10 Alvin I. Goldman uses the term "mentalizing" as an alternative to mind reading, ostensibly since it points to the process of representing others' mental states in our own minds: "Mentalizing may be the root of our elaborate social nature. Would there be language and discourse without mentalizing? Would the exquisitely coordinated enterprises of cultural life, the structures of love, politics, and games, be what they are without participants' attending to the mental states of others? Would there be a human sense of morality without an understanding of what others experience, of what their lives are or might be like?" (Goldman 3).

11 For conflicting conclusions about the ToM of primates, see B. Hare, J. Call, and M. Tomasello, "Do chimpanzees know what conspecifics know and do not know?" and D. J. Povinelli, K. E. Nelson, and S. T. Boysen, "Inferences about guessing and knowing by chimpanzees (*Pan troglodytes*)," *Journal of Comparative Psychology* 104 (1990): 203-10.

12 The development of ToM manifests itself at around the same time as pretend play, which requires the ability to model the epistemic states of others and distinguish these from one own's epistemic state (Baron-Cohen, *Mindblindness* 56).

13 Ann McCullough states: "Perceval's complete lack of social skills is a result of the strange education his mother gave him." (48). See also Claude Luttrell's "The Upbringing of Perceval Heroes."

14 While current research is trying to develop screening tools to detect autism in children younger than two, since improved outcomes are associated with early intervention (cf. the research of Rebecca Landa of the Kennedy Krieger Institute), in a survey reported in *Neurology* in 2000, most parents recognized a problem by the time their child was eighteen months old and sought medical assistance by the age of 2, although the average age of official diagnosis was 6 years (Filipek, Accardo, Ashwal et al. 469).

15 Boys could enter service as a squire at a young age, but most would not be dubbed until adolescence.

16 "Del doel del fil morut li pere." "The father died of grief for his sons" (v. 481), but he has already sustained a serious injury from combat.

17 Cf. P. Carruthers and P. Smith, *Theories of Theory of Mind*. On simulation theory especially, see Gallese and Goldman.

18 Evelyn Birge Vitz, "Rereading Rape" (19). She argues that Chrétien is falsely accused of setting up scenes of rape to provide opportunities for knights to rescue damsels, and notes that there are no scenes of rape in any of his romances (6).

19 The authoritative source for the signs and symptoms of autism is the American Psychiatric Association's *Diagnostic and Statistical Manual of Mental Disorders*, fourth edition, Washington DC: American Psychiatric Publishing, Inc., 1995. The signs and symptoms of autism are also widely published in generally available pediatric pamphlets, articles in the popular press, and Internet sites.

20 Alexandre Micha, "Le Perceval de Chrétien de Troyes (roman éducatif)"; Jean Frappier writes of "les apprentissages de Perceval....L'initiation à la chevalerie est au savoir-vivre est suivie d'une initiation aux délices sentimentales de l'amour courtois, puis d'une initiation plus difficile et plus lente à la vie spirituelle" (*Chrétien de Troyes et le mythe du Graal* 68).

21 A notable exception is Peggy McCracken's reading of the scene through its corollary in the *Perlesvaus*. Following Poirion's insight that the scene should be read in conjunction with the scene in which Perceval encounters the lady in the tent, which we have discussed above, McCracken suggests reading the scene as symbolic of "a myth of social order that is grounded on the sacrifice of women" (168).

22 For example: Carolyn Whitson, "Why Does the Lance Bleed? Whom Does the Grail Serve? Unasked Questions from a Working-Class Education"; Anna-Marie Ferguson, "Percivale and the Grail: Always Ask the Foolish Question"; Michel Stanesco, "Le Secret du Graal et la voie interrogative"; T. J. Cherian, "To Ask or Not to Ask the Question: East-West Encounters in the Perceval Legend"; Anton Janko, "Parzivals Fragen"; Harry F. Williams, "The Unasked Questions in the *Conte del Graal*."

Acknowledgments

I would like to thank my colleagues Howard Mancing, Rich Schweickert, and Jen William for reading an earlier draft of this paper and offering perceptive commentary and suggestions.

Works Cited

Anacker, Robert. "Chrétien de Troyes: The First French Psychological Novelist." *The French Review* 8:4 (March 1935): 293-300. Print.

Baron-Cohen, Simon. "Autism: A Specific Cognitive Disorder of MindBlindness." *International Review of Psychiatry* 2 (1990): 79-88. Print

---. *Mindblindness: An Essay on Autism and Theory of Mind*. Cambridge, MA: MIT Press, 1995; 1997. Print.

Boorman, John. Dir. *Excalibur*. 1981. DVD. Warner Home Video, 1999.

Busby, Keith. "The Illustrated Manuscripts of Chrétien's *Perceval*." In *Les Manuscrits de Chrétien de Troyes: The Manuscripts of Chrétien de Troyes*. Eds. Keith Busby, Terry Nixon, Alison Stones, and Lori Walters. Faux Titre: Études de langue et de littérature françaises 71. Amsterdam: Rodopi, 1993. 2 vols. I, 351-63. Print.

Carruthers, P., and P. Smith. Eds. *Theories of Theory of Mind*. Cambridge: Cambridge University Press, 1996. Print.

Cherian, T. J. "To Ask or Not to Ask the Question: East-West Encounters in the Perceval Legend." *South Asian Review* 19:16 (December1995): 91-99. Print.

Croen, L. A., D.V. Najjar, B. Fireman, and J. K. Grether. "Maternal and Paternal Ages and Risk of Autism Spectrum Disorders." *Archive of Pediatric Adolescent Medicine* 161 (2007): 334-340. Print.

Diverres, Armel H. "The Grail and the Third Crusade." *Arthurian Literature* 10 (1990): 13-109. Print.

Eckhardt, Caroline D. "Arthurian Comedy: The Simpleton-Hero in *Sir Perceval of Galles*." *The Chaucer Review: A Journal of Medieval Studies and Literary Criticism* 8:3 (1974): 205-20. Print.

Enders, Jody. "Memory and the Psychology of the Interior Monologue in Chrétien's *Cligés*." *Rhetorica* 10:1 (Winter 1992): 5-23. Print.

Ferguson, Anna-Marie. "Percivale and the Grail: Always Ask the Foolish Question." *Parabola: Myth, Tradition and the Search for Meaning* 26:3 (Fall 2001): 44-7. Print.

Filipek, P. A., P. J. Accardo, S. Ashwal, et al. "Practice parameters: Screening and Diagnosis of Autism: Report of the Quality Standards Subcommittee of the American Academy of Neurology and the Child Neurology Society." *Neurology* 55 (August 2000): 468-79. Print.

Fourrier, Anthime. "Remarques sur la date du *Conte del Graal* de Chrétien de Troyes." *Bibliographical Bulletin of the International Arthurian Society* 7 (1955): 89-101. Print.

---. "Réponse à Madame Rita Lejeune à propos de la date du *Conte del Graal de Chrétien de Troyes*." *Bibliographical Bulletin of the International Arthurian Society* 10 (1958): 73-85. Print.

Frappier, Jean. *Le Roman breton*. Paris: Centre de Documentation, Sorbonne, 1960. Print.

---. *Chrétien de Troyes et le mythe du Graal*: étude sur "Perceval ou le Conte du Graal." 2nd ed. Paris: Société d'édition d'enseignement supérieur, 1979. Print.

Frith, Uta. *Autism and Asperger Syndrome*. Cambridge: Cambridge University Press, 1991. Print.

Gallese, V., and A. Goldman. "Mirror Neurons and the Simulation Theory of Mind-reading." *Trends in Cognitive Sciences* 2 (1998): 493-501. Print.

Gilliam, Terry, and Terry Jones. Dirs. *Monty Python and the Holy Grail*. 1975. DVD. Sony Pictures, 2001.

Goldman, Alvin I. *Simulating Minds: The Philosophy, Psychology, and Neuroscience of Mindreading*. Oxford: Oxford University Press, 2006. Print.

Grandin, Temple. *Thinking in Pictures: And Other Reports from My Life with Autism*. New York: Doubleday, 1995. Print.

Groos, Arthur, and Norris J. Lacy, eds. *Perceval = Parzival: A Casebook*. New York: Routledge, 2002. Print.

Hare, B., J. Call, and M. Tomasello. "Do chimpanzees know what conspecifics know and do not know?" *Animal Behavior* 61 (2001): 139-151. Print.

Janko, Anton. "Parzivals Fragen." In *Literature, Culture and Ethnicity: Studies on Medieval, Renaissance and Modern Literatures: a Festschrift for Janez Stanonik*. Ed. Mirko Jurak. Ljubljana, Slovenija: Department of English, Filozofska Fakulteta, 1992. 267-75. Print.

Johnson, Robert A. *He: Understanding Masculine Psychology*. King of Prussia, Penn.: Religious Publishing Company, 1974; rev. New York: HarperCollins, 1989. Print.

Lacy, Norris J., Geoffrey Ashe, and Debra N. Mancoff. *The Arthurian Handbook* 2nd edition. Garland Reference Library of the Humanities, volume 1920. New York: Garland, 1997. Print.

Lejeune, Rita. "La date du *Conte del Graal* de Chrétien de Troyes." *Le Moyen Âge* 60 (1954): 51-79. Print.

---. "Encore la date du *Conte del Graal* de Chrétien de Troyes." *Bibliographical Bulletin of the International Arthurian Society* 9 (1957): 85-100. Print.

Levinson, Barry. Dir. *The Natural*. 1984. DVD. Sony Pictures, 2007.

Luttrell, Claude. *The Creation of the First Arthurian Romance: A Quest*. Evanston: Northwestern University Press, 1974. Print.

---. "The Upbringing of Perceval Heroes." *Arthurian Literature* 16 (1998): 131-69. Print.

Mahoney, Dhina B., ed. *The Grail: A Casebook*. New York: Garland, 2000. Print.

Mavroudis, Christophe. Dir. *Perceval*. Bulldog Studios, in production.

McCracken, Peggy. "The Poetics of Sacrifice: Allegory and Myth in the Grail Quest." *Yale French Studies* 95: *Rereading Allegory: Essays in Memory of Daniel Poirion* (1999): 152-168. Print.

McCullough, Ann. "Criminal Naivety: Blind Resistance and the Pain of Knowing in Chrétien de Troyes's *Conte du Graal*." *Modern Language Review* 101 (2006): 48-61. Print.

Méla, Charles, ed. Chrétien de Troyes: *Le Conte del Graal*. Paris: Livre de poche, 1990. Print.

Micha, Alexandre. "Le Perceval de Chrétien de Troyes (roman éducatif)." *Lumière du Graal: études et textes*. Ed. René Nelli. Paris: Cahiers du Sud, 1951. 122-31. Print.

O'Connell, Sanjida. *Mindreading: An Investigation into how we learn to love and lie*. New York: Doubleday, 1997. Print.

Palmer, Alan. *Fictional Minds*. Lincoln: University of Nebraska Press, 2004. Print.

Poirion, Daniel. "Du sang sur la neige: Nature et fonction de l'image dans le *Conte du Graal*." *Voices of Conscience: Essays on Medieval and Modern French Literature in Memory of James D. Powell and Rosemary Hodgins*. Eds. Raymond J. Cormier and Eric Sellin. Philadelphia: Temple University Press, 1977. 143-65. Print.

Povinelli, D.J., K.E. Nelson, and S.T. Boysen. "Inferences about guessing and knowing by chimpanzees (*Pan troglodytes*)." *Journal of Comparative Psychology* 104 (1990): 203-210. Print.

Premack, David, and Guy Woodruff. "Does the Chimpanzee have a Theory of Mind?" *Behavioral and Brain Sciences* 1:4 (1978): 515-26. Print.

Roach, William, ed. Chrétien de Troyes: *Le Roman de Perceval ou Le Conte du Graal*. Textes littéraires français. Geneva: Droz, 1959. Print.

Rey-Flaud, Henri. "Le sang sur la neige. Analyse d'une image-écran de Chrétien de Troyes." *Littérature* (Palaiseau, France) 37 (1980): 15-24. Print.

Richardson, Alan. *British Romanticism and the Science of the Mind*. Cambridge: Cambridge University Press, 2001. Print.

Rockwell, John. "Review / Theater; On West German Stages, 3 Opera-Related Dramas." Rev. of *Parzival: On the Other Side of the Ocean*, by Robert Wilson, *New York Times* (8 May 1988). Print.

Rohmer, Eric. Dir. *Perceval le Gallois*. 1978. DVD. Fox Lorber, 2000.

Rondan, Cecile, and Christine Deruelle. "Global and Configural Visual Processing in Adults with Autism and Asperger Syndrome." *Research in Developmental Disabilities* 28 (2007): 197-206. Print.

Sargent-Baur, Barbara Nelson. "'Avis li fu': Vision and Cognition in the *Conte du Graal*." *Essays on Medieval French Literature and Language in Honor of John L. Grigsby*. Eds. Norris J. Lacy and Gloria Torrini-Roblin. Birmingham, Al: Summa, 1989. 133-44. Print.

Schmolke-Hasselmann, Beate. *Der arthurische Versroman von Chrestien bis Froissart: zur einer Gattung*. Tübingen: Niemeyer, 1980. Print.

Simons, Penny. "Pattern and Process of Education in *Le Conte du Graal*." *Nottingham French Studies* 32:2 (Autumn 1993): 1-11. Print.

Stanesco, Michel. "Le Secret du Graal et la voie interrogative." *Travaux de Littérature* 10 (1997): 15-31. Print.

Vitz, Evelyn Birge. "Rereading Rape in Medieval Literature: Literary, Historical, and Theoretical Reflections." *Romanic Review* 88:1 (January 1997): 1-26. Print.

Whitson, Carolyn. "Why Does the Lance Bleed? Whom Does the Grail Serve? Unasked Questions from a Working-Class Education." *Minnesota Review: A Journal of Committed Writing* 61-2 (2004): 115-28. Print.

Williams, Gladys, Corrine R. Donley, and Jennie W. Keller, "Teaching children with autism to ask questions about hidden objects." *Journal of Applied Behavior Analysis* 33:4 (Winter 2000): 627-30. Print.

Williams, Harry F. "The Unasked Questions in the *Conte del Graal*." *Medieval Perspectives* 3:1 (Spring 1988): 292-302. Print.

Wise, Naomi. Rev. of *Perceval le Gallois*, by Eric Rohmer (1978), *Film Quarterly* 33:2 (Winter, 1979-80): 48-53. Print.

Zunshine, Lisa. *Why We Read Fiction: Theory of Mind and the Novel*. Columbus: The Ohio State University Press, 2006. Print.

Whose Mind's Eye? Free Indirect Discourse and the Covert Narrator in Marlene Streeruwitz's *Nachwelt*

JENNIFER MARSTON WILLIAM

I can see it in my mind's eye. Whether in reference to a fully imagined or a remembered image, this common expression reveals how the mind's workings are often conceptualized. In this simplified view of cognition, the mind becomes analogous to an optical system with a separate "eye" mechanism that processes experience and makes imagination and recollection possible. This metaphor implies a uniquely subjective standpoint; a mind's-eye view can be described, but not directly shared. This essay explores the metaphor of the mind's eye[1] in relation to the phenomenon of free indirect discourse. By way of example I consult Marlene Streeruwitz's *Nachwelt*, a novel that relies heavily on free indirect discourse (FID)[2] as a means of conveying its protagonist's thoughts and emotions. Starting with the premise of Ann Banfield's revolutionary theory of "unspeakable sentences," with its emphasis on the voicelessness of FID utterances, I argue for a further reconceptualization of FID by examining it in light of the mind's eye metaphor. This approach leads to a more productive reading of the narrative dynamics of Streeruwitz's novel in particular, and to a greater understanding in general of how a character's thoughts are conveyed through language in a third-person text. The following demonstrates how deictic shifts (which I will analogize as the focal shift from one mind's eye to another) in a third-person narrative need not indicate the narrator's Theory of Mind (ToM) or the characters' thoughts as filtered through the narrator, as conventional and intuitive conceptions of FID would imply. Rather, FID points toward the author's temporary silencing of the narrator, providing the reader with more direct glimpses into the protagonist's mind. The reader is thereby given an opportunity to practice mind reading without the narrator's involvement.

Although contemporary narratologists have offered numerous definitions for FID, the technique is best illustrated through specific instances from literature. Since Gustave Flaubert was one of the earliest authors who relied on FID, a passage from his novel *Madame Bovary* serves as an appropriate example (FID is italicized):

> Ce qui l'exaspérait, c'est que Charles n'avait pas l'air de se douter de son supplice. La conviction où il était de la rendre heureuse lui semblait une insulte imbécile, et sa sécurité là-dessus de l'ingratitude. *Pour qui donc était-elle sage? N'était-il pas, lui, l'obstacle à toute félicité, la cause de toute misere, et comme l'ardillon pointu de cette courroie complexe qui la bouclait de tous côtés?* (145)
>
> [What exasperated her was that Charles did not seem to be aware of her torment. His conviction that he was making her happy looked to her a stupid insult, and his self-assurance on this point sheer ingratitude. *For whom, then, was she being virtuous? Was it not for him, the obstacle to all happiness, the cause of all misery, and, as it were, the sharp clasp of that complex strap that buckled her in all sides?*] (77)

The first two statements of this passage are clearly related by the narrator, who is reporting on the emotions of the desperate Emma Bovary. There is an apparent shift in the two questions that follow, however; while conceivably these queries could stem from the narrator who directs them toward the reader, it is much more likely that the questions depict Emma's own state of mind—these are the questions she is asking herself as she reflects on the marriage she finds so constraining. Flaubert uses FID here to temporarily diverge from the narrator's report, taking us directly "into the head" of Emma instead.

Not surprisingly, given its frequent ambiguities, many scholars have issued caveats about relying on FID as a useful category for analysis of literary discourse. In her valuable work *The Fictions of Language and the Languages of Fiction*, for example, Monika Fludernik comprehensively outlines problems with the tripartite model of viewing narrative communication as consisting of the two poles of direct and indirect discourse, with FID situated somewhere between the two. She also reviews and extends the criticisms from Banfield and others of Roy Pascal's celebrated theory of a "dual voice" that allegedly combines the voices of narrator and literary characters (see Fludernik 322 ff.).[3] In his path-breaking book *Fictional Minds*, Alan Palmer asserts that speech categories like FID—which, as he points out, is often misidentified—are not especially useful in analyzing presentations of fictional thought, and he notes that "the high regard in which free indirect discourse is held can lead theorists into inaccuracy" (61). Such warnings are wise; the zeal to neatly classify complex linguistic structures can hinder rather than further narrative analyses. At the same time, we need a useful framework for better understanding and discussing FID, which holds an important key to the fictional minds created by a text's author. I propose that the mind's-eye metaphor[4] helps illuminate the nuances and the very nature of FID, providing us in turn with greater insight into the disparate but interconnected Theories of Minds of readers, writers, and fictional figures.

A review of some commonly asserted characteristics of FID makes the connections between it and ToM immediately clear. Readers practice mind reading when engaged with a third-person narrative;[5] an utterance in FID then provides them with some confirmation or denial of what they could previously only infer about characters' thoughts, feelings, and motivations. FID, often less formal in style than that of the surrounding text, may be realized as a casual observation, an exclamation, or as a character's self-interrogation. The appearance of a question such as "What had she gotten herself into?" in a third-person narrative[6] is often thought to reduce, if only temporarily, the mental proximity between the narrator and character in question, as well as between the reader and that character. FID need not signify a direct or indirect quotation, an important point to which I will return shortly, and it remains in the third person. But upon encountering FID, the reader senses having been granted a glimpse into the character's inner world. FID thus allows readers to shift their gaze from the external standpoint that the third person usually promotes to a more internal one.[7] This viewpoint approaches but does not quite reach the first-person perspective, in part because the pronouns used tend to remain in the third person. Generally speaking, FID is employed to convey characters' thoughts that remain unuttered. As readers we are not quite "in the head" of the character—as we might believe to be while reading a first-person narration—we do not have enough access to the character's mental space to lay claim to a mind's eye view, although it might seem as if the narrator does have that privilege. However, conceding that the narrator retreats from narrating altogether at such times alleviates this kind of suspicion and allows us a greater appreciation of FID as the linguistic interpretation of the character's thoughts. This verbalization is not that of a mind-reading narrator, but simply that of the text's author. I propose that in considerations of third-person FID, we follow the lead of Ann Banfield in her radical divergence from the notion of an omnipresent and ever-narrating narrator:

> Represented speech and thought is neither an interpretation of the reported speech or thought which implies an evaluating speaker, nor a direct imitation or presentation of the quoted speaker's voice. Instead, the speech or thought of the SELF represented retains all its expressivity without suggesting that its grammatical form was that uttered by an original speaker, whether aloud or silently. (Banfield 108)[8]

In other words, we must remember that the representation of consciousness effected through FID is not the same as simply turning a direct utterance into an indirect one. One could perhaps argue for FID as the expression of the narrator's reading of the main character's mind. Yet it seems that an author relying on her third-person narrator to this extent generally does so in the direct reportive form of "She thought . . . ," or through thought report.[9] The author's decision to use FID instead of these forms indicates that s/he relieves the narrator of any reportive tasks at those moments, thereby shifting the narrator to a covert position within the narrative world, as the following analysis demonstrates.

Streeruwitz's novel *Nachwelt*, published in 1999, provides fertile ground for exploring the nuances of FID. A highly autobiographical novel, the narrative perspective toggles between straight third person and third-person FID. Streeruwitz's preference for a third-person over a first-person narrator reinforces the distinction between her narrator's voice and her own, despite the many details in the novel that overlap with the author's biography. *Nachwelt* documents ten days in the life of Austrian dramaturge Margarethe Doblinger, who travels to Los Angeles to conduct research and interviews for a biography of the émigré sculptor Anna Mahler, the daughter of composers Gustav Mahler and Alma Mahler-Werfel. Instead of concentrating on this project, Margarethe becomes absorbed with her personal life, particularly relationship troubles and various health concerns. The account of the protagonist's trip begins on 1 March 1990, but the novel pays only minimal attention to this significant historical period at the Cold War's end, as the preoccupied protagonist skims newspaper articles or listens halfheartedly to newscasts about the watershed events happening in Europe. The mentions of these news items are but one component of the novel's multilayered narration, which also includes Margarethe's personal stories, conveyed primarily via FID, as well as details about Anna Mahler's life, as reported in first-person voice by sources in varying degrees of proximity to the artist. Margarethe originally plans to incorporate the fragmented stories from these primary sources into Mahler's biography, but she quickly grows weary and wary of her role as a mediator between past and present, ultimately casting the project aside as futile and mercenary. Meanwhile, she is distracted by, and at times obsessed with, the complexities of her personal life, especially a deteriorating relationship with her partner back in Austria.

Author Marlene Streeruwitz has quite a bit in common with her protagonist Margarethe Doblinger, even beyond their hometown of Vienna and the first three letters of their forenames. Like Streeruwitz, a dramatist with a number of successful plays brought to the stage over the past fifteen years, Margarethe feels at home in the realm of theater. But also like Streeruwitz, her intellectual and creative pursuits are not confined to the theatrical. Before writing *Nachwelt*, Streeruwitz had also attempted to write Anna Mahler's biography, for which she embarked on a research trip to Los Angeles, where the artist had resided after fleeing Europe during the Nazi period. But like her protagonist, Streeruwitz also abandoned this endeavor after realizing the impossibility of condensing a woman's life into biographical form. Margarethe's less than sympathetic depiction prompts questions about the possible connections between these autobiographical aspects and the author's decisions in regard to narrative perspective. It would have been feasible, and arguably easier, for Streeruwitz to portray the innermost thoughts of Margarethe through a first-person voice. Yet the author opted instead for a style that underscores the division between author and protagonist, while providing considerable insight into the mental world of the latter.

By virtue of its frequent and at times muddled deictic shifts, *Nachwelt* demonstrates the potential of FID to both convey a literary character's thoughts and ToM as conceived by the author, and to complicate clear-cut distinctions between the various minds of a fictional world (e.g., narrator versus character whose story is narrated). The novel's opening invokes immediate uncertainty regarding the narrative perspective. Because the first section is headed with the boldfaced date of Thursday, 1 March 1990, the reader's reasonable expectation might be that a first-person journal entry is to follow. The first several sentences provide no evidence to the contrary: "Im Haus war es warm. Roch nach Krankheit. Desinfektionsmittel und Urin. Stechend. Und süß" (7)

["In the house it was warm. Smelled like illness. Disinfectant and urine. Pungent. And sweet"].[10] The particular subjectivity of the senses evoked in the descriptive opening statements, namely the very proximal senses of touch and smell, suggests that these are Margarethe's own perceptions, and not those of the third-person narrator. Indeed, these opening impressions need not be understood as presented by the narrator, who does not seem to appear until the sixth sentence, "Manon führte sie durch Zimmer" ["Manon led her through rooms"]. Here it becomes clear that the narrator is not of the first-person variety, as Margarethe is introduced to the reader via the third-person feminine object pronoun *sie*. In retrospect, the novel's first five sentences appear to have been written in FID through Margarethe's mind's eye, and not until the sixth sentence does the deictic center shift to that of the narrator.

Streeruwitz conveys Margarethe's impressions of Los Angeles in a similarly direct fashion through her tendency toward strings of short utterances. We are provided with a list of sites passed by Margarethe as she drives around in unfamiliar territory:

> Sie fuhr Venice Boulevard bis Sepulveda. Holzhäuser. Einfamilienhäuser. Tankstellen. Burger Kings. Bestattungsinstitute. Kirchen. Motels. Holzhäuser. Keine Bäume. Die Büsche staubig und grau. Kaum Menschen unterwegs. Autos. Aber nur wenige. Die Sonne hinter einem Wolkenschleier. Das Licht blendete. Sie fuhr kurz auf Pico. (128)
>
> [She drove Venice Boulevard to Sepulveda. Wooden houses. Single-family houses. Gas stations. Burger Kings. Undertakers. Churches. Motels. Wooden houses. No trees. The bushes dusty and gray. Hardly any people on the way. Cars. But only few. The sun behind a veil of clouds. The light dazzled. She drove quickly onto Pico.]

The reader gleans some insight here into the state of Margarethe's mind, which at this point is not formulating concrete thoughts as much as it is accumulating impressions. The nearly complete lack of verbs in this passage enhances the immediacy of the listed images, and makes them appear to the reader not as narrative descriptions, but as flashes of the protagonist's consciousness. While we receive no explicit commentary on her reactions to the succession of buildings and desolate surroundings, we sense implicitly Margarethe's feelings of alienation as she is immersed in this new environment. Whether this type of stream-of-consciousness can be classified strictly as FID is up for debate, but more significant to the present discussion is that the third-person narrator seems to disappear in between the two framing statements ("She drove . . ."). A narrator is not necessary (and perhaps would be unable) to mediate these observations from Margarethe's mind's eye; indeed, the role of the narrator in this novel is reduced to providing fairly bland statements of actions—there are no instances of narrative thought report, as Streeruwitz relies only on FID to convey the protagonist's ruminations.

The deictic shifts between the third-person narrator and protagonist Margarethe are even more pronounced in those statements that would be more readily classified as FID. The following passage is representative in its revelation of Margarethe's thought processes as she procrastinates on her research project and anxiously attempts to pass the time in her Los Angeles apartment:

> Und warum saß sie allein. Hier. Warum war er nun wirklich nicht mitgekommen. War sie schon wieder dabei, sich von ihm etwas einreden zu lassen. Sie hätte ihm die Telefonnummer nicht geben sollen. Zwei Wochen nicht anrufen. Nicht reden können. Aber das hätte sie wieder nicht fertiggebracht. Es war nach neun Uhr. Was sollte sie hier tun. Konnte man wirklich nicht hinaus. Sie konnte doch nicht jeden Abend nach Einbruch der Dunkelheit hier herumsitzen. (17)
>
> [And why was she sitting alone. Here. Why had he actually not come along. Was she already prepared to be persuaded by him. She should not have given him the telephone number. Two weeks not calling. Not able to talk. But she would not have been able to manage that either. It was after nine o'clock. What should she do here. Could one really not get out. She could not just sit around here every evening after nightfall.]

Such long passages of FID permeate the novel, interspersed with third-person narrative reports comprised largely of trivial details about mundane activities. Streeruwitz stresses the protagonist's temporal and spatial position through repeated deictic references, such as two instances of *wieder* (again), and three instances of *hier* (here).[11] As Fludernik notes, "Deictic expressions (including their syntactic equivalents)—in so far as they are *shifters* or indicative of a SELF's point of view—are intrinsically 'subjective'"; they often "refer to a SELF's referential deictic centre" (431). Yet Fludernik claims the language itself, even when presented in FID, still marks "the language of the current speaker or text" (432). In *Nachwelt*, the language remains in third person, but the mind's eye represented is often clearly that of Margarethe. Thus it makes little sense to speak of a "third-person narrator" at those points containing FID, as it is clearly not the case that her thoughts are being filtered through the narrator's mind's eye.

Through FID characterized by deixis, and through other linguistic means,[12] Streeruwitz shifts the deictic center frequently back to that of the protagonist's self. In the sample passage above, the statement-question "What should she do here" does not imply that the character necessarily said or thought the exact words, "What should I do here"; FID is, in such a case, an approximation of a thought process that need not have a direct verbal equivalent. It seems then that what is communicated via FID has nothing to do with the omniscient narrator's perspective on the character's thoughts.[13] Rather, it signifies the author's attempt to translate thought, or at times ToM, into language. We need not assume the assertion of a narrative voice at junctures of FID; as Banfield demonstrates in her work, "Subjectivity is not dependent on the communicative act, even if it is *shown* through language. And if it is not subordinated to the communicative function, then language can contain speakerless sentences" (70). A focus on the question of whose mind's eye is represented at a given narrative moment allows for a clear dissociation of FID and a narrative voice.

At times the reader of *Nachwelt* must determine whether an utterance is intended as FID or third-person narrative, accentuating the different challenges involved in reading fictional minds as opposed to mind reading with an actual person. When presented with a question of character motivation, such as "And why was she sitting alone. Here" from the above passage, we rely on context and the text's particular narrative patterns to tell us whether it reflects the character's self-questioning, or a critical stance of the narrator that has nothing to do with the character's own thoughts. Given the premise that thought is generally not directly translatable into the written word (i.e., in all likelihood Margarethe was not thinking verbatim "Why am I sitting alone?"), FID becomes a convenient means of inviting us to read the literary figure's mind. As readers we receive the essence of the thought, but we are still required to fill in the gaps in regard to impetus and emotion behind it (e.g., Margarethe's loneliness and her apparent ambivalence toward going out). During this interim, the narrator becomes completely covert,[14] even when the third-person pronoun remains as a reminder that this is not a first-person account, and the reader becomes privy to a more direct view of the fictional mind.

This determination of narrative perspective—that is, of knowing on whose mind's eye to focus at a given time and of sensing when the narrator is actually covert—might be easier in *Nachwelt* than in many other third-person texts, due to the narrator's consistent lack of involvement in reporting Margarethe's thought processes throughout. Geoffrey Leech and Michael Short have pointed out the difficulties of distinguishing the "mind-styles"[15] of narrator and literary characters, since "novelistic descriptions, having different discourses embedded inside one another often 'flow,' in a manner difficult to pin down, from say, a narratorial description, to a description where the narrator and the character's perspective are fused and back again" (Short 32). This kind of flow strikes me as a problem only if scholars of narrative choose to constitute it as one. That is, regardless of how we choose to label the discourse at a given textual moment, the fact remains that a fictional mind's eye guides our reading gaze at that moment, and the shifts between the mind's eye of the third-person narrator and that of characters are hardly unexpected by the mind-reading reader. Seeing through a literary mind's eye involves much more than looking at a narrative situation from another visual vantage point, as the metaphorical mind's eye encompasses the subjectivity of a character's prejudices, predispositions, and previous experiences. Deictic references like those found in the sample passage from *Nachwelt* above are thus significant not only because they signify a particular spatial and temporal position occupied by the character, but because they remind us that the fictional mind dealing with relative concepts such as *here / there* and *now / then* also carries with it the implication of a different set of experiences from those of the narrator—and perhaps from those of the author.

As I suggested earlier, the prevalence of FID in this novel as well as its similarities to a personal diary beg the question of why Streeruwitz did not simply compose it in the first person. There are a few possible reasons for this stylistic choice. First, Streeruwitz has remarked in interviews and essays on her desire to find a new, anti-patriarchal, and anti-hierarchical language.[16] Arguably, a unique literary style that ultimately privileges neither the narrator's nor the protagonist's mind would mark a start in that direction. Second, because her novel is so autobiographical, a logical presumption would be that Streeruwitz had hoped for her readers to view through *her* mind's eye some of her experiences from Los Angeles while working on the Anna Mahler research project.[17] At the same time, she might not be eager for readers to equate this often pathetic character Margarethe [18] with herself—a fallacy more easily committed when faced with a first-person narration. In any case, the pervasiveness of FID does not tell the whole story about what makes Streeruwitz's novel work so well despite its concentration on the protagonist's mundane activities and procrastination tactics. Frequent shifts of the deictic center from narrator to protagonist allow Streeruwitz to provide the mind-reading reader with considerable access to Margarethe's thoughts and mental representations that remain unmediated by the narrator. The reader's mind-reading abilities are thus engaged by the lack of narrative hints regarding the motivations and emotions behind these thoughts.

The conclusions reached through this analysis of FID in *Nachwelt* can be extrapolated to considerations of third-person narratives in general. First, insofar as the mind's-eye view in represented thought is purely that of the literary character in question, FID implies the temporary silencing of the third-person narrator's voice. Sentences written in the style of FID are best regarded as "speakerless," as Banfield has argued, and the subjectivity inherent in the mind's eye metaphor helps to clarify both why this is the case and why it matters for literary studies. Second, accepting the possibility that even an overt narrator becomes covert in such sentences enables us to more comfortably view FID as a verbal approximation of characters' nonverbal thoughts and motivations; these expressions can be viewed as guideposts for the mind-reading reader. Finally, in analyzing literary works with strong autobiographical elements, a mind's-eye view can illuminate the stylistic choices made by the author in the process of fictionalizing her own story.

NOTES

1 See Lakoff and Turner, *More than Cool Reason*, 151. See also Barnden's chapter in *Two Sciences of Mind*, especially 317 ff., for a summary of the linguistic-philosophical debates surrounding the cognitive metaphors of COGNIZING AS SEEING and MIND AS PHYSICAL SPACE.

2 There are at least a dozen variations on the term describing this narrative phenomenon, and related ones, as Alan Palmer lists in his book *Fictional Minds* (55). Besides "free indirect discourse" and "narrated monologue," the French and German terms *style indirect libre* and *erlebte Rede* are often used and left untranslated. While the phenomenon may have different implications depending on the language in which it is expressed, and debates abound among literary theorists regarding exact definitions, the general concept of a non-reportive style remains constant. I use the common and easily abbreviated term "FID" here, although I prefer Ann Banfield's more descriptive but more cumbersome term "represented speech and thought" (12). See Fludernik, especially chapter 2, for the history behind the terminology and details on previous studies of the phenomenon.

3 The dual voice concept, put forth by Pascal in 1977, is still endorsed by many narratologists in one form or another. For instance, Palmer describes "Free Indirect Thought" as a form that "combines the subjectivity and language of the character,

as in direct thought, with the presentation of the narrator, as in thought report" (54).

4 Although in common usage "the mind's eye" tends to refer to visual mental imagery, here I expand the metaphor to describe an individual's perceptions of the external and internal world (using all the senses as well as ToM) and the recollection and retelling of those perceptions through narrative. It differs from "perspective" in that a mind's-eye view is wholly individual, whereas a perspective can be shared by two people (or multiple literary figures, or a narrator and literary characters).

5 Cf. Zunshine, *Why We Read Fiction*, for a comprehensive analysis of this phenomenon.

6 FID is found in first and second-person narratives as well (see Fludernik 85), but here I will concentrate on the particular deictic shifts that result from the switch between third-person, omniscient narration and third-person FID representing a character's thoughts.

7 At the same time, the often abrupt appearance of FID marks an interruption in the reading process that may produce an alienating effect. The absorbed reader becomes momentarily conscious of the text's fictionality, and of the fact that s/he is reading and practicing mind reading with fictional characters rather than with real people.

8 Among other scholars, Palmer does not agree with Banfield's "dogmatic antiverbal approach"; he asserts that "sometimes thought is highly verbalized and can accurately be described as inner speech; sometimes it is not and so cannot" (65). Palmer's criticism is reasonable but not especially relevant for my purposes here, as I concentrate on the deictic shift that occurs with FID and renders the narrative voice silent, regardless of whether a character's thoughts are represented verbatim or in an approximated fashion. The main point I am borrowing from Banfield is that a sentence containing represented thought can be speakerless and need not be understood as conveyed by a narrator.

9 Also known as "psycho-narration," thought report is a technique employed to "touch on states of consciousness or feeling that the character may be *unaware* of (in which case this implies a narrator's external description) or of which s/he may only be dimly cognizant, and certainly not in the terms of description supplied by the narrative" (Fludernik 297).

10 Translations from *Nachwelt* are my own.

11 The German adverb *hinaus* in this passage is also notably deictic, as is its opposite *heraus*; both can be translated into English as "out," but the directional prefixes *hin-* (to) and *her-* (from) determine the spatial reference point.

12 For example, extreme syntactic reductionism and fragmentation that reflect Margarethe's distracted and frazzled thought patterns.

13 The complexities behind the concept of the narrator's mind warrant careful consideration as well, but begin to go beyond the scope of this essay. See Fludernik, 58 ff., for a summary of some debates regarding the essence of narrators in fictional texts.

14 Although "covert" and "overt" are common narratological terms to describe the level of active involvement from a narrator within a text, I am using the term "covert" here to describe the narrator specifically at the juncture of FID. While the narrator of *Nachwelt* happens to be only minimally involved and thus largely covert throughout the novel, I am suggesting that all third-person narrators, even otherwise overt ones, become temporarily covert through FID. My own use of "covert" to describe the narrator's position during instances of FID also alludes loosely to Catherine Emmott's application of the term to literary characters within a primed contextual frame that are not being specifically referenced in a sentence, but which the reader still assumes to be present (cf. Emmott 132). To say that the narrator is "absent" altogether at such times seems too extreme, since the reader is hardly surprised when the narrator takes over again.

15 The term "mind-style" was coined by Roger Fowler in his book *Linguistics and the Novel* (1977) to describe the phenomenon of how worldviews are projected by the language of a text; the concept was developed further by Leech and Short in their work *Style in Fiction*. Mind-style characterizes "the reader's interpretation of certain consistent linguistic choices in novels as reflecting the way characters . . . perceive the world" (Short 31).

16 "Die bekannten Sprachen müssen verlassen werden. Der Subjekt/Objekt-Grammatik der Rücken gekehrt werden. Langsam. Schrittchenweise. Vorsichtig. Langweilig vorsichtig" ["The familiar languages must be left behind. Back turned on the subject-object grammar. Slowly. Tiny step by tiny step. Carefully. Slowly carefully"] (*Hexenreden* 26).

17 This dynamic recalls Zunshine's discussion of the mind-reading writer who engages the mind-reading reader out of a kind of "cognitive necessity" (160).

18 Britta Kallin, who has written an otherwise astute analysis of the novel, would likely disagree with my negative assessment of Margarethe. Kallin labels the protagonist "a self-confident woman," "a successful agent," and "a woman who pursues professional goals and can take care of herself" (341).

ACKNOWLEDGMENTS

I would like to express my gratitude to Atsushi Fukada, Paula Leverage, Howard Mancing, and Richard Schweickert for their insightful comments on previous drafts of this essay.

WORKS CITED

Banfield, Ann. *Unspeakable Sentences. Narration and Representation in the Language of Fiction*. Boston: Routledge and Kegan Paul, 1982. Print.

Barnden, John A. "Consciousness and Common-sense Metaphors of Mind." In *Two Sciences of Mind: Readings in Cognitive Science and Consciousness*. Eds. Seán Ó Nualláin, Paul McKevitt, and Eoghan Mac Aogáin. Amsterdam: John Benjamins, 1997. 311-39. Print.

Emmott, Catherine. *Narrative Comprehension. A Discourse Perspective*. Oxford: Clarendon Press, 1997. Print.

Flaubert, Gustave. *Madame Bovary.* New York: Dell, 1964. Print.

---. *Madame Bovary. Backgrounds and Sources, Essays in Criticism*. Ed. and trans. Paul de Man. New York: Norton, 1965. Print.

Fludernik, Monika. *The Fictions of Language and the Languages of Fiction. The Linguistic Representation of Speech and Consciousness.* London and New York: Routledge, 1993. Print.

Fowler, Roger. *Linguistics and the Novel.* London: Methuen, 1977. Print.

Kallin, Britta. "Marlene Streeruwitz's Novel *Nachwelt* as Postmodern Feminist Biography." *The German Quarterly* 78.3 (Summer 2005): 337-56. Print.

Lakoff, George, and Mark Turner. *More than Cool Reason. A Field Guide to Poetic Metaphor*. Chicago: University of Chicago Press, 1989. Print.

Leech, Geoffrey N., and Michael H. Short. *Style in Fiction: A Linguistic Introduction to English Fictional Prose*. London: Longman, 1981. Print.

Palmer, Alan. *Fictional Minds.* Lincoln, NE: University of Nebraska Press, 2004. Print.

Pascal, Roy. *The Dual Voice. Free Indirect Speech and Its Functioning in the Nineteenth-Century European Novel.* Totowa, NJ: Rowman and Littlefield, 1977. Print.

Short, Michael H. "Mind-Style." *The English European Messenger* 1.3 (Autumn 1992): 31-34. Print.

Streeruwitz, Marlene. *Hexenreden*. Eds. Gisela von Wysocki and Birgit Vanderbeke. Göttingen: Wallstein, 1999. Print.

---. *Nachwelt. Ein Reisebericht.* Frankfurt am Main: Fischer, 1999. Print.

Zunshine, Lisa. *Why We Read Fiction: Theory of Mind and the Novel.* Columbus: The Ohio State University Press, 2006. Print.

Attractors, Trajectors, and Agents in Racine's "Récit de Théramène"

Allen G. Wood

Racine's tragedy *Phèdre* (1677) is one of the most famous, most produced, and most analyzed texts of seventeenth-century French classicism. Generations of French schoolchildren have memorized and recited passages from the play, especially the extremely important and emotionally-charged account of the death of the young hero Hippolyte, as told by his mentor and guardian Théramène. Occurring in the fifth act, the narrative *récit* is a long (almost one hundred lines), static, and nearly monologic interlude in the otherwise dialogic, interactive drama. It has often been characterized as a *morceau de bravoure*, a virtuoso speech, similar in cultural stature and popularity to Hamlet's soliloquy or Cyrano's description of his nose. Théramène's *récit* relates the events of the young prince Hippolyte, who, falsely accused of an incestuous love for his stepmother Phèdre, is banished by his father Thésée. Upon leaving the city of Trézène, Hippolyte and his followers are attacked by a sea monster, sent by Neptune in response to Thésée's hasty prayer. Hippolyte fights the creature, which, wounded, startles his horses. The prince is thrown from his chariot, becomes entangled in the reins, and is dragged to his death.

The passage is crucial in the performance of the play, and it has received much attention from a wide range of literary critics. Leo Spitzer analyzed the philological stylistics of the text as primarily ornamental rhetoric, and Philip Butler considered it a baroque element in a classical play. Psychological critics such as Charles Mauron have examined the passage for signs of repressed desire, the return of the repressed, and signs of the maternal. Other critics have looked to thematic elements to emphasize historical, mythological, theological, and intertextual aspects. Yet one approach that should also be utilized is that of cognitive poetics, which is rich in possibilities for explaining the ways in which both the characters themselves, as well as spectators of the play, process the information in the passage, make sense of an event that is to some extent "senseless," and react emotionally to it.

It is indeed a passage that moves characters and audiences. Aristotle proposes a cathartic purpose for tragedy in his *On Poetics*, that it should cause emotions of terror and pity for the audience, and this is echoed by Racine in the "Préface" to *Phèdre* when he states that Hippolyte possesses all the characteristics of a hero "qui sont propres à exciter la compassion et la terreur" (745) [which are appropriate to arouse pity and terror]. Appearing in the penultimate scene of the play, the *récit* is the focal point for these emotions.

Théramène's long speech is different from the surrounding text because it is a monologic narrative; the action of the play is suspended as the just recently transpired death is recounted. Yet this unique situation is not without irony, since most of the action in the play consists of talk, whereas this concentrated talk contains the most (physical) action in the play, as Hippolyte fights for his life, and loses. His death is a physical, real consequence to a series of previous situations and speech acts that make his death, and the *récit de Théramène*, a summary of the preceding play. In the midst of the theatrical spectacle, in which the audience sees and hears the characters interact (in movement and words), the *récit de Théramène* appeals to the spectators' imagination, to a mental playing out of the events related. The mental images are stronger and more effective than any staging of the events, which could not credibly handle the dimensions or extraordinary nature of the action. What could devolve into the laughable on stage is instead horrific in verbal imagery.

In the beginning of the fifth act, Thésée has already begun to doubt his hasty judgment of his son's guilt based on the false accusation from Phèdre's nurse. Aricie confirms Hippolyte's claim that he was really in love with her, not Phèdre, and the nurse, Oenone, is reported to have committed suicide. The condemnation of his son, which Thésée claimed was based on "témoins certains, irréprochables" (1441) [reliable, irreproachable witnesses], quickly loses credibility, as the witnesses become "peu fidèles" (1485) [hardly trustworthy]. Thésée realizes he was perhaps wrong about his son, wants to recall him from exile, and hopes Neptune did not carry out his request for vengeance. It is at this moment that Théramène enters to give his account.

Théramène cannot know that the king has begun to doubt his erroneous belief that his son is guilty of an incestuous desire for Phèdre. His account of Hippolyte's death must stress both the heroism and the innocence of the prince, in order to change Thésée's mind. The *récit* needs to function as an UpDater in modern mind-reading theory:

> Though we have no idea how the process of belief updating works, it is obvious that it *does* work and that it generally happens swiftly, reasonably, accurately, and largely unconsciously. So there must be a cognitive mechanism (or a cluster of them) that subserves this process. We will call this mechanism the *UpDater*. (Nichols and Stich 30)

Although Théramène has just gone through the catharsis of the experience, is still shocked, and drained of all emotions except for a few tears, he must frame his account to be effective. He can accomplish this task since he is a master rhetorician, and a teller of tales of the king's former exploits against mythic creatures (74).

The king sees that his son's guardian, who has been entrusted with the care of the prince since his early childhood: "Je te l'ai confié dès l'âge le plus tendre" (1489) [I have entrusted him to you since his tenderest youth]. He has returned to the palace unexpectedly, and is crying. Théramène immediately responds that the prince has died: "Hippolyte n'est plus" (1492) [Hippolyte is no more]. This removes any narrative suspense from the *récit*, since we are aware of the final outcome from the beginning. As spectators we process the information, not to construct a meaningful conclusion that will occur sequentially and inductively, but for the details that support an already-given conclusion. The narrative is thus ultimately circular, in that when it arrives at the recounting of Hippolyte's death, it fulfills the news that was initially announced. And Théramène knows the mind of the king, and constructs his account accordingly, thereby illustrating the following phenomenon:

> Indeed, to initiate conversation at all, speakers make judgments about the other person's willingness and ability to participate in the desired interaction. These mental models about the hearer's presumed belief and intention states must shift constantly as conversation proceeds, as new information is exchanged. (Barker and Givón 224-25)

The *récit* is informative, but it is also performative rhetoric, in that it persuades the characters and audience. The passage is exculpatory, in that it answers Thésée's accusation "Qu'as-tu fait de mon fils?" (1488) [What did you do to my son?], as Théramène makes clear that it was a monster, sent from the sea, that led to both Hippolyte's heroic act, and ultimately his death. On the surface, the language is objective and dispassionate, although a strong unstated or understated affective purpose is clear. One way of examining the highly organized details in the *récit* comes from Gestalt theory, and strategies for distinguishing prominence and pertinence of various elements. Théramène does not allow his account to appear frantic or disjointed, despite his need to discuss multiple subjects engaged in various actions simultaneously. Théramène's task is to tell a credible tale about an incredible event.

Recently many literary texts have been the object of insightful studies using principles of cognitive theory. Peter Stockwell notes that "[p]erceiving a figure and ground in a . . . field involves *selection for attention*" (15). Visually this may involve greater size, unity, or detail of an item that attracts our attention more than others.

> A literary text uses stylistic patterns to focus attention on a particular feature, within the textual space. . . . attention will only be maintained by a constant renewal of the stylistic interest, by a constant process of renewing the figure and ground relationship. . . . literature is literally a *distraction* that pulls attention away from one element onto the newly presented element. I will call these objects or devices **attractors** in this context. (Stockwell 18)

An examination of the attractors in the *récit de Théramène* reveals a dynamically shifting pattern of figures and grounds, found in a sequence of changing nouns (usually subjects) and pronouns that refer to those entities with a main role in the event. As Russell Tomlin notes, an item occurring in the foreground "is characterized as information which is more central or salient or important to the development of the discourse theme" (89).

Théramène's narrative begins with the well-known "A peine nous sortions des portes de Trézène" (1498) [Scarcely had we left the gates of Troezen], where the vaguely undetermined "nous" [we] refers to Théramène himself (as he initially places himself into the account), to Hippolyte, and his followers. But the focus does not remain on this "nous," as it becomes the ground against which the prince, unmistakably referred to by the pronoun "il" [he], is described in the next eight lines. Hippolyte is given vertical and social prominence, since he is "sur son char" [on his chariot], and both his guards and horses imitate the somber mood of the unjustly exiled prince making his way along the shore. In fact, his horses are so much under his control that Hippolyte lets their reins fly freely. This detail is pushed to the background at this point, but later both horses and reins will figure prominently in the action.

While visual images formed the initial, cognitive figure of Hippolyte, presented in the "silence" (1500) maintained by the prince and his guards, a loud, unexpected auditory interruption prepares for the next attractor. We hear it before we see it (or rather they heard it before they saw it), and it is not clear where to look or what will be seen. A frightening roar ("un effroyable cri" 1507) comes from the water, and a formidable voice responds from deep within the earth. The backgrounded characters are briefly recalled; the men, the previous "us," were afraid—"notre sang s'est glacé" (1511) [our blood was frozen]—and the horses' hair stood on end. All look to the sea, which rises vertically as a "montagne humide" (1514) [wet mountain], but the object itself is obscured by the water in which it is still submerged. The huge mass comes to shore as a wave and finally it is revealed to be a "monstre furieux" (1516) [furious monster]. Its horns and body are described in the following five lines (1517-21), with possessive pronouns referring back clearly to the newest figure, the water born half-bull, half-dragon. The next five lines (1522-26) indicate the effect the beast has on various natural elements (earth, air, and water) and how "chacun" (1525) [each one] sought refuge.

But the "chacun" was inaccurate, since one person alone dared to confront the dangerous beast. Our attention is focused again on Hippolyte, who stopped his horses, grabbed his javelins, and threw one at the monster. What follows is a confusing and fast succession of these three prominent figures (prince, monster, and horses) at the heart of the *récit*. The monster is hit and comes to land at the feet of the horses (1530-33), where it covers them with flame causing them to take off in a panic (1534-41). The chariot breaks apart, and Hippolyte is caught up in the reins (1542-44). It is at this point that the narrator interrupts himself, for although he had presented a rather rhetorically-composed, dispassionate account, the image of his pupil and prince caught in the reins makes him pause and excuse himself before his king:

> Excusez ma douleur. Cette image cruelle
> Sera pour moi de pleurs une source éternelle.
> J'ai vu, Seigneur, j'ai vu votre malheureux fils
> Traîné par les chevaux que sa main a nourris. (1545-48)

> [Forgive my grief. This cruel image
> Will be for me an eternal source of tears.
> I've seen, my lord, I've seen your unfortunate son
> Dragged by the very horses his hand has fed.]

And while the horses continued to flee, the young prince suffered such injuries that his body was soon little more than a mass of wounds. References to the plural pronouns of the horses rapidly alternate with singular, third-person references to the dying prince.

When the horses finally stop, Théramène interjects for the first time in the *récit* his own first-person narrative of his actions. Up to this point his account had been objective, told primarily in the third person, as he had formed part of the background, the group that had accompanied the main figure, Hippolyte. Théramène had been part of the initial "nous" (we) that set out from the gates of the city, then one of the "chacun" (each one) who had fled for safety from the monster. But as his prince lay dying, Théramène is foregrounded when he states that "I run there, sobbing" (1555) with the guards and others following him (a detail reminiscent of their following Hippolyte in the opening line). The guardian then relates how "I reach him, call him" (1559), using a historical present that, when combined with the first-person narrative, creates a strong sense of immediacy and nearness.

The prince has just enough life left in him to rally one final moment to attract our attention. He extends his hand, opens a dying eye, and speaks. His final action is to speak. In the six and one-half lines that are reported verbatim, Hippolyte's dying request is that his father, once he learns of his son's innocence, treat Aricie with kindness. The focus of attention, the speaking prince, utters his final words and immediately becomes no more than a thing, "triste objet" (1569) [lamentable object], in Théramène's arms.

The effect upon the king is conveyed at this point by his interrupting the narrative, and it is clear that his previous anger against his son, and accusation of fault by Théramène, have changed to grief and awareness of his own culpability. The *récit* was performatively effective, as the king laments that his son was a "cher espoir que je me suis ravi" (1571) [a dear hope that I have taken from myself] and this will be a source of considerable "regrets" (1573).

Théramène concludes his *récit* with an account of the final figure, that of Aricie. Her gestures are at first similar to those of the guardian—she arrived at the spot, approaches her beloved, and has difficulty recognizing him in his current state—although Hippolyte is now dead. But unlike him, she accuses the gods, faints at Hippolyte's feet, and is brought back to life by her servant. At this point Théramène leaves the scene to return to the palace with his horrible news.

The *récit de Théramène* is a narrative recounting the death of Hippolyte, and indeed the prince is the primary figure, the one who grammatically and semantically attracts the most attention throughout the passage. He is kept in the foreground to increase the grief felt by his father and the audience. The two other main figures are the sea monster, and collectively his horses, and the central portion of the narrative contains a dynamic interchange, as our attention switches rapidly among the three. It is significant to note, however, that once the monster and the horses have fulfilled their primary function (of scaring the horses, of dragging Hippolyte) they do not just fall into the background, but they disappear, from the narration and our consideration. It is not clear if the monster died of the wound that the prince inflicted, making Hippolyte triumphant in his final hour, or if, being after all a supernatural phenomenon sent by Neptune, he simply vanished once the horses were frightened. And the horses, once they finally stop of their own accord—"At last their mad, wild galloping abates" (1553)—are simply not mentioned again. As it were, in their absence, the new figures of Théramène himself, and then Aricie, become secondary figures, called upon to interact with the dying, and react to the dead, young hero.

In the beginning of the *récit* Hippolyte presents a strong, positive figure, magnificent even in exile, who is young, noble, and handsome. Because of his many admirable qualities, he attracts much attention. The prince is serene, almost immobile in his composure, as his horses first carry him away from the city. When he is called to action, his courage and skill are singular when he wounds the monster. But from the moment he falls, entangled in his horses' reins, he is broken, losing figural integrity as he is both literally and symbolically disfigured. He disintegrates from the pronominal whole of "Il" in "Il veut les rappeler" (1549) [He wants to recall them] to the next line with "son corps" (1550) [his body] that so soon becomes "un corps défiguré" (1568) [a disfigured body], in other words a "Triste objet" (1569) [lamentable object]. The dictates of French classicism required Racine to describe Hippolyte's death in a decorous, unshocking manner, and so the extent of his injuries are only vaguely evoked, as when Aricie finds his body unrecognizable: "Elle voit Hippolyte, et le demande encore" (1582) [She sees Hippolyte, and still calls for him]. Previous versions of the play, however, especially those of Seneca and the French baroque poet Garnier (1573), were not bound by such niceties, and in fact often reveled in gory details. As Hippolyte was dragged along, details abound concerning his dismemberment, an eye dangling here, a leg thrown there. There is certainly not enough of him left to say anything when he is finally found by his men, who start picking up the scattered pieces to bring back to king Thésée. Hippolyte is no longer physically, literally attractive, nor is he a narrative attractor except in the memory of his wholeness.

Another structuring device in the *récit de Théramène* that can be analyzed using cognitive theory involves figures that are foregrounded as trajectors. Whereas a figure can be presented in stasis, a trajector attracts attention by its motion. Leonard Talmy indicates that "[t]he Figure is a moving or conceptually movable entity whose site, path or orientation is conceived as a variable, the particular value of which is the relevant issue" (19). Stockwell comments on specific terms involved in such movement: "the moving figure can be seen to follow a **path**. . . . Within the image schema, though, the element that is the figure is called the **trajector** and the element it has a grounded relationship with is called the **landmark**" (16).The opening line of the *récit*, "A peine nous sortions des portes de Trézène" (1498) [Scarcely had we left the gates of Troezen], reveals these very elements, with the landmark being the gates of the city Troezen, from which the "we" (Hippolyte, Théramène, and his followers) issued forth, the point of origin or terminus a quo. The path they were following, "le chemin de Mycènes" (1501) [the road to Mycenes], is also clearly specified, forming a second landmark, the *terminus ad quem*, at which they never arrive.

From out in the middle of the sea, "du fond des flots" (1513) [from the depths of the waves], first arises a terrible cry, then "sur le dos de la plaine liquide" [on the back of the wet plain] arises an enormous wave. The watery landmark is perhaps not precise, but clearly denotes Neptune's realm. The mass is not static, however, as it moves for the shore: "L'onde approche, se brise, et vomit à nos yeux, / Parmi des flots d'écume, un monstre furieux" (1515-16) [The wave approached, broke and vomited before our eyes / From among the frothy waves a raging monster]. The initial trajectory of Hippolyte's travel along the shore to Mycenes is intersected by the perpendicular path of the monster, forming a deadly crossroads.

Michel Serres observes that in Greek mythology and literature, the topos of the crossroads serves as a place of crisis and decision. At the chiasmus occurs a clash of disparate intents and fates, and it is often a place of death and revenge. Oedipus encounters unknowingly his father at a crossroads, and "it is a place so catastrophic and so confined that he must kill his father" (47). Ubersfeld speaks of the crossroads as an "impossible place where the horses of the forest have their deadly encounter with the monsters of the wave" (204).

At the approach of the monster, all of Hippolyte's men leave the road, but their flight is scattered, lacking figural unity, and limited in narrative scope—"tout fuit" (1525) [all fled]—as they seek safety in a nearby temple. Even nature abhors the monster, since the wave that brought it in rolls back, frightened. Only Hippolyte moves toward the monster, as he throws a spear, in a line that foregrounds for the first time in the *récit* his name, his lineage, and his bravery: "Hippolyte lui seul, digne fils d'un héros" [Alone, Hippolyte himself, worthy son of a hero] (1527).

After the injured monster falls dying at the feet of the horses and frightens them, they take off. Whereas the previous trajectories indicated a clear teleological landmark for completion (Hippolyte headed to Mycènes, the monster bearing down on the shore and Hippolyte, all the attendants fleeing to the temple, the wounded monster approaching the horses), the frightened horses are directionless, without any guidance from their master Hippolyte. And as they run, they drag him along, in a trajectory that causes his death. The horses' flight is a deviation from his path; he is thrown off course and into the wilderness that will kill him. Théramène and the other men are able to find Hippolyte by following the bloody trail that he leaves:

> De son généreux sang la trace nous conduit:
> Les rochers en sont teints; les ronces dégouttantes
> Portent de ses cheveux les dépouilles sanglantes. (1556-58)
>
> [The trail of his generous blood led us:
> The rocks were colored by it, the dripping brambles
> Wear the bloody remains of his hair.]

The less decorous, earlier versions of the tragedy portray an even more gruesome path, littered with the prince's body parts. Racine's *récit de Théramène* ends with Aricie also following the path to her beloved fiancé, and the guardian making his return to the palace. This is done in order to fulfill the promise of the dying prince who begs him to have the king protect Aricie, as well as inform, convince, and move Thésée. A circular motion occurs that takes the narration, and our imaginations, out to the scene of death and back again to the palace.

The main figures in Théramène's account are brought into focus for our cognitive processing by their nominal positions grammatically and semantically as attractors; they move along a trajectory, and they are agents of action. Craig Hamilton explains the distinction between agents and patients:

> To profile objects conceptually first as figures and then as trajectors linguistically entails marking some objects as *agents* and others as *patients*; things that are more active in relation to less active things, or things that act versus things that are acted upon. (58)

At a grammatical level, the concept is often tied with subject or object positions of transitive action verbs.

The first section of the *récit de Théramène* is more concerned with motion than with other actions. Hippolyte and his group leave the city (he does not even have to guide his horses); the sea monster appears, comes on shore, and seems threatening. The prince figures most prominently as an agent when he seizes his javelins and throws one at the beast. Wounded, the monster is weak (it rolls over) and not capable of much more action than exhaling some flames at the horses. But this is enough to frighten the horses, or perhaps there was another agent in this. Théramène admits at this single juncture a different voice into his narration, the vague "on" [somebody] of other witnesses to the event: "On dit qu'on a vu même, en ce désordre affreux, / Un Dieu qui d'aiguillons pressait leur flanc poudreux" (1539-40) [Some even say they saw, in this frightful disorder / A god who pricked with spurs their dusty flanks]. Whatever the cause, the horses ran, and Hippolyte could not control them. This is the first instance of powerlessness, and the transition from the prince as agent to that of patient. He falls, is entangled in the reins, and the still fleeing horses drag him to his death. It is an accident, the horses did not intend to kill him, and so they are unwittingly, perhaps even unknowingly, agents of his death. The rest of the *récit* involves the reactions and consequences of this chain of agents (or rather of instruments used by an agent)—the horses drag Hippolyte to his death, but they were acted upon by the monster, sent by Neptune, at the request of Thésée. It was the king, Hippolyte's father, who was the originating agent and cause of the prince's death, although chance, the accidental fall, complicates a strict causal chain.

An analysis of the *récit de Théramène* using principles of gestalt perception and cognitive poetics, namely attractors, trajectories, and agents reveals multiple ways in which Hippolyte is foregrounded (which play out in the pattern of nouns, pronouns, and verbs), and the dynamic interplay of and mind reading between the other main figures (the monster, the horses, even Théramène himself, who is both narrator and actor). And it reveals a particularly pertinent line of inquiry, as we see the intersecting trajectories of Hippolyte and the sea monster. It was a fateful and fatal encounter, one that changed Hippolyte's initial and intended path, as he effortlessly guided his horses to exile in Mycènes and beyond, to a path of destruction, as he was dragged by his horses, resulting in death by dismemberment, and a lack of figural unity. It is a tale that arouses terror for both the king and the audience, and not just terror at the horrendous aspects of the monster, but at the injustice of both human and divine persecution of an innocent prince. The cold clarity of Théramène's focused account brings about a complete change in Thésée, who has not only recognized his own role in his son's death, but reconciles himself with his former enemy Aricie as the play closes.

Works Cited

Aristotle. *On Poetics*. Trans. Seth Bernardete and Michael Davis. South Bend: St. Augustine's Press, 2002. Print.

Barker, Marjorie, and T. Givón. "Representation of the Interlocutor's Mind during Conversation." *Other Minds: How Humans Bridge the Divide between Self and Others*. Eds. Bertram F. Malle and Sara D. Hodges. New York: Guilford Press, 2005. 223-38. Print.

Butler, Philip. *Classicisme et baroque dans l'oeuvre de Racine*. Paris: Nizet, 1959. Print.

Hamilton, Craig. "A Cognitive Grammar of 'Hospital Barge' by Wilfred Owen." *Cognitive Poetics in Practice*. Eds. Joanna Gavins and Gerard Steen. London: Routledge, 2003. 55-66. Print.

Mauron, Charles. *L'inconscient dans l'oeuvre et la vie de Racine*. Paris: Gap, Éditions Ophrys, 1957. Print.

Nichols, Shaun, and Stephen P. Stich. *Mindreading: An Integrated Account of Pretence, Self-Awareness, and Understanding Other Minds*. Oxford: Clarendon, 2003. Print.

Racine, Jean. *Phèdre. Œuvres completes*. Vol. 1. Ed. Raymond Picard. Paris: Gallimard, 1950. 735-803. Print.

Serres, Michel. "Language and Space: From Oedipus to Zola." *Hermes: Literature, Science, Philosophy*. Eds. Josué V. Harari and David Bell. Baltimore: Johns Hopkins University Press, 1982. 39-53. Print.

Spitzer, Leo. "The Récit de Théramène." *Linguistics and Literary History: Essays in Stylistics*. Princeton: Princeton University Press, 1948. 87-134. Print.

Stockwell, Peter. *Cognitive Poetics: An Introduction*. London: Routledge, 2002. Print.

Talmy, Leonard. "Concept Structuring Systems in Language." *The New Psychology of Language*. Vol. 2. Ed. Michael Tomasello. Mahwah, NJ: Lawrence Erlbaum Associates, 1998. 15-46. Print.

Tomlin, Russell. "Foreground-Background Information and Syntactic Subordination." *Text* 5.1-2 (1985): 85-122. Print.

Ubersfeld, Anne. "The Space of Phèdre." *Poetics Today* 2.3 (Spring 1981): 201-10. Print.

The Importance of Deixis and Attributive Style for the Study of Theory of Mind: The Example of William Faulkner's Disturbed Characters

INEKE BOCKTING

INTRODUCTION

Teaching William Faulkner's *The Sound and the Fury* to English major students in Holland, Norway, and France, I have always been asked why Faulkner made the story so difficult to read, the choice of words so bizarre, the syntax so convoluted, and the situation in time and space so extremely complex. To this question I have come to answer: because he wants to create compassion for the characters. He wants you to feel as deserted as they do—that is why I avoid explaining anything about the book beforehand—he wants you to be as desperate, as lost as they are. I might have said: he is testing your Theory of Mind and soliciting it to the fullest, expanding it beyond its everyday use.

I use the term Theory of Mind, here, not just as the ability of individuals to perceive other people to "know, want, feel, or believe things" that may be different from what they themselves know, want, feel, and believe, per Simon Baron-Cohen (37-46), but as an actual capacity to understand what it is that they "know, want, feel or believe"[1]—what Lisa Zunshine calls "our mind-reading ability" (47)—and, going further, to even experience it in their place. This is why I prefer to talk about the capacity to step into the shoes of someone else, seeing the world from his or her point of view. This taking "the other fellow's point of view," to use the words of the linguist Charles Fillmore in his *Santa Cruz Lectures on Deixis* (44)—or viewpoint shift—is not an unusual phenomenon at all. Douglas Hofstadter, in his majestic work *Gödel, Escher, Bach: An Eternal Golden Braid*, expresses it as follows: "I can fire up my subsystem for a good friend and virtually feel myself in his shoes, running through thoughts which he might have, activating symbols in sequences which reflect his thinking patterns more accurately than my own" (386). Faulkner's text is just more challenging in this respect than what our everyday experience teaches us.

The fact that Faulkner's style is so extraordinary, of course, makes any kind of linguistic study of his work worthwhile, but it is a real gold mine for an analysis of the ways in which Theory of Mind is realized linguistically in the text. I will look here at the linguistic nitty-gritty of its artistic creation, both in terms of what is presented and in terms of how that is done, starting, therefore, with a discussion of the textual markers of viewpoint shift, or *deictic projection* (Lyons 579), and subsequently analyzing the various forms the attribution of mental activity to a subject may take, discussing both the different mental verbs (including perception verbs) and their complements.

Cognitive linguistics, of course, has taught us that reality is not simply out there to be discovered, named, and talked about, but rather a construction in the individual mind consisting, basically, of three elements: *universal reality* (that which we all share because we are humans; that which is "hardwired" into our brains); *social reality* (those preexisting social relations we are born into); and *personal reality* (that which our own psychological makeup and our own personal experiences add to the previous two). An interactive mixture of these three elements, both determined by and determining our position in the world, makes up our individual point of view. Language offers different types of linguistic terms that will encode this individual point of view into the language we use: the so-called *deictics*. Indeed, deictics normally point to things in the world from the position of the language user. This position is called the *deictic center* (Levinson 664), the point to which all deictics are "anchored."[2] If we say, then, that language is egocentric in nature, it means that, normally speaking, all phenomena in the world are related to the position of the language user. To illustrate this, I will briefly review the different classes of deictics.

Temporal deictics function to relate the time of an event to the time of the deictic center, that is to say, to the speech event, the major ones being the adverb (*now*, indicating simultaneity, *then* anteriority, and *soon* posteriority of the event),[3] and the system of the tenses (present tense indicating simultaneity, past tense anteriority, and future tense posteriority of the event). Tense, in fact, shows the profound way in which, at least in our Western culture, human beings are embedded in time, and it is hard to avoid them, every well-formed sentence in English containing at least one of its elements. (One might cite Shakespeare's "To be or not to be . . ." as a counter-example, were it not that the next sentence brings us back into time, with its "whether t'*is* best . . ."; emphasis added.)

Spatial deictics function to relate the position in space of a phenomenon to the position of the deictic center and include the common demonstratives *this / these* and *that / those*, and the adverbs *here* and *there*, which indicate physical closeness to or farness from the deictic center. The spatial deictics may also indicate emotional stance. By using the deictic *this*, for instance, a speaker may not only evoke spatial proximity, but also emotional nearness, which John Lyons calls "emphatic deixis" (677). Certain motion verbs, in addition, have built-in deictic aspects, such as *come* and *go* and *bring* and *take*, indicating directions or destinations toward and away from the deictic center.[4]

That temporal deixis and spatial deixis are closely related, finally, is clear, and this shows itself for instance when Faulkner makes one of his characters say: "You've been running a long time not to've got any further off than meal time" (*Sound and Fury* 81).

Social deixis concerns kinship terms, which include a relation of superiority to the deictic center (such as *parent*, *mother*, and *father*, *grandmother* and *grandfather*, *aunt* and *uncle*), of inferiority to the deictic center (such as *child*, *daughter*, and *son*, *niece* and *nephew*), or equality with the deictic center (such as *sister* and *brother*, and *cousin*), as well as hierarchical terms, again including superiority, inferiority, or equality with regard to the deictic center (for instance *boss*, *pupil*, and *colleague*, respectively).

Personal deixis, finally, concerns the set of personal pronouns, of which the first person pronouns *I* and *we* (as well as their derivatives *me*, *us*, *mine*, and *ours*) create and sustain the deictic center itself (a personal one, or one shared with another person), the pronoun *you* (as well as *your* and *yours*) relate the deictic center to a speech partner, or speech partners, and the pronouns *he*, *she*, *it*, *and they* (and *his*, *her*, *its*, *their*, and *theirs*) posit a subject or subjects as outsider or outsiders with regard to the language event. Indeed, in the present tense, the s of the third-person singular can be seen as a visible and sonorous marker of absence from the speech event (Joly and O'Kelly 415-16).

The pronoun *I* obviously occupies a special position, as it is the one through which the deictic center establishes itself. At birth, the young individual—as psychologists agree—is still undifferentiated, not yet occupying any subject position at all. Then follows the mirror stage, which the psychoanalyst Jacques Lacan saw as an essential stage in human development, when the child starts to recognize itself as a separate individual. Subsequently, as the child starts to speak, the deictic center—that is, the encoding of his or her personal position as a language user—starts to fall into place. However, with their unstable reference—that is why they are sometimes called "shifters"—deictics are notoriously difficult to learn how to use. Young children will therefore use the proper name—as a sort of "proto-deictic"—until they have mastered this difficulty, and require others to do so well.

We may turn to the first chapter of William Faulkner's novel *The Sound and the Fury* now, where Caddy Compson, returning from her day at school, sees her brother holding on to the fence around their house, looking distressed, and says to him: "Did you come to meet Caddy. . . . What is it. What are you trying to tell Caddy" (7).

By using her proper name rather than the pronoun *me* to refer to herself, Caddy can be seen to take the point of view of her brother; indeed, she has "stepped into his shoes" and uses a proto-deictic, as he would (as a matter of fact, she might have used two proto-deictics and have said "What is Benjy trying to tell Caddy," but presumably her brother has enough information if he just understands "telling Caddy" or else he is already in the process of learning the deictic system, being able to accommodate one deictic). In any case, Caddy's Theory of Mind is in place. She is able to project herself into the point of view of somebody else, her brother. In linguistic terms, she is able to use *deictic projection*.

A more everyday, yet instructive, example of deictic projection is where we find Mr. Compson—Benjy's and Caddy's father—using the noun phrase "your grandfather" in a discussion with his eldest son, Quentin. The social deictic that performs the deictic projection—that is, which shows the workings of Mr. Compson's Theory of Mind—is the term *grandfather*. Indeed, it is the term that Quentin himself would use to refer to this relative, not, of course, his father. Without the deictic projection, the term used by Mr. Compson would have been *father*. What is important to notice, however, is that the deictic projection is not complete. While the social deictic *grandfather*, indeed, shows the deictic projection, the personal deictic *your* remains anchored to the deictic center, that is, to the position of the speaker, Mr Compson. After all, it is the term that Mr. Compson uses to refer to his son, not the term Quentin would use to refer to himself. If his deictic projection had been total, Mr. Compson would have said "my grandfather," which would have created total confusion.

This simple, everyday example shows, in fact, that deictic projection must always remain anchored, otherwise chaos will occur. That is to say, for Theory of Mind to be successful, one must be able to perform deictic projection while at the same time holding steady one's own deictic center. This anchoring function is essential. Apart from the social and artistic conventions of role-play and acting in the theater or the movies, which are beyond the scope of this paper, this anchoring can in spoken language be indicated by changes in speed, rhythm, and tone of voice and in written language be taken up by graphological signs—the comma, the colon, and quotation marks—as well as by deictics and by the system of attribution.

Faulkner's novels form a gold mine for showing what happens if deictic projection is disturbed, that is, if it is either absent or unanchored. From the way his sister talks to him, we can deduce that Benjy is not yet able to perform deictic projection; that is, his Theory of Mind is not yet in place: he cannot yet see the world from Caddy's point of view. This observation will be confirmed in the rest of the chapter, for instance where he has drunk from the champagne at his sister's wedding. Remembering how his brother Quentin had to lead him, Benjy's text reads: "The ground kept sloping up. . . . Quentin held my arm and we went towards the barn. Then the barn wasn't there and we had to wait until it came back" (23).

By using the deictic *we*, Benjy creates a combined deictic center for himself and his brother, thus showing that because he is dizzy—seeing everything turn before his eyes—he believes that his brother is too. This would not be surprising, indeed, in a child of three. But Benjy is thirty-three, an adult autist rather than a child. The grown man he is shows that he is unable to perform deictic projection or, in Baron-Cohen's terms, that he is incapable of perceiving other people to feel things that are different from what he himself feels, which is seen as one of the diagnostic symptoms of autism. Indeed, in their work *The Language of Psychosis,* Bent Rosenbaum and Harly Sonne argue that in contrast to other types of special needs children, the problems of language acquisition that autistic children show are especially in the area of deictics (52).[5]

The other example I want to present here is that of Benjy's older brother, Quentin. In contrast to Benjy's text, in which deictic projection is limited or perhaps not realized at all, it is easy to see that in Quentin's text it has run wild. Indeed, we can recognize that Quentin's viewpoint shifts are largely unanchored, missing both lexical anchors—the pronouns that are supposed to remain anchored to the deictic center—and graphological ones—the comma, the colon, and the quotation marks. Here is a sample from the first page of the chapter narrated by him:

> When the shadow of the sash appeared on the curtains it was between seven and eight o'clock and then I was in time again, hearing the watch. It was Grandfather's and when Father gave it to me he said I give you the mausoleum of all hope and desire; it is rather excruciatingly apt that you will use it to gain the reducto absurdum of all human experience which can fit your individual needs no better than it fitted his or his father's. I give it to you not that you may remember time, but that you might forget it now and then for a moment and not spend all your breath trying to conquer it. (86)

In addition to the absence of lexical and graphological anchors, his text shows very few attributive clauses, and when they occur they often sound like afterthoughts, added at the last minute, such as in: "It's always the idle habits you acquire which you will regret. Father said that. That Christ was not crucified: he was worn away by a minute clicking of little wheels. That had no sister" (87). The result is that Quentin, for more than half a page at a time sometimes, takes over the viewpoint of his father without any markers at all. We can say that, in contrast to Benjy's lack of Theory of Mind, Quentin's has become so expansive—so unanchored—that he can no longer distinguish what his father knows, wants, believes, or feels from what he does himself.

Critics have diagnosed Quentin as a psychotic, his language as schizophrenic,[6] and although the usefulness of such labels is debatable, of course, it is true that the collapse of the deictic system that Quentin's text shows has been described as a symptom of schizophrenia. As Rosenbaum and Sonne put it, in schizophrenic language the "otherwise relatively firm boundary between internal and external, between self and surroundings" becomes "penetrable" (105), until finally the speech of many different persons becomes merged in totally unanchored deictic projection, as Quentin's text shows it in the following passage:

> *Three times. Days. Aren't you even going to open it* marriage of their daughter Candace *that liquor teaches you to confuse the means with the end* I am. Drink. I was not. Let us sell Benjy's pasture so that Quentin may go to Harvard and I may knock my bones together and together. (200)

As Theory of Mind thus runs rampant, operations upon language become more and more central, as a last attempt to hold together some sort of personal viewpoint.[7] In Quentin's text one can see clearly how thinking becomes, in Rosenbaum and Sonne's words, "metonymically substitutive" (64), with concepts following each other not because they form part of an integrated conceptualization of the world, but as a result of "phonetic and semantic similarities and contiguities." Such "sliding," as it is called, may as if by accident land on the crucial point, which is clear in the following passage:

> *the first car in town a girl Girl that's what Jason couldn't bear the smell of gasoline making him sick then got madder than ever because a girl Girl had no sister but Benjamin Benjamin the child of my sorrowful if I'd just had a mother so I could say Mother Mother.* (197)

The text finally presents the total collapse of Quentin's deictic center when the personal deictic "I" is written as a lower case "i" in a memory of a direct confrontation with his father. Quentin, here, "confesses" the incest he has not committed:[8]

> . . . and i i wasnt lying i wasnt lying and he you wanted to sublimate a piece of natural human folly into a horror and then exorcize it with truth and i it was to isolate her out of the loud world so that it would have to flee us of necessity and then the sound of it would be as though it had never been and he did you try to make her do it and i i was afraid to i was afraid she might . . . (175-76)

From the study of schizophrenic language it is known that with the "fragmentation of the imaginary body"—that is, when the "I" loses its "body-bound identity," as Rosenbaum and Sonne put it (105)—certain body parts take over, thus becoming its acting and speaking counterparts, as where Quentin remembers confronting his sister's lover: ". . . then I heard myself saying Ill give you until sundown to leave town. . . . My mouth said it I didn't say it at all" (183).

We see here that Quentin uses an attributive clause—*I heard myself saying*—to attribute mental activity to himself at an earlier time. In other words, Quentin steps into the shoes of his younger self, the past tense of the verb—*heard*—providing the anchor to his deictic center while the pronoun "I" with its reflexive *myself* and the progressive form of the verb *say* perform the deictic projection.

Even if this passage happens to be anchored somewhat more firmly than some of the passages we have seen before, it has an unsettling quality. One reason is the splitting in "behaver and observer" that the deictic projection produces, which specialists of schizophrenia have recognized as characteristic of the affliction (Bernheim and Lewine 56), the other is the syntactic form of the attributive clause itself. This brings me to the second part of my discussion, the importance of the attributive clause for the study of Theory of Mind.

If Theory of Mind concerns the attributing of mental activity to a subject—whether this goes all the way to "virtually feel[ing] [oneself] in his shoes," as Hofstadter puts it, or stays within the more distanced realm of "mind reading"—it seems useful to me to study the specific mental activity verb that is used when this attributing of mental activity is represented in the text—the verb *hear* in this case—as well as the form of the complement (the clause *myself saying . . .*). By using *not* a "that-clause," such as *I heard that I was saying . . .* (in which Quentin would have attributed to his younger self a conclusion based on prior existing knowledge), *not* a "how-clause," such as *I heard how I was saying* (which would have signified his awareness of a process going on inside him), and *not* a "to-infinitive," such as *I heard myself to be saying . . .* (which would have expressed his assessment of himself based on immediately available knowledge), but instead a so-called "small-clause." Quentin, as narrator or "attributor," expresses the mental experience of his younger self in a pure and intellectually unprocessed way.

As defined by the linguist Frederike van der Leek, the term *small-clause* refers to the complement of a mental activity verb—in this case the verb *hear*—which, if it is verbal, is non-finite and not accompanied by the infinite marker *to* (1-28), such as the clause *myself saying* used here. This small-clause complement of a mental activity verb, rather than conveying the assessment of a situation (as does the to-infinitive), the awareness of a process (as does the how-clause), or the conveying a conclusion (as does the that-clause), refrains from making any reference to a truth-judgment on the part of the experiencing character, conveying his or her experience "raw," as it were.[9] As a matter of fact, the grammatical form of the small-clause actually prohibits the addition of an epistemic evaluation, this becoming clear if we use a verb that includes such an evaluation, such as "I *knew* myself saying," or "I *concluded* myself saying," which are clearly ungrammatical.

Because the small-clause conveys phenomena as experienced rather than epistemically—that is, in terms of what is considered true of the world—such a construction lends itself especially well to the attributing of states of altered consciousness to an experiencer, such as reveries, dreams, psychological stress, drugs-induced conditions, hallucinations, and mental deficiency, when truth-judgment is avoided, deferred, disturbed, altered, impaired, or plainly impossible. Faulkner's stories and novels, with their concentration on deviant states of mind, contain many other beautiful examples, for instance *Light in August*, where Joe Christmas's depersonalized behavior is described: "He heard his voice say . . . and he watched his hand swing" (261); as well as in the story "Pantaloon in Black," where the young man Rider has to bury his wife after only six months of marriage: "He stood in the worn, faded, clean overalls which Mannie herself had washed only a week ago and heard the first clod strike the pine box" (*Go Down, Moses* 131).

In each case the mental activity verb *heard* occurs in combination with a small-clause. To take the last example, instead of using attributive clauses such as *He heard that the first clod was striking the pine box*, so as to give Rider's conclusion; or *He heard how the first clod was striking the pine box*, so as to convey Rider's awareness of a process witnessed; or else *He heard the first clod to be striking the pine box*, to indicate Rider's assessment of the situation before his eyes, the narrator uses his Theory of Mind to present the character's unmediated, "raw" experience.

Rider's text, however, is not totally devoid of other types of attribution. One finds, in fact, a small number of that-clauses. Consider the following sentence, in which the external narrator ascribes mental activity to the character Rider:

> Then he could stop needing to invent to himself reasons for his breathing, until after a while *he began to believe he had forgot* about breathing since now he could not hear it himself above the steady thunder of the rolling logs; whereupon as soon as *he found himself believing he had forgotten it, he knew that he had not* . . . (140-41; emphasis added)

At first glance only one that-clause is obvious: "he knew that he had not." In this construction the narrator, in order to enter Rider's state of mind, combines the truth-judgment on his—Rider's—part, which the that-clause conveys, with a choice of the attributive verb *knew.* This attributive verb, *know*, belongs to a group called factives, normally presenting the type of mental activity that a subject engages in, and at the same time indicating narratorial consent; that is to say, the narrator vouches for the truth of the matrix subject's observation. That this is so becomes clear when one makes the consent explicit. We can see easily that the sentence "he knew that he had not forgotten his breathing, and he was right" is redundant, while conversely "he knew that he had not forgotten his breathing, but he was wrong" is obviously paradoxical. Thus it is clear that speaker consent is part of the intrinsic meaning of the verb *to know.*

Two other that-clauses can be found in the passage:

a) he began to believe [that] he had forgot about breathing;

b) he found himself believing [that] he had forgotten it.

Obviously, the intellectual mediation attributed to Rider, because of the ellipsis of *that*, is of a more covert type here, and what is more, it is combined with the attributive verb *believe*, which refrains from any truth-judgment on the part of the narrator. This again becomes clear if the implicit is made explicit: "he believed that he had forgotten it and he was right" and "he believed that he had forgotten it but he was wrong" are both possible. This proves that no truth-judgment is part of the intrinsic meaning of *to believe.* The second that-clause, furthermore, is embedded within the small-clause, "he found himself believing," which casts the whole experience as a "raw" sensation that the reader shares with Rider. This effect is still further enhanced by the depersonalizing reflexive "he found himself."

The passage reveals as further treasures for the study of Theory of Mind its temporal organization. Changing from the adverb *then* in the first clause, to *now* in the third, the text shows well the temporal flexibility, or as Cohn calls it the "elasticity," of "psycho-narration" (38).[10] Rider's experience, thus, is captured again through deictic projection, as the narrator, through the usage of *now* and further on of terms such as "six months ago" instead of "six months before" (134), projects himself into the time perspective of the experiencer, that is to say, steps into the shoes of this young black laborer gone crazy with grief over the death of his young wife and takes us, his readers, with him.

CONCLUSION

I hope that I have been able to show that for the study of Theory of Mind in literature it is worthwhile to descend into the linguistic nitty-gritty of the text, first of all because linguistically speaking, Theory of Mind is a matter of deixis. As we have seen, the stepping into the shoes of another, and presenting the world from the point of view of that other, necessitates both the anchoring and the shifting of deictics. Secondly, Faulkner's texts have shown, I hope, how it can be worthwhile to study closely the specific mental verbs (and that includes perception verbs) through which a narrator, using his Theory of Mind, attributes mental activity to an experiencer, including himself at a younger age. In addition, we have seen that the specific attributive verb chosen may or may not include a truth-judgment on the part of this narrator himself, while the form of the complement of the attributive clause itself indicates the degree of intellectual awareness of the experiencer, going from a totally conscious conclusion to an intellectually unmediated, "raw" perception.[11] It is not just a matter of having a Theory of Mind or not; it is a matter of how, when, and to what degree. One day, hopefully, brain imaging will be subtle enough to show us these differences on film.

Notes

1 See also Douglas Frye and Chris Moore.

2 See also Duchan et al., who bring together a series of essays concerned with "deictic shift theory," the various ways in which "readers and writers of narratives sometimes imagine themselves to be in a world that is not literally present" (14).

3 In the case of the "if . . . then" conditional, Barbara Dancygier and Eve Sweetser argue, the deictic *then* creates a mental space of temporal dimensions (144-46).

4 As a matter of fact, the motion verb *come* is more complex, as it may stipulate a movement toward the deictic center (as in *The mail has finally come*), toward an addressee (as in *I don't mind coming to get you*), or toward the home-base of either (as in *Why did you come all the way to my house?; I could have come to yours*).

5 See also Harold I. Kaplan and Benjamin J. Sadock 557. For a discussion of Benjy's autism, see Sarah McLaughlin 34-40.

6 Joseph Blotner calls him Benjy's "psychotic older brother (213). Bruce Kawin speaks of a young man "who is not just chaotic and allusive, but frankly psychotic" (17). John Irwin argues that Quentin's narration shows the "bipolarity typical of both compulsion neurosis and schizophrenia" (29). The literary critic and psychiatrist Jay Martin believes he is best qualified as a male hysteric (personal communication).

7 See Julius Laffal 19; Sigmund Freud 203; and Rosenbaum and Sonne 64.

8 Faulkner explained this omission of capitals as follows: "because Quentin is a dying man, he is already out of life, and those things that were important in life don't mean anything to him any more." In Frederick L. Gwynn and Joseph Blotner 18.

9 A beautiful example of the small-clause is found in Henry James's short story "The Beast in the Jungle": "He saw the Jungle of his life and saw the lurking Beast; then, while he looked, perceived it, as by a stir of the air, rise, huge and hideous, for the leap that was to settle him." In Morton Dauwen Zabel, ed., 327-83. (See also James Phelan's interesting discussion of the story "The Beast in the Jungle" in *Reading People, Reading Plots*, 61ff.). But the narrator might have allowed for some form of epistemic evaluation of the experience on the part of the matrix subject by choosing the *to-infinitive* ("he perceived it *to be rising*"), the *how-clause* ("he perceived *how it rose*"), or the *that-clause* ("he perceived *that it rose*").

10 This form of narration often moves seamlessly into what Cohn calls "narrated monologue" (38), also known as free indirect discourse.

11 The approach developed here is, of course, not limited to William Faulkner's works. Indeed, deictic projection and attributive style are worthwhile subjects of study in connection with Theory of Mind for many other literary works. In Flannery O'Connor's short story "Parker's Back," for instance, the main character, the

non-believer Parker, crashes his truck into a tree, causing what amounts to a religious vision: "All at once he saw the tree reaching out to grasp him. A ferocious thud propelled him into the air, and he heard himself yelling in an unbelievably loud voice, 'GOD ABOVE!'" (520). The small-clauses "he saw the tree reaching" and "he heard himself yelling" give the experience "raw," here, showing that neither Parker nor the narrating voice—this because of the truth-neutral attributive verbs *saw* and *heard*—questions his experience. In the second small-clause, the depersonalizing reflexive adds to the supernatural effect of the passage. In this context the exclamation "GOD ABOVE!" can no longer simply be seen as a case of blasphemy. For the third time in the story, Parker ends up on his back—he had fallen twice before—as the tractor crashes "upside down into the tree" and he sees his shoes "quickly being eaten by the fire" (another small-clause). Yet this is the first time Parker reaches some intellectual awareness. Indeed, the small-clauses, here, are followed by the attributive that-clause: "He only knew that there had been a great change in his life, a leap forward into a worse unknown, and that there was nothing he could do about it" (521). By making use of the that-clause and the factual attributive verb *know*, the attributive clause "he knew that there had been a great leap forward" in this passage shows at once Parker's intellectual grasp—he is able to form a conclusion on the basis of his experience—and the narrator's consent. This conclusion is paired with a pure and simple explanation that cannot be contested, and that is strongly reminiscent of Christ's words on the cross: "it was for all intents accomplished" (521). (John 19:28 reads, "After this, Jesus knowing that all things were now accomplished, that the scripture might be fulfilled, saith, I thirst." One notices, here, the that-clause "knowing that," as well as the past participle "accomplished," which are also essential in Parker's awareness. In verse 30, moreover, Jesus says: "It is finished"; the Greek verb form is *tetelestai* in both cases). From the "raw" sentiment of being brought out of himself and carried away, conveyed by the small-clauses "he saw the tree reaching out" and "he heard himself yelling," Parker has moved into the intellectual awareness—he "knew"—that he must let himself be moved toward the Christ on the cross.

WORKS CITED

Baron-Cohen, Simon, Alan M. Leslie, and Uta Frith. "Does the Autistic Child have a 'Theory of Mind'?" *Cognition* 21 (1985): 37-46. Print.

Bernheim, Kayla F., and Richard R. J. Lewine. *Schizophrenia: Symptoms, Causes, Treatments*. New York: Norton, 1979. Print.

Blotner, Joseph. *Faulkner: A Biography*. New York: Random House, 1984. Print.

Cohn, Dorrit. *Transparent Minds: Narrative Modes for Presenting Consciousness in Fiction*. Princeton: Princeton University Press, 1983. Print.

Dancygier, Barbara, and Eve Sweetser. *Mental Spaces in Grammar*. Cambridge: Cambridge University Press, 2005. Print.

Duchan, Judith F., Gail A. Bruder, and Lynne E. Hewitt, eds. *Deixis in Narrative*. Hillsdale, NJ: Laurence Erlbaum, 1995. Print.

Faulkner, William. *The Sound and the Fury*. New York: Vintage, 1987 [1929]. Print.

---. *Light in August*. New York: Vintage, 1987 [1932]. Print.

---. *Go Down, Moses*. New York: Vintage, 1987 [1942]. Print.

Fillmore, Charles. *Santa Cruz Lectures on Deixis*. Berkeley: The University of California Press, 1971. Print.

Freud, Sigmund. *The Standard Edition of the Complete Works*. Vol. 14. London: The Hogarth Press, 1978. Print.

Frye, Douglas, and Chris Moore. *Children's Theories of Mind: Mental States and Social Understanding*. Hillsdale, NJ: Lawrence Erlbaum, 1991. Print.

Gwynn, Frederick L., and Joseph Blotner, eds. *Faulkner in the University: Class Conferences at the University of Virginia 1957-1958*. Charlottesville: The University of Virginia Press, 1959. Print.

Hofstadter, Douglas. *Gödel, Escher, Bach: An Eternal Golden Braid*. New York: Vintage, 1980. Print.

Irwin, John. *Doubling and Incest, Repetition and Revenge: A Speculative Reading of Faulkner*. Baltimore: The Johns Hopkins University Press, 1975. Print.

Joly, André, and Dairine O'Kelly. *L'Analyse linguistique des textes anglais*. Paris: Nathan, 1989. Print.

Kaplan, Harold I., and Benjamin J. Sadock. *Synopsis of Psychiatry: Behavioral Sciences, Clinical Psychiatry*. Baltimore: Williams & Wilkins, 1988. Print.

Kawin, Bruce. *Faulkner and Film*. New York: Frederick Ungerer, 1977. Print.

Laffal, Julius. *A Source Document in Schizophrenia*. Hope Valley, RI: Gallery Press, 1979. Print.

Leek, Frederike van der. "Significant Syntax: The Case of Exceptional Passives." *DWPELL* 27 (1992): 1-28. Print.

Levinson, Stephen C. *Pragmatics*. Cambridge: Cambridge University Press, 1983. Print.

Lyons, John. *Semantics*. Vol. 2. Cambridge: Cambridge University Press, 1977. Print.

McLaughlin, Sarah. "Faulkner's Faux Pas: Referring to Benjamin Compson as an Idiot." *Literature and Psychology* 33:2 (1987): 34-40. Print.

O'Connor, Flannery. "Parker's Back." In *The Complete Stories*. London: Faber & Faber, 1990. 510-31. Print.

Phelan, James. *Reading People, Reading Plots*. Chicago: The University of Chicago Press, 1989. Print.

Rosenbaum, Bent, and Harly Sonne. *The Language of Psychosis*. New York: New York University Press, 1986. Print.

Zabel, Morton Dauwen, ed. *The Portable Henry James*. Harmondsworth: Penguin, 1977. Print.

Zunshine, Lisa. *Why We Read Fiction: Theory of Mind and the Novel*. Columbus: The Ohio State University Press, 2006. Print.

Alternative Theory of Mind for Artificial Brains: A Logical Approach to Interpreting Alien Minds

Orley K. Marron

We have come to regard Theory of Mind (ToM) as a natural process through which readers interpret and comprehend characters in fiction. Authors such as Jane Austen or Virginia Woolf, writing books about human characters like Emma or Mrs. Dalloway, expect their readers to infer characters' motivations and feelings by assuming a similarity to the readers' own thinking and feeling bodies. The authors often construct their characters as human beings with ToM skills similar to the reader. However, writers may also undermine readers' and characters' assumptions that they correctly perceive others' intentions, by deliberately depicting mistakes in their construction of other people's minds—or *misconstruction*—thereby creating complex webs of misunderstanding and misinterpretation between people of different cultures or even those growing up in the same home (as in Shakespeare's *Othello* or *A Midsummer Night's Dream*). My interest in this essay is with authors who go so far as to construct test-cases of Theory of Mind by creating interactions between characters that are clearly human and characters that are artificial constructs, harboring alien, uncharted minds. Robots, golems, moving statues, speaking pictures, and dynamic chess pieces—objects visually and cognitively marked as different from humans and thus as more than normally unpredictable, may be presented in narratives as reliable resources for absolute "truth" and reflectors of the human soul, or, at other times, as completely opaque. By describing the interaction between human and nonhuman bodies, and the clash of cultural and biological expectations with alien neuron systems, the texts question and probe the limits of humanity and human expectations, and force the reader to rethink and reconsider reactions that seem "natural." Fantastical worlds and artificial minds provide a perfect laboratory for examining how human characters contend with, adapt to, and overcome—or fail to overcome—obstacles to their own survival and success. Such worlds allow for "extreme case analysis" and provide readers with optional cognitive "playgrounds" for their own thinking and feeling brains.

My examples here are taken from Isaac Asimov and Charles Lutwidge Dodgson (also known as Lewis Carroll), in their engagements with science fiction and fantasy. These authors probe the question of how can humans, when confronted with an alien mode of thinking or behavior, understand the reasoning inside such brains? Stanislaw Lem in *Solaris* maintains that such feats are impossible: there are entities too great and too obscure for human minds to understand or even to approach (namely the ocean).[1] Humans hardly understand their own hidden desires and motives, their obscure biology—how can they comprehend others? But authors like Asimov and Dodgson take the approach that even a partial success is worthwhile, and they optimistically create human characters that learn not to rely on intuitive human ToM skills, but rather to deploy a "Theory of Artificial Minds" (ToAM) in order to succeed or even survive in complex fictional environments. Their protagonists acquire ToAM skills as players acquire a game's rules and strategy, assuming the method in which logicians and scientists approach a problem: they study the environment and its constraints, they observe alien creatures' behaviors, collect as much empirical and background (or historical) information as possible, and then they deduce a set of premises, or game rules. These rules are used in turn to predict the creatures' responses, and must be modified according to the success or failure of their projections. Of course in a simple game scenario there is an underlying assumption that the alien behavior will be consistent, but occasionally inconsistency is also taken into account, and the human characters must live with uncertainty and develop heuristics to reduce this instability. By endowing their characters with an approach that is similar to Dodgson's description of formal logic—that is, take whatever "rules" or premises you observe (whether they seem true or false in the "real world") and follow them to their logical conclusion[2]—the authors reduce the emotional and even intuitive aspects of character to character interactions. The human character has the propensity for reacting emotionally, but it manages to control its spontaneous reaction (which may be very negative) and to use inference and logic instead to comprehend the alien one. A nonemotional reaction, however, does not mean inhumane. Frequently the protagonists that are most logical and least emotional, like Powell in *I, Robot,* also prove to be the most open and accepting of alternative ways of thinking. The highly popular character Spock in the Gene Roddenberry *Star Trek* series refrains from emotional reactions and uses logical inference to understand the needs of other species; he has become a model of respect for diversity and difference in both the television series and *Star Trek* books. Alice in Dodgson's books for children is just a child, easily moved to tears or anger, but she manages often to control her emotional behavior and apply logical thinking in order to interact with and learn from alien beings. Dodgson and Asimov's human protagonists mediate for the reader a rational access to alien minds and thus encourage readers to adjust to new ways of thinking and alternative perspectives.

Isaac Asimov's *I, Robot,* published in 1950, was groundbreaking in its inventiveness. Asimov introduced the robot with a positronic brain, the forefather of Data in *Star Trek: The Next Generation.* Science fiction differs from fantasy, explains Larry Niven,[3] in that (at the time it is written) you cannot prove that it cannot happen: the premises upon which the sci-fi worlds are constructed must seem plausible and believable within the current scientific community (readers often argue about the details and authors like Niven relate to their concerns, as with Niven's *Ring World* series). Fantastical worlds, however, while they need to be consistent within their own narrative schema, do not have to seem scientifically plausible (like Terry Pratchett's utterly flat Discworld, which rides on the back of four elephants standing on the back of Great A'Tuin the turtle). Asimov's artificial, human-constructed, positronic robot brain is consistent with a science fiction approach, and a hierarchy of three basic rules built into its logic prescribes the robot's behavior (or "motivation"). A robot may not injure a human being or, through inaction, allow a human being to come to harm; it must obey orders given it by human beings except where such orders would conflict with the first law; and it must protect its own existence as long as such protection does not conflict with the first or second law. However, how these rules are construed by the robot's electronic mind is often surprising, and the human characters face the problem of what happens "when one is face to face with an inscrutable positronic brain, which the slide-rule geniuses say should work thus and so. Except that it doesn't" (56). In "Runaround," Isaac Asimov's story of a drunken robot, two human robot specialists, Mike Donovan and Greg Powell, find themselves in dire need of a robot's services, but the robot, named Speedy, does not function as planned. Rather than bringing back selenium from a certain pool on Mercury's surface, the robot circles the pool again and again, swaying drunkenly and quoting lines from Gilbert and Sullivan. The narrator describes the desperation of the two men: unless they understand why Speedy behaves as it does, and motivate it to act differently, they will burn to death within a few hours. Having a Theory of Artificial Mind becomes here a matter of life or death: thus the story provides for the reader an extreme, nearly bare-bones testing ground of human versus machine thought. Asimov's narrative is constructed as a conundrum or dilemma similar to the detective story. As in detective stories, there is a riddle or problem that must be resolved, and the basic "rules of the game" are already known ahead of time: what are the given physical realities, and what are the possible motivations for the culprit's behavior. Using all the relevant facts, human characters combine Theory of Mind skills with deductive reasoning to construct a solution. In *I, Robot*, the protagonists know that the three laws of robotics determine Speedy's behavior (rather than love or power or money found in human detective stories), and they must use the same rules to devise a solution to their problem. Lisa Zunshine suggests that detective stories exercise readers' metarepresentational ability, or the ability to keep track of sources of representations (who said what, when), to store such data under advisement and to reevaluate their truth-value once more information becomes available. Detective stories provide pleasure in the cognitive training of this ability (123). In addition, however, these "whodunits" provide the reader with the enormous satisfaction of solving riddles and bringing open questions to a neat and logical conclusion—a response shared by mathematicians, scientists, crossword puzzle solvers and novel readers alike. While Asimov's stories exercise readers' metarepresentational skills to some extent, they emphasize more the gratification of riddle resolution—provided by detective like scientists and robopsychologists with unusual ToM skills.

In "Runaround," Asimov's human characters model two distinct approaches to artificial behavior interpretation. The narrator employs language patterns, action, and thought descriptions to stress the difference. Mike Donovan represents the average human point of view: he reacts very emotionally to the stressful situation, and becomes frustrated and angry, attributing human agency to the robot's mind. Donovan construes the robot's behavior as deliberately antagonistic and menacing. When he calls Speedy *drunk*, he suggests the negative connotations of tales of self-induced inebriation (e.g., the biblical Noah and Lot), and when he applies the word *thinks* he implies that Speedy is an independent, free-willed thinker. He thus attributes a malevolent intention to Speedy's refusal to obey orders. By suggesting that Speedy is playing a game Donovan conjures an intentionally irresponsible, even teasing, and aggravating attitude: "'To me, he's drunk,' stated Donovan, emphatically, 'and all I know is that he *thinks* we're playing games. And we're not. It's a matter of life and very gruesome death'" (43). Greg Powell, on the other hand, is more rational and inclined to proceed logically, and he does not easily fall back on intuitive human ToM. Powell refuses to treat Speedy as a human, nor does he assume deliberate insubordination. Refuting the negative implication of self-induced inebriation, he replies, "Speedy isn't drunk—not in the human sense, because he's a robot, and robots don't get drunk. However, there's *something* wrong with him which is the robotic equivalent of drunkenness" (43).

When readers first read Donovan's allegations, they may construct a certain view of Speedy's agency and motivation. However, once Powell reacts, Donovan's view will come under advisement. Powell's approach asks the reader to revise an earlier opinion of Donovan's highly emotional message. He refutes Donovan's humanization of Speedy's intentions, by objectifying Speedy, saying that: "A robot's only a robot. Once we find out what's wrong with him, we can fix it and go on" (43). As do investigators in detective stories, Powell attempts to reconstruct the scenario before Speedy "went bad," so as to imagine what could have brought about Speedy's bizarre behavior. Powell thus acts for the reader as a mediator to the artificial mind. He analyzes the environment around the pool, pointing out that while Speedy is perfectly adapted to normal Mercurian environment, the particular region they are in is abnormal and particularly toxic to the Robot's iron body ("There's our clue"). He then requires Donovan to reiterate exactly what he asked of Speedy and realizes that Donovan failed to emphasize the urgency of the request. Powell, using the basic laws of robotics upon which Speedy's positronic brain is constructed, analyzes the miscommunication and the electronic conflict that occurred in the machine brain. Speedy's Rule 3 (saving himself) was strengthened as a result of his costly construction, given that he is "expensive as a battleship." Although obeying Rule 2—human commands—is in general of higher priority than Rule 3, the orders given by Donovan were given casually and without special emphasis, so the Rule 2 potential was rather weak. Powell concludes that the conflict between potentials is what drove Speedy to the pool and away from it, causing him to circle it; the point where the potentials strike an equilibrium is the distance from the pool that Speedy maintains. This explains the drunken attitude, says Powell:

> And that, by the way, is what makes him drunk. At potential equilibrium, half the positronic paths of his brain are out of kilter. I'm not a robot specialist, but that seems obvious. Probably he's lost control of just those parts of his voluntary mechanism that a human drunk has. (46)

Thus using inference and logic, Powell shows the reader how a specific combination of decision states, or algorithmic possibilities, caused a conflict of interest that confused the machine brain. The lack of urgency in Donovan's command, given a low priority level by the machine brain, is what triggered the conflict with Speedy's unusually high priority instruction to protect his expensive iron body. Powell alerts the reader to a more rational representation of the particular reality of machine "thought"—a type of short-circuiting of metal neurons. This human character thus acts like a detective, psychologist, and computer analyst in one. He probes the source of conflict that could cause a robot to appear malevolent and confrontational, without making the mistake of thinking that the robot has an autonomous, self-governed inner self to which his actions are clues. Powell's deductions prove correct and they allow him to devise a solution that brings Speedy out of his confused state and back to normal functioning, saving the lives of the two humans. The scientist puts himself at risk (effectively triggering a response to a No. 1 Rule), overriding Speedy's circuit malfunction with a higher priority command that forces Speedy into positive action. Once Speedy returns to normal and realizes how poorly he performed, he apologizes profusely, thereby disproving Donovan's insinuation of deliberate robot insubordination and reinforcing Powell's approach.

Many of the stories in *I, Robot* repeat this pattern of strange robot behavior followed by detective-like logical analysis, or ToAM, that explains it. The author thus encourages readers to adopt analytic and deductive thinking when dealing with initially incomprehensible brains. Zunshine suggests that high intensity detective stories pay a price for their demanding cognitive exercise. Such stories must be more focused and emphasize a certain plotline above all others. They do not, for example, give equal time to romance and mystery, since that may create competition with the "metarepresentational framing required to process the detecting elements of the story" (143, 147). Emphasizing aspects of romance or other genres may weaken the mystery plot by compromising readers' ability to keep track of characters' states of minds, especially when they are under advisement. Asimov's stories, too, focus on specific dilemmas, and they rarely create multiple plot lines or complex intentionality levels. Rather, they concentrate on the "artificial mind" problem at hand. Readers need to concentrate on the state of mind of the people trying to understand the machines, the current artificial world rules, and the possible options for robot thought processes. Readers (along with human characters) are working within a type of symbolic logic framework, in which each new premise that the author introduces is used in constructing or testing the next stage.

An exception to this focus on logic is Asimov's "Liar!," a story in which the schema is reversed: instead of humans trying to read the minds of robots, a mind-reading robot attempts to exercise theory of human minds. This strange creation has on the one hand direct access to human thoughts (literally "reading them"), but on the other it has no human judgment or evaluative skills nor any human intuition and common sense. The robot's behavior is structured upon the three rules embedded into its logic and its positronic brain, the first of which is not to hurt people, and the second of which is to obey orders. His interpretation of these commands is wish-fulfillment: when he perceives a certain desire or wish within the human characters, for example a romantic affection for someone or an ambition to take over another's position, the robot attempts to fulfill this desire through stories, or lies. Because the robot lacks the ability to generate embedded narratives of the minds he reads, he cannot imagine the full story of the humans' reactions, and thus he cannot predict the consequences of any actions he takes based on his privileged knowledge. Disregarding the misery that will result in feeding humans on fantasies, he misleads the human characters with invalid "facts," promising them what they cannot have. They, in turn, assume that a machine cannot lie, they fail to verify his input, and act foolishly on false assumptions. When he tells the robopsychologist Susan Calvin that her affections for one of the scientists are reciprocated by that person, even though the man in fact loves another woman, Susan acts on his information and makes futile overtures. The robot does not understand relative magnitudes of human pain, and that the shame of being openly rejected and losing one's pride may be far worse than living with unrequited love. The tenuous balance between the fear of being made to look like a fool in contrast to obtaining one's desire is not apparent to a robot brain. "Liar!" thus provides a test case depicting what happens when one's mind is bound by certain fixed rules, and is privileged with special knowledge, but does not have access to human cultural and biological requirements and expectations. While the robot fails to develop a correct theory of human mind, Susan does figure out how his artificial mind works. She realizes that her assumption that a machine is unbiased and therefore provides true facts was wrong, and that all her coworkers fell for the same illusion, eager to have their fantasies fulfilled. Incensed by being made to look a pathetic fool, she destroys the robot by charging him with causing pain to humans and thus driving him mad.

About a century before Asimov, Charles Lutwidge Dodgson also created worlds full of artificial beings. Dodgson was a professor of mathematics and loved math and logic, observing a unique type of truth and beauty in these subjects. He believed everyone should be trained in logic theory and mathematics, as it provided enjoyment and an excellent way to develop the mind. Using various visual aids he developed teaching methods fit for different audiences, including those not expected to study logic in Victorian England—young children, high school girls, and women teachers. In his first volume of *Symbolic Logic*, which appeared in February 1896, he addressed schoolteachers in a separately printed prospectus, where he points symbolic logic out as a healthy mental recreation in the education of young people between twelve and twenty:

> I claim, for Symbolic Logic, a very high place among recreations that have the nature of games or puzzles; and I believe that any one, who will really try to understand it, will find it more interesting and more absorbing than most of the games or puzzles yet invented. (45)

Dodgson claimed that people harbor three false ideas about the study of logic: "that it is too hard for average intellects, that it is dry and uninteresting, and that it is useless." He rebutted all three, and concluded that this fascinating subject will be "of service to the young" and should be taken up in high schools and by families.[4]

Similar to Asimov's construction of robotic mind-riddles for youth and adults, Dodgson invented for children fascinating games, puzzles, and riddles that engaged their attention and encouraged them to solve problems and to experience the satisfaction of coming up with clever solutions. I suggest that Dodgson's Alice books themselves (*Alice in Wonderland* and *Through the Looking Glass*), the first originally written for Alice Liddell,[5] were a powerful means of expressing to thousands of children and adults, across generations, the beauty and wit and power of logic and math. In these books, Dodgson creates a new model protagonist who acts out his ideas, a heroic paradigm that boldly seeks new and unknown regions—not just physical, but also of the mind.[6] Dodgson's Alice models a logician's approach to alternative ways of thinking and to the understanding of alien minds.

Dodgson's imaginative worlds, created for a young audience, are different from Asimov's more serious, scientific-sounding constructs, and they do not claim to be possible technologically. The inhabitants are purely fantastical, a combination of mythological creatures, characters out of fables, political cartoons, and *humanobs* (humanlike, man-made animated objects). While the stories seem like a wild collage of children's memories and scenes from pretend games, they display Dodgson's remarkable acuity as a teacher for children. He uses objects and concepts that are familiar to many Victorian children (e.g., poetry, puns, and visual art) to introduce new ideas, and thus he provides a type of learning lab for the character Alice—and for the children who read her story. Unlike Powell and Donovan, Alice does not come equipped with a predetermined set of premises through which she can interpret alien behaviors. There are no "three laws of Wonderland creatures." Like a child in a bewildering and alien adult world, she is unprepared and must undergo a complex process of learning to interpolate world rules and acquire meaning. Many of the *Wonderland* or *Looking Glass* world creatures with which Alice interacts, especially the playing cards and chess game pieces, are comparable to elements of formulas and sets that Dodgson presented in his mathematic lectures and game theories. They have values and attributes that can be used to categorize them as elements of sets, and they are bound by specific game or world principles. Pawns, for example, can only move in specific directions, and in the *Looking Glass* world creatures must sometimes walk backward in order to move forward. When Alice approaches them with her Victorian child's conceptions, she often finds that they cannot be understood simply through her own embodied ToM. Her critical, reasoning mind is the bridge that enables her to close the gap between human expectations and alien modes of thought, allowing her to construct a ToAM. Alice develops her ToAM gradually, by using—as Powell did—empirical information, inference, and deduction. At every new encounter she gains more knowledge. As she compiles a set of rules of behavior by which the strange creatures abide, she improves her ability to predict their reactions, and she devises adaptive strategies to deal with them and to maneuver toward her goals. Dodgson, through the narrator character (a type of "fond uncle"), constructs Alice as a curious, independent, and humorous person with deductive powers, as well as frustrations and concerns—someone with whom children can identify and whose learning methods they may imitate. Alice's learning process thus becomes a model through which Dodgson promotes logic and inference as tools for dealing with new ideas and unconventional minds.

How does Dodgson convey this process to the reader? Like Asimov, he uses his protagonist to mediate the access to alien minds. Such mediation may not be necessary when alien creatures exhibit humanlike emotions and behaviors, such as fear or anguish or anger. The narrator uses what Alan Palmer terms a thought-action (or action-disposition) type of description—for example, the gardener Five "had been anxiously looking across the garden," and when the Queen appears "the three gardeners instantly threw themselves flat upon their faces" (Palmer 108). These behaviors are easily interpreted by both Alice and readers, and evoke immediate responses: Alice pities the frightened gardeners when they are threatened with decapitation, and she hides them in a flowerpot. But behaviors that are remarkably bizarre and cannot be understood intuitively, such as physical reactions based on prediction of the future or disembodied responses, require mediation and cognitive analysis. For example, many of the characters seem to ignore physical risk to themselves and to others, and they misinterpret each other's (and Alice's) needs. The Red Chess Queen, after an exhausting race, offers Alice dry biscuits to "quench her thirst" rather than water. The footman nearly gets his nose smashed, but utterly ignores the event.[7] And the Duchess rocks her wailing baby under a barrage of flying pots and pans, insensitive to the blows and callously ignoring the danger to the baby's well-being—in contrast with Alice, who (in keeping with her humane character) becomes greatly anxious ("jumping up and down in an agony of terror") for the poor child's welfare (84). In addition, the physical world rules of the fantastical worlds shape the physical reactions and assumptions of the inhabitants. They must run extremely fast to stay in the same place, or move backward to advance. In the *Looking Glass* world where future events are known in advance (that is—creatures "live backwards"), the characters frequently act on the knowledge of a future or potential event rather than in response to a direct physical cause. Cakes must be served before they are cut. People are punished before they are found guilty, and injuries are tended to before they occur. The white chess Queen cries in pain—anticipating a pinprick from her brooch, but remains smiling when the event actually takes place, and refrains from screaming again having "done all the screaming already." The Queen thus displays a disembodied emotional response to a physical event occurring on her body, as if she is insensitive to pain resulting from the prick.[8] The earthly empirical concept of direct "cause and event," with which Alice is familiar, becomes distorted by the effect of "living backwards."[9] At this more complex level of behavior, Dodgson's artificial creatures seem quite inscrutable, and Alice's ToM inference falls short of predicting their reactions or guiding her as to how she should best respond.

The narrator has several ways of revealing the internal workings of alien minds to readers. He can give authorial commentary, or expose the alien mind to the reader directly, or use the protagonist, Alice, to figure out the ToAM for the reader. As it turns out, like many other science fiction and fantasy narratives including Asimov's robot stories, the narrator creates an asymmetric mode of mind exposure. Unlike Alice's broadly exposed contemplations and embedded narratives, the alien characters' minds are opaque: the narrator does not expose them for viewing and there are no descriptions of their thought processes, nor of their embedded narratives. That is, there are no unequivocal authoritative statements such as "the Gardener felt sure that his end was near . . ." or "he hoped that Alice would save his life, despite her youth." Nor does the text describe the cards' mental plan to escape their plight, and the Queen's attempt to prevent them. This mental opaqueness dehumanizes the artificial characters, and keeps the reader from "seeing through" their eyes and from adopting their point of view, maneuvering the reader to focus on Alice and look through her perspective. Alan Palmer describes a similar narrative technique in Evelyn Waugh's *Vile Bodies*, where the narrator dehumanizes even human characters by hiding their thoughts and embedded narratives from the readers.[10] It is Alice's analytical and probing deliberations, revealed to the reader, that allow, as do Powell's inferences, access to the characters.

But because Alice cannot rely on intuitive (or previously developed) understanding and intuition, she needs to adopt a more formal analytical approach. Alice needs to collect empirical data by observing the characters' conduct (including their reaction time and cause-and-effect schema), by listening to their input and by repeatedly questioning them. She needs to acquire new terms and language skills to better comprehend their world and to understand their obscure language and its implications (just as logicians and mathematicians require a definition of terms). Alice must then extrapolate new world rules from the creatures' speech and body motions, test these rules by experimentation, draw conclusions, and finally apply them—both to social situations and to physical maneuvers en route to her goal.[11] Thus fantastical worlds such as these encourage in Alice the exercising of a logician's type of ToAM. Since Alice's thoughts *are* described by the narrator, the reader becomes privy to the deductive processes, inferences, and conclusions she generates as she constructs a schema of new world rules and behaviors.

One example of the process of deliberation and new schema construction is the remarkable question and answer dialogue between the White Queen and Alice. In this discussion Alice studies the idea of futuristic causality, a phenomenon that explains alien creatures' disembodied behavior as well as their ability to conceive "impossible things." In a world where potential events are seen as if they already occurred, empirical data is not immediately necessary for something to be proven as true and believable, but only the *expectation* or potential that it will occur. Thus, explains the White Queen, the King's Messenger is already sitting in prison, being punished, "and the trial doesn't even begin till next Wednesday, and of course the crime comes last of all." Alice expresses her confusion about such a system of causal rules: what if the event does not occur—that is—it becomes a failed alternative? The Queen insists that it may be so much the better, but Alice has a hard time accepting this alien notion, and especially its ethical implications. Not only will there be effect without cause, but conventions of justice based on the concept of punishment only of the guilty may be altogether eradicated. Alice's encounter with alien world rules thus makes her aware of cultural conventions she (and readers) have taken for granted:

> "Suppose he never commits the crime?" said Alice.
> "That would be all the better, wouldn't it?" the Queen said . . .
> Alice felt there was no denying *that*. "Of course it would be all the better," she said: "but it wouldn't be all the better his being punished."
> "You're wrong there, at any rate," said the Queen. "Were you ever punished?"
> "Only for faults," said Alice.
> "And you were all the better for it, I know!" the Queen said triumphantly.
> "Yes, but then I had done the things I was punished for," said Alice: "that makes all the difference."
> "But if you *hadn't* done them," the Queen said, "that would have been better still; better, and better, and better!" . . .
> Alice was just beginning to say "There's a mistake somewhere—", when the Queen began screaming . . . (248)

Alice's analytical acquisition of a theory of alien minds seems to be highly conscious and goal-oriented, perhaps similar to the descriptions of autistic savants' attempts at learning to read human faces and intentions.[12] It seems to differ from the automatic or nonconscious manner in which normal human children acquire ToM skills. However, it may be that the basic cognitive / neurological structures underlying both automatic and self-aware ToM acquisition are alike or even common to both. The manner of acquisition of ToM skills by children is still debated by researchers, a crucial question being of the relative weights of innate capabilities versus social training. Some researchers emphasize a more modular and "innate" approach, while others, such as Jay L. Garfield, Candida C. Petterson, and Tricia Perry, argue that the acquisition of ToM is "dependent as well on social and linguistic accomplishment, and that it is modular in only a weak sense" (505). Garfield et al. present a developmental model that is "social and ecological as opposed to being individualistic." I suggest that for any model of automatic ToM acquisition in normal children, underlying that capability is a basic biological capacity for rule acquisition, or positive-negative value acquisition, (perhaps using neurological constructs such as those as found in conditioning described by Larry Squire and Eric Kandel, 57). That is, infant brains, on the basis of social and environmental interaction, must be able to construct certain cause and effect rules—albeit automatically and not in a language form. For example—"Given milk, the pain in my stomach disappears," or "the light is turned on, someone will come to me," and eventually "if I hit someone, they will feel pain, shout at me, or hit me back." Children's ability to read visual body cues and to comprehend others' intentions may develop automatically (or without awareness) through social interaction, but it relies on a neurological logical-comparative mechanism, which enables the child, unconsciously, to test inferences and to discern and remember causal rules. I believe this comparative mechanism comes into play, and becomes more noticeable to the interpreting person when an obscure or alien mind crops up, and the interpreter finds that he or she has to consciously extract information and generate new causal rules to comprehend that mind. Authors like Dodgson and Asimov, a logician and a scientist who use analytical thinking in their work, externalize and expose the logical process in their narratives by depicting the interaction of human and alien characters. They seem to suggest humans should recognize the limitations of their normal human intuition and, when confronted with seemingly alien modes of behavior, they should adopt a more formal logical approach. Like their fictional protagonists, readers should observe others, collect empirical data and extrapolate new world—or cultural—rules. This approach can encourage readers to adopt a more flexible, and perhaps sympathetic, approach to different modes of thinking. Many science fiction and fantasy writers (including *Star Trek* producer Gene Roddenberry), believed that their narratives could thus encourage a more pluralistic society.[13]

Notes

1 Stanislaw Lem, 1921-2006, was a science fiction writer whose works explore philosophical themes such as the impossibility of mutual communication and understanding. The official Lem site is *Solaris*, ed. Stanislaw and Tomasz Lem 2000-2007 http://www.lem.pl/.

2 Morton N. Cohen, *Lewis Carroll, a Biography* (New York: Alfred A. Knopf, 1995) 446.

In 1886 Dodgson wrote *The Game of Logic*, in which he explains that it does not matter what the beginning premises are, as long as they are followed logically to the end:

> I don't guarantee the Premises to be facts . . . It isn't of the slightest consequence to us, as Logicians, whether our Premises are true or false: all we have to make out is whether they lead logically to the Conclusion, so that, if they were true, it would be true also.

3 The prolific science fiction writer Larry Niven has written over sixty books, among them the *Ring World* series, and has created the unique alien the Pierson's Puppeteer; personal interview, March 18, 2008, Bar Ilan University Creative Writing Visitor Lecture.

4 In his introduction to his *Symbolic Logic* book, Charles Dodgson (a.k.a. Lewis Carroll) writes:

> this is, I believe, the very first attempt . . . that has been made to popularize this fascinating subject . . . But if it should prove, as I hope it may, to be of real service to the young, and to be taken up, in High Schools and in private families, as a valuable addition to their stock of healthful mental recreation, such a result would more than repay ten times the labor that I have expended on it. (47)

5 Alice Liddell was one of Dodgson's favorite child-friends. Morton Cohen in the biography of Dodgson describes the famous trip that took place on July 4, 1862, in which Charles Dodgson, Robinson Duckworth (Fellow of Trinity College), and three Liddell sisters set off for Godstow for one of their picnics. On the way, Charles told Alice her story, and Alice petitioned that the tale might be written out for her, and *Alice's Adventures Underground* (later "in Wonderland") was created (89).

6 For discussion of the new paradigm in Dodgson's books, see Orley Marron, "Fictions Beyond Fiction: A Cognitive-Literary Study of Human-like Animated Objects in the Fiction of Lewis Carroll and Nathaniel Hawthorne," diss., Bar-Ilan University, 2008.

7 The footman in *Alice's Adventures in Wonderland* does not react as a normal human would to a near catastrophe:

> At this moment the door of the house opened, and a large plate came skimming out, straight at the Footman's head: it just grazed his nose, and broke to pieces against one of the trees behind him.
> "—or next day, maybe," the Footman continued in the same tone, exactly as if nothing had happened. (81)

8 In *Through the Looking Glass* (hereafter *TLG*), the White Queen displays anticipatory responses before she is injured, crying out loudly, and then explaining to the worried Alice that "I haven't pricked it yet, . . . but I soon shall—oh, oh, oh!" (249).

9 The essence of "living backwards" as explained by the White Queen in *TLG* 247 is that "one's memory works both ways." Alice explains that her memory works "only one way" and that she "can't remember things before they happen."

> "It's a poor sort of memory that only works backwards," the Queen remarked.
> "What sort of things do you remember best?" Alice ventured to ask.
> "Oh, things that happened the week after next," the Queen replied in a careless tone. (247)

10 Palmer discusses presentation of consciousness in *Vile Bodies* by Evelyn Waugh:

> The key to the fictional minds in Vile Bodies is that there is a good deal of intermental thinking but very little evidence of doubly embedded narratives. There is very little indication of the existence of one character in the mind of another...The lack of doubly embedded narratives demonstrates some very solipsistic states of mind . . . [it] contributes substantially to the callous and unfeeling quality of the novel. (233-34)

11 For example, by conversing with the talking flowers in *TLG*, Alice learns to walk backward in order to move forward toward the Queen.

12 Autistic savant Temple Grandin wrote the book *Animals in Translation: Using the Mysteries of Autism to Decode Animal Behavior*. Temple attributes her success as a

humane livestock facility designer to her ability to recall detail, which is a characteristic of her visual memory. She has become aware of details to which animals are particularly sensitive, giving her insight into their needs, and allowing her to design humane animal-handling equipment. Her site is http://www.grandin.com/.

13 Gene Roddenberry's *Star Trek* scripts promoted many forms of interracial relations, exemplified by the first interracial kiss broadcast on television. Actress Nichelle Nichols, who played Lieutenant Uhura, discussed the importance of this symbolic event as well as Martin Luther King's conviction that her role in the series provided an immensely important non-stereotypical model for African-Americans. She was presented on an equal basis, on a level of dignity and authority, and with the highest of qualifications. Interview and text can be found in the "Trek Nation" news site, "Nichols Talks First Inter-Racial Kiss," *Trek*, ed. Christian Hohne Sparborth, 5 Sept. 2001, http://www.trektoday.com/news/050901_05.shtml.

WORKS CITED

Asimov, Isaac. *I, Robot.* New York: Bantam Dell Books, 2004. Print.

Bartley, William Warren. "Introduction." *Lewis Carroll's Symbolic Logic, Part I & Part II*. 1896. By Lewis Carroll. Comp. and ed. William W. Bartley. New York: Potter, 1977. Print.

Carroll, Lewis. *The Annotated Alice: Alice's Adventures in Wonderland & Through the Looking Glass Today.* Comp. and ed. Martin Gardner. London: Penguin Books, 1970. Print.

---. *Lewis Carroll's Symbolic Logic, Part I & Part II*. 1895. Ed. William Warren Bartley, III. New York: Potter, 1977. Print.

Cohen, Morton N. *Lewis Carroll, a Biography*. New York: Alfred A. Knopf, 1995. Print.

Dodgson, Charles Lutwidge. *The Game of Logic.* London: McMillan & Company, 1887. Print.

Gardner, Martin. "Introduction and Notes." *The Annotated Alice: Alice's Adventures in Wonderland & Through the Looking Glass.* By Lewis Carroll. London: Penguin Books, 1970. Print.

Garfield, Jay L., Candida C. Peterson, and Tricia Perry. "Social Cognition, Language Acquisition and the Development of Theory of Mind." *Mind and Language* 16.5 (2001): 494-541. Print.

Hambly, Barbara. *Ishmael (Star Trek No. 23)*. New York: Pocket Books, 1985. Print.

Palmer, Alan. *Fictional Minds.* Lincoln: University of Nebraska Press, 2004. Print.

Squire, Larry R., and Eric R. Kandel. *Memory: From Mind to Molecules.* New York: Henry Holt and Company, 2003. Print.

Waugh, Evelyn. *Vile Bodies.* Boston: Little, Brown and Company, 1930. Print.

Zunshine, Lisa. *Why We Read Fiction: Theory of Mind and the Novel.* Columbus: The Ohio State University Press, 2006. Print.

Reading Phantom Minds: Marie Darrieussecq's *Naissance des fantômes* and Ghosts' Body Language

Mikko Keskinen

> l'absence de mon mari à mes côtés me désigne plus que jamais comme un corps étranger.
> —Marie Darrieussecq, *Naissance des fantômes*

> the absence of my husband at my side marks me more than ever as a foreign body.
> —Marie Darrieussecq, *My Phantom Husband*

Currently, Theory of Mind could be dubbed Practice of Body without losing much of its functional content. Actual people, real readers, and fictional characters are all accustomed to interpreting human body language as indicative of thoughts and feelings, that is, of otherwise hidden mental structures. This move from body to mind usually happens so automatically that to call it a *Theory* of Mind is something of a misnomer.[1] But the theory in Theory of Mind becomes more justifiable than the practice in Practice of Body, when the default reading cannot take place. This failure in the mind reading ability may be due to a number of reasons. The person occupying the position of the mind reader may be suffering from autism or Asperger's syndrome, making the subject incapable of such immediate inference. Or, on the other side of the process, there may not be a body present to infer a mind from.

In this essay, I address the latter case by analyzing Marie Darrieussecq's 1999 novel *Naissance des fantômes* (*My Phantom Husband*).[2] In that novel, the female narrator's husband suddenly disappears, and possibly dies, leaving her in a state that develops from the initial disquietude to numbness and eventually to hallucinations (or, alternatively, to witnessing actual visitations).[3] The wife's mind reading activities necessarily—and radically—differ from those usually performed by fictional characters. Since her husband is not corporeally present, she cannot interpret his body language and behavior as indicative of his mental structure or state. Instead, she must rely on her memories and the residual markers of his past behavior.

Not surprisingly, her very first mind reading activities relate to the possible reasons for his disappearance, to his corporeal absence. The speculation on the workings of his mind or on his mind-set in general is made explicit on the novel's opening page:

> Mon mari a-t-il disparu parce que, se soir-là, après des années de négligence de ma part, excédé, fatigué par sa journée de travail, il en a eu subitement assez de devoir, jour après jour, redescendre nos cinq étages en quête de pain? (11)
>
> [Has my husband disappeared because that evening, after enduring years of my negligence, exasperated, worn out by his day at work, he was suddenly fed up with having to go back down our five flights of stairs, day after day, in search of bread?] (1)

The investigators provide some more scenarios, based on the statistical data of two hundred missing persons a day, ranging from the possibility of his going on a vacation with a beautiful blonde to that of a suicide. Soon, however, it becomes evident that there is no cunning plan, no scheming mind behind the mysterious disappearance. The husband is probably as dull and unimaginative as the mundane dreams ("d'une quotidienneté consternante" [45]; "distressingly ordinary" [35]) he has of his business or of shopping at the local bakery. Significantly, it is his wife ("beaucoup ennuyée" [42]; "extremely bored" [32]) who makes up Freudian interpretations of his dreams. He is, indeed, in the real estate business, with the main emphasis on the first word, whereas she is busy being unreasonable or even surreal. Narrationally, this means that she can seamlessly move, in free direct discourse, from reporting the investigators' utterances to her own speculative details of forensic precision, and back again:

> d'autres encore passaient la frontière et il ètait sage, là, de renoncer à tout espoir, d'autres enfin se jetaient dans la mer, échouaient tout gonflés sur les plages, les yeux et la langue mangés par les crevettes, des colonies de bigorneaux dans le rectum, il valait mieux s'épargner ce genre de retrouvailles. (12)
>
> [while others cross the border, in which case it's wisest to renounce all hope, and still others throw themselves into the sea, washing up bloated on the beaches, eyes and tongue eaten by shrimp, bodily crevices colonized by sea snails, it's best to spare yourself this type of reunion.] (2)

Immediately after her rambling digression into the corporeal decay, she resumes the investigators' crucial question: "Les enquêteurs m'ont demandé si mon mari était dépressif" (12); "The police asked me if my husband was prone to depression" (2). That question could justifiably be posed to herself as well.[4]

Her husband turns out to be, in the police investigation, curiously ambiguous and semi-transparent even before his disappearance. The real estate clients he meets on the day of his mysterious vanishing fail to remember his facial features (12 / 2), and the baker does not recall his customary visit to the corner *boulangerie* (21 / 12). Objective evidence also testifies to his vacillating physical appearance. Trying to get a "un sens de la réalité" (49) ("sense of reality" [40]), the narrator looks at her wedding photo but notices that her husband's image is (or has become) vague: "La photo avait bougé. Elle était devenue floue [...]. C'était la photo de sa disparition" (49–50); "The picture had moved. It had blurred [...]. It was the photograph of his disappearance" (40–41). This man without qualities (if not without qualia) thus resembles a ghost or a zombie even before his possible death.

Although the husband is both physically unassuming and mentally unimaginative, the narrator has, at three o'clock in the morning, an illumination that he had framed his disappearance for a purpose:

> mon mari n'avait mis en scène le scénario de sa disparition que pour me rendre à la conscience de cet amour, à seule fin, lorsqu'il aurait eu la prevue (à son tour) de mon désespoir, de revenir en conquérant recevoir les multiples gifles que je ne manquerais pas de lui administrer, quel abruti, après m'avoir livrée combien de temps aux épouvantes du veuvage. (35)
>
> [my husband had stage-managed the scenario of his disappearance only to bring me to an awareness of my love, in the sole aim of making a triumphal return as soon he (in his turn) wielded the proof of my despair; to receive the multiple blows I would not fail to administer, what a jerk, after having abandoned me for how long to the terrors of widowhood.] (26)

This plan, cunning as it may seem, only generates a third- or fourth-order intentionality: she thinks or believes that her husband wants to make her aware of her love, giving him the reason to return to receive his punishment. The final phrase starting with "de revenir" is not likely part of the husband's plan but, rather, in its detailedness, her wishful thinking. So is the whole speculation, as she herself admits in the next paragraph when she does some source-monitoring (in disguise of self-scrutiny) fifteen minutes after her illumination: her husband is "un homme dépourvu d'imagination, et, de plus, extrêmement gentil" (35); "a man devoid of imagination, and in addition extremely kind" (26). The whole elaborate scheme derives from one source: her mind. She is the ultimate (and only) mastermind behind the theory that seeks to solve the mystery by casting it as a love plot or test of love. The explanation she provides is therefore essentially susceptible. She seems to be an unreliable narrator in the sense that she misreports, misreads, and misregards, which forces the audience to discard her "words and reconstruct an alternative" (Phelan 219) to get the things right. On the other hand, that she admits she was wrong in this particular case makes her tend toward reliability. She is systematically neither. Just as a narrator can be "unreliable in different ways at different points" (Phelan 52), s/he can also fluctuate between reliability and unreliability in the course of narration (which makes the audience's role all the more challenging). This kind of narrator, by being alternately or in degree reliable and unreliable, is always to be doubted (Phelan 53), which makes him or her, basically, unreliable until found truthful at a particular point. Hence, not even the narrator's unreliability is always reliable.

In Darrieussecq's case, the situation is even more complex than that. First, the nature of the phenomena that she perceives and reports defy accurate narrating beyond reasonable doubt. The very ontology of a ghost is questionable, as is the epistemology of its human perception. One could dub the novel's ghost an "unreliable character," were it not an unnecessary term for a persistently reticent agent.[5] The narrator could not, even if she wished, be totally reliable in connection with ghosts. Second, even when giving an unreliable account of the world around her, she performatively provides a reliable or at least truthful-seeming representation of her inner world, the workings of her own mind.

READING GHOSTS' BODY LANGUAGE

The first complication, mentioned above, relates to the novel's main concern, made explicit in its French title, the birth (and consequent existence) of ghosts. Ghost, in the meaning of "the soul of a deceased person, spoken of as appearing in a visible form, or otherwise manifesting its presence, to the living" ("Ghost," def. 8a) is a matter, albeit an immaterial one, of belief, not a verifiable fact. It is symptomatic that we ask if someone believes in ghosts, in the plural, rather than in *a* ghost, in the singular. The ghosts' mode of existence problematizes not only reliability, but also the very idea of Theory of Mind or mind reading as constructs or activities based on corporeal data.

The ghosts do not have bodies (of their own) to base a theory or a reading on. Ghost, in the meaning of the "immaterial part of man as distinct from the body or material part" ("Ghost," def. 3a), seems, by definition, bodiless. The ghost does not have a proper body, even doubly so. When still in the living body of its host, the immaterial part (the soul or spirit) of a human is not called a ghost. Ghost as the "soul of a deceased person" appears "in a visible form" or otherwise manifests its presence ("Ghost," def. 8a). The visible form of a ghost is the body of another, an artifactual or prosthetic body, or an ambiguous entity like fog (Derrida 7, 126, 194).[6] A corollary of this state of affairs is that visuality or, more accurately, physical resemblance is not the ghost's primary attribute. Not only does a ghost's appearance differ from what used to be its original bodily host, the ghost is also unidentical with its *present* physical appearance in the sense that it is traditionally believed to lack a mirror-image. Therefore a ghost will not recognize itself in a mirror, but *others* will recognize it as one by this very token (Derrida 156). Nevertheless, the very distinction of the ghost as mind, spirit, or soul from the body demarcates its invisible contours by negation. A ghost is what body or matter is not. Without what frames it, a ghost would be not only imperceptible, but also unspeakable.

The incarnation of spirit in *some* body other than the one it inhabited while still alive, indeed gives birth to a ghost (cf. Derrida 127). A ghost is, thus, engendered posthumously, but the most important aspects of its mind derive, to create a preposterous neologism, from the subject's "pre-posthumous" phase.[7] Hence, perhaps, the *birth* of phantoms in Darrieussecq. The *ghost's spirit*, conceived of as preceding incarnation, would be an impossibility, for the possessive case contradicts, in spectral logic, the state of not being possessed. What all this means to Practice of Body (also known as Theory of Mind) is that the ghost's body language is, by definition, a second language, a language articulated or, rather, gesticulated in and by a foreign body.

In *Naissance des fantômes*, ghosts appear in the narrator's life as metaphors and representations before there are any manifestations proper. She has been afraid of ghosts since her childhood and has shown exceptional talent in dreaming up their qualities in dreadful detail (43 / 33). She is afraid of ghosts, not because of their snatched, horrendous bodies, but because of their evil minds. She does have a Theory of Posthumous Mind based on a Practice of Invaded Body. Ghosts are, in her reading of their semi-vaporous corporeality, malicious and scheming, stalking innocent humans with "des griffes, des dents, des ventouses" (43); "claws, teeth, suckers" (34). She has a number of ghostbusting means, the most important of which is her husband and his steady breathing at night (31). With her husband gone, she is exposed to the shadows of the night and left with her old, less efficient ghost-repelling tricks: thinking of her own madness ("folie" [43]), light reading (even gory horror, but not fantasy or flat realism), repeated turning on of lights, and staying awake all night long (43–44 / 33–34).

In a dreadful twist commonly found in modern ghost stories, spectrality draws so near that it verges on incorporating the narrator: she momentarily acquires visual attributes of the very entities she fears. When she spreads, for cleansing purposes, green paste on her face, it makes her look, besides an alien and creature of the depths, like "un fantôme vieux modèle" (37); "like an outdated model of ghost" (28). She is, thus, a veritable mirror-image of a ghost, of an entity that allegedly has none. Reflective absence is conventionally a token of a ghost's presence. That she can see her face in the mirror indicates that she only resembles, and not actually is, a ghost.

To her surprise and awe, she witnesses a manifestation in broad daylight, which deviates from the usual midnight appearance of the classic specters she is accustomed to dreading.[8] Significantly, the narrator does not explicitly call the apparition a "ghost" but a "shadow" (*ombre*). It could be read as referring to another kind of (supernatural or unnatural) entity besides a phantom, but, in the context of literary ghosts, it rather reads as a euphemism reminiscent of some staged apparitions in Marlowe and Shakespeare (cf. Greenblatt 156, 170). The odd presence is a "densification de l'espace" ("densification of space") and "un épaississement de l'air" ("thickening of [. . .] air," a three-dimensional "colonne de l'air dans l'air" ("column of air in the air") and, although an "ombre" ("shadow"), "si claire, si fluctuante dans la lumière" ("so bright, so fluctuating in the light") (54–55 / 46). She also tries to make contact with this strange phenomenon, but it does not react to her gestures ("il n'y avait pas d'effet de miroir" [55]).[9] Astonishingly, the entity is not completely immaterial: when the narrator steps inside it, she feels "une pression, une prise" (55); "a pressure, a hold" (46) In any case, the narrator seems to presume that the phenomenon is a living entity, perhaps even having a mind, but she does not regard it, unlike she does the imagined nocturnal ghosts, as malicious or frightening.

Some thirty pages later, the thickening and densification of space is specified as that of a "solidification du vide" (86); an emptiness or "solidification of void" (77). That empty space is, predictably, created by the disappearance of her husband. It is not exactly an absence, a vacuous space formerly occupied by him, but an invisible entity substituting for that space ("Le vide s'était fait à l'endroit même qu'il occupait" [86]).[10] The difference is significant, since it implies that her husband, or his soul or mind, has returned, as the aptly named revenants customarily do, incarnated in another, albeit indiscernible, "body." This state of affairs reminds one of Derrida's formulations in *Specters of Marx*: "there is never any becoming-specter of the spirit without at least an appearance of flesh, in a space of invisible visibility, like the dis-appearance of an apparition" (126). Again, the only thing that the narrator reads in this fluctuating texture of a body is that it relates to the *existence* of a substituting intending subjectivity, specifically to that of her husband, but without any modalities.

Soon the narrator does, however, arrive at a conclusion concerning the reading of phantom minds, on both general and specific levels. In general, she concludes, "[m]ême nommés, touchés ou traversés, les fantômes ne perdent ni en puissance ni en indulgence" (96); "[e]ven when named, touched or crossed through, ghosts lose none of their power or indulgence" (87). And, in particular, "[m]on mari, copiant les morts, allait me faire signe et me rendre à l'éxistence" (96); "[m]y husband, copying the dead, was going to give me a sign and return me to existence [. . .]" (88). Neither of these readings is based on actual bodily information. The first is a generalizing statement, a deductive *idée reçue* of sorts. The second is speculation disguised as logical necessity:

> Mon mari était forcément quelque part, gazeux peut-être, à la limite de sortir de l'univers, mais quelque part forcément, penché sur les bords (ce qu'il faut bien supposer de bords) et me regardant; comme les morts dont les vivants savent qu'il sont encore là [. . .]. (96)
>
> [My husband was necessarily somewhere, vaporous perhaps and on the verge of exiting the universe, but necessarily somewhere, leaning over the edge (whatever edge we must suppose there is) and watching me; like the dead whose living know they are still there [. . .].] (88)

The postulated, gas-like body becomes visible a few pages later at a supermarket where "[l]e bac fumait et dans cette fumée se devinait un corps gazeux informe et flottant, doué pourtant d'une sorte de volonté [. . .]" (109–10); "[t]he freezer gave off a vapor and in that vapor a gaseous body could be distinguished, formless and floating, though endowed with a kind of will [. . .]" (101). The materialization is not only visual but also haptic: "je tendais la main et cela me caressait délicatement les doigts, me pressait amoureusement la paume" (110); "I stretched out a hand and it caressed my fingers delicately, amorously pressed my palm" (102). In both manifestations, then, the almost incorporeal body is readable or at least indicative of a will or emotion.

The next phase in the gradual materialization of the phantom (or shadow, or whatever it should be called, for it is not unequivocal that the supernatural entity is the same one on each occasion) is the predictable manifestation of the husband. At her mother's farewell party toward the end of the novel, the narrator and some other guests witness the husband's semitransparent figure emanating before their very eyes. The narrator-wife reads his mind more specifically than that of the supermarket specter: "mon mari sembla hésiter, vacillant sur le seuil" (144) ("my husband seemed to hesitate, trembling on the threshold" [136]); "[m]on mari, malgré son teint lumineux, avait l'air anxieux et comme délavé" (145) ("[m]y husband, despite his luminous hue, looked anxious and washed-out" [138]). When she tries to touch him, he disappears, leaving behind only some residual light on her fingers and eyes (149 / 140).

The novel ends with the narrator returning home and finding her husband there, looking exactly the same as the day he disappeared. She reads his body language and infers from it even more complicated intentions than at the party: "il semblait attendre quelque chose, comme si c'était à moi de l'accueillir, de lui demander, que sais-je, s'il avait bon voyage" (157); "he seemed to be waiting for something, as if it were up to me to welcome him, to ask him, what do I know, if he had had a nice trip" (149–50). He embraces her with his "mains peu matérielles" ("barely material hands") thus without exactly touching her but charging her with a particular energy, and disappears (161–62 / 153–54). This also puts an end to her kind of supernatural (and natural, in the sense of faunal) mind reading activities:

> je sais seulement avoir cessé, à ce moment-là, de me demander si mon mari (si les chats, les oiseaux, les poissons et les mouches aux yeux à facettes) sentait et voyait tout de même ce que moi je sentais et voyais. (162)
>
> [at that moment I stopped wondering whether my husband (or cats, birds, fish and flies with their many-faceted eyes) felt and saw what I felt and saw.] (154)

This last sentence of the novel may be read as a statement implying that all the apparitions she has recounted so far do in fact relate to her as a feeling and seeing narrator, and therefore are not necessarily reliable accounts of actual happenings in the storyworld, but, rather, projections of her own mind.

As is commonplace in ghost stories, either ghosts actually exist in *Naissance des fantômes*'s storyworld or the narrator only believes she sees them (possibly because she is mad). In the latter case, it is the narrator's and not the supernatural entity's mind that is foregrounded, and the recursiveness easily becomes self-referential: the mind represents itself even when ostensibly representing others' minds (or any constituents of the storyworld). The "architectural truth" (cf. Cosmides and Tooby 60–61) of the narrator's metarepresentations is possibly that of a haunted house.

The epigraph taken from *Alice's Adventures in Wonderland* by Lewis Carroll relates to the function and traumatic nature of the apparitions in Darrieussecq's novel. Trying to find a way to escape a possible beheading, Alice notices a "curious appearance in the air" that soon turns out be a grin; she says to herself, "It's the Cheshire-Cat: now I shall have somebody to talk to" (Carroll 112). Darrieussecq's autodiegetic narrator can be seen as endeavoring to cope with the shock of her husband's possible death by dreaming up or conjuring an apparitional addressee or, rather, silent companion (for she does not address her words to the entity, nor does it, or he, ever verbally respond to her). In any case, curiosity and airiness connect the two entities at the initial stage. The Cheshire Cat also ties in with the narrator's own spectral qualities. Listening to her friend's relentless speech, the narrator produces a veritable *risus sardonicus* on her face:

> Je m'enforçai à un sourire que j'espérais aimant, attentif, et le plus convaincant possible, mais qui dut ressenbler, à mon corps défendant, à une manifestation physique aussi étrange que les coquetteries du chat du Cheshire [. . .]. (78–79)
>
> [I forced myself to give a smile that I hoped was loving, attentive, and as convincing as possible, but that must (against my will) have seemed a physical manifestation as strange as the coquetries of the Cheshire cat [. . .].] (69)

This feline metamorphosis is all the more prominent as it comes immediately after the extended section in which the narrator is metaphorically cast as a dog (75–76 / 66–67).

MINDWORKS

Naissance des fantômes contains not only heightened descriptions of (possibly) supernatural entities and their relation to posthumous minds, but also minute accounts of natural processes inside the brain and nervous system. The workings of the mind are hence depicted in quite a literal sense of the term. Narrationally, the posthumous and the neural are equally paranormal in the sense that they are invisible to the naked eye and only available to the mind's eye. The narrator repeatedly zooms in on the molecular level of the mind but also brings metaphoric language (drawn mainly from the source of mechanical domain) into play. She, as it were, reverses her narrational strategy of projecting her mind to the outside world by introjecting external realms to thematize the structure and processes of the mind.

When telephoning her mother-in-law in the novel's second chapter, the narrator describes what she hears happening:

> Je n'ai plus entendu qu'une respiration raidie, la pulsation presque palpable d'influx cérébraux, la forme que peut prendre, entre deux personnes en contact dans le noir, un effort ou un vacillement de la mémoire. (27)
>
> [I heard nothing but a tense breathing, the almost palpable impulse of every nerve cell in the brain, the form that contact between two people in the dark can take, a straining or flickering of memory.] (17)

Elsewhere, she continues the mechanical or machinic metaphor and conceives of her neurons as "rouillé" (92); "rusting" (84). She also takes a cue from the moving sea foam she sees during a walk in conceptualizing her mind:

> J'imaginais ainsi mon cerveau, soumis à la pression et vaporisé, toutes les connexions de mon cerveau peu à peu défaites, brumeuses et floues [. . .], et ma pensée se vaporisait à son tour [. . .]. (68–69)
>
> [That was how I imagined my brain, subjected to great pressure and vaporized, all its connections undone little by little, foggy and slack [. . .], and my mind was vaporized in turn [. . .].] (59)

In addition, she repeatedly refers to the molecules of thought, thinking, and body (94, 98, 125, 140–41 / 86, 89, 116, 132–33).

The narrator even gives lively accounts of how the animal mind functions. These takes on the animals' inner worlds are hypothetical, since she presumably cannot enter their "consciousness" or the organs where it possibly resides. She is not, in other words, omniscient in any reliable way as regards these strata of the storyworld. The narrator makes both normal and paranormal contact with a sea lion on the beach:

> de toutes mes forces j'ai lancé un caillou, pile entre les deux yeux que l'abruti a ouverts un peu plus grands, l'information a cheminé à travers ses synapses bardées de lard, deux neurones ont réussi à se détacher de leur graisse pour inaugurer leur roulement à billes [. . .]. (67)
>
> [I threw a pebble with everything I had and got him [the dominant male sea lion] right between his two large eyes, which the brute opened a little wider, the information made its way along his lard-encased synapses, two neurons succeeded in detaching themselves from their bed of fat to set the marbles rolling [. . .].] (57–58)

Another animal mind is described through the narrator's metaphoric metamorphosis into a dog. Listening to her friend Jacqueline, the narrator finds herself, dog-like, only reacting to a familiar string of sounds:

> Je restais béate devant cet étonnant phénomène, et comme les chiens, dont on dit que dans le discours le plus assertif de leur maître ils n'entendent, salivants, que la répétition martelée de leur nom [. . .], j'étais assise sur mon derrière, la bouche ouverte et le poil lissé, une queue presque tangible battant dans mon dos au rythme bien marqué des paroles de Jacqueline [. . .]. (75–76)
>
> [I sat and gaped at this astonishing phenomenon like a dog that supposedly understands, as it listens, drooling, to its master's most vehement speeches, only the hammering repetition of its name [. . .]; I was sitting on my hindquarters, mouth open and panting, fur smoothed down, an almost tangible tail thumping behind me to the heavy beat of Jacqueline's words [. . .].] (66)

The extended canine metaphor generates a "dog schema" for reading the poor metamorphosed creature's (that is, her own) mind: "j'écoutais fascinée, salivant toujours davantage, attendant quoi, un sucre, la promenade, qu'on me flatte du plat de la main" (77); "I was listening [. . .] in fascination, still drooling copiously and waiting—for what? a sugar cube, my walk, someone to pat me with an outstretched hand?" (67). There is a connection here to the "spectral schema" that the narrator applies, at the beginning of the novel, to the phantoms' or shadows' minds. The received knowledge or *idées reçues* is triggered almost unwittingly, but might as well turn out to be Barthesian *doxa*, false knowledge. Whatever their truth value, these schemata are versions of the narrator's paranormal and supernatural Theories of Mind.

ELECTRONIC MEDIA AND SPIRITUALISTIC MEDIUMS

The narrator is not content with speculating on minds or with trying to reach them by means of extended metaphors. She also has recourse to several methods of making supernatural contact. Most of these attempts appear as ordinary media use on the surface, but the novel clearly taps many occult streaks discernible in media history (for spiritualism and electronic telecommunication, see Sconce, and Keskinen 93–119).

The first medium in her search for her disappeared husband is the telephone. She tries to call him at his real estate agency, but the only response she gets is a sonic verification that he is not present (or not answering the phone): "J'entendais de très loin les pointillés de l'absence de mon mari" (22–23); "I heard the stipplings of my husband's absence from very far away" (13). She also calls her friend Jacqueline, her mother-in-law, and, finally, the police. What is common to all these calls is that she does not primarily want to reach the person or instance at the other end of the line but to make contact with her husband, or at least to learn that he is alright. In this sense, she uses the telephonic medium in a spiritualistic fashion, since she cannot be certain whether he is dead or alive, and whether his well-being is posthumous or not.

In the midst of her telephone calls she turns on the television, which seems more like an automatic gesture than a conscious reach for information. Soon, however, the program flow begins to relate, in her hypothetical mind, to her husband: "il me semblait qu'à tout moment le présentateur prendrait une mine grave pour annoncer la disparition de mon mari [. . .]" (18); "any moment now, I thought, the announcer would put on a serious face to announce the disappearance of my husband," who would have ended up in a variety of freak accidents (9). After calling the police, she turns on the TV again, this time "très fort" ("very loud"), and the debate on "choses concrètes" ("hard facts") between two electoral candidates sounds strangely soothing to her (30 /20). The medium itself does not, however, remain concrete or stable: "L'image bleue de la télé semblait surgir hors de son cardre et dégoutter en l'air, suspendue dans l'espace comme un rideau de douche" (31); "The blue image on the TV seemed to overrun its frame and precipitate in the air, suspended in space like a shower curtain" (21). Analogously, she senses that he is, as a bodily person, gone forever. What the overrunning and precipitating image resembles is ectoplasm oozing from a spiritualistic medium's mouth. It can refer to another kind of hope, to that of a paranormal encounter or contact with the absent husband. Later the TV screen sheds green light (originating from a documentary about the Amazon) (32 / 24), and the narrator's emotions sympathize with the vistas represented in the documentary, ranging from the low angle (panic and anguish) to the high (relief and newly kindled hope):

> D'un coup, comme un hélicoptère s'élevait droit par-delà les arbres, dévoilant le trajet du fleuve et la pelote de ses affluentes, d'un coup comme je reprenais mon souffle dans le ciel grand ouvert je dis que [. . .] il était évident et obligatoire que je dormirais avec mon mari [. . .]. (36)
>
> [Suddenly, as a helicopter rose straight into the sky over the trees revealing the path of the river and the tangled mass of its tributaries, suddenly, as I began to

> breathe again in the wide open sky, I told myself that [. . .] I would be sleeping with my husband [. . .].] (27)

In her next phase of supernatural or at least paranormal media use, she is even more formally mediatic at the cost of the message or program content: "Je changeais de chaîne sans regarder, j'essayais de sentir sa présence quelque part, dans les rues, dans la ville, sur la planète" (38); "I changed the channels without watching, I was trying to feel his presence somewhere, in the streets, in the city, on the planet" (29). She explicitly conceives of her channel-hopping as technologically assisted "telepathy"—both in the literal and metaphorical senses of the term: "je voulais croire qu'en atteignant la bonne longueur d'onde j'allais pouvoir retrouver mon mari par la seule vibration de mes antennes [. . .]" (38); "I wanted to believe that if I achieved the correct wavelength I would be able to find my husband again by mere vibration of my antennae [. . .]" (29).

The narrator's attempts at making contact with her husband turn out to be, in spite of their apparent resemblance to detecting electronic voice phenomena (EVP), paranormal rather than supernatural (for EVP, see Sconce 85–91). She tries to reach her *living* husband on the spiritual or mental level, not to reach him in the afterlife. In a fit of depression she comes to the following conclusion: "si je ne parvenais pas à joindre mon mari [. . .], c'est qu'il était mort" (38); "I could not succeed in reaching my husband [. . .] because he was dead" (29). There is, however, a spiritualistic streak in her paranormal activities. This is especially pertinent to her use of the computer. In her search for her husband, she repeatedly goes to his real estate agency, sits at his desk, and uses his computer.[11] The computer provides a window on a world beyond the normal perception. She finds out that her husband's business goes on as usual, with the commissions bringing in money, although he is only virtually, not bodily, present in the transactions:

> autant d'opérations qui n'avaient sans doute de référence qu'informatique, mais indiquaient très réellement, sous les modifications spectrales des pixels, que peut-être, quelque part, mon mari (ou quelque esprit tutélaire) continuait de penser à moi. (114)
>
> [undoubtedly none of these operations had any reference outside of cyberspace, but they indicated in a very real way, beneath the spectral modifications of the pixels, that perhaps, somewhere, my husband (or some tutelary spirit) went on thinking about me.] (104)

Again, she reads the mind of her husband in the absence of his body, on the basis of unsubstantial evidence.

Sitting in his chair and participating in "ce qui avait été son atmosphère" (113–14) ("in what had been his atmosphere" [104]), she virtually becomes him, or at least assumes a number of his roles. She makes appointments in his name, visits the Web sites he had been to, and engages in online chats with strangers, possibly using his alias name. She, in a way, becomes a medium who channels her husband's gestures and words at electronic séances of sorts. The computer also figures as a writing implement, and thus functions in a more traditional manner, in her paranormal or supernatural pursuits. She starts writing the story of her husband's disappearance and her wait, that is, the narrative that constitutes the novel *Naissance des fantômes*. She writes about her writing: "frappant sur le clavier j'essayais ainsi [. . .] de me clarifier peut-être les idées [. . .]" (114); "I tried, tapping on the keyboard, [. . .] perhaps to clarify my thoughts [. . .]" (104–05). The rapping or knocking[12] and the clairvoyant vision implied in the diction of her account of writing can be read as indicative of the spiritualistic or supernatural facet of her project. Indeed, the computer keyboard functions, formally, as an Ouija board, with the standardized QWERTY system making automatic-seeming (supernatural or paranormal) contact via writing possible. In practice, however, the act of writing marks separation rather than connection. The narrator finds the "writing to the moment" principle, routinely encountered in epistolary and diary fiction, to be impossible:

> je n'écrivais pas aussi vite que je vivais, et pourtant cette vie était lente. Et dans le retard accumulé, qui semblait mimer la disjonction temporelle dont je souffrais parfois si violemment [. . .], dans ce retard je reconnaissais le temps que je vivais mieux que si j'avais pu l'écrire sans écart. (115)
>
> [I didn't write as quickly as I was living, yet this life of mine was slow. And in the accumulating lag, which seemed to mimic the temporal disjunctions from which I sometimes suffered so violently [. . .], I recognized the time I was living through better than if I had been able to write it without the lag.] (105)

Thus, she makes contact with her own life rather than with her husband's possible afterlife. In fact, the very act of narrating, which could function as a connecting channel, generates a hiatus that becomes an emblem of the couple's temporal and ontological separation:

> le retard que prenait sur ma vie le récit de cette disparition, ou plutôt de ses effets en négatif, ce retard était celui que je me sentais prendre sur mon fantôme de mari, parti plus loin que moi dans des espaces qui m'échappaient. (116)
>
> [the growing lag between the story of this disappearance, or rather of its effects in the negative, and my life was the same one I felt widening between myself and my phantom husband, gone much farther than I into the spaces that eluded me.] (106–07)

The contact with herself, or with her own life, that the narrator's act of storytelling creates by widening the lag and gap between the two strata of happening, is also of a supernatural nature. During the process, the narrator herself acquires spectral attributes:

> Mais s'il ne restait de moi qu'une coque vide, ce que j'avais été se dissolvait dans l'atmosphère pour participer presque harmonieusement à la réalité de l'absence et du vide, d'une façon désormais plus gazeuse qu'immobile. (116)
>
> [What remained of me was only an empty shell, what I once had been dissolved in the atmosphere to participate almost harmoniously in the reality of absence and void, in a way that became more ethereal than immobile.] (106)

"Gas-like" or "vaporous" are the usual attributes attached to the "shadow" or phantom in the novel, and this choice of epithet connects the narrator to these semi-immaterial entities. She may be one of the ghosts raised that the plural in the novel's French title suggests. When she becomes semi-immaterial or incorporeal, she must perform her mind reading activities (aimed at herself) without a discernible body and articulate body language. In this case, too, her Theory of Phantom Mind equals Practice of Absent Body.

Reading written minds: From the unnatural to the supernatural

But perhaps reading the phantom minds of absent or dead bodies is not, after all, as curious an activity in fiction as I have suggested. I could turn the spiritualistic table and state that it is, in fact, the unmarked feature of reading literary language also known as narrative fiction.

This primordial supernaturalness or at least paranormality of narrative fiction can be crystallized in one word, albeit with a double meaning: character. Firstly, characters, in the sense of personages, only exist in writing, as inscribed representations of their bodies and minds. Both are absent as actual or bodily entities. In most cases, that absence is of an ontological nature, since fictional characters usually lack worldly referents. Fictional characters are thus, in an important sense, "posthumous" from the outset. They are dead because they never were alive, or, rather, they arise after their primordial death and give the impression of being living people. To emulate Lisa Zunshine, the problem of *why* we read fiction turns into *how* we *can* read fiction (and claim that we read characters' minds).

Secondly, character, in the sense of a graphic sign, or a letter of the alphabet, is a synecdoche of language. Literary language can be thought of as a subset of natural or ordinary language, a heightened or second-order version of the everyday linguistic mode. In this sense, literary language is "unnatural." On the other hand, it is debatable whether "natural language" is natural at all. De Saussure and the majority of modern linguists would claim that language is an arbitrary and conventional system developed for communicative purposes, without any relation to "nature."[13] In this constellation, the language of fiction appears even more unnatural or abnormal.

Consequently, reading becomes not only an unnatural, but a supernatural activity. All fiction conjures absent characters, gives them life and voice, preserving, in the residue of writing, what would not be otherwise present either on account of death or primordial nonexistence. Ghost stories perform these literary conjuring tricks explicitly, but the house of fiction is always, implicitly, haunted. The nature of fiction as make-belief is thus profoundly supernatural, and the reader's willing suspension of disbelief amounts to belief in literature's ghost world. By the same token, many of the acts performed by narration are not only unnatural, but paranormal. The narrator's telepathic or prophetic omniscience and superhuman mind reading capabilities are just the most obvious examples of literary paranormality.[14]

In addition to talking about natural narratives (Fludernik) or unnatural narration (Richardson), we could also mind the supernatural aspects of (reading) narrative fiction.[15] If "*on one level* our evolved cognitive architecture indeed does not fully distinguish between real and fictional people" (Zunshine, *Why We Read Fiction* 19), the same could hold true of living and dead persons when they are not present. And if "fiction engages, teases, and pushes to its tentative limits our mind-reading capacity" (Zunshine, *Why We Read Fiction* 4), one of the boundaries tested is the ultimate one, the one between life and death, between shared presence and irrecoverable absence. In this sense, the cognitive reward of reading fiction can turn out to be of an extreme kind.

Notes

1 Summing up the theory-theory branch of ToM, Alan Palmer writes, "No one suggests that what people use is a self-conscious and fully worked theory. All agree that it is used intuitively and non-consciously" (143). Presumably the same could be said of the simulation theory in ToM as well. For a discussion of the seeming facility of mind reading, see also Zunshine, *Why We Read Fiction* 3–4, 13–16. In her recent article, Lisa Zunshine emphasizes that, in actual practice, "*theory* in Theory of Mind and *reading* in mind-reading" do not imply intentional and conscious attribution of mind ("Theory of Mind" 67; emphasis in original). For a metapsychological critique of the "theory" in ToM, see Costall and Leudar.

2 Marie Darrieussecq (1969-) is an internationally renowned experimental author of French Basque origin. She has written eight novels, a collection of short stories, a play, and an unpublished dissertation on autofiction in French literature. Darrieussecq's first novel, *Truismes* (1996; *Pig Tales*), turned into an international success, which enabled her to leave her teaching position at the University of Lille and to become a full time writer of fiction. *Naissance des fantômes* (1999; *My Phantom Husband*) is her second novel. I quote *Naissance des fantômes* and Esther Allen's translation of it parenthetically in the text.

3 Strange disappearances are not uncommon in folklore and literature, and the explanations given to these mysteries often tend toward the paranormal. Two examples of the disappearance novel may suffice to demonstrate the dynamic within the subgenre. Tim O'Brien's *In the Lake of the Woods* (1994) reverses Darrieussecq's basic situation by making a wife vanish and her husband search for her, or at least for a reason for her disappearance. Although the supernatural is not explicitly suggested as a solution to the mystery, ghosts do figure in the husband's Vietnam War secrets. In Georges Perec's lipogrammatic novel *La Disparition* (1969; *A Void / A Vanishing*), a character's disappearance takes place doubly in the sense that both a fictional personage, Anton Voyl, and the letter E are entirely absent from it. In Perec's *Les Revenentes* (1972; *The Exeter Text*), the ghostly E returns *en masse*, since it is the only vowel used in the whole novella.

4 The possible death of her husband is not the only case of demise in her immediate family. She has had several miscarriages during her seven-year marriage, and one of her pregnancies even lasted almost six months. The dead fetuses, the ghosts of her unborn babies, or at least the idea of pregnancy, can be seen as haunting her, albeit in a subdued way, in brief references to real or pseudo pregnancies (52,

54, 106 / 43, 45, 97) and to metaphorically or literally dead children (70, 130 / 61, 121). Her unsuccessful work of mourning could be interpreted as having turned into melancholia, resulting in apparitions in the classic Freudian manner (cf. Rickels 16). *Naissance des fantômes* features themes also found in Darrieussecq's other works, and posthumous presence of sorts is a veritable leitmotif in her fiction. The disappearance of family members recurs in *Le Mal de mer* (1999; *Undercurrents / Breathing Underwater*), and the persistent grief over a dead child is focused on in both *Bref séjour chez les vivants* (2001; *A Brief Stay with the Living*) and *Tom est mort* (2007; *Tom is Dead*). *Le Bébé* (2002; *The Baby*) shows that a living child, too, can haunt his parents. For critical essays on *Naissance des fantômes*, see Robson; Horvath; Narjoux; and Jordan.

5 In addition to being ontologically fragile, a ghost can, when articulating, be as unreliable as any other narrator; cf. the lying ghost in Akira Kurosawa's 1951 film *Rashomon* (Richardson 3, 94).

6 In this essay I mainly utilize Derrida's concise account of the lore and study of ghosts. Derrida's conception of specters is paradoxically ahistorical or at least synthetic, but its heuristic force lies elsewhere. Re-evaluating ontology in the tradition of continental philosophy, Derrida coins the neologism *hauntology*, which comprises both ontology and haunting: "This logic of haunting would not be merely larger and more powerful than an ontology or thinking of Being [. . .]. It would harbor within itself, but like circumscribed places or particular effects, eschatology and teleology themselves" (10). In Thomas Mical's reading, hauntology is "an intellectual conjuring trick where the spectral after-image of the thought of ontology becomes its prior foundation—by situating hauntology as prior to ontology [. . .], as the unexpected chain-rattling return of repressed difference within any sweeping static ontological claims." I find hauntology productive in reading Darrieussecq's novel whose central concern pertains to the absent husband's ontological status. For contextualizing readings of ghosts in literature, see Greenblatt; Wolfreys; Dickerson; and Kolmar and Carpenter, eds.

7 In popular tradition, ghosts are earthbound spirits who will haunt the living "until a wrong done to them or by them has been set right" (Gillie 540). In Rickels's reading of Freud's *Totem and Taboo*, "the hostility the dead, while still alive, had aroused in the still living is attributed to the phantoms of the deceased who now persecute the survivors" (16). The ghost's motivation or mind-set, whether actual or attributed, hence originates from the realm of the living.

8 Midnight is traditionally the specters' most common showtime, although some ghosts are also believed to make an appearance in the day (Greenblatt 41, 114–15, 274n77). Darrieussecq's novel follows a medieval and Renaissance pattern in the sense that "[t]he ghost generally appears shortly after death, while the memory of the deceased [. . .] is still fresh" in the mind of the loved one (Greenblatt 41, 291n45).

9 In Allen's translation, this sentence reads somewhat vaguely "it didn't move" (46); Helen Stevenson renders it more literally as "there was no mirror effect" (45). The mirror is important in at least three ways in the scene. The lack of the mirror effect,

that is, of reflection, momentarily makes the narrator resemble a ghost in front of a looking glass. Second, that she can step inside and through this airy "mirror" puts her in the position of Lewis Carroll's Alice; this intertextual connection is further reinforced by the Darrieussecq novel's Cheshire Cat epigraph. Thirdly, the mirror effect relates, in the context of cognitive science, to mirror neurons and simulation theory (cf. Goldman); the shadow's reluctance to imitate the narrator's gestures may point to its autism, not being a primate, or fundamental nonexistence.

10 In Allen's wording, "Void had sprung up in the place he once filled" (77), and in Stevenson's, "The emptiness had appeared in the very place where he'd once been" (77). The ghost's invisibility equals perfect transparency. In this sense, invisibility is not a matter of "embodied transparency," that is, "perfect access to other people's minds via their observable behavior" (Zunshine, "Theory of Mind" 72), because there is no discernible body to observe. Nor is it exactly a matter of a "transparent mind" in Dorrit Cohn's sense; the ghost's consciousness is not psycho-narrated but merely rendered as translucent as its "body."

11 Blond and curious, the narrator acts, in this scene, like a cyber-age Goldilocks. Another juvenile blonde, Carroll's Alice, and via her the fantastic in children's literature, are evoked throughout the novel. One example will suffice to demonstrate this economy of simultaneous allusion to supernatural technology and transgressive figures. Maniacally cleaning her apartment, the narrator has recourse to a homonymy of the mysterious oceanic element where spirit beings were once believed to travel, the ether (cf. Sconce 63–66): "I sprinkled all the windows with ether [. . .] and rubbed hard until they were spotless, you could pass right through them" (91).

12 There are also references to posthumous rapping, both imagined and (presumably) real, by skeletons or spirits in the novel (96, 139 / 88, 131).

13 In contrast with Saussurian arbitrariness, some contemporary linguists emphasize "natural factors affecting and motivating linguistic forms and functions" (Fludernik 18). Mark Turner's take on the naturalness / arbitrariness debate "naturalizes" what is usually regarded as the second-order language in both schools' literature. Turner claims that story, parable, and metaphor precede language and are basic to thought. In his model, language follows from mental capacities that are, primordially, literary.

14 In cognitive psychology, the concept of "mind-reading has nothing to do with plain old telepathy" (Zunshine, *Why We Read Fiction* 6), but in criticism, it may have, as in Nicholas Royle's thematization of literary omniscience.

15 If Monika Fludernik is able to call her theory of natural narratives, which she defines on the basis of "the *cognitive frames* by means of which texts are interpreted," *natural narratology* (12, 312–15), perhaps my tentative coinage *supernatural narratology* could have, at least in a jocular frame of mind, some heuristic value.

Works Cited

Carroll, Lewis. *Alice's Adventures in Wonderland* and *Through the Looking-Glass*. Harmondsworth: Penguin, 1966. Print.

Cohn, Dorrit. *Transparent Minds: Narrative Modes for Presenting Consciousness in Fiction*. Princeton: Princeton University Press, 1978. Print.

Cosmides, Leda, and John Tooby. "Considering the Source: The Evolution of Adaptations for Decoupling and Metarepresentations." *Metarepresentations: A Multidisciplinary Perspective*. Ed. Dan Sperber. New York: Oxford University Press, 2000. 53–116. Print.

Costall, Alan, and Ivan Leudar. "Where Is the 'Theory' in Theory of Mind?" *Theory & Psychology* 14.5 (2004): 623–46. Print.

Darrieussecq, Marie. *Naissance des fantômes*. 1998. Paris: Gallimard, 1999. Print.

---. *My Phantom Husband*. Trans. Esther Allen. New York: The New Press, 1999. Print.

---. *My Phantom Husband*. Trans. Helen Stevenson. London: Faber and Faber, 1999. Print.

Derrida, Jacques. *Specters of Marx: The State of the Debt, the Work of Mourning, and the New International*. Trans. Peggy Kamuff. New York: Routledge, 1994. Print.

Dickerson, Vanessa D. *Victorian Ghosts in the Noontide: Women Writers and the Supernatural*. Columbia: University of Missouri Press, 1996. Print.

Fludernik, Monika. *Towards a 'Natural' Narratology*. London: Routledge, 1996. Print.

"Ghost." *The Oxford English Dictionary Online*. 2nd ed. 28 Feb. 2008. Web. http://www.oed.com.

Gillie, Christopher. *Longman Companion to English Literature*. London: Longman, 1972. Print.

Goldman, Alvin I. *Simulating Minds: The Philosophy, Psychology, and Neuroscience of Mindreading*. New York: Oxford University Press, 2006. Print.

Greenblatt, Stephen. *Hamlet in Purgatory*. Princeton: Princeton University Press, 2002. Print.

Horvath, Christina. "Le fantastique contemporain: un fantastique au feminin." *Iris* 24 (2002–2003): 171–80. Print.

Jordan, Shirley. "Saying the Unsayable: Identities in Crisis in the Early Novels of Marie Darrieussecq." *Women's Writing in Contemporary France: New Writers, New Literatures in the 1990s*. Ed. Gill Rye and Michael Worton. Manchester: Manchester University Press, 2002. 142–53. Print.

Keskinen, Mikko. *Audio Book: Essays on Sound Technologies in Narrative Fiction*. Lanham: Lexington Books, 2008. Print.

Kolmar, Wendy, and Lynette Carpenter, eds. *Haunting the House of Fiction: Feminist Perspectives on Ghost Stories by American Women*. Knoxville: University of Tennessee Press, 1991. Print.

Mical, Thomas. "Introduction: Hauntology, or Spectral Space." *Perforations* 29 (2007). 28. Feb. 2008. Web. http://www.pd.org/~chea/Perforations/perf29/p29–intro.pdf.

Narjoux, Cécilie. "Marie Darrieussecq et 'l'entre-deux-mondes' ou le fantastique à l'oeuvre." *Iris* 24 (2002–2003): 233–47. Print.

Palmer, Alan. *Fictional Minds*. Lincoln: University of Nebraska Press, 2006. Print.

Phelan, James. *Living to Tell about It: A Rhetoric and Ethics of Character Narration*. Ithaca: Cornell University Press, 2005. Print.

Richardson, Brian. *Unnatural Voices: Extreme Narration in Modern and Contemporary Fiction*. Columbus: The Ohio State University Press, 2006. Print.

Rickels, Laurence A. *Aberrations of Mourning: Writing on German Crypts*. Detroit: Wayne State University Press, 1988. Print.

Robson, Kathryn. "Virtual Reality: The Subject of Loss in Marie Darrieussecq's *Naissance des fantômes* and Régine Detambel's *La Chambre d'écho*." *Australian Journal of French Studies* 41.1 (2004): 3–15. Print.

Sconce, Jeffrey. *Haunted Media: Electronic Presence from Telegraphy to Television*. Durham: Duke University Press, 2000. Print.

Turner, Mark. *The Literary Mind*. Oxford: Oxford University Press, 1996. Print.

Wolfreys, Julian. *Victorian Hauntings: Spectrality, Gothic, the Uncanny and Literature*. London: Macmillan, 2001. Print.

Zunshine, Lisa. "Theory of Mind and Fictions of Embodied Transparency." *Narrative* 16.1 (2008): 65–92. Print.

---. *Why We Read Fiction: Theory of Mind and the Novel*. Columbus: The Ohio State University Press, 2006. Print.

Theory of Mind and Metamorphoses in Dreams: *Dr. Jekyll and Mr. Hyde,* and *The Metamorphosis*

Richard Schweickert and Zhuangzhuang Xi

Introduction

An author has an opportunity to adopt a special point of view in a story when one character metamorphoses into another. In the famous opening of *The Metamorphosis,* Franz Kafka immediately immerses the reader into the mind of the central character:

> When Gregor Samsa woke up one morning from unsettling dreams, he found himself changed in his bed into a monstrous vermin. He was lying on his back as hard as armor plate, and when he lifted his head a little, he saw his vaulted brown belly, sectioned by arch-shaped ribs . . . His many legs, pitifully thin compared with the size of the rest of him, were waving helplessly before his eyes. "What's happened to me?" he thought. It was no dream. (Kafka 3)

The entire story, except the epilogue, is told from Gregor's point of view: "Magically, the story adopts the victim's perspective, which produces both brief comic moments and a lasting pathos" (Adler 82).

However, a metamorphosis does not always prompt an author to attend to an accompanying mental change. In *Dr. Jekyll and Mr. Hyde,* Robert Louis Stevenson describes Mr. Hyde transforming into Dr. Jekyll as seen by another person, Dr. Lanyon:

> He put the glass to his lips and drank at one gulp. A cry followed: he reeled, he staggered . . . there came, I thought, a change—he seemed to swell—his face became suddenly black . . . I leaped back, my mind submerged in terror . . . What he told me in the next hour, I cannot bring my mind to set on paper. (Stevenson 75)

The opportunity to tell the reader what Dr. Jekyll experienced is declined. Only the final chapter, the narrative of Dr. Jekyll, is written from the metamorphosed character's perspective, and there, as Joyce Carol Oates says, "It is significant that the narrator of Jekyll's confession speaks of both Jekyll and Hyde as if from the outside" (xv).

A character attributing perceptions, thoughts, feelings, and so on to another character is said to be using Theory of Mind (ToM). Recent work by Alan Palmer and Lisa Zunshine pays close attention to mental activity of characters, and of readers and authors as well, as a way of understanding the function of literature and of enriching the experience of reading.

Authors Stevenson and Kafka were both influenced by their dreams. In "A Chapter on Dreams," Stevenson says the source for the above scene in *Dr. Jekyll and Mr. Hyde* was a dream (more precisely, a dreamlike-state, see Karen Goodwin). "For two days I went about racking my brains for a plot . . . on the second night I dreamed the scene at the window, and a scene afterwards split in two, in which Hyde . . . took the powder and underwent the change . . . " (Stevenson 103). For Kafka, dreams do not seem to be a direct source of material, but he reports his dreams in his diaries and letters, and says in the *Diaries*, "My talent for portraying my dreamlike inner life has thrust all other matters into the background . . ." (qtd. in Corngold xvii).

Metamorphoses of one character or animal into another occur in roughly 1% of dreams (Hall and Van De Castle 168). In a study of metamorphoses in a particular dreamer, G. William Domhoff found the most common type to be human-to-human, but there are also human-to-animal, object-to-object, and so on (131). Studies by David Kahn and J. Allan Hobson and by Kahn, Edward Pace-Schott, and Hobson show that mind reading and other ToM activities frequently occur in dreams. With a metamorphosis of characters, where there was one mind, now there is another. Are mental states of transformed characters attended to in dreams, or do they pass unnoticed? Is one or the other of our two metamorphosis stories more like a dream in this respect?

We can pursue the questions with dream reports from a large collection on a Web site by Adam Schneider and Domhoff at the University of California at Santa Cruz. We find there reports of inner states of a metamorphosed character, for example:

> (Hall / VdC Norms: Female: #0288)
>
> I, as my maiden aunt, was standing in the front yard of my home in the country. I was not myself, but my aunt. A car drove by in which were my sister (my mother, my aunt's sister) and her husband. I did not determine whether her son and daughter were in the car. I felt very sad that I had no husband while she did. I envied her. Immediately, I changed back to myself, although the setting remained the same . . . (Schneider and Domhoff)

In another report the idea of minds transforming when bodies transform seems to be understood in the midst of dreaming:

> (Barb Sanders: #1985, 11 / 15 / 91)
>
> . . . Now Troi and I are in bed together cuddling. . . . Troi and I then exchange bodies so I can experience what it is like to be free of my own patterns of thought and feeling I've built up since birth, and to experience her way of feeling her own feelings. It's a delightful experience. Then I see her push a table over and hit her ankle and limp with pain. I go and kneel in front of her and

> try to be sympathetic. "Does it hurt?" I ask. She grimaces and says, "I'm fine." (Schneider and Domhoff)

The transformation is brief, and soon the dreamer has to ask about the pain when Troi hits her ankle.

On the other hand, there are also reports indicating that a metamorphosis does not automatically call attention to a possible change in mental experience. A good example is in the following part of a dream report of a woman in her thirties:

> (Merri: #032 6 / 12 / 1999):
>
> ... There was a family and I was the little boy and on Saturdays we had to line up and get a big plastic cup and have it filled with sulfuric acid. Then we had to stick our hand in the acid (my right hand) and scrub—hard. I had to scrub the 4 sides of the light post. It was trapezoid in shape. ... There was an underwater cave murder. There was a pocket of air in the underwater cave and 3 guys were there. One was the culprit, one was the victim, and one was the survivor. The victim knew the end was coming and he became very calm. ... (Schneider and Domhoff)

The woman adult dreamer has the form of a male child, but the hand of this child in sulfuric acid produces no comment about inner feelings. A little later, however, the dreamer knows somehow that a different character, the victim, knows the end is near. In this dream report, a ToM event occurs, but quite unrelated to the metamorphosis.

Ignoring a metamorphosis is a little like the phenomenon of change blindness. A rather large change in a scene can pass unobserved unless the observer is attending directly to it, as Daniel J. Simons and Daniel T. Levin have shown. In one of their demonstrations, a male experimenter asks directions from a woman on a street. While they are talking, a person carrying a door blocks the woman's view for a moment, and, changing places with the experimenter, replaces him in the conversation. The woman continues the conversation, not noticing one person has been replaced by another. This suggests that some metamorphoses in dreams are overlooked. A metamorphosis must have been noticed in a dream for the dream report to mention it, but the consequence that a mind was transformed sometimes passes unremarked.

The examples show that mental states of metamorphosed characters are noted in some dreams but not in others, so *The Metamorphosis*, which attends to such states, and *Dr. Jekyll and Mr. Hyde*, which ignores them, are each faithful to dreams in this respect, albeit to different dreams. The examples do not suffice to determine whether ToM is typical or not when a metamorphosis occurs in a dream, and we take up this issue now with a sample of dream reports. A frequent and reasonable objection to using material from dream reports is that one must assume the reports are accurate accounts of what occurred in the dreams. Unfortunately, there is no way to test the accuracy of dream reports. Some indirect evidence for accuracy is summarized in Domhoff (40). At this time, if we want to study dream content we have no choice but to study dream reports, with the working assumption that they are accurate.

OBSERVATIONS

Description of the study here is necessarily brief; more details are in the paper by Richard Schweickert and Zhuangzhuang Xi. All available dream reports in English from individuals on the Schneider and Domhoff Web site were searched for words and phrases indicating a metamorphosis. Phrases such as "change," "transform," and "turn into" were included, in addition to "metamorphosis" (see also Domhoff 132). Dream reports containing such phrases were read and selected for further study if a sentient or robotic entity was involved in a metamorphosis. A report was included if one of the metamorphosed entities was an object, for example, a chair turning into a cat, but not if all metamorphosed entities were objects. Reports were also selected for further study if a group, for example, a flock of sheep, was involved in a metamorphosis, but only dream reports of metamorphoses involving single entities will be discussed here.

More dream reports are available from some dreamers than others, so the number of dream reports in the sample from each dreamer is not the same. To prevent the sample from being dominated by dreamers with a large number of reports, no more than ten dream reports with a metamorphosis were selected from any one dreamer.

The Web site provides a procedure for selecting reports from a dreamer at random, with upper and lower bounds for the word length of the selected reports. Using this procedure, for each of the dream reports with a metamorphosis a control dream report from the same dreamer was selected at random, within plus or minus twelve words of the length of the corresponding report with a metamorphosis. A control report was replaced if it happened itself to contain a metamorphosis. Dream reports were put in a random order and printed with dreamer's names and word-lengths removed.

One coder (the first author) listed the characters, animals, sentient and robotic entities, and groups of such entities in each dream report. The coding system is a modified version of that of Calvin S. Hall and Robert Van De Castle; see also Schweickert.

Two other coders (one of whom is the second author) coded ToM events in the dream reports. The coding system was developed from ideas of Zunshine, of Kahn and Hobson, and, most directly, from a coding system for children's literature by Kimberly Wright Cassidy, Lorraine V. Ball, Mary T. Rourke, Rebecca Stetson Werner, Nohr Feeny, June Y. Chu, Donna J. Lutz, and Alexis Perkins. Briefly, each coder looked for phrases referring to internal states of entities. Internal states include what an entity is perceiving, feeling, believing, knowing, thinking, wondering, remembering, wanting, or intending. Each coder also looked for phrases referring to higher order internal states that themselves refer to internal states, for example, "Mary believed Harry was sorry." Results for higher order ToM events will not be discussed here.

Instructions were to "Underline with one line a word or short phrase identifying the entity whose internal state is referred to," and "Circle a word or short phrase mentioning the internal state." For example, if the dream report said "Mary was sad," the coder was to underline Mary and circle sad. A word or phrase mentioning a higher order mental state was to be circled twice, and the entity with this higher order state was to be double underlined. Coders were not informed that half the dream reports contained a metamorphosis and half did not, but the instructions said "If one entity transforms into another, consider the entities before and after the transformation as different."

RESULTS

Each ToM event identified by a coder attributes a mental state to a particular character or other entity. The average over the two coders of the number of ToM events attributed to each entity was calculated. There are 65 dream reports from 21 dreamers.

METAMORPHOSIS OF DREAMER

In 10 of the 65 dream reports with a metamorphosis, the dreamer was metamorphosed. For example, a dream report of the adult woman Alta says, "I have turned into a male policeman."

In these 10 dreams with a metamorphosis of the dreamer, 6.6 ToM events per dream are attributed to the dreamer in one form or another, on average. In the 10 corresponding control dreams, 7.0 ToM events per dream are attributed to the dreamer, on average. These rates are about equal; in other words, the frequency of ToM events referring to a form of the dreamer is about the same, whether or not the dreamer is metamorphosed.

Because each dreamer did not contribute the same number of dream reports, averages were calculated in the following way. The number of ToM events per dream was calculated for each dreamer. Then these numbers were averaged over the dreamers; hence each dreamer contributes one number to the average. All averages reported here were calculated this way.

In the dreams in which the dreamer is metamorphosed there were 21 dreamer forms (sometimes a dream report begins with the dreamer already transformed, and sometimes a dreamer undergoes more than one metamorphosis, so the number of dreamer forms is not exactly twice the number of dream reports). In dreams with a metamorphosis of the dreamer there are fewer ToM events per dreamer form, 4.8 on average, than in dreams without a metamorphosis of the dreamer, 8.1 on average. This happens, of course, because there are more dreamer forms when the dreamer metamorphoses. To summarize so far, the dreamer, in whatever form, refers to his or her (or its) mental states the same number of times per dream, on average, whether or not the dreamer metamorphoses.

METAMORPHOSIS NOT OF DREAMER

In 55 dream reports the dreamer did not undergo a metamorphosis, but at least one other entity did. For such dreams, there was an average of 2.3 ToM events per dream. This is quite close to the average of 2.4 ToM events per dream for the corresponding 55 control dream reports without a metamorphosis. (Because we have already discussed the dreamer, the dreamer is excluded from these calculations.) For entities other than the dreamer, we reach the same conclusion as for the dreamer. The frequency of ToM events in dreams is the same for nondreamer entities, on the average, whether there is a metamorphosis or not.

When an animate entity in one form changes into another form, followed perhaps by other changes in form, let us call the set of forms a *line*. When the dreamer changes from one form to another, the number of characters and animals is increased, but there is a single underlying line. Over all dreams with metamorphoses, the average number of forms is 6.2. Over all control dreams this average is smaller, 4.5. But, over all dreams with metamorphoses, the average number of lines is 4.9, about equal to that of control dreams, 4.5. A metamorphosis does not increase the number of lines. Putting this together with our result that the number of ToM events in a dream is the same for dreams with and without a metamorphosis, we conclude that the number of ToM events on a line is the same, whether or not there are metamorphoses along the line.

To summarize, one might expect the dreamer's attention to be drawn to an entity undergoing a metamorphosis, so the number of ToM events attributed to such entities would be larger than for other entities. However, the number of ToM events per dream is the same, whether or not there is a metamorphosis. Contrary to our initial intuition, the average number of ToM events per entity for metamorphosed entities is less than or equal to that for nonmetamorphosed entities. This is puzzling, perhaps, until we consider that a metamorphosis increases the number of entities, and thus decreases the average. It is as though the dreamer attends to mental states at a certain rate (not necessarily periodically). The focus of attention depends on who is present, but the rate does not. A metamorphosis does not call the dreamer's attention to the mental states involved, even if it is the dreamer who is metamorphosed.

DISCUSSION

In dreams mental states of a character are referred to, or not, quite independently of whether the character has undergone a metamorphosis. Stevenson and Kafka drew on different dream experiences and produced two different types of metamorphosis story. *The Metamorphosis*, one type, presents the feelings and thoughts of a metamorphosed character. *Dr. Jekyll and Mr. Hyde*, the other type, largely ignores the inner life of metamorphosed characters.

What does ignoring or attending do for the story? The story of *Dr. Jekyll and Mr. Hyde* is better served by ignoring the minds of Jekyll and Hyde. In our day "Jekyll and Hyde" is a well-worn phrase, but Stevenson intended the metamorphosis to be a surprise. A contemporary review says "Mr. Stevenson evolves the idea of his story from the world that is unseen, enveloping everything in weird mystery, till at last it pleases him to give us the password" (137). For this to succeed, thoughts of Jekyll and Hyde cannot be revealed, of course. Moreover, because the description of the mind of Hyde is omitted, when Hyde is described as unlikable or evil, the reader fills in details, perhaps more luridly than the author would have dared to.

On the other hand, attention to the mind of the metamorphosed character provides opportunities for comparisons, as in *The Golden Ass*, when Lucius says, "That wonderful magic of yours has equipped you with an ass's shape and an ass's hard life, but not his thick skin" (Apuleius 107). Opportunities also arise for irony, as in *The Metamor-*

phosis when Gregor thinks "'This getting up so early,' . . . 'makes one a complete idiot. Human beings have to have their sleep'" (Kafka 4).

What might dreams have done for the authors? It is well known that Stevenson wrote *Dr. Jekyll and Mr. Hyde* in great haste. He refers to dream images as the sources for Jekyll and Hyde. According to Ernest Hartman, many dreams have a central image that is vivid, emotion laden, and memorable (28). If, as seems to be the case, Stevenson held a dream image in mind while he wrote about the scene the image portrayed, he would feel the emotional impact the image had on him, and would know that a good description of the image would suffice for an impact on the reader. Mental states not accompanying the image need not be invented. The image guides what to write about and what not to write about.

Dreams also may have influenced the description of inner states of metamorphosed characters, when they are described. Not all mental states can be produced by the dreaming brain, because of biological limitations. A dreamer can experience flying because views of the ground from high up, feelings of wind, and so on are available in the dreamer's memory and imagination. But consider this dream report of Merri:

> (Merri: #224 1 / 04 / 2000):
>
> . . . I did a few lines of coke with a girl on the floor. She had a whole lot of coke in a clear plastic round cylinder, the size of a film canister but bigger circumference. We left there. They wanted me to see some other artists' work at this school I had gotten a scholarship to. . . .

No change of inner state is reported after the dreamer takes coke, perhaps because the dreaming brain cannot produce the experience of being high.

Let us take a closer look at one of the few passages in *Dr. Jekyll and Mr. Hyde* where the mental experiences of the main character are described. In Henry Jekyll's full statement of the case Jekyll says:

> . . . I . . . woke the next day in bed with odd sensations. It was in vain I looked about me; in vain I saw the decent furniture and tall proportions of my room in the square . . . something kept insisting that I was not where I was . . . I began lazily to inquire into the elements of this illusion . . . in one of my more wakeful moments, my eyes fell upon my hand. . . . It was the hand of Edward Hyde. (82)

It is curious that Hyde does not notice he is Hyde through his mental state. His inner state hints he is not where he thinks he is, but it does not hint he is not who he thinks he is. He learns who he is by observing the hair on his hand. Hyde is said to be the very embodiment of evil; surely this must be manifest in his own mind. But what exactly could the writer describe of this? The author can conceive of a mind of pure evil, but he cannot produce the experience in his imagination or dreams.

Jekyll learns on waking that he has transformed into Hyde by looking at his hand, just as Gregor learns he has been transformed into a vermin by looking at his legs. No inner feeling informs either character that his mind has undergone a transformation.

Kafka does not present the mind of a vermin—what words could he write? The voice is third person narrative. As dream reports are naturally in first person, the voice emphasizes that this is no dream. Kafka presents, as a dream would, a body changed to vermin, with a mind continuing on, half-asleep, but mostly human. Kafka's talent for describing his dreamlike inner life is shown in maintaining a steady pitiful reasoning through page after page of struggle with an absurd reality.

One might wonder whether in Kafka's dream reports, metamorphoses are accompanied by descriptions of inner states. In the following dream, the last known of his life, Kafka dreams he is transformed into the woman Milena:

> Last night I dreamt about you. What happened in detail I can hardly remember, all I know is that we kept merging into one another. I was you, you were me. Finally, you somehow caught fire. Remembering that one extinguishes fire with clothing, I took an old coat and beat you with it. But again the transmutations began and it went so far that you were no longer even there, instead it was I who was on fire and it was also I who beat the fire with the coat. But the beating didn't help and it only confirmed my old fear that such things can't extinguish a fire. In the meantime, however, the fire brigade arrived and somehow you were saved. But you were different from before, spectral, as though drawn with chalk against the dark, and you fell, lifeless or perhaps having fainted from joy at having been saved, into my arms. But here too the uncertainty of transmutability entered, perhaps it was I who fell into someone's arms. (qtd. in Hall and Lind 124)

The dreaming brain of a man cannot produce the experience of being a woman, so little is said about the inner experience of the dreamer as a woman. There is no report of sensation when her body is on fire, and at the moment of a hint of joy, her inner life is impossible because she has died, or, perhaps, has fainted.

Often we think of dreams as a source of wild ideas. But sometimes in a dream there is an equanimity disproportionate to a strange situation, which, if all is carefully described, can produce a curious effect in a story. The inner nature of Mr. Hyde remains a mystery even after his identity with Dr. Jekyll is revealed. For juxtaposition of the fantastic with the ordinary in *The Metamorphosis*, dreams are a source for the ordinary as well as the fantastic.

ACKNOWLEDGMENTS

We thank Sonya Basaran for help with coding, and G. William Domhoff, Paula Leverage, Howard Mancing, and Jennifer Marston William for helpful discussion.

WORKS CITED

Aldler, Jeremy. *Franz Kafka*. New York: Overlook Press, 2001. Print.

Apuleius. *The Golden Ass*. Trans. E. J. Kenney. London: Penguin Books, 1998. Print.

Cassidy, Kimberly Wright, Lorraine V. Ball, Mary T. Rourke, Rebecca Stetson Werner, Norh Feeny, June Y. Chu, Donna J. Lutz, and Alexis Perkins. "Theory of Mind Concepts in Children's Literature." *Applied Psycholinguistics* 19 (1998): 463-70. Print.

Corngold, Stanley. "Introduction." *The Metamorphosis*. By Franz Kafka. New York: Bantam Books. Ed. and trans. Stanley Corngold. New York: Bantam Books, 1986. xi-xxii. Print.

Domhoff, G. William. *The Scientific Study of Dreams*. Washington, DC: American Psychological Association, 2003. Print.

Goodwin, Karen. "Drug Took Stevenson Face to Face with Hyde." *Sunday Times* 20 Mar. 2005. Web. http://www.timesonline.co.uk/tol/newspapers/sunday_times/scotland/article432698.ece.

Hall, Calvin S., and Richard E. Lind. *Dreams, Life, and Literature: A Study of Franz Kafka*. Chapel Hill: University of North Carolina Press, 1970. Print.

---, and Robert L. Van de Castle. *The Content Analysis of Dreams*. New York: Appleton-Century-Crofts, 1966. Print.

Hartman, Ernest. *Dreams and Nightmares: The Origin and Meaning of Dreams*. Cambridge, MA: Perseus, 1998. Print.

Kafka, Franz. *The Metamorphosis*. Ed. and trans. Stanley Corngold. New York: Bantam Books, 1986. Print.

Kahn, David, and J. Allan Hobson. "Theory of Mind and Dreaming: Awareness of Thoughts and Feelings of Others in Dreams." *Dreaming* 15 (2005): 48-57. Print.

---, Edward Pace-Schott, and J. Allan Hobson. "Emotion and Cognition: Feelings and Character Identification in Dreaming." *Consciousness and Cognition* 11 (2002): 34-50. Print.

Oates, Joyce Carol. Foreword. *The Strange Case of Dr Jekyll and Mr Hyde*. By Robert Louis Stevenson. Lincoln: University of Nebraska Press, 1990. ix-xviii. Print.

Palmer, Alan. *Fictional Minds*. Lincoln: University of Nebraska Press, 2004. Print.

Rev. of *The Strange Case of Dr Jekyll and Mr Hyde*, by Robert Louis Stevenson. *The Times* 25 January 1886. In *The Strange Case of Dr Jekyll and Mr Hyde*. Ed. Martin A. Danahay. Peterborough, Ontario, CA: Broadview Literary Texts, 2000. 136-38. Print.

Schneider, Adam, and G. William Domhoff. *DreamBank*. Department of Psychology, University of California Santa Cruz. 16 December 2006. Web. http://www.dreambank.net/.

Schweickert, Richard. "Properties of the Organization of Memory for People: Evidence from Dream Reports." *Psychonomic Bulletin & Review* 14 (2007): 270-76. Print.

---, and Xi, Zhuangzhuang. "Metamorphosed Characters in Dreams: Constraints of Conceptual Structure and Amount of Theory of Mind." *Cognitive Science* 34 (2010): 665-84.

Simons, Daniel J., and Daniel T. Levin. "Failure to Detect Changes to People during a Real-World Interaction." *Psychonomic Bulletin & Review* 5 (1998): 644-49. Print.

Stevenson, Robert Louis. "A Chapter on Dreams." *The Strange Case of Dr Jekyll and Mr Hyde*. Ed. Martin A. Danahay. Peterborough, Ontario, CA: Broadview Literary Texts, 2000. 93-104. Print.

---. *The Strange Case of Dr Jekyll and Mr Hyde*. Ed. Martin A. Danahay. Peterborough, Ontario, CA: Broadview Literary Texts, 2000. 29-92. Print.

Zunshine, Lisa. *Why We Read Fiction: Theory of Mind and the Novel.* Columbus: The Ohio State University Press, 2006. Print.

Mother / Daughter Mind Reading and Ghostly Intervention in Toni Morrison's *Beloved*

KLARINA PRIBORKIN

Toni Morrison's *Beloved* explores a triangular relationship between a mother (Sethe) traumatized by the horrors of slavery, her youngest daughter (Denver), and the ghostly figure of her deceased daughter (referred to as Beloved). The circumstances of Beloved's death as well as the mother's past experiences as a slave are the "unspoken secrets" that define the mother / daughter relationship in the novel. Growing up in a terrifying atmosphere, with the ghost of her dead sister haunting the house, Denver is unaware of the true reasons for the haunting. When she finds out that her mother killed Beloved to save her from slavery, she also notices the community's hostility toward her family. Not only the community, but Sethe's family and children, too, continuously misinterpret her intentions. Adopting the environment's interpretation of her mother's deed, Denver alienates herself emotionally, creating a demonic image of her mother. While Sethe understands the murder of her daughter as an act of love intended for that child's protection, Denver, similarly to other members of her family and community, believes that something horrible in her mother "makes it all right to kill her own" (Beloved 205).

This paper will examine three incidents, two early in the narrative and one toward the end, in which Denver's Theory of Mind (ToM) seems at first to fail, but finally succeeds in functioning. The change, I claim, is enabled by Beloved—the ghost of the murdered daughter—who facilitates Denver's acquisition of mind-reading skills. Beloved's mediation—the mediation of a ghost—is the narrative device that allows Denver's development of ToM, and its consequent application to her mother's stories. By encouraging Denver to visualize the details of her mother's narrative, Beloved compels her to change perspectives, recreating what Sethe must have thought, felt, and experienced as a slave mother. Such cognitive exercises, as well as continuous paralinguistic interactions with Beloved, gradually improve Denver's mind-reading skills. When Denver learns to retell her mother's story from her mother's perspective, rather than from her own, she learns to imagine Sethe's mental and emotional states. This allows her to fill in the gaps in the narrative, retell her mother's story, and eventually to succeed in interpreting her mother's mental states empathically. I will first discuss the reasons for Denver's difficulty in developing efficient ToM and then show the cognitive processes she undergoes as she learns to reinterpret her mother's states of mind.

The atmosphere of secrecy produced by Sethe's inability and unwillingness to share her traumatic memories with her daughter not only impedes mother / daughter communication, but also hampers Denver's cognitive and personal development. In "Mother-Child Reminiscing and Children's Understanding of Mind," Elaine Reese and Emily Sutcliffe suggest that mothers who discuss mental and emotional states and memories with their children advance their children's understanding of mind. These children relate richer and more elaborate autobiographical memories (18-19). Tragically, Sethe's failure to discuss the horrors of slavery and her own traumatic past with her daughter prevents Denver from developing the skills necessary for successful mind reading.

According to Nicolas Abraham and Maria Torok's theory of trauma, "secret discourse" or "cryptonymy" (the practice of word hiding) is symptomatic of traumatized individuals who experience difficulty talking about their past. Abraham and Torok claim that family secrets are transmitted without words and it is the offspring's suspicion that something has been left unsaid that impels the younger generation to listen for clues and hints in their parents' speech.[1] This is precisely what happens in *Beloved*. Although Denver subconsciously knows that her mother killed her sister, she does not know why she did it or what led her to do it. Since Denver cannot discuss her assumptions regarding the murder with her mother, Sethe cannot correct her daughter's mistaken inferences regarding her original intentions.

Not only has no one ever corrected Denver's mistaken understanding of her mother's mind, but Denver's brothers and grandmother, Sethe's mother-in-law, and other members of the community[2] also misinterpret Sethe's intentions. The boys tell Denver "die-witch!" stories that teach her how to kill her mother "if [she] ever needed to" protect herself" (205). Although Denver loves her mother, she also fears her. In Denver's words: "I love my mother but I know she killed one of her own daughters, and tender as she is with me, I'm scared of her because of it. She missed killing my brothers and they knew it" (205). When the brothers are old enough, they escape the haunted house without confronting their mother or talking with her about the murder.[3] Denver, too, is secretly indulging the fantasy of leaving her mother; she is waiting for her father, who apparently failed to escape the slaveholders, believing that he will redeem her from her mother's potential violence.[4] The children's inability to communicate with their mother is reinforced by their grandmother, who had been bought out of slavery by her son, and with whom Sethe and her children live on the outskirts of Cincinnati after they escape from the South.

Although Denver initially learns about the murder from her grandmother's cryptic narratives, Baby Suggs's stories conceal much more than they reveal. Denver remembers her grandmother telling her that she need not fear the ghost: "she said the ghost was after Ma'am and her, too, for not doing anything to stop it. But it would never hurt me. I just had to watch out for it because it was a greedy ghost and needed a lot of love, which was only natural, considering . . ." (209).[5] Baby Suggs hints at but does not explain the murder to Denver. Indeed, she adds an additional layer of secrecy to the atmosphere of horror that already exists in the house. Instead of reducing Denver's fear of her mother by explaining to her the sociocultural context of the murder, Baby Suggs transfers the unspeakable secret to the next generation, reinforcing the tradition of reticence and secrecy.

Denver, thus, participates in a community of interpreters or rather misinterpreters of Sethe's intentions.[6] Failing to react empathically to Sethe's tragedy or to try to understand her intentions, Denver's brothers, the grandmother, and the community of Cincinnati condemn Sethe's violence. They establish a cognitive framework of reference that Denver instinctively assimilates as her own. The environment, thus, shapes Denver's interpretation of her mother's violent act, leading the daughter to develop a demonic image of her mother.

In "Intermental Thought in the Novel," Alan Palmer defines intermental units as "groups [such as large organizations, as well as families, couples and friends] that regularly employ intermental thinking" (429). Palmer explains that this kind of thinking "is joint, group, shared, or collective, as opposed to intramental, individual, or private thought. It is also known as socially distributed, situated, or extended cognition, and as intersubjectivity" (427). Since all adult members of Sethe's community share the traumatic experience of slavery, they usually succeed in understanding each other's unspoken traumas and cryptic references to the past. This intermental communication is necessary for what Palmer refers to as an "intermental mind: these are intermental units that are so well defined and long lasting, and where so much successful intermental thought takes place, that they can be considered as group minds" (430). By attributing a common mind to a group of seemingly separate individuals, it is possible to analyze their social conventions in contrast to a single, private mind that may choose to rebel against a society.

Another vivid example of an intermental-group thought in the novel has to do with racial discrimination. According to the slaveholders, "slaves not *supposed to* have pleasurable feelings on their own; their bodies *not supposed* to be like that, but *they have to* have as many children as they can to *please whoever owned them*" (*Beloved* 209, emphasis mine). The words I marked belong to the white's "group mind" that imposed its conceptions on the black community. The white people communicate this racist message of enslavement to the blacks, making them incorporate it as an integral part of their own culture. In *Beloved*, Baby Suggs tries to instill the opposite message, based on self-love and self-respect, thus attempting to reconstruct the black community and create a new group mind. As the spiritual leader of her community, Baby Suggs communicates with her people intermentally: "After situating herself on a huge flat-sided rock, Baby Suggs bowed her head and prayed silently. *The company* watched her from the trees. *They knew she was ready when she put her stick down*" (87, emphasis mine). The communal mind reading constructed at the spiritual site creates an unspoken understanding between Baby Suggs and her community. Baby Suggs's blessing and motivating speech that comes right after the ritual signifies intermental thinking, implying complete understanding between the leader and the group.

Binding the different characters in the novel into one intermental communal unit, Morrison exposes her readers to the cognitive processes of remembering and forgetting that the black community undergoes coming to terms with its past. According to Garciela Moreira-Slepoy, Toni Morrison's *Beloved* provides an alternative to "the historical monolithic accounts dealing with slavery" (3) by integrating the scattered personal testimonies into a comprehensive account of these characters' past. These "series of local or private narratives . . . need to be told and retold once and again in order to reconstruct and come to terms with the past in a liberating way" (3). As Christopher Powers suggests, "Morrison creates characters whose consciousness of time is in fact spatialized, because it is part of her innovation as a writer to show how people experience memory synchronically" (34). Unlike Moreira-Slepoy, Powers does not believe that Morrison's main purpose is to undo "master narratives," rather, he claims that Morrison "spatializes time" and "synchronizes narrative" in order to "simulate subjective experience" of self-construction (33-34).[7] While Morrison's focus on individual narratives indeed illuminates the characters' personal development, it is the connection between these stories that makes an authentic recovery of the past possible. When the individual voices in *Beloved* are joined to tell a story, their personal testimonies confirm and legitimize each other, establishing a communal voice that reconstructs the white narratives about slavery.

According to Palmer a mind can "consist of more than one brain" (432). I suggest that the communal group mind constructed through Baby Suggs's rituals, cooperative remembering, and storytelling can recover truths that remain inaccessible to an individual mind. When several minds work together they form an intermental unit that consists "of individual minds pooling their resources and producing better, or at least different, results" (430). It is therefore through the cooperation between the members of the community that the individual self can access and come to terms with the communal past that shapes individual experience.

Although this group mind in *Beloved* is initially determined to keep its past at a safe distance, Beloved's murder brings the horrors of slavery back to the people's lives. They attempt to repress it by ostracizing Sethe and her family. When Sethe challenges the cultural and moral presuppositions about the nature of motherhood and slavery, she becomes a rebel and an outsider in both white and black societies. By comparing Sethe's interpretation of her own beliefs and behavior to the ways white and black communities perceive them, it is possible to explain the workings of these distinct yet interrelated groups. Sethe challenges the social codes of the white community, insisting on her natural rights as a mother in spite of her supposedly inferior race and social status.[8] Furthermore, she challenges the black community's moral standards. Sethe's community does not justify infanticide in the face of slavery, yet she rebels against this cultural or intermental construction. Sethe reinterprets her act of violence as an act of love and protection. Yet since this view does not correlate with the others' social codes, they create the intermental construct based on meaningful silence that everybody in the community understands. This silence defines Sethe as "the other," a murderer who broke a basic moral law.

When Sethe saw the slaveholder, called Schoolteacher, approaching her home to take her and her children back to the farm where she had been a slave before escaping, she rushes with her children to the shed and slashes the throat of her "crawling already!" baby daughter. She intends to kill all her children and herself, but her mother-in-law stops her. Stunned by her act, the white men conclude that Sethe is far too rebellious, and perhaps even mad, and therefore cannot be enslaved again. The people of the community, equally shocked, observe Sethe as she is taken to prison by the sheriff. Yet Sethe

> walked past *them* in *their* silence and *hers*. She climbed into a cart, her profile knife-clean against a cheery blue sky. A profile that shocked *them* with its clarity. Was her head a bit too high? Her back a little too straight? Probably. Otherwise the singing would have begun at once . . . some cape of sound would have quickly been wrapped around her, like arms to hold and steady her on the way. (152, emphasis mine)

This compelling mind reading interchange between Sethe and her community is relayed by the third-person narrator who makes assumptions regarding both Sethe's and the community's mental states. The double mind reading, between the narrator and the characters, as well as between Sethe and her community, allows readers to participate in the creation of an intermental or group mind that observes and judges Sethe's behavior.

Since the readers are provided with Sethe's observable actions, such as holding her head too high or her back too straight, they understand, and perhaps participate in, the community's misinterpretation of Sethe's intentions. Showing no apparent or observable remorse through her body language, Sethe intentionally or unintentionally conveys her contempt and disrespect for the community, which simultaneously rejects her in return. Sethe later says that she could never explain why she killed her daughter "for anybody who had to ask. If they didn't get it right off—she could never explain" (163).[9] Sethe refuses to communicate her motives to anyone but her reincarnated daughter Beloved, who, she believes, is the only one that can understand her motives without verbal explanation.[10] This lack of linguistic or paralinguistic input makes Sethe rather opaque to her community and her family, leading them to draw incorrect assumptions regarding her mental states.[11]

In order to become conscious of the family secret, children of traumatized parents must decode the cryptic language of the adults. This is traumatic, especially when the ultimate revelation of the secret comes from a person that does not belong to the family. Although the atmosphere of secrecy oppresses Denver for years, it is only when she is directly asked about her mother's deed that she realizes her secret. Misreading not only her mother's, but also her peers' paralinguistic signals, Denver does not notice that her classmates often make "excuses and alter their pace not to walk with her" (102). By communicating their contempt to Sethe and her family through body language, the children subtly reject the outsiders, thus participating in the construction of the communal group mind. When one of her classmates confronts Denver about her sister's murder, she realizes her failure to read both her mother's and other people's minds. One of her fellow students asks Denver: "didn't your mother get locked away for murder? Wasn't you in there with her when she went?" Denver does not laugh the question off, because "something leap[s] up in her, when he asked; it was a thing that had been lying there all along" (102). The question brings Denver's subconscious knowledge about the murder into her everyday reality, thus allowing the daughter to start attributing meaning to the hints she has heard all her life.

Denver's realization that she has failed to understand her mother's and her community's intentions leads to her mistrust of language and communication. This is symbolized by her psychosomatic deafness and self-imposed isolation from social contact. She stops attending school and secludes herself in the house, concentrating on the ghostly presence of her dead sister. Although Denver's hearing impairment symbolizes her detachment from the outside world, it brings her closer to familial secrets and the ghost. Denver is capable of playing with the ghost without using verbal language: "that's how come me and Beloved could play together. Not talking. On the porch. By the creek. In the secret house" (206).

Assuming that Beloved's ghostly figure is not real, but rather belongs to the realm of Denver's imagination, the ghost can be thought of as Denver's imaginary friend. According to developmental psychologists, interacting with imaginary friends plays a positive role in a child's development both cognitively and emotionally, allowing children to practice managing social situations and handling conflict in a safe context. Cognitively it helps them to deal with abstract symbols and to start thinking about their own identity.[12] Interacting with Beloved is indeed essential for Denver's cognitive development. Their silent communication, within the context of Denver's deafness, provides an essential learning experience; it trains her to read other people's faces and to "learn how to figure out what people were thinking, so [she] did not need to hear what they said" (206).

While the cognitive psychologists suggest that development of mind-reading abilities depends both on successful language acquisition and social interaction (Garfield, Peterson, and Perry 494), in *Beloved* it is precisely Denver's detachment from society and language that allow her to sharpen her mind-reading abilities. Even if Denver did acquire some basic mind-reading skills as a child, they proved insufficient for decoding her traumatized mother or the community's paralinguistic signals. Denver learns the hard way that what people say does not necessarily correlate with what they think. However, although Denver rejects verbal communication, she hones her ToM skills to an exceptional degree. Mind reading becomes Denver's survival strategy; it allows the daughter to interpret her mother's facial expressions, watching out for murderous thoughts that she believes may be crossing her mother's mind.

Although the ghost teaches Denver to decode people's faces, it does not teach her to interpret her mother's intentions on a more complex level. Still fearing that her mother might kill her, Denver does not ask Sethe to tell her about the murder. She chooses to repress the story, thus protecting herself from additional traumatic revelations. As the novel progresses, however, the ghost of Sethe's murdered daughter establishes her physical presence in the house. This opens a new phase in Denver's relationship with Beloved. If prior to Beloved's reincarnation the sisters used to communicate in silence, Beloved's embodied presence initiates verbal interaction. The ghostly figure influences Denver's patterns of speech and storytelling, thus transforming the youngest daughter's relationship with her mother.

Prior to Beloved's intervention, the only story Denver is willing to hear from her mother is the story of her own birth. This can be interpreted as her refusal to accept Sethe as a separate individual with a personal history. Denver acknowledges only those parts of Sethe's past that are relevant to her. Since Sethe's function in Denver's life is defined mostly through her role as a mother, the daughter does not perceive her as a separate individual and therefore blocks those parts of her mother's story that define her as such.

In *Reproduction of Mothering*, Nancy Chodorow claims that since mothers and daughters are of the same sex, their separation and individuation processes are more problematic and complicated than those of mothers and sons. While boys tend to define themselves in opposition to their mothers, girls experience themselves as contingent with them. For a girl there is no "absolute change of love object" and even her "libidinal turning to her father is not at the expense of, or a substitute for, her attachment for her mother" (125). Thus mothers and daughters maintain elements of their primary relationship throughout their lifetimes, and their ego boundaries remain unstable because they develop a relational, rather than an individualistic, sense of self.[13]

As Jessica Benjamin argues in *The Bonds of Love*, a healthy relationship between a mother and child is made possible through intersubjective connection and mutual recognition rather than through individuation and separation.[14] Benjamin's intersubjective view suggests that "we actually have a need to recognize the other as a separate person who is like us yet distinct. This means that the child has a need to see his mother . . . as an independent subject" (23). Thus, paradoxically, it is only by acknowledging each other as individuals that the mother and daughter's identities can develop in relationship. In *Feminism and Psychoanalytic Theory*, Chodorow shows that although mother / daughter relationships are extremely close across cultures, in matrifocal and traditional societies these relationships are less problematic. This is because "the people surrounding a mother while a child is growing up become mediators between mother and daughter, by providing a daughter with alternative modes for personal identification and objects of attachment, which contribute to her differentiation from her mother" (62).

The intersubjective communication and subsequent mutual recognition is hampered in Sethe and Denver's relationship, since the mother and daughter are ostracized by the community throughout most of Denver's childhood. As a result, Denver has very little social interaction with potential mediating figures in the community. Therefore, it is through Beloved's mediation that Denver is finally exposed to alternative modes of social interaction. Beloved's verbal intervention in Denver's storytelling practices facilitates the daughter's retelling of her birth as her mother's, and not only her own history. This rhetorical exercise develops Denver's creativity and independence, enabling her to imagine her mother's perspective as separate from her own, thus undermining the unhealthy patterns of dependence between the mother and daughter.

In "Explaining the Emergence of Autobiographical Memory in Early Childhood," Katherine Nelson suggests that by learning to tell stories about themselves children develop their autobiographical memory and thus construct their personal identity.[15] In order to learn the skill of self-narration children must learn to "tell a coherent story, to tell the truth, get the facts right," and so on; "In doing all this, the child must become reasonably adept at taking the perspective of another, and of viewing events from a somewhat detached, meta-representational distance" (377). When Beloved teaches Denver to tell the story of her birth from her mother's perspective, she both evokes the daughter's empathy toward her mother and initiates the processes of the daughter's self-construction.[16] Paradoxically, by telling her mother's story, Denver creates the necessary distance between Sethe and herself to recognize her own and her mother's individuality. As Paul Eakin suggests in *How Our Lives Become Stories*, "mothers and daughters are so intimately bound in the process of identity formation that to tell the story of the one is necessarily to tell the story of the other" (179). By facilitating this relational storytelling, Beloved helps Denver to assert her individuality in relationship, rather than in opposition to her mother.

Moreover, by interacting with Beloved, Denver learns to read minds. This extensive exercise of her ToM enables Denver to apply her cognitive skills to her mother's as well as to other people's minds. At first Denver learns to understand the meaning behind Beloved's gazes:

> Beloved seldom looked right at her, or when she did, Denver could tell that her own face was just the place those eyes stopped, while the mind behind it walked on. But sometimes at moments Denver could neither anticipate nor create— Beloved rested cheek on knuckles and looked at Denver with attention. (118)

Denver differentiates between Beloved's absentminded and meaningful gazes by employing the embodied ability of mind reading that, as Lisa Zunshine suggests, allows her to "ascribe to a person a certain mental state on the basis of her observable action" (6). Beloved thus uses paralinguistic communication in order to engage in an intersubjective relationship with Denver: "it was lovely. Not to be stared at, not seen, but being pulled into view by the interested, uncritical eyes of the other. Having her hair examined as a part of her self, not as material or a style" (118). Denver enjoys being a subject rather than an object of observation. Beloved's recognition allows her to recognize herself as an independent individual in relationship, and later to apply this experience of self-assertion to her relationship with Sethe.

The changes in the narrative patterns between the two versions of Denver's retelling of her birth, which I now consider, reflect the transformations in Denver's perception of her mother. The first time Denver tells the story of her own birth, she basically repeats her mother's words instead of engaging in a creative retelling. Since Denver is not experienced in the techniques of self-narration, she is not accustomed to using her own narrative voice or to creating imaginative strategies in order to tell her own story. Thus she first renders the story through her mother's narrative voice, using reported speech: "she had good hands, she said. The whitegirl, she said, and then little arms but good hands. She saw that right away, she said" (76). Beloved, however, is not satisfied by Denver's abrupt narration and therefore provokes more elaborate storytelling by "asking questions about the color of things and their size" (77). Since Sethe has not assisted her daughter in the development of remembering and retrieving processes, Denver's storytelling techniques remain rather scant. Sethe's inability to discuss her past hampers not only Denver's cognitive abilities, but also the development of her autobiographical self-perception. Thus Beloved's assistance in the creation and shaping of life stories is essential for Denver's self-construction.

According to Reese and Sutcliffe, cooperative reflection on the past also enables parents to train children to shift perspectives. This serves as a powerful context for understanding minds (36). Indeed, when Denver, with Beloved's help, learns to perceive her birth story from her mother's perspective, she also becomes aware of her mother's mental and emotional states. Beloved facilitates Denver's storytelling by encouraging her sister to generate the visual details of Sethe's story. By joining in imaginative constructions, the two sisters come to share their mother's past, thus creating a mutual system of references that binds them both cognitively and emotionally into a new interpretive community.

In order to imagine her mother's thoughts and emotions when running away from the slaveholders, Denver has to change the narrative's perspective. This is conducted through the sisters' cooperation, since as a dyad, Denver and Beloved possess more interpretive authority to add details and develop the emotional framework of Sethe's story. Moreover, as mentioned above, Denver lacks the necessary interpretive background to engage in a complicated rhetorical enterprise. Although Beloved's guidance is necessary for Denver's cognitive and emotional development, the reincarnated sister does not overpower the narrative process.

On the contrary, Beloved refrains from imposing her own voice on Denver's narration. Instead, she facilitates a dialogic, intersubjective narration in which Denver and Beloved have equal parts. According to Mikhail Bakhtin, the intersection between voices, consciousnesses, or worldviews does not necessarily imply one voice overpowering another, but rather a "dialogic concordance of unmerged twos or multiples" (289). Bakhtin's concept of dialogism suggests simultaneous interdependence and autonomy in relation to the other. Since language, according to Bakhtin, is fundamentally social, the process of our self-construction[17] depends on interaction with others. This view corresponds with Jessica Benjamin's concept of intersubjectivity that maintains that "the individual grows in and through the relationship to other subjects" which occurs through "mutual recognition" (20, 16). Both Bakhtin and Benjamin emphasize the possibility of individual development in relationship; interdependence need not negate personal freedom.

Indeed, in *Beloved*, constructive narration becomes possible as a duet rather than as a monologue. By serving as Denver's audience, Beloved silently participates in the narration and encourages the storytelling process by creating an atmosphere of mutual support: "Denver spoke, Beloved listened and the two did the best they could in order to create what really happened" (78). By asking Denver to narrate the story: "'Tell me,' Beloved said. 'Tell me how Sethe made you in the boat,'" (76) Beloved undermines the patterns of silence and secrecy in which Denver has been growing up. She asks Denver to narrate that which has been indirectly relayed to her by her mother, brothers, grandmother, and the community at different times and under different circumstances. Denver is asked to transform the implicit into explicit: "[Denver] swallowed twice to prepare for the telling, to construct out of the strings she had heard all her life a net to hold Beloved" (76).

Beloved's rhetorical guidance helps Denver to identify with Sethe to such a level that she can fill in the missing traumatic details Sethe was unable to narrate. By helping Denver to describe events she has not actually witnessed, Beloved impels her sister to imagine; that is "to *see* what she was saying and not just to hear it" (77, emphasis mine). At first, Denver recreates the mother's story from the perspective of the observer. However, as she goes on, she identifies with her mother so much that she starts not only seeing but also feeling the story through Beloved: "feeling how it must have felt to her mother. Seeing how it must have looked" (78). The change in perspective develops Denver's mind-reading ability, enabling her to experience the story from her mother's (i.e., the participant's) perspective. While in Sethe's storytelling about her own mother Beloved helps to transform visual, field memories into narrative memories, with Denver, Beloved initiates an opposite process, transforming the remembered story into visual images, which enhances Denver's identification with her mother.

According to John A. Robinson, "remembering can be organized through various perspectives or points of view. Subjectively, the rememberer may reexperience the event as a participant or a spectator." The participant's perspective enables imaginative participation in the events as if experienced firsthand. The spectator's point of view, on the contrary, registers "the self engaged in the event as an observer would," that is, without particular emotional involvement (206). Robinson further claims that flashbacks associated with post-traumatic stress disorder and other traumas tend to occur as participant memories (207). This may suggest that the participant's perspective is more emotionally loaded than a spectator's point of view. Since Denver's initial imagination of her mother's story occurred merely from a spectator's perspective, it blunted her emotional involvement in the story. Beloved's intervention allows Denver to develop an additional perspective. Although she maintains the initial observer's stance to a certain degree, after shifting her point of view she can also participate in the story as if she was actually present when the events took place.

However, even though Denver becomes emotionally involved in the story, she is not as traumatized by the events as her mother. This is because she now possesses a double vision as both an observer and a participant; she can both identify with her mother and maintain her own separate self. The novel's narrative strategy brings this out. Morrison narrates Denver's second retelling in the third person, rather than in the first, which is more immediately associated with personal testimonies. The third person voice provides the necessary distance for Denver's narration of her mother's story: "there is this nineteen-year-old slave girl—a year older than herself—walking through the dark woods to get to her children who are far away. She is tired, scared maybe, and maybe even lost" (77-78). On the one hand, the observer's perspective is maintained when Denver describes her mother, as if observing her from a distance. Yet, on the other hand, the daughter can relate to her mother's situation and narrate her emotions. By mentioning that her mother was her age when running away, the daughter brings her mother's past closer to her own present and can therefore understand how exhausted and scared her mother had been.[18]

When Sethe acknowledges Beloved as her daughter, she tries to amend their relationship. Beloved, however, refuses to forgive; instead, she attempts to avenge her own murder by killing Sethe. She makes Sethe quit her job and play with Denver and herself. Then, she drives Denver away from their play. Constantly asking for food and sweets, Beloved almost makes Sethe and Denver starve to death. Observing this deteriorating situation, Denver finally succeeds in drawing the right conclusions regarding the Sethe-Beloved relationship: she understood that Sethe "was trying to make up for the handsaw; Beloved was making her pay for it." Denver, however, also realizes "there would never be an end to that, and seeing her mother diminished, shamed and infuriated her. Yet she knew that Sethe's greatest fear was the same one Denver had in the beginning—that Beloved might leave" (251). Denver understands her mother's state of mind when comparing it to her own fear. By recognizing her own emotional connection and similarity to her mother, she establishes an intersubjective bond that allows her to read her mother's mind.

Beloved's intervention, despite its negative impact on Sethe's mental and physical health, promotes changes in Denver's assumptions. At first, Denver watches Sethe and Beloved's interaction alert for "any sign that Beloved was in danger . . . her eye was on her mother, for a signal that the thing that was in her was out, and she would kill again. But it was Beloved who made demands" (240); "The job [Denver] started out with, protecting Beloved from Sethe, changed to protecting her mother from Beloved. Now it was obvious that her mother could die" (243). Denver thus takes the initiative into her hands and turns to the black community of Cincinnati for help.

Interestingly, the same community that ostracizes Sethe for her violence at the beginning of the novel embraces her at the end of the novel, exorcising Beloved through vocal collaboration. The community once again creates an intermental unit that shares a common goal and a common mind. When the black women gather to banish Beloved, they use no words: "in the beginning there were no words. In the beginning was the sound, and they all knew what that sound sounded like" (259). The women's collective memory of the right sound allows them to access the primary, prelinguistic experience that precedes speech in order to accept Sethe back into their community.[19] The women's collaboration during the exorcizing ritual reestablishes the intermental bond between the members of the community: "building voice upon voice," the women search for the right key, and when it is found, they produce "a wave of sound wide enough to sound deep water and knock the pods off chestnut trees" (261).

The community's silence, immediately after the murder juxtaposes with this later vocal attempt to help Sethe overcome her horrible past. In fact, after the women succeed in banishing Beloved physically, they begin the cognitive process of mental exorcising or—as Morrison puts it—"disremembering."

> Disremembered and unaccounted for, she [Beloved] cannot be lost because *no one* is looking for her, and even if *they* were, how can *they* call her if *they* don't know her name? . . . *They* forgot her like a bad dream. After *they* made up their tales, shaped and decorated them, *those* that saw her that day on the porch, quickly and deliberately forgot her. . . . Occasionally, however, the rustle of a skirt hushes when *they* wake, and the knuckles brushing a cheek in sleep seem to belong to the sleeper. Sometimes the photograph of a close friend or relative – *looked at* too long—shifts, and something more *familiar* than the dear face itself moves there. *They* can touch it if *they* like, but don't, because *they* know things will never be the same if *they* do. (274-75, emphasis mine)

The cognitive framework of stories the community constructs in order to disremember[20] Beloved creates an intermental web that connects the community members into what Palmer refers to as a group mind. This mind is shown to have an uncanny experience of the ghostly presence that keeps haunting this group's imagination. The haunting past becomes an integral part of the communal knowledge or the communal mind. It becomes their common knowledge that memory, even though it is recreated in the group's mind, may reincarnate and change the present.[21]

After years of misunderstanding, mutual rejection, and loneliness, not only Denver, but the community, too, realizes their mistaken assumptions about Beloved's murder. When it turns out that Sethe does not only feel guilty for her violent act, but may die immersing herself in her destructive remorse, Denver appeals to the community and receives help. In order to understand Sethe empathetically, Denver has to reject the community's original conception of her mother. When this is achieved, the daughter can reenter the communal intermental unit and change it from within. The individual's impact on the community is thus revealed—Denver explains her mother's mental states to others, thus changing the group's opinion about the murder.

When Denver must ask for help, she realizes that "nobody was going to help her unless she told it—told all of it" (253). The daughter makes amends for her mother's silent pride through verbal communication. She tells part of the story about Beloved's haunting to some women in the community, explaining her mother's deteriorating mental and physical condition. Although Denver revises the story of the haunting, representing Beloved as a cousin who came to visit, got sick, and bothered her mother (254), the women of the community reinterpret the story in much more supernatural terms:

> the news that Janey got hold of she spread among the other coloredwomen [sic]. Sethe's dead daughter . . . had come back to fix her. She was worn down,

> speckled, dying, spinning, changing shapes and generally bedeviled. . . . It took them days to get the story properly blown up and themselves agitated and then to calm down and assess the situation. (255)

By revising Denver's story and creating their own interpretation the women cognitively reprocess Sethe's past and present and alter their communal mind.

Using her enhanced mind-reading skills Denver eventually understands her mother's victimization; she empathizes with Sethe's suffering as a slave-mother who is forced into violence against her own children by the system of slavery. While Beloved has been the victim of her mother's violence, Sethe has been the victim of slavery and of her own ambiguous choice. Reinterpreting Sethe's motivation through empathy, Denver finally effaces the demonic mother figure she has imaginatively constructed. Ironically, by using her imagination, the daughter finally succeeds in coming to terms with her real mother.

NOTES

1 Developing Abraham and Torok's argument, in *Family Secrets*, Esther Rushkin suggests that phantoms or ghosts are an unconscious, repressed formation, too horrible or shameful to be represented in words (28). The phantom image generated in the subconsciousness of the traumatized parent is indirectly transmitted to the child by means of cryptic discourses, thus becoming an integral part of the child's subconscious worldview. According to Rushkin, the child that inherits the gap in her parent's speech actually inherits parts of the parent's subconsciousness (29).

2 After some members of Sethe's community witness Beloved's murder, they stop visiting Sethe's house and treat the whole family as social outcasts. Stamp Paid seems to be the only character who succeeds in interpreting Sethe's intentions empathically. In his words: "She love those children. She was trying to outhurt the hurter" (234). Even though, just like the rest of the community, Stamp Paid has been avoiding Sethe, toward the end of the novel he admits that unlike others he does not perceive Sethe as crazy, but rather as an extremely devoted mother who tried to overpower the system of slavery through the murder of her own child.

3 After the brothers leave Denver continuously has nightmares and fantasies about her mother's violence. She dreams about her mother cutting her head off "her pretty eyes looking at me like I was a stranger. Not mean or anything, but like I was somebody she found and felt sorry for. Like she didn't want to do it but she had to and it was not going to hurt. That it was just a thing grown-up people do" (206). Denver makes an attempt to understand her mother's violence by attributing it to the inexplicable realm of the grown-up's world. This, however, does not justify the mother's deed, and therefore, just like the readers, Denver experiences continuous difficulties in understanding her mother's motives and intentions.

4 While Sethe and her children mange to flee from the slaveholders, the father of the family, Halle, fails to escape. His fate remains a mystery for years until Paul D, who was enslaved on the same farm as Sethe and her family, arrives at her house. He

tells Sethe that the last time he saw Halle on the farm, he was smearing butter over his face. Paul D assumes that "something broke" Halle, but it is only after Sethe tells him that prior to her escape she was violated and beaten by the slaveholders that he understands what happened to Sethe's husband. Paul D concludes that Halle must have witnessed the horrible scene of his wife's violation, and unable to protect her, he lost his mind.

5 It is possible that Sethe's deed remains unnamed because the grandmother, as well as other people in the community, lack suitable words to express it. Stamp Paid, who witnessed Sethe's offense, also experiences difficulty talking about the murder directly; he refers to it as "Sethe's Misery," thus expressing both the child's and the mother's victimization.

6 In *Is There a Text in This Class?* Stanley Fish argues that "meanings are the property neither of fixed and stable texts not of free and independent readers but of interpretive communities that are responsible for the shape of a reader's activities and for the texts those activities produce" (322). According to Fish, our "consciousnesses are constituted by a set of conventional notions" that we assimilate from our sociocultural environment. Using these notions to interpret our reality, we produce the culturally accepted meanings that allow us to participate in the interpretive community set by our social environment.

The concept of "interpreting communities" in relation to *Beloved* was initially brought to my attention by Rita Horvath, whose manuscript "Murdered Joy: A Reading of Henry James's 'The Figure in the Carpet'" discusses what it means to enter a reading community and what factors enable or prevent one to enter a community of interpreters / readers.

7 Powers claims that Morrison's narrative manipulates time by "fastforwarding and rewinding of the temporal setting through flashbacks and stories of the past related by characters or through the meandering, history-purveying eye of an omniscient narrator. Rather than a chronological, diachronic storyline that weaves the evidence of the past into an ordered, *de facto*, meaningful narrative, time in Morrison synchronizes various pats into one level narrative space, which in turn is subjected more to the demands of characterization than to those of narration" (33).

8 The slaveholders perceive Sethe and her children as their commodity and therefore do not believe in Sethe's right to mother her children. In these circumstances, the only motherly act Sethe can impose on the white society is the murder of her own child.

9 For Sethe the truth was simple: she had to protect her children from the Schoolteacher even if she had to kill them. As the narrator puts it: "she just flew. Collected every bit of life she had made, all the parts of her that were precious and fine and beautiful, and carried, pushed, dragged them through the veil, out, away, over there where no one could hurt them" (163).

10 This, however, proves to be incorrect, since Beloved forces Sethe to explain her intentions again and again, draining Sethe's emotional and physical strength.

11 The community's stony silence after the murder contrasts with the silent mutu-

ality between Baby Suggs and her congregation. Although both reactions involve paralinguistic communication and signify intermental thinking, the former silence testifies to utter misunderstanding between Sethe and her community, while the latter implies cooperation and understanding between the leader and the group.

12 Schwarz, Joel. "65% of school-age children have an imaginary companion by age 7," *Medical News Today* 7 Dec. 2004, 21 Oct. 2007, http://www.medicalnewstoday.com/articles/17426.php.

According to developmental psychologists, children who report having imaginary companions also have more developed ToM abilities. Research with 152 preschoolers found that having an imaginary companion or impersonating an imaginary character was positively correlated with ToM performance. School-age children who did not impersonate scored lower on emotion understanding (Taylor et al.)

13 The term "relational" or "collective identity" was developed in feminist criticism to describe the characteristics of female identity as different from a male individualistic, autonomous self. For a useful review of models of identity, see Paul Eakin's *How Our Lives Become Stories* (46-53).

14 Although Benjamin discusses the relationships between mothers and infants in general, her theory is particularly relevant to mother-daughter bonds. Since the daughters' identification processes are more problematic than the sons', they find alternative ways to relate to their mothers. Benjamin's intersubjective view illuminates the processes of identification and construction of relational identity through mutual recognition.

15 As Kay Young and Jeffrey Saver argue in "Neurology of Narrative," the ability to construct narrative is inseparable from personhood. Brain-injured individuals "who have lost the ability to construct narrative . . . have lost their selves" (780).

16 In "Narrative Empathy," Suzanne Keen suggests that empathy is not only an emotional, but also a cognitive process: "empathy itself clearly involves both feeling and thinking. Memory, experience, and the capacity to take another person's perspective (all matters traditionally considered cognitive) have roles in empathy" (213). Beloved's intervention in Denver's cognitive processes not only develops her ToM, but also her emotional capacities. By changing the narrative perspective of her birth story Denver empathizes with her mother. She begins to understand Sethe's emotional and physical difficulties as a slave mother, struggling to protect her children and keep her family together. This emotional and cognitive process finally allows Denver to arrive at an understanding of why Sethe killed Beloved.

17 I can become "myself only while revealing myself for another, through another, and with help of another" . . . "I must find myself in another by finding another in myself (in mutual reflection and mutual acceptance)" (Bakhtin 287).

18 "Expressive writing has been shown as a powerful therapeutic tool for resolving the intense effects engendered by traumatic experiences" (Robinson 207). By adopting an observer's perspective, at least while narrating the story, victims of trauma learn to reconstruct meaning and attain some sense of control over their experience. By splitting the narrating self from the experiencing self the traumatized person dis-

tances himself or herself from the past, transforming his or her participant perspective into a spectator's perspective. Denver, however, has to go through an almost reversed process: to add a participant's point of view, thus making her mother's story more emotional and relevant to herself.

19 It is unclear where the women gain the experience or knowledge of the sound. It is possible that the community has been using this sound at the spiritual meetings they held when Baby Suggs, or Baby Suggs Holy as they referred to her, was alive. The memory of Sethe's mother-in-law, to whom the community is spiritually indebted, also propels mutual forgiveness and reconciliation.

20 As opposed to forgetting, disremembering is a deliberate process of healing by putting the past behind. The horrors of slavery cannot be forgotten, but rather put aside in order to continue living.

21 According to psychological research, remembering is a creative, rather than a precise and unchanged retrieval of past events. As studies on flashbulb memories, Deese-Roediger-McDermott illusions, and eyewitness testimonies demonstrate, present recall may distort the original memories of past events. For further details see Roediger and McDermott as well as Schacter. However, as Daniel Schacter also demonstrates in *Searching for Memory*, emotional and especially traumatic memories influence the rememberer's present and may even change this person's character. The great majority of individuals who experienced traumatic events repeatedly recollect these events to the point where they cannot fully enjoy their present lives. The traumatic memories "impose" themselves on the individual "cast[ing] a shadow" over the victims' lives (196, 203). Thus, past and present inform and shape each other. On the one hand, present events evoke the memories of the past, which may distort or change them, yet on the other hand, when the recall of the past occurs it may influence the present life of the remembering person.

WORKS CITED

Abraham, Nicolas, and Maria Torok. *The Wolf Man's Magic: A Cryptonymy*. Trans. Nicholas Rand. *Theory and History of Literature*. Vol 37. Minneapolis: University of Minnesota Press, 1986. Print.

Bakhtin, Mikhail. *Problems of Dostoevsky's Poetics*. Trans. Caryl Emerson. Minneapolis: University of Minnesota Press, 1984. Print.

Benjamin, Jessica. *The Bonds of Love: Psychoanalysis, Feminism and the Problem of Domination*. New York: Pantheon, 1988. Print.

Chodorow, Nancy J. *The Reproduction of Mothering. Psychoanalysis and the sociology of Gender.* Berkeley: University of California 1978. Print.

---. *Feminism and Psychoanalytic Theory*. New Haven and London: Yale University Press, 1989. Print.

Eakin, Paul John. *How Our Lives Become Stories. Making Selves*. Ithaca and London: Cornell University Press, 1999. Print.

Fish, Stanley. *Is There a Text in This Class? The Authority of Interpretive Communities.*

Cambridge: Harvard University Press, 1980. Print.

Garfield, Jay L., Candida C. Peterson, and Tricia Perry. "Social Cognition, Language Acquisition and the Development of the Theory of Mind." *Mind and Language* 16.5 (2001): 494-541. Print.

Horvath, Rita. "Murdered Joy: A Reading of Henry James's 'The Figure in the Carpet.'" Unpublished Essay, 2008.

Morrison, Toni. *Beloved*. London: Vintage, 1997. Print.

Moreira-Slepoy, Garciella. "Toni Morrison's Beloved: Reconstructing the Past through Storytelling and Private Narratives." *Revue de Recherche Interdisciplinaire en Textes et Médias* 2 (2003). Web. February 2008. http://www.post-scriptum.org.

Nelson, Katherine. "Explaining the Emeregence of Autobiographical Memory in Early Childhood." *Theories of Memory*. Ed. Alan F. Collins et al. Hove, East Sussex: Lawrence Earlbaum Associates, 1993. Print.

Palmer, Alan. "Intermental Thought in the Novel: The Middlemarch Mind." *Style* 39.4 (2005): 427-39. Print.

Powers, Christopher. "The Third Eye: Love, Memory, and History in Toni Morrison's Beloved, Jazz and Paradise." *Narrating the Past: (Re)Constructing Memory, (Re)Negitating History*. Ed. Batra Nadita and Messier Vartan. Newcastle upon Tyne: Cambridge Scholars, 2007. Print.

Rashkin, Esther. *Family Secrets and the Psychoanalysis of Narrative*. Princeton: Princeton University Press, 1992. Print.

Reese, Elaine, and Emily Sutcliffe Cleveland. "Mother-Child Reminiscing and Children's Understanding of Mind." *Merrill Palmer Quarterly* 52.1 (2006): 17-43. Print.

Robinson John A. "Perspective Meaning and Remembering." *Remembering our Pasts*. Ed. David C. Rubin. Cambridge: Cambridge University Press, 1996. Print.

Roediger, Henry. L. III, and Kathleen B McDermott. "Creating False Memories: Remembering Words not Presented in Lists." *Journal of Experimental Psychology: Learning, Memory, and Cognition* 21.4 (1995): 803-14. Print.

Rushdy, Ashraf H. A. *Remembering Generations. Race and Family in Contemporary African American Fiction*. Chapel Hill and London: The University of Carolina Press, 2001. Print.

Schacter, Daniel L. *Searching for Memory. The Brain, The Mind, and The Past*. New York: Basic Books, 1996. Print.

Taylor, Marjorie et al. "The Characteristics and Correlates of Fantasy in School-Age Children: Imaginary Companions, Impersonation, and Social Understanding." *Developmental Psychology* 40.6 (2004): 1173-87. Print.

Young, Kay, and Jeffrey L. Saver. "The Neurology of Narrative." *SubStance* 30.1 (2001): 72-84. Print.

Zunshine, Lisa. *Why We Read Fiction: Theory of Mind and the Novel*. Columbus: The Ohio State University Press, 2006. Print.

Changing Minds: Theory of Mind and Propaganda in Egon Erwin Kisch's *Asien gründlich verändert*

Seth Knox

The foremost goal of every propagandist is to affect audience cognitions. In order to accomplish this, the propagandist must construct a plausible and probable "audience mind" that has the capacity to be affected. The construction of an audience mind clearly falls within Flavell's definition of metacognition as "any knowledge or cognitive activity that takes as its object, or regulates, any aspect of any cognitive enterprise" (104). As propagandists take as their object of study the cognitions of others, the Theory of Mind (ToM) of cognitive psychology holds particular promise for the analysis of their techniques of mind reading and manipulation. This paper will examine Egon Erwin Kisch's propagandistic travel book *Asien gründlich verändert* (*Changing Asia*; 1932, translated 1935) through an approach informed by cognitive studies and ToM. Two mind reading and manipulation techniques that are deployed throughout *Asien gründlich verändert* will be analyzed here: resonance and high source-tracking load. A cognitive approach to these techniques illuminates how they may create the illusion of independent reasoning and self-generated belief in the mind of the propagandee.

When discussing a topic as politically and emotionally sensitive as propaganda, it is helpful to have a working definition of the term. Unfortunately propaganda seems to resist a precise and non-controversial definition, despite the fact that propaganda studies have attracted scholarly work since the end of World War I from several disciplines, including political science, history, sociology, psychology, and communications. Defining propaganda is complicated by its associations in modern English with brainwashing and immoral attempts to manipulate mass audiences with clever falsehoods. Further, it may be tempting to label as propaganda any persuasive communication that one disagrees with (and deny as propaganda any persuasive communication that one finds appealing).

This paper seeks a definition of propaganda that focuses on communicative function. Taylor, in his historical study of propaganda, defines it as "the conscious, methodical and planned decisions to employ techniques of persuasion designed to achieve specific goals that are *intended to benefit those organizing the process*" (6; emphasis in the original). Jowett and O'Donnel similarly define propaganda as "the deliberate and systematic attempt to shape perceptions, manipulate cognitions, and direct behavior to achieve a response that furthers the desired intent of the propagandist" (4). It is clear from these definitions that propaganda is a subcategory of persuasion; persuasion is, however, distinct from propaganda in that persuasion is an "interactive process in which a sender and a receiver are linked by symbols, verbal and nonverbal, through which the persuader attempts to influence the persuadee to adopt a change in a given attitude or behavior because the persuadee has had perceptions enlarged or changed" (O'Donnel and Kable 9). Whereas persuasion is interactive and ostensibly more voluntary, and it is even possible that the persuader could become the persuadee over the course of the exchange, propaganda does not attempt to engage the audience in a truly participatory dialogue. Instead, propaganda is one-sided communication that anticipates and attempts to manipulate the cognitions of the propagandee in a way that is beneficial to the propagandist. Whether this is ultimately beneficial to the propagandee is either secondary or irrelevant. The conclusions to be drawn from persuasive communication are somewhat flexible due to its interactional nature; the conclusions and attitudes of propagandistic communication are fixed and absolute.

Propaganda is typically classified into three shades: white (overt), gray, and black (covert). This classification is based on the degree to which the propaganda source is obscured and sometimes the accuracy of the information presented. *Asien gründlich verändert* is an example of overt, or white, propaganda. This means that the source of the propaganda (Kisch) is clearly identified, the information presented is accurate in so far as the book describes an actual journey undertaken by Kisch, and the book's self-selecting audience would have been aware of Kisch's membership in the Communist Party and his pro-Soviet bias. *Asien gründlich verändert* is a travel account of Kisch's 1931 journey with an international authors' brigade to the youngest Soviet Republics of Uzbekistan and Tajikistan. At the time, Kisch was working as a professor at the University of Kharkov in the Ukraine and as a speaker on Radio Moscow, whose propagandistic broadcasts could be heard in Germany (Patka 122). The deepening global economic crisis and the growing disillusionment of the German reading public with the United States as a viable economic model for Germany increased interest in and sales of his earlier travel books on the Soviet Union (*Zaren, Popen, Bolschewiken* 1927) and the United States (*Paradies Amerika* 1930) (Djukic-Cocks 26).

These three travel works formed a propagandistic trilogy that resonated with the vague, conspiratorial "anti-System" thinking that dominated political discourse in the Weimar Republic. Anti-System theories were embraced by both the nationalist right and the Communist left; they differed most noticeably in their choice of villains behind the international political system supposedly responsible for Germany's ruin (Lieberman 358-63). Kisch's travels to America and the Soviet Union provided readers with eyewitness accounts of the inevitable misery wrought by capitalism and the inspiring collective achievements of Communism. Kisch's earlier travel works, however, were not as overtly propagandistic as *Asien gründlich verändert*. *Zaren, Popen, Bolschewiken* is an often dry, if highly selective, presentation of facts and statistics of the early Soviet Union. *Paradies Amerika* is an entertaining mosaic of Kisch's frequently amusing and sometimes shocking experiences from his journey through "Gottes eigenes Land" ("God's own country"; *Gesammelte Werke* 5: 9).

Zaren, Popen, Bolschewiken and *Paradies Amerika* give the reader the impression that they are travel works about their destinations (the propagandistic tendencies of these works are more subtly embedded in the travel narrative). *Asien gründlich verändert*, however, bridges the two earlier travel narratives and makes clear that this travel trilogy is about the near future of the world (and, more importantly, Germany). Kisch's work on Central Asia also clearly promotes Communism as the most preferable system for the coming new world order. Whereas *Zaren, Popen, Bolschewiken* and *Paradies Amerika* were highly successful in financial terms (and, important for their propagandistic value, in reaching a large audience), *Asien gründlich verändert* was available in only its first edition in Germany before being banned by the Nazi government (before the ban, Kisch was also able to publish a hastily compiled collection of travel writings on China). The second German-language edition was published in exile in Moscow. It is thus impossible to know whether *Asien gründlich verändert* could have had the same popular appeal and market success as its two predecessors.

A mind reading technique that Kisch employs throughout *Asien gründlich verändert* is the deployment of anchors to create the effect of resonance. Resonance refers to a complex of values expressed in propaganda that is shared by the propagandist's intended audience, and an anchor is a belief, value, or attitude that is already present in the cognitive system of the propagandee (Jowett and O'Donnell 25-26). For example, if one were creating propaganda targeting self-described environmentalists, anchors might include assertions of the efficacy of government regulation in reducing pollution, the scientific consensus on man-made causes of global warming, and so on. Anchors should repeat beliefs already held by the target audience. The net effect of anchors is resonance—the activation of beliefs, values, and attitudes that ideally creates the illusion that the propagandized message is coming from within the subject rather than as a message imposed from without.

Anchors may make the propagandee more susceptible to propagandized content by activating the believability effect observed by Evans, Barston, and Pollard, who found that people are likely to accept conclusions that appear to be based on their preexisting assumptions. If propagandized content is presented as conclusions derived logically from well-placed anchors (even if the logic is weak or faulty), the propagandee may be more likely to accept it. Of course, in order to determine the content that is suitable for use as anchors, the propagandist must first imagine the mind of the propagandee. This construction of the audience is necessarily an inexact abstraction, and fits well into the idea of problematization formulated by Michel Foucault (Bratich 243-44). In *Asien gründlich verändert*, Kisch must problematize his imagined audience and anticipate probable group-identities in order to identify potentially effective anchors. Several anchors used by Kisch serve to encompass Kisch (and by extension his propagandized messages) and his audience in a common group-identity.

Throughout *Asien gründlich verändert*, Kisch refers to himself as a "Western European," a "German," and a "Berliner" (this is despite the fact that he is actually from Prague). Such descriptors clearly link Kisch with the group-identity of his German-speaking audience. However, in *Zaren, Popen, Bolschewiken*, Kisch went to great lengths to bring Soviet Russians into the sphere of the German group-self. In addition to emphasizing the ways in which Russians resembled Germans, both linguistically and in similar customs, Kisch attributed to Russians those qualities that most Germans (and most people) aspire to: dedication, nobility, honesty, and a strong work ethic (Knox 80-81). This attempt to include Soviet citizens in the group-identity of his German-speaking audience continues in *Changing Asia* as Kisch depicts Soviet Communists as liberating Uzbeks and Tajiks from the tyrannies of czarist colonialism, capitalist exploitation, and Islamist sexism, terror, and oppression.

The representation of Soviets as existing within the German group-self is simultaneously reinforced through a starkly polarized depiction of others existing outside the group-self. To achieve this, Kisch calls upon an effective technique used by the British during World War I: atrocity propaganda. Two examples of Kisch's use of atrocity propaganda are particularly striking. After a visit to the Sindan, a former dungeon prison for enemies of the Emir of Bokhara, Kisch recounts the story of the imprisoned uncle of Olim Kahn. Conditions in the prison were so severe that this man attempted to gnaw off his shackled arm at the shoulder (*Gesammelte Werke* 4: 247, *Changing Asia* 54-55). Later in the book, Kisch records the story of a Ukrainian woman's ordeal in 1918 during the civil war. When the Whites entered her village and broke into her home, they raped her as they murdered her three year-old daughter and five year-old son before shooting her husband, who was a local revolutionary leader (*Gesammelte Werke* 4: 283-85, *Changing Asia* 111-14). Both stories, along with other atrocities, are presented as barbarous practices that are being stamped out by the Soviets.

The rigid moral dichotomy established in *Asien gründlich verändert* serves to achieve resonance between Kisch's readership and the declared objectives of Soviet activities in Central Asia. Also, in anticipation of his readers developing a sense of hopelessness after reading his atrocity propaganda, Kisch highlights the accomplishments of the Soviets and the hopeful words of Uzbeks and Tajiks who are delighted with the Soviet presence and look forward to an increasingly bright future. Kisch assures his readers that, despite what they read in the press, the Central Asian Republics are achieving independence in cotton production. Increasing numbers of girls are attending Soviet-built schools, literacy rates are advancing at an impressive clip, more and more women are giving up their veils and working outside the home, and Islamist terrorists, secretly funded by imperialist England, are being decisively defeated. All of this strongly encourages resonance between the perceived motivations and attitudes of the Soviets with those of the propagandee.

In one chapter, "Was hat sich geändert in Chodschent?" ("What Are the Changes in Khojent?"), Kisch anticipates doubt in the reader caused by newspaper articles he is likely to have read. After referring to specific articles and answering the charges raised by each, Kisch shares his frustration with his reader (who, if Kisch's propaganda has been successful, also shares his frustration):

> Wenn sich nichts geändert hätte auf diesem Sechstel der Erdoberfläche, als daß die Ausbeutung weggefegt worden ist—auch ohne die Abschaffung der Arbeitslosigkeit, des Kinderelends, des Analphabetismus, der Religionsverdummung, der Korruption, auch ohne die Erfüllung von hundert Millionen Menschen mit werktätiger Begeisterung, mit Wissen und Kultur, auch ohne all dies, nur um dieser Beseitigung der Ausbeutung willen verlohnte es sich, Zeitgenosse unserer Zeit zu sein.
>
> Aber wer begreift das? Der in kapitalistische Verhältnisse hineingeborene und von ihrer Ideologie benebelte Mensch findet das furchtbarste Unheil nicht furchtbar; er hat sich an die soziale Ungleichheit gewöhnt, die lange vor der Geburt des Menschen beginnt und mit seiner Grablegung noch lange nicht endet. Er empfindet es nicht als grausam, er empfindet es bestenfalls als unabwendbar, daß Hunderttausende Menschen für einen roboten müssen; wer durchschaut die Mittel der Massenverdummung, die diese Verhältnisse künstlich und künstlerisch aufrechterhalten?
>
> Der Leser hat obige Abweichung ins Leitartikelhafte mit Unwillen gelesen. Diese ausnahmsweise Überschreitung ist jedoch notwendig, weil hier unerfreuliche Details nicht nur nicht verschwiegen, sondern oft kraß skizziert wurden und daher auch angegeben werden muß, daß die verschiedenen Skizzen verschiedene Maßstäbe haben: die Originalgröße der unerfreulichen Details ist verschwindlich klein im Verhältnis zum erfreulichen Gesamtbild. (*Asien gründlich verändert* 350-51)
>
> [If there had been no other changes on this sixth part of the surface of the globe but that exploitation has been done away with—leaving aside the eradication of unemployment, of the misery of children, of illiteracy, of religious superstition, of corruption, leaving aside the fact that a hundred million human beings have been filled with constructive enthusiasm, with knowledge and culture, leaving aside all this—if only for the sake of abolishing exploitation, it would be worth while to live in our day and age.
>
> But how many people understand this? A man born into capitalistic conditions, his mind befogged with capitalistic ideology, sees nothing horrible in the most horrible squalor. He is accustomed to a social inequality which begins before birth and continues after burial. He does not deem it cruel—at best he feels it to be regrettable, but inevitable—that hundreds of thousands must act as robots for a single man who is clever enough to exploit the stupidity of the masses.
>
> The reader has read this editorial digression with displeasure. But one such digression becomes obligatory to balance unfavourable evidence which cannot be glossed over—which indeed should be repeatedly and emphatically pointed

> out. In other words, the reader must be reminded that these pictures are drawn to scale, and details which are derogatory if studied as isolated phenomena take on minor proportions when regarded in their relation to the picture as a whole, which is decidedly favourable.] (*Changing Asia* 203-04)

In this remarkable chapter, Kisch draws the reader's attention to potential reasons to doubt the assertions of his travel narrative. This passage, however, simultaneously instructs the reader on how to process Kisch's claims in the context of competing sources of propaganda. By insisting that evidence that does not speak well of Soviet efforts will not be "glossed over," but rather emphasized, Kisch is explicitly manipulating the cognitions of the reader so that his text will be perceived as balanced and objective. (The verb "manipulate" is used here in a negative sense, since, despite Kisch's claim, evidence suggesting that Soviet efforts are anything but advantageous to Central Asians is quite scarce in the book.) The text has a good chance of appealing to the propagandee, since it is inherently flattering to the self-selecting readership of *Asien gründlich verändert*: they, Kisch implies, can see clearly (without minds "befogged with capitalist ideology") and will not be manipulated like "robots" by a malicious individual who knows how to take advantage of the average person's stupidity. Kisch's readers, unlike the common crowd, will not be taken in by propaganda.

The lengthy passage above achieves resonance by appealing to the propagandee's vanity. Kisch suggests what most readers probably already believe: that their intelligence is above average, they are perceptive and able to grasp the big picture, and they are not gullible. If the propagandee already believes these things (and such self-flattering notions are probably reliable anchors), then it may seem as if Kisch is giving voice to the propagandee's own thoughts. This could further place the propagandee in a more suggestive state and more receptive to Kisch's representations of the out-group (men whose minds are befogged with capitalism).

Considering that Kisch has provided repeated stimulation of negative representations of capitalists in *Paradies Amerika* and *Asien gründlich verändert*, and considering that Kisch's audience is self-selecting, these propagandized representations could have an effect on the base-rate bias of the propagandee's allocation system. In other words, as a result of repeated exposure to the propagandized representations of capitalists, these representations could be evoked more and more frequently when encountering (or reading about) really existing capitalists. In his discussion of the cognitive allocation system, Brase refers to this phenomenon as "initial base-rate bias," also referred to as "chronically accessible schemas" in social psychology (19-20). Brase describes a chronically accessible schema as "a particular way of representing events that is used by a person in a habitual manner, such as when a person represents all social events as being related to race relations (or politics, or sex, or ethnicity, or any other specific frame of reference)" (19). If propagandized representations of capitalists are repeated often enough, then such representations will be most easily available in memory and habitually activated when capitalists (or discussions of capitalists) are encountered. Kisch's instinct that effective propaganda relies at least in part on repetition is well founded, as a study by Skurnik, Yoon, Park, and Schwarz found that previous exposure to a written statement increased the probability that a person would find the statement credible. In this manner, it might be possible for a book-length work of propaganda such as *Asien gründlich verändert* to create new anchors in the propagandee that deviate subtly from already existing anchors.

In addition to achieving resonance (and possibly a chronically accessible schema), Kisch employs several techniques to tax the propagandee's source-tracking ability. This claim may seem strange, given that *Asien gründlich verändert* is an example of overt propaganda. Kisch is clearly identified as the author (source) of the text. Kisch is also known to his readers as a Communist revolutionary and one-time leader of the Austrian Red Guard. In fact, Kisch could only function effectively as an overt propagandist precisely because of his carefully cultivated public image. His image as a journalist and celebrity was carefully controlled. His public persona was that of the *rasende Reporter*, the tireless journalist who would do anything for his story, scribbling notes hastily to capture as many facts as possible. This, coupled with his association with the *Neue Sachlichkeit*, or "New Objectivity," movement, gained him a reputation as a reliable and trustworthy source.

Also strongly linking Kisch to his work is the fact that *Asien gründlich verändert* belongs to the non-fiction genre of travel literature. Readers of travel literature expect an account of an actual journey made by a really existing author. While the author's personal opinions are typically tolerated, there is an expectation that the author will describe the voyage essentially as it was experienced. Thus travel literature affords the reader a form of vicarious travel. It also affords the propagandist the assumption of a certain amount of objectivity on the part of the propagandee. Yet despite the seeming advantages of genre and reputation, Kisch employs techniques that weaken source tags linking him to the representations in his book. Applying the concept of mind reading to travel literature provides a plausible explanation for this behavior and why it is advantageous to the propagandist.

The model below is based on Baron-Cohen's description of the Shared Attention Mechanism in the human mind reading system (44-45). For a very basic understanding of the Shared Attention Mechanism, one can imagine a child and a parent sitting on a park bench and watching a bird. The Shared Attention Mechanism enables the child to realize that his or her parent is attentive to the same bird that he or she is watching. In regard to any representation in the text *Asien gründlich verändert*, both Kisch and the reader are aware that the other is attending to the same representation. When, for example, Kisch describes the Sindan prison, the reader is aware that Kisch is the source of the representation (and hence aware of it), and the reader may also be aware that Kisch knows the reader will be attending to the representation. Conversely, Kisch is obviously attending the representation, and he is also aware that his reader will as well. Kisch is also aware that the reader will know he is attending the representation. This model, however, implies naïveté on the part of the reader. To borrow and adapt Baron-Cohen's explanation of the subject's search for "relevance," the reader "assumes that the meaning of [a representation] will be relevant to the [author's] current intentions" (27). In other words, the reader will likely ask the question, "Why is Kisch showing me this?"

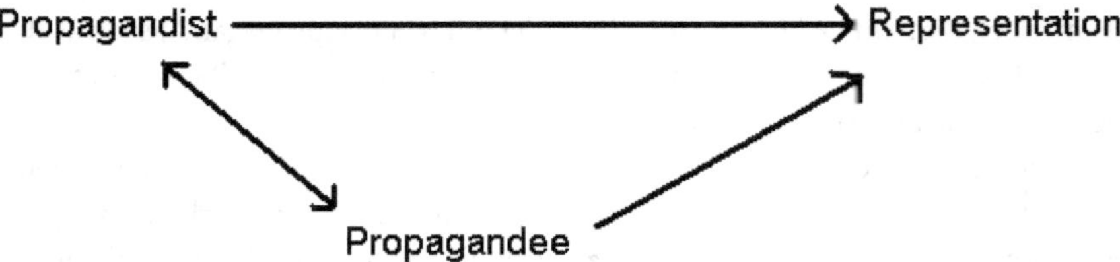

Figure 1. Naïve metarepresentation.

This probable search for relevance, especially with a text that attempts political persuasion, could easily lead to the realization illustrated in the second model: the reader realizes that Kisch determines what is seen and not seen, and who is heard and not heard on this journey. This realization, coupled with Kisch's representations of the minds of Uzbeks, Tajiks, and foreign Communists, could result in a suspicion of metarepresentation. When this situation occurs during the reading of a detective novel, it is part of the fun. The reader can play the game of asking, "Why is the author showing me *this* and not *something else*? Is it a clue? Is it a trick?" This sort of intellectual game is stimulating and engaging in a detective novel. Such suspicion of metarepresentation in propaganda, however, can greatly weaken, if not negate, its effectiveness.

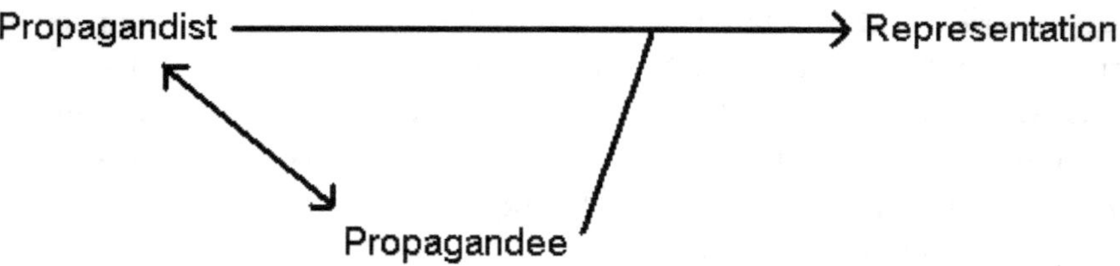

Figure 2. Suspicion of metarepresentation.

It is thus in the best interest of the propagandist to discourage the creation of source tags that link him or her to propagandized representations. One technique used by Kisch to accomplish this is pronoun confusion. Except for a chapter detailing an illegal tiger hunt in Afghanistan, Kisch eschews the first-person singular pronoun and repeatedly uses the plural form "we." While this could often be interpreted in the text as his membership in the traveling authors' brigade, the pronoun is frequently ambiguous and seems to encompass author and reader. There is no ambiguity, however, at the conclusion of the final chapter, where Kisch compares the achievements and enthusiasm of Central Asian cotton farmers with the conditions of African-American cotton farmers:

> . . . und *wir* denken an Dixie, den Baumwollgürtel Amerikas, das Land, wo die Sklaverei herrscht wie vor Lincolns Zeit. [. . .] *[W]ir* denken an dieses Land, wo *wir* zerlumpte, schlotternde, ausgehungerte, ausgebeutete Gestalten sahen, wo *wir* von torkelnden Säufern angerempelt, auf Schritt und Tritt von Kindern

> angebettelt wurden, wo weißgelockte Neger die weißgelockte Ware schleppten, die hier wie dort gedeiht. (386-87; emphasis mine)
>
> ... and *we* think of Dixie, the cotton belt of America, where there are slaves, actually, just as before the time of Lincoln. [...] *We* think of that country, where *we* saw figures in rags, hungry, plundered figures, where staggering drunkards jostled into *us*, children begged from *us* at every step, and white-haired Negroes "toted" the white burden, which thrives both here and there. (258)

This is a reference to Kisch's earlier travel book *Paradies Amerika*. The "we" in this paragraph cannot possibly refer to the authors' brigade, as they did not accompany Kisch to America. This "we" includes Kisch and his readers, who have traveled with him vicariously from America to Russia to Central Asia. His experiences are his readers' experiences, thus weakening him as the ultimate source of representations in his travel works.

Kisch also introduces multiple sources of representations. This creates a high source-tracking load, which can further weaken the ability of the propagandee to assign Kisch as the source of all the representations in *Asien gründlich verändert*. The book is populated with characters who gesticulate and narrate their experiences of living in a Central Asian Soviet Republic. When they appear and speak, they are the sources of the information they provide (it would take an especially astute reader to continuously tag Kisch, the narrative editor, as the ultimate source of these representations). Kisch also quotes passages from *The New Republic* that are quite critical of social and economic prejudice in the United States, thereby pitting an American media voice against the excesses of capitalism. In addition to contributing a sense of credibility to the work (i.e., multiple voices confirming Kisch's observations), these additional voices also stress the reader's source-tracking ability. With so many new minds on which to exercise mind reading skills, Kisch can fade as the ultimate source of the representations before the reader. Simultaneously, Kisch's selective presentation of Central Asian speakers has a high probability of distorting the propagandee's estimation of the popularity of Soviet activities in the Central Asian Republics. Weaver, Garcia, Schwarz, and Miller found in a recent study that the assertions of just one member of a group, if repeated often enough, were likely to be considered representative of the shared opinion of the entire group.

Another means by which Kisch achieves a high source-tracking load is to require the reader to monitor multiple levels of intentionality. In the chapter "Ein Bezirk am Pamir" ("A District on the Pamir"), Kisch recounts the story of visiting a few Tajik comrades in Garm. Kisch admits to the reader that his weight and the excessive heat of the region conspire to make the Tajik custom of squatting on the ground and drinking tea particularly uncomfortable (although Kisch specifically describes how uncomfortable the experience is for "us"). One long-winded Tajik comrade regales Kisch with the endless improvements the Soviets have made in the province of Pamir. Occasionally Kisch attempts to stand, which his comrade interprets as impatience to see these improvements. His comrade quickly insists that Kisch sit and enjoy his tea—as there will be plenty of time for exploring. One can easily imagine Kisch's urgency as this routine repeats itself several times.

The joke is dependent on the reader's understanding that Kisch knows that his comrade thinks that he is eager to venture off and verify what he is being told, and this motivates the comrade to insist that Kisch should enjoy his hospitality a while longer. Of course, the comrade's belief is false and Kisch is only behaving in this manner because he does not want his comrade to think him rude. This routine is sustained over several pages (*Gesammelte Werke* 4: 323-28; *Changing Asia* 169-78). Humor of this type can stress the ToM mechanism with multiple levels of intentionality, thus distracting the propagandee from the ultimate source of the metarepresentations—the propagandist.

Most of the techniques that have been discussed here are not new to the study of propaganda from communications and social science perspectives. The concept of mind reading, however, offers an additional perspective on these techniques. Paul Kecskemeti has observed that in order "to be persuasive, the propaganda theme has to be perceived as coming from within" (849), and others have also noted that successful propaganda must seem as if it were merely reflecting beliefs and attitudes already present in the propagandee. ToM may explain how this is possible. The anchors used by propagandists to achieve resonance are, ideally, semantic memories (representations that lack a source tag and form part of a person's general, accepted knowledge about the world). Zunshine's literary application of Cosmides and Tooby's work on representational quarantine is especially relevant here (50-53; 54-58). She explains Katerina Ivanova Marmeladova's (from Fedor Dostoyevski's *Crime and Punishment*) striking confusion of fantasy and reality as a "failure to monitor properly the source of her representations," that is, herself (57). It is the task of the propagandist to induce a very similar cognitive failure in the propagandee. By using techniques that limit the propagandee's ability to track the propagandist as the ultimate source of propagandized representations, these representations have a greater chance of being stored without source tags. Lacking source tags and resembling semantic memories, these representations could then evade systems of representational quarantine and migrate more freely through the propagandee's cognitive architecture. Reinforced and made more accessible through repetition, such representations, lacking external source tags, would seem to come from within. Propaganda that succeeds in this manner would not appear as propaganda at all; rather it would appear merely as a mirror held up to reflect and affirm the preexisting beliefs, attitudes, and affects of the propagandee.

WORKS CITED

Baron-Cohen, Simon. *Mindblindness: An Essay on Autism and Theory of Mind.* Cambridge: MIT Press, 1995. Print.

Brase, Gary L. "The Allocation System: Using Signal Detection Processes to Regulate Representations in a Multimodular Mind." *Evolution and the Psychology of Thinking: The Debate.* Ed. David E. Over. Current Issues in Thinking and Reasoning. Hove: Psychology Press, 2003. 11-32. Print.

Bratich, Jack Z. "Amassing the Multitude: Revisiting Early Audience Studies." *Communication Theory* 15.3 (2005): 242-65. Print.

Djukic-Cocks, Ana. "Die Komposition der Kisch-Reportage in *Paradies Amerika*." *Focus on Lituratur: A Journal for German-Language Literature* 1.1 (1994): 23-35. Print.

Evans, J. St. B. T., J. Barston, and P. Pollard. "On the Conflict between Logic and Belief in Syllogistic Reasoning." *Memory and Cognition* 11.3 (1983): 295-306. Print.

Flavell, J. H. *Cognitive Development*. 2nd ed. Englewood Cliffs, NJ: Prentice Hall, 1985. Print.

Jowett, Garth S., and Victoria O'Donnel. *Propaganda and Persuasion*. 2nd ed. Newbury Park: Sage, 1992. Print.

Kecskemeti, Paul. "Propaganda." *Handbook of Communication*. Ed. I. D. Pool et al. Chicago: Rand McNally, 1973. 844-70. Print.

Kisch, Egon Erwin. *Asien gründlich verändert*. Berlin: Reiss, 1932. Print.

---. *Asien gründlich verändert*. Moscow: Verlagsgenossenschaft Ausländischer Arbeiter in der UdSSR, 1933. Print.

---. *Changing Asia*. Trans. Rita Reil. New York: Knopf, 1935. Print.

---. *Egon Erwin Kisch beehrt sich darzubieten: Paradies Amerika*. Berlin: Reiss, 1930. Print.

---. *Gesammelte Werke in Einzelausgaben*. Ed. Bodo Uhse and Gisela Kisch, cont. by Fritz Hofmann and Josef Polá ek. 12 vols. Berlin: Aufbau, 1993. Print.

---. *Zaren, Popen, Bolschewiken*. Berlin: Reiss, 1927. Print.

Knox, R. Seth C. *Weimar Germany between Two Worlds: The American and Russian Travels of Kisch, Toller, Holitscher, Goldschmidt, and Rundt*. New York: Lang, 2006. Print.

Lieberman, Ben. "The Meanings and Function of Anti-System Ideology in the Weimar Republic." *Journal of the History of Ideas* 59.2 (April 1998): 355-75. Print.

O'Donnel, V., and J. Kable. *Persuasion: An Interactive Dependency Approach*. New York: Random, 1982. Print.

Patka, Marcus G. *Egon Erwin Kisch: Stationen im Leben eines streitbaren Autors*. Ed. Klaus Amann and Friedbert Aspetsberger. Literatur in der Geschichte, Geschichte in der Literatur 41. Vienna: Böhlau, 1997. Print.

Skurnik, I., C. Yoon, D. C. Park, and N. Schwarz. "How warnings about false claims become recommendations." *Journal of Consumer Research* 31 (2005): 713-24. Print.

Taylor, Philip M. *Munitions of the Mind: A History of Propaganda from the Ancient World to the Present Day*. 3rd ed. Manchester: Manchester University Press, 2003. Print.

Weaver, K., S. M. Garcia, N. Schwarz, and D. T. Miller. "Inferring the Popularity of an Opinion from Its Familiarity: A Repetitive Voice Can Sound like a Chorus." *Journal of Personality and Social Psychology* 92.5 (2007): 821-33. Print.

Zunshine, Lisa. *Why We Read Fiction: Theory of Mind and the Novel*. Columbus: The Ohio State University Press, 2006. Print.

Functional Brain Imaging and the Problem of Other Minds

DAN LLOYD, VINCE CALHOUN, GODFREY PEARLSON, AND ROBERT ASTUR

Once upon a time a rainbow appeared to two friends, Bert and Ernie. Knowing all about rainbows, Bert and Ernie decided to set out for the pot of gold they knew to be at the rainbow's end. Bert clearly saw the bow fall between two hills, and proposed a path between them. Ernie just as clearly saw the rainbow intersect the hilltop to the right, and proposed to climb straight to the summit. An argument and wrestling match ensued, during which the rainbow disappeared, leaving the friends to ponder a deep mystery of the human condition. Or perhaps a not-so-deep mystery about optics, since their disagreement about the location of the bow was a consequence of their different viewpoints. Rainbows form as rays of light strike water droplets, each a tiny prism, refracting and reflecting the shades of the spectrum at fixed angles from about 40 degrees (violet) to 42 degrees (red). Every droplet reflects and refracts at exactly these angles and wavelengths; to catch a colored ray from any drop you need to be in its path. Accordingly, any one rainbow is really many—there is a rainbow seen from your standpoint, but myriad different rainbows to be seen from other spatial viewpoints. Bert and Ernie were in the unusual position of perceiving two contradictory visual worlds, but nonetheless perceiving these worlds accurately, as they were in fact. There really are rainbows. Indeed, the sky is filled with rainbows just waiting to be seen. We resolve the seeming inconsistency among rainbows by recognizing that their location is essentially perspectival.

Without an understanding of optics, Bert and Ernie might have drawn a different moral from their two rainbows. An object cannot be in two places at the same time. Their observations of the rainbow contradict this principle, so the rainbow must not be a real object. Its appearance, accordingly, must be entirely subjective, rooted in something about Bert and Ernie that is not a part of physical reality.[1] Bert (or Ernie) might call this "the problem of other rainbows." "I can see a rainbow right there," declares Bert, "but I can't see the rainbow you claim to see. Of course I believe you are sincere in your rainbow claims—it's just that I cannot confirm them in anything like the way I confirm my own—directly, incorrigibly, and privately. I must infer your rainbow percept indirectly, via a complicated and dubious analogy. In fact you might not be experiencing anything at all like the rainbow I see." Bert might therefore call rainbows a type of mental event. Moreover, if either Bert or Ernie happened to be a student of philosophy, he might appeal to several current arguments that claim to show that the phenomenal, subjective appearances of things are beyond the reach of materialist, objective science. For example, Thomas Nagel writes:

> It is impossible to exclude the phenomenological features of experience from a reduction in the same way that one excludes the phenomenal features of an ordinary substance from a physical or chemical reduction of it—namely, by explaining them as effects on the minds of human observers. If physicalism is to be defended, the phenomenological features must themselves be given a physical account. But when we examine their subjective character it seems that such a result is impossible. The reason is that every subjective phenomenon is essentially connected with a single point of view, and it seems inevitable that an objective, physical theory will abandon that point of view. (437)

But with respect to rainbows these metaphysical gyrations turn out to be completely unnecessary. Rainbows are perfectly well-behaved natural phenomena. After a little optics, any special difficulty with rainbows simply evaporates, so completely do they reduce to their sole physical ingredients, light and water. As the subjectivity of rainbows collapses into the objectivity of optics, neither Bert nor Ernie need abandon his point of view, however. Their perceptual claims remain true and are in fact vindicated. In this case objectivity and point of view coexist.

Ever since Descartes, modern philosophy has grappled with the problem of other minds, much like the problem of other rainbows as confronted in Bert and Ernie's optical innocence. The experienced world is thoroughly perspectival, but the machinery that leads to alternative appearances has been mostly unknown. The classical problem of other minds confronted a double barrier: the metaphysical distinction between mind and brain mirrored a physiological accident, namely, that brains hid in skulls. The obvious correlation between mental and neurological conditions could be glimpsed only in snatches and indirectly. Lately, that has changed. Neuroscience has married the clever experimental strategies of cognitive psychology to some amazing observational technology, with a resulting explosion in research correlating brain and behavior. The brain, with its hemispheres, lobes, ridges, and folds is perhaps *the* scientific icon of our generation, easily overshadowing the mighty atom of an earlier era and in a tight race with the double helix. The gray matter is rarely merely gray; upon it, like a screen, are projected the transient fires of cognition, typically as hot orange blobs, the simmering symptoms of human perception and action, in both normal and abnormal brains. The neuroimages thus reflect both the anatomy and function of the brain, in studies of gray and orange.

The impression that there is a great deal of research in this area is entirely true. Although functional magnetic resonance imaging is just one of many tools for brain exploration, a search of the PubMed database on the joint topic of "fMRI and brain" yields more than 68,000 articles, of which over 6,000 were published in the last year. The heralded "golden age of brain science" would seem to have arrived. Bear in mind that this is indeed science. The majority of these papers report on controlled experiments with multiple subjects. Their conclusions, accordingly, are generalizations that have a better than 95% chance of being true of the general population. For the most part, all these studies are true of you and me. This one consideration alone almost entirely defangs the traditional problem of other minds. In the parable of the rainbow, during their initial state of ignorance Bert and Ernie had no basis for comparing their experiences. Bert's was simply given, and from his point of view Ernie's was simply wrong, and insofar as it was wrong had no point of comparison with Bert's own. Without a circumspect view of their situation, their perceptions were simply contradictory. But, in the case of perception overall and functional neuroimaging, we do learn something important from the science, namely that there are identifiable commonalities between you and me in hundreds or even thousands of situations. That something is the "area of activity" represented in the characteristic brain images. (Ask not for whom the blob shines. . . .) It is easy to forget that this common ground among us all is a contingent fact, as is the fortunate interplay of neural function and blood flow, since it is the latter that functional neuroimaging usually detects.

However, in pursuit of this scientific common ground we can observe the very process that Nagel described. The "single point of view" of the individual has been "abandoned" for the sake of hypotheses about brains in general. Again the parable of the rainbow is instructive. Bert observed an unproblematic visual fact—there is a rainbow—until his observation collided with Ernie's. The parable suggests that the problem of subjectivity is actually a problem of intersubjectivity. Or in other words, subjectivity is not encountered in the commonalities among subjects, but in their differences. In fact the friends need not enroll in a course in optics to determine that rainbows are real. All they need to do is trade places. Once they learn how the apparent location of the rainbow changes with one's standpoint, they can coordinate their differing perceptions. Prior to the reductive explanations of light and water, there appears to be a prereductive explication. We can refer to this prereductive inquiry as "standpoint mapping."[2] In this example, standpoint mapping links spatial viewpoints with apparent positions of rainbows. Importantly, standpoint mapping describes how changes in standpoint lead to changes in what is perceived. Standpoints are related by describing how to exchange one point of view for another. That is, standpoint mapping describes the dynamics of points of view. Bert and Ernie can determine that rainbows are real (though insubstantial) by confirming that the rules of dynamic standpoint mapping are constant for each of them. Moreover, note that Bert and Ernie can establish that rainbows are both real and subjective without appeal to reductive explanation at all. The optics of water droplets need not be mentioned.

"Dynamic standpoint mapping" is a deliberately abstract characterization of an activity that pervades our lives. How will Bert and Ernie communicate the interrelated changes of standpoint and perception? Their most natural impulse will be to tell each other stories. In their simplest forms, their stories will narrate how moving oneself also moves the rainbow. Implicit in their first-person narratives will be a generalization to the second and third persons. That is, the audience for such a story is invited to see if the same story holds from her or his viewpoint as well. In short, one function of narrative is to exchange dynamic standpoint maps, and this in turn enables communities to resolve fundamental distinctions between the objective and subjective. Standpoint mapping—storytelling—is a general topic beyond this chapter, of course. Here two points are relevant. First, the myriad forms of narrative in the service of standpoint mapping remind us that the subjective is neither monolithic nor sharply demarcated from the "objective." Through stories individuals coordinate their worlds; some areas of agreement are solid, while others are fluid, subject to debate. Second, this intricate human activity precedes science. It sorts the universe into the personal and the interpersonal, the singular and the shared, and in so doing distinguishes what is to be explained from what is available to do the explaining. Over time, the landscape of knowledge and speculation shifts. As the mapping progresses, the personal and idiosyncratic elements are subsumed into a logical edifice of causal generalization, that is, science. But science arrives late to a world already sorted into objective facts and subjective experiences.

With standpoint mapping in mind we can identify a gap in contemporary neuroimaging. In the quest for common ground cognitive neuroscience reduces the subject to a single standpoint; the dynamic and transitive mapping from one viewpoint to another disappears in this process. There are many reasons for this: First, science itself requires uniformity. A relatively new science will search first for the common ground and later for the effects of individual change and differences. Second, the technology of neuroimaging is not exact. From image to image changes are usually too small to be reliably detected, and often effects only emerge when multiple subjects are averaged. Experiments depend on repeating conditions both by single subjects and across subjects. Accordingly, only large, stable, relatively static effects appear. Imaging is also relatively slow. Each 3-dimensional image takes a second or more to assemble, and because the signal is small, often many images are averaged together to cancel out the randomly varying noise and preserve the more consistent signal. This does not enable the detection of faster dynamic processes. Finally, to achieve uniformity in the face of noise, experiments in imaging generally describe brain activity in correlation with conditions in the task environment. (The "task environment" is the combination of stimuli and the task posed by the experimenters. In other words, it is the set of experimental conditions defined for the particular study.) For example, if experimenters are interested in face perception, they will present subjects with images of faces in alternation with some other stimulus or task (for example, a blank screen or a scrambled image of light and dark patches). For analysis, the face scans are grouped and averaged. Methodologically, this assumes that brains are clamped to the face perception task in the same way throughout the face presentations, and equally disengaged from face perception in the nonface blocks of the experiment.

In short, the path from data to analysis is one of merging and averaging; along this path individual standpoints and their dynamic variation disappear. These methodological blinders lead to skepticism about the prospects for imaging in application to the problem of subjectivity. But they are largely arbitrary conventions of the discipline, rather than a priori limits. These conventions are inevitable only if no other interpretive method yields significant results. Accordingly, one way forward is to try something different, and see what's there—alert to the possibility that the answer may be nothing.

If the standard approach is objective, then we might characterize the alternative as the subjective strategy for brain research. Exactly this will occupy the remainder of this chapter, a descent into the data of one neuroimaging study, which is ongoing at the Olin Neuropsychiatry Research Center in Hartford, Connecticut.[3] We will examine this study in a nonstandard way, driven by a need to preserve, not blur, subjectivity. In this experiment, participants drive a simulated automobile through a virtual landscape, controlling their route with a steering wheel and brake and gas pedals. The experiment is divided into three runs, and each run has the same structure of three parts: First, subjects see a black screen with a plus sign, a "fixation cross," in the middle, for thirty seconds. Then the virtual reality simulation begins, and subjects drive through the simulated landscape, for ninety seconds. Then subjects move through the simulated landscape again, but it is as if they are passengers in the automobile, merely observing but not driving. This lasts for sixty seconds. This same sequence of Fixate, Drive, and Observe repeats three times without intermission, and is followed with a final thirty seconds of fixation. The whole session, then, comprises this sequence:

> Fixate—Drive—Observe—Fixate—Drive—Observe—Fixate—Drive—Observe—Fixate

With three runs, the experiment lasts about nine minutes. While the subjects are driving, a number of behavioral variables are recorded. This includes the current position of the car in the virtual landscape, steering, accelerating, braking, and others. Each session yields 375 whole-brain images, collected every 1.5 seconds.

Although no one would confuse the experience in the scanner with actual driving, it is nonetheless a compelling and immersing perceptual and behavioral task. Complex and open-ended, the task comes closer to simulating a natural interaction with the world than the host of button-pushing stimulus-response experiments designed to probe specific narrowly defined facets of perception or cognition. In addition, each session in the scanner comprises three very different subjective states, Fixation, Driving, and Observing, which interweave and repeat. In their phenomenology the three conditions are certainly diverse: one of them requires action, while two are passive. One presents a nearly blank screen, while two are visually rich and dynamic.

Facing this experiment, the standard neuroimaging approach would begin by assuming that the three main conditions will correlate with three distinct patterns of activity in the brain. Standardly, we would seek similarity among these patterns in all subjects, and from there localize brain activity, ultimately to explain the behaviors elicited by the experiment as the joint production of functionally specific brain regions. Here, however, we are interested in a less objective analysis, one revealing of subjective differences. We seek the interplay of standpoints. This suggests questions outside of (and prior to) the standard analysis. For example, in what respects do individuals differ in their brain responses during this experiment? In each subject, do the three conditions coordinate with three distinct patterns of activity in the brain? If so, then these correlations will link the brain activity to the objective conditions of the experiment, rather than to subjective variation.

The standard approach seeks to confirm the uniformity of brain activity in conformity to environmental conditions. In pursuit of this goal, standard interpretive methods are blind to deviations from the working assumptions.[4] A different approach would begin with individual subjects and apply interpretations subject-by-subject. Moreover, a nonstandard approach would not assume that the three experimental conditions map perfectly onto three distinct brain patterns. Just as your rainbow and mine are different, the sufficient mark of subjectivity is difference in perception despite similarity of objective (environmental) conditions.

Considering subjects one by one is an easy emendation. But how can we probe for different subjective responses to the same stimuli? Some experiments in cognitive neuroscience use subject reports to flag perceptual shifts, but in this analysis we use a more direct approach of letting the brain "speak for itself." That is, we analyze each image independently of any assumption about its objective correlations with the task environment. To make sense of the series of images as a whole, they are grouped by similarity. Similar images reflect similar brain states realized at different time points in the experiment. On this basis, then, we can carve the experiment at its joints, as signaled by the brain, independently of the switches among driving, observing, and staring at a fixation cross.

In more detail, the alternative method works as follows. Like other digital images, functional brain images are ultimately number strings (vectors) and as such one can measure similarity and dissimilarity between any pair of images. Think of dissimilarity as an abstract "distance" between images. So, with any set of images, some will be relatively similar/near each other, and some will be dissimilar/far apart. The image series accordingly can be retooled as an abstract space of brain activity, with unknown constellations of brain patterns scattered about. The similarities that structure brain space take into account entire images, that is, global patterns of activity that involve the whole brain. Perhaps the distances derive from localized differences in the images, but this analysis does not assume localization. Instead, the measure of distance encompasses whole-brain patterns that may be partly focalized, or not. Importantly, relations of near and far in "brain space" are not necessarily related to the temporal order of images, nor are they necessarily aligned with objective environmental conditions in the experiment.

Brain space is not conveniently depicted in two or three dimensions. (Mathematically, an image series traverses as many dimensions as there are pixels in the images.) Instead, we can subdivide brain space into neighborhoods, and assign each image to its region by virtue of similarity with its neighbors. There are several methods for "cluster analysis," each seeking to maximize the similarity within neighborhoods while also maximizing the dissimilarities of separate neighborhoods from one another.[5] We used one common method to perform this analysis with several subjects in the driving study described above. To get oriented to the method, we begin with a division of the 375 images for one subject (who happens to be the first author of this chapter) into two broad clusters (Fig. 1).

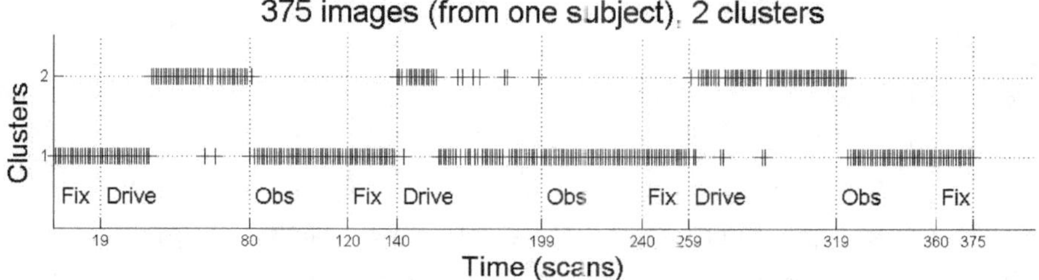

Fig. 1. Two-cluster division of 375 brain images for one subject in the driving study. Each plus sign is one image (i.e., a representation of brain activity at one point in time), and separate lines denote separate clusters in "brain activation space." (When a series of consecutive images fall in the same cluster, the plusses overlap in cross-hatching.) The Fixate, Drive, and Observe conditions are abbreviated, and elapsed time (in 1.5 second intervals, the time taken to collect each image) indicated. The second cluster appears to partially match the Drive condition.

The two clusters appear on separate lines, with each image (at each time point) symbolized with a small plus. (Plusses overlap when consecutive images fall in the same cluster.) Here we have divided the entire set of images (for one subject) into two groups or "clusters." Within each cluster, images are more similar to each other than to the images collected in the other cluster. In other words, the analysis assigns each image to a type, which we can think of as a global brain state or pattern of activity. In this case, then, there will be two distinct patterns or global brain states, and our subject oscillated between them over the course of the experiment. The analysis shows when the subject brain is in each of the two states. The first cluster comprises images collected at the time points marked on the first line, and the second image comprises the remaining time points. (The numbering of the clusters is arbitrary. The same analysis might be represented with lines 1 and 2 interchanged.) Reading the figure from left to right, we observe that this subject was in one broadly defined brain state for approximately the first forty scans (about sixty seconds), as shown in the dense cross-hatching of plusses on the first line. Then the brain activity changed to better resemble a second, different overall pattern, as shown by plusses along the second line. These two coarsely distinguished brain states alternate through the experiment. When the brain images are collected in two clusters, one cluster matches the third Drive epoch well, along with segments of the two preceding Drive periods.

A critical question, then, is whether a three-cluster interpretation maps well onto the three experimental conditions. If so, then the standard assumption that the brain is clamped to the objective task environment would be confirmed. A three-cluster analysis is depicted in Fig. 2.

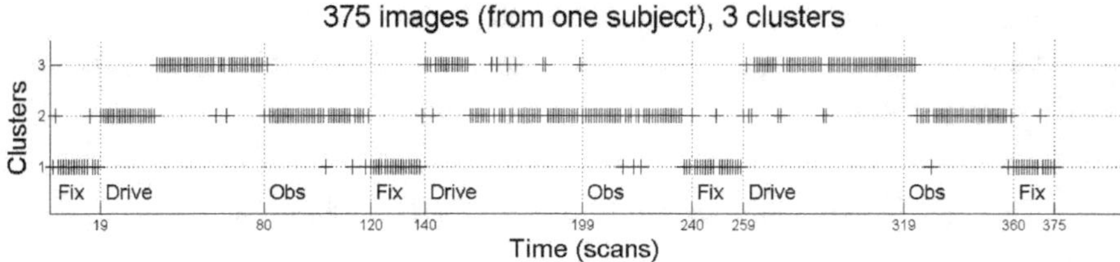

Fig. 2. Division of images for one subject into three clusters. Although the image neighborhood boundaries often correspond to changes in task condition, only the Fixation condition is consistently represented by a single brain image type.

For this subject, only the Fixation condition has a single neighborhood to call home. The Drive and Observe conditions do not sort images to conform to experimental expectations. In other words, if we divide all the patterns of global brain activity in this subject's session into three types, we find that the types cut across the conditions of the experiment. The Drive condition is represented by two different patterns, as are the Observe conditions. Moreover, single patterns often encompass differing experimental conditions; there is no overall scheme of "meaning" to assign to the three global brain conditions. Nonetheless, the clustering is not entirely random. In general, the global brain activity remains similar for periods of time, and is most likely to switch to a new state at a transition in the experiment. The Fixation condition seems generally represented by a single type of brain image. But even these generalizations have exceptions. In this case, then, the brain has a mind of its own—experimental conditions in the task environment do not entirely determine global patterns of brain activity. This motivates some further subdivision to see in greater detail how the experimental sequence is represented in the brain. Fig. 3 divides one subject's brain space into eight compartments.

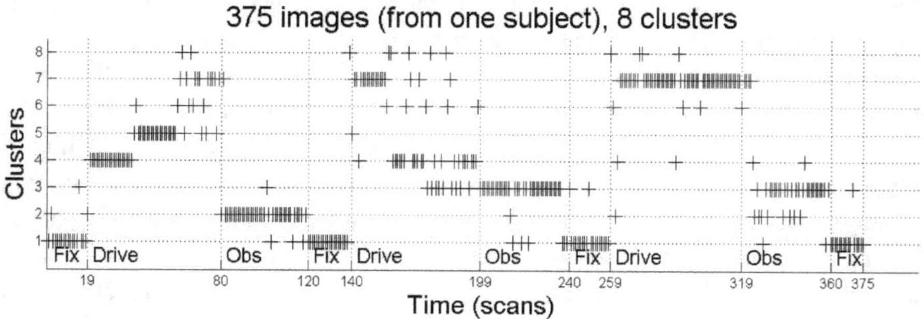

Fig. 3. Brain space (for one subject) divided into eight regions.

Five clusters—five global brain activity patterns—are devoted to the Drive conditions. One cluster spans the third Drive condition; the other Drive epochs are spread among clusters. At this level of analysis, several sporadic clusters appear (6 and 8, for example). These represent distinct patterns of brain activity that are realized briefly and intermittently. In short, for this subject major transitions in brain state only partially reflect differences in the task environment. Something "nonobjective" characterizes this brain.

Before continuing this interpretation, we examine the second issue of subjectivity, namely, individual differences. Figure 4 compares ten subjects, each image series divided into three clusters. To enable comparisons among the subjects, we symbolize the three image clusters with black, gray, and white bands. Accordingly, each numbered line of Fig. 4 represents a single subject, rather than a single cluster (as in figures 1 through 3). Subject 1, for example, moves through brain states that nicely correspond to the task conditions of the experiment, Fixation (in black), Drive (gray), and Observe (white). However, the other subjects march to different drummers. Most of them divide the Drive condition into two clusters, and conflate the other two conditions in a single cluster. However, three subjects display a distinctly different categorization of brain scans, dividing the experiment temporally into beginning, middle, and end.

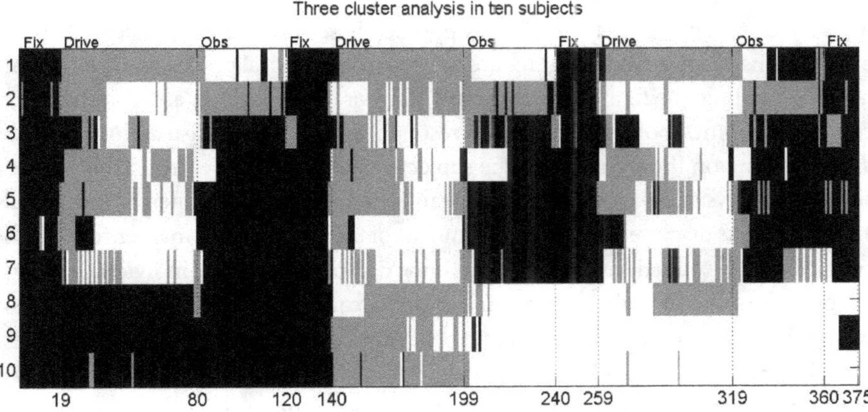

Fig. 4. Image series for ten subjects, sorted in three clusters each. Each subject is represented by a gray-scale horizontal band spanning the experimental conditions (375 scans). The three clusters are arbitrarily encoded as black, gray, or white. Subject 1 comes closest to matching the experimental conditions of Fixation (black), Driving (gray), and Observing (white). Subject 2, who also appears in figures 1 through 3, displays a single recurring image type during the Fixation condition, but the other clusters do not correspond consistently to the experimental conditions. For subjects 3 through 7, the Drive condition is divided into two clusters and the other two conditions conflated. Finally, subjects 8 through 10 tend to divide the session by time.

So far, this interpretation has emphasized several departures from the generalized and generalizing assumptions of the standard approach. The standard approach would assume that the brain displays distinct patterns of activity specific to the three main conditions of the experiment. The subjects in Fig. 4 support this assumption at moments of transition from one condition to the next. Most of the time, the change from Fixation to Driving (for example) is reflected in a global shift of brain state. Similarly, in several subjects brain activity remains in the same neighborhood of global similarity during each condition. Each Fixation condition, for example, is characterized by a fairly continuous series of states within the same cluster. However, this interpretive strategy has also disclosed some interesting departures from the expectations built into the standard interpretation. During some experimental conditions, brains change from one global state to another. For some subjects, brain states endure across significant changes in the experimental conditions. Finally, in different ways in these image series we observe representations of the passage of time. Three subject brains almost entirely sort the time series into successive sections.

In this experiment, we might have expected that to drive is to drive is to drive—that is, as conditions repeat the brain should as well. Objectively, in the task environment, this is exactly what happens. But in the brains of volunteers for this experiment, something else is happening as well: brain states oscillate and interweave in patterns that are distinctive and ultimately unique to each subject. In short, when this complex experience is parsed according to each individual's trajectory in brain space, we observe an interplay of distinction, progression, and repetition. Following this interpretation, we return to Nagel's claim that "every subjective phenomenon is essentially connected with a single point of view, and it seems inevitable that an objective, physical theory will abandon that point of view." Our approach here was entirely physiological. The observations collected in the figures are derived from physical processes. Commentary notwithstanding, the figures above project from brain to page via an "objective" process from cell metabolism to magnetic resonance to signal reconstruction to cluster analysis to ink on these pages. But the subjective has not disappeared in this progression. The analysis displayed features of brain activity distinct to different individuals, and all subjects displayed activity independent of the conspicuous markers of task and condition. One could develop increasingly fine distinctions among individuals, enlarging both the space of brain activity but also demarcating finer distinctions in behavior. As this research program proceeds, one behavioral domain will be of special interest, namely, language. Our subjects can answer questions about their experiences. Indeed, they can tell their stories. These too can be unwoven in brain space.

Will the subjective disappear in a research program such as this? Yes, if the subjective is understood as essentially private, incommunicable, and ineffable. Nor does this research strategy achieve objectivity, if the objective identifies strict causal relationships between conditions in task environments and brain activity, where these one-to-one relations are conceived as common to all. But, as the parable of the rainbow suggests, the subjective/objective distinction is a negotiation between subjects, a continual pursuit of commonality and difference. It overcomes solipsism but precedes science. In the middle ground is standpoint mapping, employing new interpretive methods, of which this paper is just one illustration.[6] The figures in this chapter are a new kind of text, which seem to share with sentences some regularities of structure and semantics, and with stories a temporal progress and beat. The patterns of activity in the brain are not a simple mirror of the world, but rather a subjective interpretation that, like the rainbow, refracts objective conditions into a spread of differing subjective responses. The temporal sequence of images encodes temporally ordered change and regularity in the environment.

In this middle ground of science and subjectivity, we cannot say exactly "what it is like" to be any of these experimental subjects in isolation. But we can say that what it is like changes at specific moments in the experiment, and we can further compare and contrast subjects as they move from one subjective condition to another. Their standpoints—their subjective take on the world—varies, and a subjective research strategy begins to map this dynamism. In this way, the negotiation between commonality and difference is displayed through the objective measures of functional neuroimaging, achieving an objective view of subjectivity. Other minds are ultimately other standpoints, and the many mappings among them are open even to brain scanning as a means of exploration. These neuroimages therefore invite us to apply the literary tools of poetics and especially narratology. In this form of brain reading, the task is not so much to translate the "language" of the brain as a fixed system of symbols and meanings. Even this preliminary investigation reveals broad variation in individuals' parsing of environmental conditions rather than a fixed semantics of brain activation patterns. Rather, we observe patterns of change, some driven by environmental changes but some driven by unknown factors in the brain itself. Without a lexicon for this obscure text, we can first look for clues in more formal and structural techniques of literary analysis, considering a brain image series as an extended text comprising various and shifting representations of the world and its changes. To declare this text a narrative is premature but plausible, considering the pervasive role of stories in every culture and medium. Brains produce narratives with great fluency; possibly narrative describes the dynamic changes in the brain itself.

Classically, philosophers conceived the problem of other minds as a metaphysical gulf between oneself and every other person, represented in papers like Nagel's as an inscrutable and insurmountable difference in viewpoint. But there is no single problem of other minds, but rather as many "problems" as there are minds. The problem of other minds does not dissolve by mining some hidden interiority, but rather by displaying the differences in the experienced worlds of different individuals. Each of these problems is open to partial solution. In practice we have continual access to partial pictures of the world from other points of view, and much of the activity of human life is dedicated to coordinating points of view. Literature and art are particularly devoted to presenting and communicating individual perspectives, to rendering the subjective in various physical, objective media. By pursuing a more subjective research strategy, humans can also display their subjectivity in the new medium of neuroimaging. The figures in this chapter are example texts in this new medium. They remain highly abstract and largely untranslated, but we hope they begin to break loose from the picture of the brain as clamped to its environment in a fixed relationship that does not vary from person to person. There are many rainbows; each is an objective fact that is nonetheless different for every person. Likewise there are many worlds, each objectively indexed to each individual. Science, with a little retooling, can join with literary studies in showing and exploring the richness and diversity of the human mind.

Notes

1 Bert and Ernie are not alone in reasoning from optical ignorance toward mystical hypotheses. See Epstein and Greenberg, "Decomposing Newton's Rainbow." A related spectral display also provoked transcendental speculations: one's shadow, cast

on a cloud, will appear to be ringed with a rainbow with its exact center at one's point of view, a phenomenon known as a "glory," "Bhuddha's light," or "Brocken spectre." Wanderers at dawn on high ridges have wondered at this visual treat, and attributed it to their state of mind in concert with some other dimension of the natural world. See C. J. Wright, "The 'Spectre' of Science."

2 "Standpoint mapping" is a new coinage, but reflects some of the ideas of standpoint epistemology developed in recent feminist philosophy of science. Standpoint epistemology pays particular attention to the processes of scientific research in their institutional, social, and political contexts, noting that one's societal position (broadly, one's position in hierarchies of power and privilege) affects the questions one deems worthy of exploration, and the hypotheses and even data that one will find legitimate. "Standpoint" in standpoint epistemologies refers to social position. In this chapter, standpoint is used in an individual and phenomenological way to refer to the many ways in which experiences can differ, depending on concrete circumstances (like Bert and Ernie's physical location), differences in learned and innate cognitive capacities and "styles," and many other contingencies. Social position is just one among many aspects of one's standpoint in this sense. On standpoint epistemology, see the papers collected in Sandra Harding (ed.) *The Feminist Standpoint Theory Reader.*

3 Publications from this study include: K. N. Carvalho, G. D. Pearlson, R. S. Astur, and V. D. Calhoun, "Simulated Driving and Brain Imaging"; V. D. Calhoun, K. Carvalho, R. Astur, and G. D. Pearlson, "Using Virtual Reality to Study Alcohol Intoxication Effects on the Neural Correlates of Simulated Driving"; V. D. Calhoun, J. J. Pekar, and G. D. Pearlson, "Alcohol Intoxication Effects on Simulated Driving: Exploring Alcohol-Dose Effects on Brain Activation Using Functional MRI."

4 For discussion, see Dan Lloyd, *Radiant Cool: A Novel Theory of Consciousness.*

5 For an introduction, see Mark S. Aldenderfer and Roger K. Blashfield's *Cluster Analysis.*

6 Functional magnetic resonance imaging (fMRI) is just one of many technologies that could be harnessed in the exploration of subjectivity. Individual brains differ in structure, in connectivity among brain regions, in electromagnetic properties measured in milliseconds, and in many other ways; an expanding toolbox of technologies is available for cognitive neuroscience. All of these technologies invite diverse interpretive methods. Moreover, recent research has employed multiple methods simultaneously. For an example and discussion, see V. D. Calhoun, T. Adalid, G. Pearlson, and K. A. Kiehl, "Neuronal chronometry of target detection."

WORKS CITED

Aldenderfer, Mark S., and Roger K. Blashfield. *Cluster Analysis.* Quantitative Applications in the Social Sciences 44. Beverly Hills, CA: Sage, 1985. Print.

Calhoun, Vince D., T. Adalid, G. Pearlson, and K.A. Kiehl. "Neuronal Chronometry of Target Detection: Fusion of Hemodynamic and Event-Related Potential Data." *NeuroImage* 30.2 (2006): 544-53. Print.

Calhoun, Vince D., K. Carvalho, R. Astur, and G. D. Pearlson. "Using Virtual Reality to Study Alcohol Intoxication Effects on the Neural Correlates of Simulated Driving." *Applied Psychophysiol Biofeedback* 30.3 (2005): 285-306. Print.

Calhoun, Vince D., J. J. Pekar, and G. D. Pearlson. "Alcohol Intoxication Effects on Simulated Driving: Exploring Alcohol-Dose Effects on Brain Activation Using Functional MRI." *Neuropsychopharmacology* 29.11 (2004): 2097-17. Print.

Carvalho, K. N., G. D. Pearlson, R. S. Astur, and V. D. Calhoun. "Simulated Driving and Brain Imaging: Combining Behavior, Brain Activity, and Virtual Reality," *CNS Spectrum* 11.1 (2006): 52-62. Print.

Epstein J., and M. Greenberg. "Decomposing Newton's Rainbow." *Journal of the History of Ideas* 45.1 (1984): 115-40. Print.

Harding, Sandra, ed. *The Feminist Standpoint Theory Reader: Intellectual and Political Controversies*. Routledge: New York, 2004. Print.

Lloyd, Dan. *Radiant Cool: A Novel Theory of Consciousness*. Cambridge, MA: MIT Press, 2004. Print.

Nagel, Thomas. "What Is It Like to Be a Bat?" *Philosophical Review* 83.4 (1974): 435-50. Print.

Wright, C. J. "The 'Spectre' of Science: The Study of Optical Phenomena and the Romantic Imagination." *Journal of the Warburg and Courtauld Insititutes* 43 (1980): 186-200. Print.

How Is It Possible To Have Empathy? Four Models

Fritz Breithaupt

This essay asks what empathy is and what kind of assumptions we have to make to explain how empathy is possible. Four basic models of empathy will discussed. Three of these derive from recent work in cognitive science, psychology, evolutionary biology, and philosophy. The fourth model, based on narratology, will be first proposed in this paper. As will become clear, the different models do not fully contradict each other. Some authors (Thompson 2001, de Waal 2006) have suggested viewing different models of empathy as progressive steps in individual development or in evolutionary processes. Nevertheless, the difference between the models shows a core disagreement of what empathy is and which (mental, evolutionary, social, cognitive) requirements need to be met for empathy to be possible. Hence, this essay seeks to clarify the difference between these models. The models are not arranged according to disciplines or schools or thoughts, but rather according to more basic operative assumptions or prerequisites, such as similarity as the basis of empathy. All models fall under the most general definition of empathy as the capacity of an observer to receive access to the emotional state or intellectual awareness of another being or fictional construct. This definition covers phenomena that range from emotional contagion and passive associations of one's body with the body of someone else to mind reading and the imaginary transposition of oneself into the "shoes" of another individual or fictional construct.

A key question of this paper is whether empathy can be sufficiently described as a process between two people alone or whether empathy, at least complex human-primate empathy, requires a social setting with at least three agents. Most (but not all) work in cognitive science takes as its starting point for investigations of empathy settings of two people or animals. This is especially obvious in work that focuses on the so-called mirror neurons, where only two people or animals are needed, but also in work on mind reading and many forms of intersubjectivity. The fourth model proposes that there need to be at least three agents for empathy to take place. Empathy shifts from the interaction between two individuals (observer and observed) to an entire narrative scene.

Hence, the three basic models that will first be discussed start with a setting of two individuals (including the possibility of a fictional construct). Each model provides a different answer to the basic requirement for empathy, and hence each model changes what exactly we mean by empathy. These models derive from similarity as the basis of empathy (model 1), the expectation of some exchange or reciprocity of sympathy (model 2), or the intellectual construction of the other in my mind (model 3). The fourth model requires a temporal-narrative setting. The condition for empathy, the model suggests, is that an observer finds himself or herself reflected in a (complex) scene of at least two (other) agents.

Whereas the three models that will be discussed first are bottom-up models that start with the simplest elements of empathy, the fourth model holds that human empathy has to be seen as a complex phenomenon to be understood in its totality. Certainly, all-or-nothing theories are suspicious. Nevertheless, there are cases where the parts do not add up to the sum. This is the case with empathy, the fourth model suggests, as it is with language. Language is either there or not there and cannot be derived in a step-by-step approach (Chomsky). This does not mean that one could not break down language or the complex form of empathy into its components. It is also still likely that there was no evolutionary leap, but that there was a transition in which the components of empathy and language came about consecutively or by chance. However, once language or empathy are in existence, they have a transformatory function with effects that cannot be explained by their parts or the steps of their development. Hence, to understand them it would not be sufficent to simplify its basic model below the interaction of at least three people (or primates). At the same time, certain aspects of the other three models play a role in model 4.

This essay operates speculatively. Further research will have to be conducted to verify its claims, especially the ones concerning model 4 (for further evidence, see my forthcoming study, Breithaupt 2009). In regard to models 1-3, the essay will synthesize existing theories and models of empathy, mind reading, and related phenomena, such as pity and sympathy. Obviously, these sketches will have to be very brief and at times overly polemical to fit this short format.

This essay is also a bit unusual in the way it suggests treating literary fiction. There would probably not be narrative fiction without empathy, that is, a "slipping into the shoes" of the characters of the narration. Narrative fiction can only exist because it invites, triggers, channels, controls, and manages empathy. Fiction probably exists in response to the capacity for narrative or situational empathy. Hence, one can assume that narrative fiction contains a lot of knowledge about empathy. However, there is a complication. Works of fiction do not only provide access to fictitious situations for the reader / viewer, but also themselves "theorize" how such access could happen. Literature is a highly self-reflexive medium that produces "allegories of empathy" by duplicating the external reader-text or spectator-theater relation as an internal arrangement within its plot. Put differently, works of fiction produce an imaginary or implied reader. To say the same thing more technically: a work of narrative fiction is a second-order observation of its implied reader, who is posited as its empathizing first-order observer.

Hence, to access the knowledge fiction has about empathy, one needs to both understand how the narrative plot triggers empathy and how the work speculates about empathy. Both are deeply intertwined—which also suggests that the narrative empathy triggers can change historically and culturally. Narrative empathy is a developing capacity with its own history. It is therefore not evident how one can access the wealth of knowledge about empathy that fiction promises to contain. The contributions to this volume may pioneer some new approaches (see also Breithaupt 2008b).

1. The model of similarity

In this model, the assumption is that we can have empathy because we are, or imagine we are, similar to other beings. We arrive at an understanding of the other individual because we derive it from ourselves, put in different circumstances. More recently, Vittorio Gallese, co-author with Giacomo Rizzolatti of many studies on mirror neurons, calls this assumption of similarity the "shared manifold hypothesis": human beings are, ultimately, deeply similar and thus can understand each other without reflection and rational thought (Gallese 2001). Enlightenment thinkers favored terms such as "universal humanity" for this deep similarity or commonality (for instance, Gottfried Lessing, Adam Smith, and, critically, Jean-Jacques Rousseau).

Assumptions of similarity have a large appeal among cognitive scientists; they allow us, among other things, to involve the idea of embodied cognition to explain how one individual seems to share, co-experience (Husserl), or understand the emotional state of another. The (imaginary) body is what we all share and hence this "body" can serve as a medium between us (Merleau-Ponty 1964). Despite its appeal, however, this model has two weaknesses. First, by postulating a deep similarity, a similarity that itself cannot be directly experienced, the model needs to slip into the register of the imaginary or projection. Second, the model is weakened by the fact that it has difficulties explaining the attraction of empathy: if we are all the same, there is no need to feel like the other. Put differently, if similarity is the core of empathy, empathy may be stuck on the level of mere emotional contagion, as Frans de Waal puts it, and would not lead to differentiations between self and other (de Waal 2006).

There is a lot of support for the assumption that similarity is the basis for empathy (and Theory of Mind, pity, and even identification). If one accepts the mirror neurons or a similar operator as the key basis for empathy that operate prior to reflection and rational motives (Gallese 2003), then one has to conclude that the readability of the emotional states of other individuals requires the immediate compatibility from one to another. It has to be noted that it is disputed which role if any the mirror neurons play in true empathy that involves emotions; thus far, we know that the mirror neurons lead observers of goal-directed movement to display similar brain patterns as if they would execute the same movement. Emotional empathy, however, is a contested area and the involvement of mirror neurons is not yet clear. Even if one employs a different notion of empathy that goes beyond the pre-reflexive mirror neurons as theorists of Theory of Mind (ToM) do, it seems impossible to object to the idea of similarity. Our imaginarily shared feeling, experiencing or understanding the emotions of another, seems to suggest that these feelings indeed can be shared and thus are the same for all of us, which means also that we are, mostly, the same. Similarity does not necessarily have to be on the level of bodily cognition. For example, the theory-theory of ToM holds that we engage in some shared treasure of cultural knowledge or folk mythology when we empathize.

Since the case for this model seems overwhelmingly strong, at least at first glance, I will skip over any further supporting evidence in this short sketch and instead turn quickly to what I perceive to be a central weakness within this model. We will come to this weakness by means of what may seem like a detour: through a reading of one of the most prominent aesthetic theories of the eighteenth century, developed by the key German Enlightenment thinker, Gottfried Lessing. The implications of our reading of Lessing, I believe, go far beyond the Enlightenment and aesthetics and are applicable for debates today.

In his *Hamburg Dramaturgy* (1769), Lessing writes:

> He [Artistotle] speaks of pity and fear . . . and his fear is by no means the fear excited in us by misfortune threatening another person. It is the fear which arises for ourselves from the similarity of our position with that of the sufferer; it is the fear that the calamities impending over the sufferers might also befall ourselves; it is the fear that we ourselves might thus become objects of pity. In a word this fear is compassion referred back to ourselves. (Lessing 179)

For pity (*Mitleid*) to occur there needs to be enough similarity between *alter* and *ego*, so that it is possible for *ego* to put himself / herself in the position of *alter*. Only because *ego* can do this, is it possible for *ego* to feel the fear of *alter* in a certain situation, since *ego* sees the danger as if it were for himself / herself. Similarity (*Ähnlichkeit*) is the condition of possibility for pity and empathy.

There is, however, another notion implicit in Lessing's primal scene of empathy. It is the notion of selfhood that emerges around 1770, that is, the idea that we are all different and unique (Wahrman 2004, Breithaupt 2008a). Lessing assumes that pity is the exception. We can access our human similarity only if we are put under a lot of stress, that is, when we feel pain or terror. We can feel like others and "with" others as in *Mit-leid* only once our individual differences and our concepts of self are bypassed or short-circuited. There can be pity (*Mitleid*, literally with-suffering) as a ribbon of community, but no *Mitfreude* (literally with-joy) since when one gains, only the jealousy of others will be aroused. The self prevents us from sharing the joy of others. Schadenfreude would be another of these disturbances.

There can be no union of selves for Lessing. Identification, empathy, pity are possible only in the complicated apparatus that we call fiction, an apparatus that operates like a nutcracker to crack the hard shell of selfhood in order to reveal the soft flesh that all beings share. There are two ways of reading this emergence of the self, that is, the emergence of a concept of selfhood as a defined entity marked by singularity, autonomy, and difference. One could think that selfhood is a *fundamental threat* for empathy; successful fiction must break it down to accomplish the effect of similarity, thereby making empathy and reader engagement possible. However, I suggest viewing the emergence of "the self" in the mid-eighteenth century as a channeling or blocking device of empathy. The self of others and of oneself allows people *not* to have empathy, not to succumb to the "compassion compulsion" (Edelman 2004), and thus allow the channeling of empathy. Narrative fiction, in this sense, would have the opportunity to mostly block empathy and thus heighten it for those special cases in which the common humanity would spark.

Hence, even if Lessing views similarity as a given underpinning of man, the perception of this similarity is not a given. The problem is that everyone thinks himself or herself to be different and as having an (individual) self. Lessing theorizes which conditions fiction needs to fulfill in order to bring about the *sensus communis*. Fiction has to bring about the similarity-effect. Fiction thus would have the task of creating those situations in which all feel the same: typically, scenarios of horror and of the overwhelming display of power. Tragedy, as it appears in Lessing's reading of Aristotle, is a site of *producing similarity*, that is, the perception of similarity, between man by stripping man of that which holds man apart, namely selfhood. Selfhood operates as the regulatory device that limits the excess of pity.

What this means for the model of similarity is that similarity, as much as it may be posed as an existing ground of unity, is always (or can also be suspected to be) a merely produced or imagined similarity, a constructed communality that has heuristic value only because it cannot be disproved. Certainly, just as Lessing indirectly admits that we do not experience ourselves as similar but rather need to employ certain situations in drama that may lead us to forget our differences, so do current cognitive researchers readily accept and employ the register of simulation. As Gallese puts it: "Embodied simulation enables the constitution of a shared and common background of implicit certitudes about ourselves and, simultaneously, about others" (Gallese 2003, 521).

However, imagined similarity is a double-edged sword. It is very close to mere projection, in which a being assumes that all others are simply like-minded even when they are not. Instead of laying bare a level of similarity, projection erases the difference of the other. Even the apparent pain of another may not really be "pain," since each individual has a different history of pain and experiences pain differently. If we replace the word "similarity" by "projection," this amounts to more than a war of words. It changes what empathy is. If empathy is a matter of projection instead of similarity, then its key resource is some form of personal memory (since we derive our knowledge, such as the knowledge of pain, from our own experiences).

In short, if one understands a deep similarity to be the core of empathy, empathy consists of the inducing of an emotional state from one to another. Empathy in this sense has to be defined as the "imaginary sharing" of an emotional state when the cause of the emotion is only directly experienced by one or some of the group, but nevertheless as if experienced by the others. Grieving with someone who has lost a relative could fall under this definition. This "sharing" of an emotional state could be explained as the result of the mirror neurons. Or it could be explained by some other trigger that might be active in emotional contagion in group behavior, when one individual induces a matching or similar emotional state in others (de Waal 2006).

However, once a form of consciousness has been reached that distinguishes conceptually between self and other, similarity is not a given platform between beings any longer. Before one could reach a level of similarity again, the difference between self and other has to be erased (Lessing [1769] 1962). Similarity thus would not be the core basis of empathy, but rather the effect of complex arrangements that sidestep other mental states.

2. Models of reciprocity

Another school of thought argues that ego is most likely to have empathy with someone who could also empathize with ego and whom ego wants to have empathy with ego. This implies that empathy is intended to be a two-way process in which the empathizer reaches out with the intention of triggering a return. Consequently, the catalyst for empathy lies in the action or status of the empathizee that makes him or her of particular interest to the empathizer's hopes for a return of empathy. Empathy thus would be more a social than a heuristic process, as evolutionary biologists argue (Humphrey 1976, Dunbar 1996). This also means that empathy is directly tied to community building since it involves some simple form of exchange communication (I understand you, therefore you ought to understand me). This model is a central assumption underlying the belief that there is a close link between empathy, sympathy, and love. It also suggests some form of an economy of social emotions (Frijda 2007). One of the consequences of this model is that there would not be much room for neutral empathy. The following sketch will put the power relations into the center of the argument.

In August 1973, a man, on leave from prison, walked into a bank where he took four hostages. He demanded that a friend of his should be brought in too, and the two of them barricaded themselves with the hostages for more than five days before the police overcame them. What has made this incident famous is what happened afterward. The first man, incarcerated, was contacted by many female admirers who had seen him in the television coverage of the holdup. He later married one of them. The second man, who was cleared from charges for this bank robbery, formed a lasting friendship with one of the female hostages. The place was Stockholm and the resulting bonds gave rise to the name Stockholm syndrome.

What is interesting here for us is how a hostage situation apparently induces an empathetic or sympathetic response by the hostage toward the hostage-taker that can outlast the hostage situation. In many cases, the hostages assume the perspective of the hostage taker to such a degree that they come to fear the police more than the hostage takers (as in the 1973 Stockholm case). But how does this work?

A key feature of Stockholm syndrome is that the hostage is more likely to relate to the hostage-taker if some sign of hope is given, often as little as passing on some food, which can be read as a clue that the hostage-taker "is not that bad" after all. Psychologists call this element the "small kindness perception" (Carver 2007). Apparently, it is not the radical power asymmetry and the confinement alone that induce Stockholm syndrome, but the hope for a return of sympathy, a strategy to form a bond with the empathizee. The finding of this hope-for-a-return is also supported by the fact that positive bonding (Stockholm syndrome) is extremely rare in cases of active torture, where the hope of "positivizing" the torturer are minimal (Regner 2000).

Stockholm syndrome leads us to consider a specific element in the model of reciprocity that may otherwise not be visible: The empathizer reacts to (what he or she perceives to be) a prior act of the powerful offender / empathizee (Regner 2000). The reaction of the empathizer is fueled by the expectation or hope that the empathizee may react to the empathy by having empathy with the hostage / empathizer. In other words, empathy could be both described as an economic endeavor (the hope for a return) or as an act of manipulation in which one hopes to modulate the initial aggressive action of a person into a sympathetic action.

In contrast to the similarity model of empathy, the reciprocity model involves a strategic element of calculation even if in a crude non-conscious form. The question is whether this investment and hope for a return could indeed serve as a non-accidental basis for empathy. Such a starting point would allow one to see empathy as a means of survival that has significant evolutionary consequences.

Indeed, evolutionary biologists often use models of reciprocity and power asymmetry to describe the development of human empathy. Robin Dunbar in particular has presented the theory that a key human advance, namely the use of language, derived from the need for social networking and that empathy (in the sense of ToM) goes hand in hand with enabling human beings to operate in larger groups than apes or monkeys (Dunbar 1992, 1996, 1998; Dunbar, Barrett, and Lycett 2007). To abbreviate Dunbar's arguments sharply: empathy becomes the basis for human communication and thus replaces the much more time-intensive grooming of the monkeys. Whoever invests in empathy does so in the hope of his or her integration into the group. The key means for this new form of empathy, which bypasses the time intensity of grooming, is language. The evolutionary purpose of language, Dunbar argues, is thus social bonding, and not the exchange of information (Dunbar 1996).

Dunbar considers a variety of forms of gossip, ranging from the social control of "free riders" to mere chitchat. I would like to elaborate on one point by Dunbar, namely on his suggestion that the participants in social conversation and gossip are very careful not to hurt the feelings of the person with whom they are talking. We know not to "rub in" our successes, especially if we know that the other lost. In conversations, the conversant tends to take the perspective and also viewpoint of the other, especially if the other has higher social status. The conversant invisibilizes his or her position and adapts the perspective and viewpoint of the other, at least in the things that are said to please the other, or at least to be considerate of his or her emotional state.

Here we find a scenario that displays a similarity to Stockholm syndrome, even if in a very mild form. In fact, it seems not far fetched to argue that there is the hope for reciprocity for one's careful considerations of the other in conversation; the other seems more likely to help us, to accept us, and to help our social status if we show signs of respect and understanding of him or her or, at least, if we do not hurt his or her feelings.

After all, paying back or reciprocity, positively or negatively, is a deep-rooted behavior (Trivers 1971, de Waal and Brosnan 2006).

Empathy according to the reciprocity model requires as its core an element of self-subjugation to assimilate the viewpoint of the other. The empathizer may hope that this (temporary) self-suppression leads to some form of payback. There is a slight paradox at the core of this form of empathy: We suppress or "invisibilize" our self to adapt the viewpoint of the other in order to strengthen our self. Certainly, this paradox can be resolved if we add the notion of a temporal delay of the return, if there will be any. However, the paradox may explain why this form of empathy is such an evolutionary exception that only a few species have adapted this form of behavior, since there is no instant gratification to be expected.

If we accept this model of reciprocity as the master model of empathy, then the tricky issue becomes to explain cases of empathy in which the hope or even desire for return seems far fetched. The monkeys of the original mirror-neuron experiment by Rizzolatti and others are a case in point (in a break of an experiment, one macaque who had an adapter helmet put on his head was given a peanut by the experimenters. His brain reaction, the monitor showed, was as if he had moved his hand). Here the semi-automatic, pre-reflexive sympathetic brain reaction of the observer seems to exclude any calculative act of empathy / sympathy. Still, there would be ways to defend the reciprocity model even for these mirror-reaction cases. One can always hope for a future return if one reveals empathy. There may be much more to empathy than mirror neurons. (Incidentally or ironically, it should be noted that the monkeys in Rizzolatti's experience are also "hostages" to the experimenters.)

Another interesting challenge to the reciprocity model derives from fiction. If empathy is indeed a form of cognitive appreciation of the other that includes a hope or expectation of a return, this seems absurd for fiction. What chance do we stand to get empathy from, say, a superhero or a complex protagonist in a novel? Where can there be reciprocity in fiction?

For one, there is a lot of empathy and mind reading going on between the characters of the novel. Hence, if we identify with one of the characters, we may be in a position to experience a lot of exchanges of empathy between various characters. More important still is the interaction between a reader / spectator (a human being) and a work of fiction (an artifact). Readers indeed do get a return. By adopting the perspective of a fictional character and looking back at our own life, it looks different, usually simpler. The character (or narrator) provides us with answers to our situations. If one chooses to empathize and identify with, say, a superhero, this superhero certainly would laugh about the business that hampers us. The situation is not that different with more sophisticated characters. They offer us a language that we can adapt and use to frame our own lives. And this is the gift of the hostage-taker character: relief, distance, freedom, even answers. One should add that the odd relation between fiction and reader shares more than one key element with Stockholm syndrome. Fiction captures us, we are absorbed. Even the least active or apathetic character in a work of fiction holds us hostage to his or her actions, thoughts, emotions. We may simply have to empathize to endure the ordeal, so to speak.

One of the weaknesses of the reciprocity model of empathy is that it can do without empathy. If the desire for the empathy / sympathy of the other drives our action, we may, after all, not need to empathize ourselves. Our wish is merely to be in the position of the other. This, as we know from Freud's drama of the Oedipus complex, is identification, the wish to re-place (*beseitigen*) the other. Another problem is that if empathy is made visible to the other, and thereby becomes something like a token of exchange, we need to ask how exactly empathy is communicated. The empathizer's reaction needs to be fed back to the empathizer in such a way to prove correct emotional understanding. However, this could be faked by some form of compassion that does not derive from an emotional understanding.

Finally, it should be mentioned that a relationship between hostage and hostage-taker may involve a third faculty: the police. It has often been observed, as in the original Stockholm holdup, that hostages adapt the perspectives of the hostage-takers to such a degree as to share the fear of the police. This implies that the hostages also see the hostage-taker as a victim or at least as the weaker side in relation to the third faculty of government officials. Hence, it is not completely implausible to consider that the hostage can view a certain likeness of his or her existence as a hostage compared to the relationship of the hostage-taker toward the police. The hostage might opt to take the side of the hostage-taker, since they both share a structural position of being the weaker side of a relation of power. The small kindness perception makes it possible to view the hostage-taker as a good guy who would act differently if there were no police. As we will see later, such an explanation would move Stockholm syndrome closer to the narrative empathy of model 4.

3. MODELS OF APPROXIMATION

Many approaches produced within the ToM school use some model of approximation: When we deal with other people, we construct or simulate their actions and emotions and make predictions based on some decision-making operators that we see at work in them ("My friend tends to make rush decisions"). The original ToM constructed others as representation in our mind (Premack and Woodruff 1978). Empathy is here seen as a medium that does not assimilate the other, but rather negotiates his or her being different by making a mental model of the other in our mind. In literary aesthetics, this form of approximation corresponds to the demand of the consistency of characters: only consistent characters allow for this predictability.

There are at least three forms that approximation can take in regard to empathy. We could call these forms the: a) *constructionist*, b) *speculative*, or c) *strategic* approach. In the following I will focus on the constructionist approach and only briefly refer to the two other variations.

The constructionist approach to empathy holds that we somehow piece together the key mental features of another being using various sources, ranging from precise observation of body language to memories of past encounters with the same person. The goal of constructionist activities is to produce a master model of the other being in our mind that lets us understand the emotional states of another or predict how the person will react in a variety of situations. These predictions can be based on simple yes / no knowledge that can be tested in false-belief scenarios. The well-known Smarties task illustrates such a form of basic positive knowledge (Gopnik and Slaughter 1991). When a child is shown a Smarties box and asked what is in the box, she will most likely say: Smarties. If it is then revealed to the child that this particular box contains pencils instead of Smarties, she has superior knowledge in regard to the box. Now comes the test: She is asked what another person who enters the room will think is in the box. If the child understands that the other person does not know what she knows, she has constructed a simple ToM of the other. Otherwise she will project her knowledge on all others and say: "Pencils." Typically, children acquire the ability to have a ToM in between 4 and 4 ½ years, whereas monkeys and apes do not.

However, this construction of the other's knowledge can also go beyond simple forms of positive knowledge, as in the Smarties task, and include complex intuitions of the psychic makeup of someone else. Such complex knowledge typically leads us to expect certain forms or styles of behavior from people if we cannot explicate our expectation in the simple form of positive knowledge. In regard to the reading of fiction, Keith Oatley has suggested that we "simulate" characters in our mind, run them in our mind like a computer program (Oatley 1994).

In fact, a trend in narrative fictions of the past two centuries can support this claim. Within the German literary canon it has become commonplace since the classics (Goethe, Schiller, Moritz) that characters can best be understood in light of their traumatic past that has shaped them and continues to haunt them (for the English context, see Pfau 2005). There are many famous works of fiction that culminate in the one moment in which readers / spectators finally get to learn the one past primal scene that has shaped a character and explains why he / she has behaved in a certain way. The first detective story of modern times, E. T. A. Hoffmann's *Mademoiselle Scudery* (1819), shows this: everything falls into place once we know that the serial killer is endlessly repeating a (prenatal) childhood trauma. Not only does this revelation immediately solve a mysterious crime, it also allows the reader to create a ToM of the serial killer by taking his prenatal experiences into account (regardless of how believable we find it).

Whereas the constructionist approach attempts to build up the other from within, the speculative approach comes from the outside and aims to build a bridge to a being assumed to be more or less incomprehensible. Instead of slipping into the shoes of the other, we are supposed to sketch the contour of the footprint in order to realize that there must be someone there. The approximation of the other can be seen as an infinite process. In fact, contemporary Continental philosophy utilizes Kant's analysis of the sublime as a paradoxical approximation of empathy for the other. Whereas it appears to be impossible to ever comprehend the other, thinkers such as Emanuel Levinas have postulated an ethical demand to engage nevertheless in the impossible hermeneutic process that aims for the other.

The strategic approach to approximation does not necessarily involve a full-fetched representation of the other in my mind, but rather identifies the areas where I and the other will collide or cooperate. It is obvious that there can be an evolutionary advantage if I understand that the other desires the same object that I desire. Once I have this insight about the other, I can adapt my behavior and develop strategies that may lead me to the object faster.[1]

It should be added that the model of approximation and the theory of similarity described in section one do not necessarily exclude each other. One could always argue that every element of approximation (reading facial expressions, making sense of past trauma, adopting a perspective of the other, etc.) is deep down based on similarity. We can read each of these elements because we implicitly assume that the other person experiences these events and feelings just as we would. Nevertheless, the basic assumption of the approximation model is that the other person is different from us, perhaps even unknowable to us, and can only be comprehended based on operations of intelligent guesswork.

Another potentially weakening aspect of this model is that it downplays the special status of empathy. If the constructionist model of approximation holds true, then empathy is little more than one of the many arenas of abstract thought. Man can construct, piece together everything in his mind, houses, machines, people. The emergence of abstract thought and the ability to detach ourselves from ourselves then would be the key evolutionary device we need to look for, not social development.

4. Narrative empathy

There is at least some evidence for each of the three basic models of empathy discussed above. As we have noted, the different models do not necessarily contradict each other. Empathy may just be an imprecise concept capturing a variety of phenomena.[2] Still, there is also some conflict between the different notions. For example, the calculation of the reciprocity model of empathy apparently is not limited to a core similarity. And the approximation model of empathy seems to come into play only because a core similarity and immediate understanding seems not to be given.

In the following, I want to suggest a fourth model that combines aspects of the three models described above. This fourth model cannot claim the beauty of radical simplicity. Instead, its beauty, so to speak, lies in providing a complex matrix from which all actual cases of empathy would be simplifications. Its starting assumption is that empathy occurs in a process that is deeply embedded in a temporal-narrative order. Another feature of this model is that it takes the basic frame of all models of empathy, namely someone observing someone (be it a person, a fellow species member, or a fictional construct), as a form that is reduplicated within the process of empathy as an internal distinction that appears in the observed action.[3]

The latter point will become clear below. For now it is enough to suggest that empathy may not just require a person A whom we observe, but an entire theatrical scene that binds an observer (empathizer) to an action executed by a character B and received by character A.

The starting point of empathy, I suggest, is an interaction that involves an active agent (B) and a passive agent (A), that is, subject and object, or perpetrator and victim. The empathizer observes this scene with two characters and their opposite tendencies (the one acting on the other). That is, already in its starting point, it is a social moment. And it is the core situation of fiction reading: the reader reads what B is doing to A. The observer (or reader) can relate to character / person A because A is in a specific setting (dominated by B) that is known to the observer. The bond between the observer and A is not necessarily based on some bodily or psychic deep similarity. Rather, there is a spontaneous commonality between the act of observing A and the suffering inflicted on A. The empathizer observes how A observes what B is doing with her or him.

This spontaneous commonality becomes more obvious when we look at what we mean when we say that we "observe" something. Observation is only partially an active process. In fact, it is possible only because of controlled inaction. We need to be quiet to observe, we do not usually intervene, and are waiting for the actions of others. Hence it would be more precise to say: "I am (passively) impressed by my (active) observations." That is, the observer shares, in a crude way, the setting with A: both are at the receiving end of the effects of actions initiated by B. Narrative empathy erects a bridge from the observer to the observed to the degree that the act of observation finds itself reflected, reduplicated in a social scene between two or more agents. Within the language of ToM we could say: empathy is possible when the observer registers what the other can see, feel, observe; the observer understands that the other is also an observer. From this it follows that one does not simply have empathy with A. It is more precise to say that one empathizes with the effect of B's action on A to the degree that it corresponds to the observer's position of observation. In other words, the (external) observer stops being a neutral bystander, but is drawn into or finds himself / herself involved in what he / she observes.

The question remains how this crude similarity or analogy between A's observation and the empathizer's observation of an observation triggers an emotional reaction by the empathizer. What allows the mere analogy of two observations to "skip" between people? Again, I can only offer a hypothesis. We have to assume that the observation of an analogy by the empathizer (which could be called a third-order observation, since it compares A's first-order observation of B to his second-order observation of A) creates the impression of identity. The observer projects identity of emotional reaction based on observed similar situations of passivity / victimization. Projection, in this sense, becomes a vehicle of cognition. If we follow this logic to its end, empathetic emotion would, thus, turn out to be the effect of affect or payback for our self-inflicted passivity of observation. Since we force ourselves to be quiet and observe, we experience the reward for our silence in the form of shared affections between our passivity and the observed objects (that we see as similar to us).

So far, I have suggested that the passive agent is the more likely recipient of empathy by an observer due to a basic passivity in observation. Our inability as observers to intervene, which is especially pronounced in media settings, may thus directly fuel our capacity to empathize. Perhaps this helps to explain why empathy favors victims and is not far from compassion or pity.[4] Nevertheless, this structure also allows for empathy with agents (B) since, in the first place, (almost) every agent can be constructed as reacting to others' actions. Even the classical hero reacts to the prior actions of others and thus can be seen as the (passive) recipient of an action. Secondly, there is also an active element involved in the observation of the empathizer, and this active element can be reduplicated in the observed. The act of choosing what to observe is the active moment in my observing that I can experience as corresponding to the activity of B.

There are two prerequisites for this narrative empathy. Each could have been decisive in its evolutionary development. A word of caution has to be added first. Evolutionary narratives have a huge appeal, not only among scientists. Perhaps the success of Darwinism can partly be explained by the lure to invent stories that favor the fittest in various settings, such as social Darwinism. Certainly, we can expect that there is a true evolutionary story of empathy. However, it is easily possible to invent ten others that also seem to make sense. I mention this as a cautionary device, since I do not think I can justify offering such an evolutionary narrative for this fourth model of narrative empathy at this point. Nevertheless, if pressed, such a narrative of the origin of narrative empathy could involve the moment of taking sides.

Social beings often find themselves in the position of observing two (or more) other members of their clan engaged in a fight. This is obviously a case of the core situation of model 4. There are situations in which it is not obvious which side the bystander / observer should take. One strategy could be to side with the dominant individual who is likely to be the victor. The benefits for the observer are obvious. If the dominant individual wins the fight as expected, and the observer showed sign of support, this may help the observer. However, there is also a benefit in taking the side of the weaker individual involved in the fight. The more such seemingly unwise support is offered, the less attractive the victory is for the dominant individual. The payback for such sympathy with the loser could be a long-term weakening of social stratification. The less glorious the victory is, that is, the less sympathy it buys the winner from the group, the weaker the hierarchies would get. And weakened social hierarchy or, put positively, a more flexible social hierarchy adds a series of evolutionary advantages. What is important here for our context is that choosing sides aligns the bystander / observer with one of the fighting parties. Even though the observer is not himself / herself active, he or she experiences the fight from the perspective of one of the parties. Hence, it seems at least plausible that the ability to take sides by social beings has a key function in developing empathy.

There is at least one popular form of behavior today that cherishes the taking of sides: watching sports. Almost all sports that enjoy large spectatorships are competitive. And apparently, the interest of the spectators is significantly heightened if they choose a side (or have already chosen such a side long before). Sport spectators commonly report that "it is more fun" to follow the events of a match by aligning oneself with one or the other team. Hence, it seems reasonable that social beings such as humans have learned to choose sides even in arbitrary situations (such as sports). Hence, the fight that emerges within a clan will certainly affect all and they react to the commotion by choosing sides, thereby getting involved. Empathy could have been a further development of this capacity of choosing a side.

Another prerequisite for narrative empathy is the awareness of one's weakness. Model 4 assumes that one is more likely to empathize with the passive agent or victim since the observer shares the structural position of being more passive with the victim. Hence, one needs to assume that there is a certain core sensibility to one's weakness, an *Ur*-experience or *Ur*-feeling of being vulnerable.

To conclude: model 4 shifts empathy from a particular person (or fictional construct or species member) to an entire situation or scene. Such a scene or situation is composed of several individuals and perhaps could be described as the simultaneity of several perspectives, as in ToM of higher intensionality (as in: I suspect that you think that she wants to steal his cookie). Model 4 assumes that the core activity of empathy, namely observation, is not neutral to empathy, but rather provides the key structure that the empathizee finds reflected within the scene he or she observes. The external observation by the observer finds itself reduplicated within the observed scene as a basic distinction, such as activeness and passivity, expression and impression, or domination and subordination. Hence, the observed scene and the observer are linked by means of some spontaneous commonality that arises from the act of observation. Empathy is, first of all, a second-order observation in which the second-order observer is drawn back into the picture of first-order observation. Perhaps this, then, is my contribution to current discussions of empathy: to complicate the act of observation by the empathizer.

Notes

1 This view is held by many evolutionary biologists, as well as literary anthropologist René Girard, who argues that love derives from a competitive or mimetic desire, namely a situation of competition that will make objects desirable to a being only because he or she observes that his competitor wants the object (Girard 1966).

2 Evan Thompson, for example, distinguishes four levels of empathy, ranging from the passive association of bodies to ethical responsibility (Thompson 2001).

3 In system theories such a reduplication of an external distinction within the system is called "re-entry" (see Spencer-Brown 1969 and the works of Niklas Luhmann).

4 Martha Nussbaum disagrees with this assessment and argues that empathy is rather neutral whereas compassion is an active, ethical process (Nussbaum 2001).

Works Cited

Bateson, Paul P., and Robert A. Hinde, eds. *Growing Points in Ethology.* Cambridge: Cambridge University Press, 1976. Print.

Berlant, Lauren, ed. *Compassion: The Culture and Politics of an Emotion.* New York and London: Routledge, 2004. Print.

Breithaupt, Fritz. *Kulturen der Empathie.* Frankfurt: Suhrkamp, 2009. Print.

---. *Der Ich-Effekt des Geldes. Zur Geschichte einer Legitimationsfigur.* Frankfurt: Fischer Verlag, 2008. Print. (=2008a)

---. "How I feel your Pain: Lessing's Mitleid, Goethe's Anagnorisis, Fontane's Quiet Perversion." *Deutsche Vierteljahrschrift* (DVjs) (Sept. 2008): 400-23. Print. (=2008b)

Carver, Joseph M. "Love and Stockholm Syndrome: The Mystery of Loving an Abuser." 1 Oct. 2007. Web. http://counsellingresource.com/quizzes/stockholm/part-2.html.

Dunbar, Robin. "The Social Brain Hypothesis." *Evolutionary Anthropology* 6 (1998): 178-90. Print.

---. *Grooming, Gossip, and the Evolution of Language.* Cambridge: Harvard University Press, 1996. Print.

---. "Neocortex size as a constraint on group size in primates." *Journal of Human Evolution* 22 (1992): 469-93. Print.

Dunbar, Robert, Louise Barrett, and John Lycett. *Evolutionary Psychology.* Oxford: Oneworld, 2007. Print.

Edelman, Lee. "Compassion Compulsion." *Compassion: The Culture and Politics of an Emotion.* Ed. Lauren Berlant. New York and London: Routledge, 2004. 159-86. Print.

Frijda, Nico H. *The Laws of Emotion.* Mahwah and London: Lawrence Erlbaum, 2007. Print.

Gallese, Vittorio. "The Manifold Nature of Interpersonal Relations: The Quest for a Common Mechanism." *Philosophical Transactions of the Royal Society of London* 358 (2003): 517-28. Print.

---. "The Shared Manifold Hypothesis: From Mirror Neurons to Empathy." *Journal of Consciousness Studies* 8. 5-7 (2001): 33-50. Print.

Girard, René. *Deceit, Desire and the Novel: Self and Other in Literary Structure.* Baltimore: Johns Hopkins University Press, 1966. Print.

Gopnik, Alison, and Virginia Slaughter. "Young Children's Understanding of Changes in their Mental States." *Child Development* 62 (1991): 98-110. Print.

Humphrey, N. K. "The Social Function of Intellect." *Growing Points in Ethology.* Eds. Paul P. Bateson and Robert A. Hinde. Cambridge: Cambridge University Press, 1976. 303-17. Print.

Kappeler, Peter M., and Carel P. Schaik, eds. *Cooperation in Primates and Humans. Mechanisms and Evolution.* Berlin, Heidelberg: Springer, 2006. Print.

Lessing, Gottfried Ephraim. *Hamburg Dramaturgy.* Trans. Helen Zimmer. New York: Dover, 1962 [1769]. Print.

Merleau-Ponty, Maurice. *The Primacy of Perception.* Evanston: Northwestern University Press, 1964. Print.

Nussbaum, Martha. *Upheavals of Thought. The Intelligence of Emotions.* Cambridge: Cambridge University Press, 2001. Print.

Oatley, Keith. "A Taxonomy of Emotions of Literary Response and a Theory of Identification in Fictional Narrative." *Poetics* 23 (1994): 53-74. Print.

Pfau, Thomas. *Romantic Moods: Paranoia, Trauma, and Melancholy, 1790-1840.* Baltimore: Johns Hopkins University Press, 2005. Print.

Premack, David, and Guy Woodruff. "Does the Chimpanzee have a Theory of Mind?" *Behavioral and Brain Science* 1 (1978): 515-26. Print.

Regner, Freihart. "Unbewußte Liebesbeziehung zum Folterer? Kritik und Alternativen zu einer 'Psychodynamik der traumatischen Reaktion.'" *Zeitschrift für Politische Psychologie* 8 (2000): 429-52. Print.

Spencer-Brown, George. *Laws of Form*. London: Allen and Unwin, 1969. Print.

Thompson, Evan. "Empathy and Consciousness." *Journal of Consciousness Studies* 8. 5-7 (2001): 1-32. Print.

Trivers, Robert L. "The Evolution of Reciprocal Altruism." *Quarterly Review of Biology* 46 (1971): 25-57. Print.

de Waal, Frans. *Primates and Philosophers: How Morality Evolved*. Princeton: Princeton University Press, 2006. Print.

---, and Sarah F. Brosnan. "Simple and Complex Reciprocity in Primates." *Cooperation in Primates and Humans. Mechanisms and Evolution.* Eds. Peter M. Kappeler and Carel P. Schaik. Berlin, Heidelberg: Springer, 2006. 85-106. Print.

Wahrman, Dror. *The Making of the Modern Self: Identity and Culture in Eighteenth-Century England*. New Haven and London: Yale University Press, 2004. Print.

Theory of Mind and the Conscience in *El casamiento engañoso*

José Barroso Castro

"I have been taught candor from my birth," said Edith; "and, if I am to speak at all, I must utter my real sentiments. God only can judge the heart—men must estimate intentions by actions." —Walter Scott, *Old Mortality*

A billiard table in the Republic of Literature

The Deceitful Marriage and *Colloquy of the Dogs* are two interrelated novels that belong to a collection that Cervantes calls *Novelas ejemplares* (*Exemplary Stories*). In the prologue of his work, Cervantes provides a fictional portrait of himself with clear physical traits and personality. He argues that the reader would be interested in knowing "el rostro y talle [de] quien se atreve a salir con tantas invenciones en la plaza del mundo" (16); "what kind of face and figure belong to him who has had the boldness to come out in the market place of the world and exhibit so many inventions" (3). This prologue brings the fictional realm closer to the frontier of the real world, an area that classic narratology has labeled as extradiegetic. In this frontier land, Cervantes seeks recognition as a distinguished member of the realm of fiction since he presents himself as the creator of inventions in what he calls "la plaza de nuestra república" ("the Republic of Literature"); inventions, not only in the ancient rhetorical sense of *inventiones*, but above all, in the new literary model sense, exemplified by *Don Quijote*. With this identity card—or passport to the fictional world—he is ready to present the novelty of these stories using an interesting metaphor, that of a billiard table:

> Mi intento ha sido poner en la plaza de nuestra república una mesa de trucos, donde cada uno pueda llegar a entretenerse, sin daño de barras; digo, sin daño del alma ni del cuerpo, porque los ejercicios honestos y agradables, antes aprovechan que dañan. [. . .] Horas hay de recreación, donde el afligido espíritu descanse. (18)

> [My intention has been to set up in the public square of our country a billiard table where everyone may come to amuse himself without harm to body or soul; for decent and pleasing pastimes are profitable rather than harmful. [. . .] There is a time for recreation, when the tired mind seeks repose.] (5)

A prologue should be the first transition from real to possible worlds. Cervantes takes advantage of it, and sets the most fundamental basis of fiction by "crossing somehow the world boundary between the realms of the actual and the possible" (Doležel 20). Consequently, he makes a "declaration of intentions" while proposing the metaphor of fiction as billiard table ("mesa de trucos"). This metaphor engenders an experience of intelligibility that provides the experience of positioning oneself in an arena of fiction. Therefore, Cervantes's main intention consists of putting the reader on the right track of that experience in such a way that his or her fictional mind ("body and soul") is ready to play inside a possible world ("a billiard table"). Now everyone has their identity card in hand and ready for a fictional world: the personal author (his figure and his soul) portrayed as an inventor and the reader engaged in an enterprise of entertainment "without harm for the soul and the body." In other words, the author has created a fictional mind for a fictional world. I insist on the term "fictional mind," for it is the author's same insistence on a body and a soul as protagonists of a possible world. In fact, Cervantes's creation of a fictional mind suggests the very definition of fiction: a "construct of the mind" (Ryan 19). However, we need to be more precise, since this fictional world belongs to the field of storyworlds, "possible worlds that are constructed by language through a performative force that is granted by cultural convention" (Palmer 33). That is why Cervantes prefers to place his billiard table in the Republic of Literature, that is, in a Republic of conventions where the user of this play has at his disposal a user's manual.

In addition, a billiard table is play, and as far as crossing boundaries of fiction is concerned, "play is a space between reality and imagination" (Bolton 220). And there is a final observation that the author emphasizes: this "performative force" granted by "cultural conventions" and available for possible worlds must keep the fictional mind immune to consequences; no moral damage should constitute the side effects of this play.

A FICTIONAL MIND FOR A FICTIONAL WORLD

However, in his prologue it seems that the author insists more on the role of the "body and the soul" as a fictional mind interacting with this fictional billiard table, than on the issue of a real world of prototypes inserted in a fictional world of characters. On the one hand, Cervantes could pursue the Renaissance formula of *imitatio* in the sense of "actual prototype" of universals being represented by "a fictional particular" (Doležel 9). On the other, since the "body and soul" is interacting with fiction, Cervantes could be pursuing a Neo-Aristotelian broader meaning of imitation, like the one stated by the Canon in *Don Quijote* who prefers that "Hanse de casar las fábulas mentirosas con el entendimiento de los que las leyeren" (*Quijote*, 548); "stories must be suitable for the intellect of the reader."[1] This comment reminds us of Doležel's warning that "persons with actual world 'prototypes' constitute a distinct semantic class within the set of fictional persons" (24-25).

In this prologue, Cervantes concerns himself with the mind, but not only the mind as a fictional agent, but also as a moral one. At first, it appears that Cervantes tries to escape a common transgression once denounced by Plato: the sin of evil *écriture*. In fact, most scholars agree that this "moral" urge to write is due to a desire to rid fiction of a bad Boccaccian "ambiguous moral reputation" of plots "full of sensuality and impudence" (García López xcv-xcvi). Indeed, Cervantes in his prologue poses a series of argumentative points that succeed, one after another, faulting all of them against this accusation of immoral transgression and defending his new literary model.

I propose that Cervantes's declaration of intentions is not designed to rid himself of the evil *écriture* reputation, but instead, to explain how the fictional mind can interact in a new fictional medium of a possible world. In addition, Cervantes claims at the end of his argumentation that "my mind [my wit] conceived" my novels (5-6). Therefore, what Cervantes wants to claim is his own fictional mind, plus that of the reader, their own semantics of fictionality, their own tricks in this new billiard table. There is no risk of doing the wrong thing: "there is not justification for two semantics of fictionality, one designed for 'realistic' fiction, the other for fantasy" (Doležel 19). We must study Cervantes's own semantics for possible world fictionality. He does not employ a real world basis with a more "essentialist" semantic, but a "transworld identity" with a more "nonessentialist" semantics (Doležel 16-17).

Therefore, what are Cervantes's semantics of fictionality? It is worth examining the mind ("wit" in Cervantes's terms) that has created it. And this mind, that of the implied author and those of his characters, can be visible by their actions and, to be precise, by their mental functioning: "their motives, intentions, and the resulting behavior and action" (Palmer 16). In a more extended definition: it is the "emotions, sensations, dispositions, beliefs, attitudes, intentions, motives, and reasons for action" (Palmer 13) of these characters that are more relevant to us. This look at the mind in action constitutes the basis of Cervantes's transworld identity that ultimately claims sovereignty over a fictional world.

Author's intentions

The implied author says: "my intention has been to set up in the public square of our country a billiard table" for entertainment without damage to the body and soul. His mind chooses a track where the exercise of reading and writing might have moral consequences and ultimately suggests a final judgment about the morality of the author's action of writing, of the reader's action of reading, and of the character's actions of representing. In other words, this mind posits a moral conscience in both parties: from the implied reader and his risk of possible moral damage and from the implied author who admits that he, too, has to account to God for his literary activity at the day of his reckoning. The implied author constructs within his fictional mind his own basis for a moral and religious conscience. He wants to make sure that the glass of his conscience of *écriture* (the glass of his fictional mind) is clean and transparent, and this is the primary condition under which he will claim his own authorship (in ethimological and moral terms "authority"). In this way, the reader imitates this same fictional semantics, and assigns a mental functioning for himself, the same as that of the implied author, implied reader, and the characters to follow.

ASPECTUAL SHAPE OF THE MIND

Therefore, in his prologue Cervantes is constructing a fictional mind ready for a fictional world. We need to study the mental functioning of this mind on its own terms. Every fictional mind has its own state of mind. In the real world, if we want to go to metaphysical levels of existence, there has to be a basic state of mind that constitutes the human consciousness also and consequently, a human being. According to Heidegger the *Befindlichkeit* is the basic mood by which human beings encounter (find) things and even their own existence (Heidegger, *Sein und Zeit* §29). There is not a neutral mood; the *Befindlichkeit* is the basic mood that constitutes our consciousness, and in turn, our own human being; we project our existence in the world ruled by this basic mood. This fundamental state of mind can be affirmative, negative, ironic, mystical, comic, parodist, tragic, and so on. I have argued in my book *Sobre la comprensión poética* that:

> El modo de percibir las cosas y de percibirse uno a sí mismo no se hace desde un estado aséptico sino desde una actitud previa o Befindlichkeit, temple o disposición envolvente (*SuZ,* §29) que perfila desde un primer momento las significaciones pues crea un ámbito de encuentro en que son bien o mal recibidas. (Barroso 39)
>
> [*Befindlichkeit* consists of the mood or the disposition by which our encounter with meaning is sketched, in such a way that from the very point of entrance to fiction we construct an atmosphere where sense is welcomed or discouraged.]

The basic mood of a fictional mind is significant for the construction of a semantics of fiction. This mood or *Befindlichkeit* has its own narrative counterpart. For instance, Alan Palmer reports Searle's theory that "every intentional state has what he calls an *aspectual shape.* This means that my conscious experiences are always from a point of view, are always perspectival . . . all seeing is seeing as" (Searle 131). Seen though Searle's perspective, Cervantes is setting a basic fictional perspective or aspectual shape (a basic state of mind) ruled by two interrelated axis: 1) an inner aspectual attitude of "play" and "recreation" of a "billiard table" ready for a mind—and in this case a soul—who is affected ("afligido" in the sense of "destressed") by the stresses of life ("donde el afligido espíritu descanse"); 2) a social aspectual disposition toward respecting a moral entertainment into which a reader's "body and soul" are welcomed into the public square of Literature and protected from any moral damage.

WRITING AND READING CONSCIENCE

In the end, in his fiction Cervantes is claiming responsibility: he claims "authority" for the author and responsibility for the reader; that is, conscience in invention and in reading. In the earlier times during which Cervantes wrote, comedy—one of the basis of the origin of the novel—was less demanding, both for the author and for the reader: there was a rhetorical manual ready for everybody, and less freedom in creating fiction. Instead, Cervantes writes with more freedom, and that is why he is claiming sovereignty over his fiction; for this reason, both an authentic attitude in shape for entertainment and a disposition of active compromise in fiction are necessary. In this sense, Cervantes constructs a fictional mind for a fictional world. This attitude of compromise extends into a transcendental mentality that is concerned with preparing himself to account to God for his actions. In the end this responsibility turns out to be a writing and a reading conscience.

Ready for tricks: three levels of invention

Now that the setting of fiction and fictional mind in the prologue has been analyzed, I would like to discuss *The Deceitful Marriage* and *Colloquy of the Dogs* by placing the "mesa de trucos" on a simple level of narrative strategies, that is, those old and new tricks, accepted or not in the world of pure narrative conventions. Cervantes is very concerned with the art of narration, with speculation and experimentation in fictional invention, but he is also committed to the search of truth and sense in his fiction. Indeed, in these two interrelated novels that I analyze here, Cervantes can be very speculative with narrative, given that he is continuously playing with different levels of fiction. In fact, the *Colloquy of the Dogs* is embedded in *The Deceitful Marriage*. One of the main characters of *The Deceitful Marriage* transcribes the *Colloquy* by memory and the other main character proceeds to read it. The reader must circulate through the different levels: the intradiegetic level of *The Deceitful Marriage*, the metadiegetic level of *The Colloquy of the Dogs* embedded in *The Deceitful Marriage* and the extradiegetic level of the Prologue where the author portraits himself and surrounds fiction with his personal portrait and his fictional metaphor of the billiard table.

A moral issue: A captive mind

A moral issue is under discussion in *The Deceitful Marriage*, since the Ensign Campuzano is forced to explain to his friend Peralta the reason why in the Hospital of Resurrection he received a sweat treatment for syphilis. Campuzano explains to his friend how his marriage was arranged between Doña Estefanía and him, a woman whom he met at an inn, and who suspiciously practiced a kind of "tapada" ("prostitution"). Campuzano is reporting to Peralta why this marriage failed. He has been deceived by Doña Estefanía but also she has been deceived by Campuzano; both of them committed to their marriage arrangement with bad intentions and with economic interests. No love and service are the basis of this marriage, if we consider these two last terms from a Christian point of view.

The levels of intelligibility of this marriage arrangement are set by Campuzano himself in terms of a mental functioning close to the Spanish Golden Age theory of the mind:

> Yo tenía entonces el juicio no en la cabeza, sino en los carcañares, haciéndoseme el deleite en aquel punto mayor de lo que en la imaginación le pintaba, y ofreciéndoseme tan a la vista la cantidad de hacienda, que ya la contemplaba en dineros convertida, sin hacer otros discursos de aquellos que daba lugar el gusto, que me tenía echados grillos al entendimiento, le dije que yo era el venturoso y bien afortunado en haberme dado el cielo, casi por milagro, tal compañera. (526)
>
> [At that time I had my judgment in my heels rather than in my head, and as the pleasure seemed just then greater even than I had imagined it, and all of that property in front of me as good as cash already, without stopping to look for any arguments beyond my own wishes, which had quite overcome my intellect, I told her that I was the most fortunate of persons to have been presented with this heaven-sent miracle, a companion like this to be the mistress of my will and possessions.] (184)

According to the Scholastic Theory of Mind (ToM), the imagination—a secondary faculty of the soul—is the intellectual process operation that results from the perception of something, a faculty that puts in mind the *phantasmata* or mental data received from the senses; in other words, the physical data are replaced by an abstraction in the intellect in terms of the concept and the image of the thing itself.[2] This mental functioning consists in an intellectual-centered practical reasoning. The thing perceived is Doña Estefanía's property, and the image and the concept in Campuzano's corrupt intellect is money ("hacienda"). On the other hand, the judgment plays its role in his mental process since it is the faculty of the soul that enables the intellect to accommodate universal intuitions of the wit to particular circumstances.[3] So ultimately, Campuzano is unable to select and translate properly and morally the data (these particular circumstances) that have been offered by Estefanía, given that wit's only universal intuition is pleasure and own wishes. Consequently, the intellect is captive to a corrupt moral context of intelligibility. The universal intuition should be a love blessed by the Holy Spirit within the context of a matrimony declared a Holy Sacrament by the Council of Trent. But neither Estefanía nor the Ensign Campuzano had respect for this sacramental component of marriage. Estefanía left him, escaped with a lover, and took his jewels, although she did not know that these jewels (especially a chain) were artificial.[4] Ultimately Campuzano faces two problems: forty days in hospital for syphilis treatment and the remorse of his conscience since he has to deal with "the evil intentions with which I had embarked on that affair" (185).[5]

Until this point, the reader has experienced the topical plot of a deceitful marriage that could be found in any Italian *novella*. However, ultimately Campuzano's imagination—as his secondary faculty of soul—is captive to his remorse in his conscience: that woman "even without looking for her, she's is always in my imagination and wherever I am my disgrace goes with me" (189).[6] He has become the victim of a bad and unblessed use of intellect and this leaves his conscience to plague him: "I was caught in my own trap; but I can't help feeling sorry for myself."[7] Later on we will see that Cervantes wants to complicate things, and open a new game in this billiard table: this attitude of remorse will become the basis for a new game: *The Colloquy of the Dogs.*

Campuzano's heart

Now that Campuzano's mental functioning has been explained by its own Golden Age semantics, let us return to one of our earlier arguments, that of fictional minds involved in fictional worlds. The reader is also engaged in the task of ascribing a fictional mind to Campuzano, in order to make sense of his mental network of intentions and motives. In this way, the readers and Peralta witness a case of embedded narrative as defined by Alan Palmer as "total perceptual and cognitive view point; ideological worldview; memories of the past; and the set of intentions, desires, beliefs, motives, and plans for the future of each character in the story presented in the discourse" (Palmer 183-84). Campuzano's mental functioning turns out to involve both practical and moral reasoning. His set of intentions could be considered in terms of beliefs and faith. In an eighteenth-century novel, such as Jane Austen's *Emma,* access to the fictional mind of a character is mostly regulated by emotions and feelings (Palmer 231). Cervantes's characters possess a fictional mind less psychologically sophisticated than *Emma,* though in its fictional presentation, it is more complex ontologically. He is concerned with a consciousness in action more than a mind in action; in other words, he prefers the mind's reflexivity in itself, but with the ingredient of practical reasoning. And whenever something subjective is presented, the issue under discussion is examined in terms of moral conscience, rather than psychology.

Let me address this mental functioning in the context of both rhetoric and the ToM present in the Spanish Golden Age. In this way, I will take as an assignment Palmer's task of answering this question: "What are the features of the fictional-mind constructions of a particular historical period that are characteristic of that period and different from other periods?" (Palmer 241). One first question to address is to ask whether it is reasonable to apply cognitive studies' current connections between cognition and emotion to a Spanish Golden Age worldview. For instance, Antonio Damasio says that "no sharp line divides thinking from feeling, nor does thinking inevitably precede feeling or vice versa" (Damasio, 313). Alan Palmer reports that "Jon Elster in *Alchemies of the Mind* (1999) continuously stresses interconnections between cognition and emotion, and argues that in practice they are difficult if not impossible to disentangle" (Palmer 19).

On the other hand, we have the medieval and Renaissance ToM of St. Augustine in which creatures are rational and intelligent in their function of being imperfect mirrors of the Trinity's mind. This divine mind is composed of memory, intellect, and will: "memoria," "intelligentia," "voluntas" (*De Trinitate* XV, 22, 42). If there is an emotion in the soul, it is the love for God, not in a psychological sense, but in an ontological sense. Therefore, intellect, memory, and love constitute human mind: "ego enim memini per memoriam, intellego per intelligentiam, amo per amorem" (*De Trinitate* XV, 22, 42: "For it is I who remember by memory, and understand by understanding, and love by love"). In St. Augustine, love and cognition are inextricably linked, since both of them are at the same time ontological mirrors of the Trinity of God's mind. In *The Deceitful*

Marriage love is a religious and moral issue because human love became an economical transaction, and for this reason is not blessed by the Holy Spirit; that is, there is not the possibility to ascribe divine love to this human love.

At some point Campuzano's mental functioning is not pure practical reasoning since there is an "emotional" counterpart that it is worth analyzing: "I was beginning to despair, and doubtless would have done so if my guardian angel hadn't come to the rescue at that moment by reminding me that I was a Christian and that the worst sin a human being could fall into was that of despair, for it was a devilish sin" (188). The words "desesperarse" and "desesperación" can be interpreted in Old Spanish terms as "to commit suicide," but it is relevant to examine the word in the context in which it appears. Campuzano looks into his heart, which is the place where a Christian—following the Bible, St. Augustine, and other Church Fathers (De Magistro XII, 40, 82)—finds God's love, and he discovers that his heart turns out to be his own conscience speaking with great "candor." With this image, I remind the reader of Walter Scott's quotation that heads this essay, which I found in Alan Palmer's *Fictional Minds*. Campuzano addresses his own conscience, which responds in the form of his "guardian angel," and discovers that he—with his attitude—is moving away from the divine love to which his moral conscience is engaged. If we follow *Diccionario de Autoridades's* definition of "desesperación" we can understand the authentic semantics of Campuzano's attitude and mental functioning. This dictionary defines "desesperación" as "complete loss of hope, and par excellence can be meant to describe complete loss of Grace."[8] In this sense, Kierkegaard illuminates very well the meaning and the mental functioning of "desesperarse": "the desperate renounces the possibility (for 'to despair' exactly means 'to renounce the possibility'); to be more precise: he insolently dares to suppose the impossibility of good" (Kierkegaard 305).[9] In other words, this is the most specific definition of "sin;" in fact, Campuzano declares "la desesperación [es] pecado de demonios" ("dispair is a devilish sin"). In this sense, it is not by chance that the *Diccionario de Autoridades* gives Alejo de Venegas's example of this particular aspect of sin present in the "despair": "since Evil displays them, his real intention is not love, but to send him into despair."[10]

In this precise moment of despair, Campuzano seeks desperately to take revenge on Doña Estefanía, but "luck, for better or worse, determined that I couldn't find Doña Estefanía, hard though I looked. I went to [the church of] San Llorente, commended myself to Our Lady, sat down on a bench, and was so upset that I fell into a deep sleep" (188). Here we find a very strong example of how Golden Age mental functioning does not relate cognition with emotion as a psychological ongoing of actions. Campuzano's cognition operates in terms of conscience, and conscience operates in terms of transcendental mediation; in other words, revelation. And the most powerful mediator is the Virgin Mary. Again, not by chance in *Diccionario de Autoridades*' definition of "desesperación," we find a very apt example of the *Flos Sanctorum*: "if you feel suffocated by your own offenses, and you fear falling into the profound abyss of despair, think of the Virgin Mary."[11] Campuzano's cognitive mental functioning works within a supernatural belief structure. In this sense, mental functioning of revelation works within the confines of dream; there is no psychological process present. In fact, in the Bible there are many cases of dreams functioning as the repository of revelation. In conclusion, Campuzano's ToM is a combination of cognition, interaction between human and divine love, and divine revelation.

Campuzano's mind

However, his supernatural mental functioning inside a religious heart works in the context of practical reasoning, intellect and faculties of the soul. Considering the times in which Cervantes lived, the ToM applied to these times owes its theoretical standpoint to the Scholastics who ascribed to the Aristotelian and the Thomist anthropology of mind. Cervantes has much in common with this anthropology, but that said, he somehow breaks the limits of the ToM present in his times by extending the mental functioning of some of his characters to both mind and consciousness. According to Anthony Kenny in Achinas's ToM, intellect and will ("intelligence and rationality") are the two essential components of mind (Kenny 16). In contrast, in Cartesian ToM, the mind can be defined as consciousness in the sense of "the realm of whatever is accessible to introspection" (Kenny 17-18). Cervantes operates in a way in between: while using rationality in mental functioning, he plays with different levels of consciousness. However, consciousness in Cervantes is not psychological introspection, but ontological consciousness. Here Morón Arroyo clarifies that "between the theological worldview of Boccaccio and the psychological of Mme Lafayette, Cervantes should be placed in a ontological level" (*Para entender* 227). For instance, love in *Don Quijote* is presented with its essential properties (ontology) and not as a psychological series of personal feelings.[12] As far as Campuzano is concerned, he is a Christian; he follows a supernatural law that creates his own existence onthologically-speaking. For instance, when Campuzano is in despair, in the greatest depths of his Christian conscience he discovers a law inscribed in his heart, which is continuously listening to God (*Romans* 2, 14-16).[13] In conclusion, the other side of Campuzano's practical reasoning is this law that creates the nature of his own existence; that is, when he examines his mind, he is exploring his own ontology.

A new set in the billiard table

Let us examine the consequences of this ontological law in Campuzano's own embedded narrative and fictional capacity. Campuzano tells Peralta that one night (the one before he had the sweat treatment for the last time) behind his bed "and in the middle of the night, when it was dark and I was lying awake, thinking of my past adventures and misfortunes, I heard talking close by [. . .] and soon after I realized by what they said that it was the two dogs 'Scipio' and 'Berganza' who were talking" (191).[14] At this point, Campuzano decides to take a dare and to participate in the billiard table of possible worlds set by the implied author in the prologue. Campuzano defends himself from the impossibility of two talking dogs by explaining in detail what happened and how he has managed to overhear the conversation, and then transcribed it as the "Tale and Colloquy":

> "Well, there's another point", said the ensign. "Since I was listening so attentively, my mind [judgment] was in a delicate state, and my memory was also delicate, sharp and free of other concerns [. . .], I learnt it off by heart and wrote it down the next day in almost the same words in which I had heard it."[15]

In his report, Campuzano explains the situation in practical reasoning terms related to the levels of senses and faculties of the soul. He also displays his moral attitude in his explanation. His senses are attentive to voices since he declares that he was using "all of my five senses as God was pleased to give them to me" (192); but they are limited, given that his eyes cannot see the dogs. Two of his own faculties of the mind, judgment and memory, are unreliable engaged in "a delicate state" (192). If we take "delicado / delicate" to mean the secondary meaning of definitions "sickly or damaged," we realize these two faculties are limited. Furthermore his moral attitude could be on exercise of penance, since he admits that his thoughts were engaged "in my past adventures and misfortunes." In conclusion, this delicate situation deprives him again of a good use of his intellect.

However, in this bad state of both imagination and intellect, Campuzano dares to make a new strike for the reader and for his friend Peralta, with consequences in the teleology of the plot, which in the end, seems to be in continuous ups and downs as if one were playing at "a billiard table." In this new fictional situation or in this fictional trick of the billiard table, the reader has to fill gaps in Campuzano's own embedded narrative. The reader could be asking questions like: what are Campuzano's intentions in conveying these thoughts? How does he present his storyworld? What is his mental functioning? In my view, the penance for his sin could be a cue of his mental functioning and his fictional mind. Campuzano's report shows that both his mind and his fictional mind function intellectually, using practical reasoning and judgment. But whenever Campuzano wants to reach into the depths of his own mind, he does not embark on a psychological path. In contrast, during this self discovery, he confronts his own mind retreated into his own conscience, that is, looking for a final judgment in the morality of his actions. There is not a psychological process in this mental functioning. Instead, he experiences essential properties that he discovers in the ontology of both his soul and conscience. I argue that Campuzano's aspectual attitude toward his own storyworld is penance in the sense of his examination of those sins that made him turn aside from the natural and ontological law of divine love. In this sense, I agree with Ruth El Saffar in this statement: "the idea that evil exists so that man may choose his salvation is behind the Catholic belief in redemption through good works, and it is reflected in the *Casamiento-Coloquio*" (20). Therefore, there is a religious attitude devoted to the penance for his sins and consequently to the return to the law that rules his own human being; this attitude is the best way to salvation. In the period of the novel, the Sacrament of Penance, in its three typical steps (*contritio, confessio,* and *satisfactio*) was a common religious practice. In fact, this Sacrament was institutionalized by the Council of Trent. In this sense, I do not find in Cervantes's religious thought a secular and natural law as stated by Américo Castro and his followers. On the contrary, I agree with Muñoz Iglesias, who believes in "the increasing moral religious rigor of [Cervantes's] works" ("el creciente rigor moral de sus escritos" 326), but I cannot agree with Descouzis[16] who claims that Cervantes was committed to the Catholic Church to the extent that he was spreading in his works the canons and decrees of the Council of Trent.[17]

Campuzano's consciousness

There is a final point on Campuzano's embedded narrative that should be discussed. I believe and agree with other scholars that Cervantes's ToM and precisely that Campuzano's ToM possesses two sides of the same coin: on one side is the practical reasoning, and the other, the "consciousness." This "consciousness" is not a Cartesian introspection, but a Baroque consciousness of self-reflection. In this sense, I propose that Cervantes's trick of placing this storyworld (*The Colloquy of the Dogs)* inside the fictional mind of a character (Campuzano) and then reading this storyworld through the fictional mind of another character (Peralta) as if it were two embedded narratives in plain interaction is the best example of auto-reflexive fictional and ontological consciousness. This consciousness is auto-reflexive because it entails a play of mirrors of different fictional levels; it is ontological because of Campuzano's return to the law that governs his heart, a return that implies penance. In addition, these auto-reflexive effects are present in the conscience of both reader and author, since both of them are concerned with the possibility of an evil *écriture*.

Intellect in good shape

Now it is Peralta's turn to play at the billiard table. He opens the notebook that contains the *Colloquy,* and starts to read while Campuzano naps. Peralta uses a mental functioning that is similar in its logic to that of Campuzano's: senses, intellect, and moral attitude. He employs his own senses by "hearing" ("oiré") the written *Colloquy,* employs the faculties of his own soul. Peralta uses his intellect as he appreciates Campuzano's wit. And finally, has a moral attitude toward entertainment and toward the fictional world.

Peralta is skeptical about two talking dogs, but he wants to enjoy the fiction: "I shall be very happy to listen to this colloquy, which as it was written down from the notes of your ingenious self [wit], Ensign, I already adjudge to be good" (192).[18] This declaration suggests that Peralta's mental functioning will circumscribe the operation of reading in the limits of pure rhetoric and fiction because he wants to limit his faculties of the soul to a rhetorical operation of fictional invention. In other words, Peralta appreciates that Campuzano's wit has made possible worlds where the *res* selected does not come from real world (talking dogs), but from fiction with its own semantics; that is, his fictional mind is ready for a fictional world. In this operation, he uses wit and judgment in its rhetoric functions. Peralta's ToM operates in the rhetorical terms used in that period. For instance, according to Morón Arroyo's analysis on Juan de Valdes's *Diálogo de la lengua, intellect* has two faculties: "*wit* as the native capacity of invention, and the *judgment* as the capacity of selection and organization of discourse."[19] Finally, since Peralta does not accept real talking dogs in the realm of a fictional world, he takes the dialogue in an aspectual shape of "laughing and apparently making a joke of all that he had heard and of what he was expected to read" (193).[20] Peralta's reaction shapes his embedded narrative and fictional mind. When he has finished reading Campuzano's *Colloquy,* he does not want to discuss again the real possibility of two dogs talking. He remarks that his reading has entertained his intellect, enabling him to experience a fictional invention of a possible world: "Ensign, don't let's return to this argument. I appreciate the art of the colloquy and the invention you've shown, and that's enough. Let's go off on the Espolón and refresh our eyes, for my mind's [intellect] has been well refreshed" (252).[21] Peralta's primary conclusion is that his *intellect* is in good shape given that he has considered the process as one of "recreation." Peralta's point to Campuzano addresses the veracity of the material or *res* selected in the invention. Peralta understands that "this colloquy may be a fake and may never have happened" (252).[22] However, Peralta does not want to enter into the true material of the invention. He distinguishes what are the semantics of a real world and the semantics of a possible world very well. His intellect is in good shape.

BAD OR GOOD USE OF INTELLECT, AND A TRANSWORLD IDENTITY

Interestingly Peralta proves to have followed the implied author's guidelines in the Prologue for access to a fictional world: that of an attitude of "recreation" and "repose." In the reading of the *Colloquy,* there is ultimate reward and repose for Peralta and for the reader because both have used recreation to practice a "good" use of their intellect, a good use of their fictional mind. Campuzano employs his intellect with remorse, and within this remorse he invents the *Colloquy* as a result of being exercised by his act of penance for his sins. In this sense, either Williamson's assumption that Campuzano is not a sincere Christian because "he couldn't forgive" ("no ha sabido perdonar" 190) or El Saffar's opinion that Campuzano is a "redeemed sinner" (20) must be examined taking into account the symbolic basis of the *Colloquy.* At the end of the dialogue between the two dogs, Cipión, who is most of the time the voice of the philosopher and moralist, emphasizes the good or bad use of intellect by saying, "Virtue and good intellect are one and indivisible, whether naked or clothed, alone or in company. Of course it is true that these things can suffer as far as people's estimation of them is concerned, but not in their real merit and worth" (252).[23] Cipión's words about intellect must be taken symbolically and ethically. This symbolic semantics could be the cue for understanding Campuzano's intentions of his storyworld. In this sense, Cervantes creates his own semantics of fiction, not as a mimetic *imitatio,* but as more autonomously *invention.* Cervantes does not use the semantics of the real world, but instead, invents a new semantics by overlaying storyworld participants who employ fictional tricks of a possible world. In terms of ToM, this embedding situation is a Cervantes's illustration of how a fictional mind should behave in a possible and fictional world. For those purposes, Cervantes has chosen the billiard table of fiction encouraging different fictional tricks. These tricks can be played by any fictional mind and yet require a high level of autoreflexive consciousness. In this play where the fictional mind is the protagonist's, there are effects in the fictional and moral conscience of every other agent (author, reader, implied author, implied reader, characters). The "exemplary" lesson could be that reading and writing are both exercises of mental functioning and a moral functioning of conscience where every agent takes responsibility and during which there can be no "harm for the body and soul."

Notes

1 Translations are my own, unless indicated.

2 "imaginatio: alicuius rei conceptio et fictio, quae mente fit; vel imaginatio est quaedam motio per quam nobis simulacra quaepiam in anima gignuntur" (*Diccionario Covarrubias*).

3 "el hábito de acomodar las intuiciones universales del ingenio a las circunstancias particulares" (Morón Arroyo "Prólogo" 133).

4 "como no es todo oro lo que reluce, las cadenas, cintillos, joyas, brincos con solo ser de alquimia se contentaron, pero estaban tan bien hechas, que solo el toque o el fuego podia descubrir su malicia" (532).

5 "iba mudando en buena la mala intención con que aquel negocio había comenzado" (528).

6 "la hallo en mi imaginación y adonde quiere que estoy tengo mi afrenta presente" (533).

7 "Bien veo que quise engañar y fui engañado, porque me hirieron por mis propios filos; pero no puedo tener tan a raya el sentimiento, que no me queje de mí mismo" (533).

8 "pérdida total de la esperanza, y por antonomasia se entiende de los bienes eternos, Lat. *Desperatio*" (*Diccionario de Autoridades*).

9 "El desesperado *sabe* también lo que la posibilidad encierra, y sin embargo renuncia a la posibilidad (ya que desesperar no es otra cosa que renunciar a la posibilidad), o dicho con mayor exactitud, él tiene la osadía insolente de *suponer* la imposibilidad del bien" (*Las obras del amor* 305).

10 "y pues el Diablo a tal tiempo se los ofrece, no lo hace de charidad, sino por trahelle a desesperación" (ibid.).

11 "si te comienzas a ahogar por la graveza de tus delitos, y temes caer en el profundo abysmo de la desesperación, piensa en María" (ibid.).

12 "el amor aparece en una serie de variables que son propiedades esenciales del amor (ontología), pero no como un sentimiento personal con altibajos, dudas, celos y reacciones provocadas por la persona amada (psicología)" (Morón Arroyo, *Para entender* 228).

13 "For whenever the Gentiles, who do not have the law, do by nature the things required by the law, these who do not have the law are a law to themselves. They show that the work of the law is written in their hearts, as their conscience bears witness and their conflicting thoughts accuse or else defend them, on the day when God will judge the secrets of human hearts, according to my gospel through Christ Jesus" (Romans 2, 14-16).

14 "pensando en mis pasados sucesos y presentes desgracias, oí hablar allí junto . . . y a poco rato vine a conocer, por lo que hablaban, lo que hablaban, y eran los dos perros Cipión y Berganza" (535).

15 Pues en esto hay otra cosa—dijo el alférez—: que como yo estaba atento y tenía delicado el juicio, delicada, sotil y desocupada la memoria [. . .] todo lo tomé de coro, y casi por la mismas palabras que había oído lo escribí otro día (537).

16 Concerning the Sacrament of Penance, see Descouzis, "Meditaciones del Cautiverio. Decreto de la Penitencia," In *Cervantes, a nueva luz,* 158-69.

17 I agree with Enrique Moreno Báez that Cervantes "los decretos del Concilio prueba que los conocía…pero no que la obra fuera determinada en su concepción o en su desarrollo por ninguno de ellos" (Moreno Báez 247).

18 "de muy buena gana oiré ese coloquio, que por ser escrito y notado del buen ingenio del señor alférez ya le juzgo por bueno" (537).

19 "el entendimiento se concreta en dos funciones: el ingenio, que es la capacidad nativa e inmediata de inventar; y el juicio, la capacidad de selección y disposición" (Morón Arroyo, "Prólogo" 133).

20 "sacó del pecho un cartapacio y le puso en manos del licenciado, el cual le tomó riyéndose y como haciendo burla de todo lo que había oído y de lo que pensaba leer" (537).

21 "Señor alférez, no volvamos más a esta disputa. Yo alcanzo el artificio del coloquio y la invención, y basta. Vámonos al Espolón a recrear los ojos del cuerpo, pues ya he recreado los del entendimiento" (623).

22 "Aunque este coloquio sea fingido y nunca haya pasado" (623).

23 "hay algunos hombrecillos que a la sombra de sus amos se atreven a ser insolentes; y si acaso la muerte o otro accidente de fortuna derriba el árbol donde se arriman, luego se descubre y manifiesta su poco valor; porque, en efeto, no son de más quilates sus prendas que los que les dan sus dueños y valedores. La virtud y el buen entendimiento siempre es una y siempre es uno, desnudo o vestido, solo o acompañado. Bien es verdad que puede padecer acerca de la estimación de las gentes, mas no en la realidad de lo que merece y vale" (622-23).

WORKS CITED

Augustine of Hippo. *De Trinitate / La Trinità.* Rome: Città Nuova Editrice, 1973. Print.

---. "De Magistro / Del Maestro." *Obras filosóficas III.* Madrid: BAC, 1958. Print.

Barroso Castro, José. *Sobre la comprensión poética.* Madrid: Visor-Antonio Machado Libros, 2001. Print.

Bolton, Derek. "Self-Knowledge, Error and Disorder." *Mental Simulation: Evaluations and Applications.* Ed. Martin Davis and Tony Stone. Oxford: Blackwell, 1995. 209-34. Print.

Cervantes, Miguel de. "Prologue." *Three Exemplary Novels.* Trans. Samuel Putman. New York: The Viking Press, 1950. 3-6. Print.

---. *Don Quijote de la Mancha.* Ed. F. Rico. Barcelona: Crítica, 1998. Print.

---. *Exemplary Stories.* Trans. C. A. Jones. London: Penguin Classics, 1972. Print.

---. *Novelas ejemplares.* Ed. Jorge García López. Madrid: Galaxia Gutenberg, 2005. Print.

Damasio, Antonio. *The Feeling of What Happens: Body, Emotion and the Making of Consciousness.* San Diego: Harcourt, 1999. Print.

Decouzis, Paul. *Cervantes, a nueva luz.* Frankfurt: Klostermann, 1966. Print.

Doležel, Lubomir. *Heterocosmica—Fiction and Possible Worlds.* Baltimore: John Hopkins University Press, 1998. Print.

El Saffar, Ruth. *El Casamiento engañoso* and *El coloquio de los perros.* London: Grant and Cutler, 1976. Print.

Genette, Gerald. *Narrative Discourse. An Essay in Method.* Ithaca: Cornell University Press, 1983. Print.

García López, Jorge. "Introducción." Cervantes, Miguel de. *Novelas ejemplares.* Madrid: Galaxia Gutenberg, 2005. XLVII-CXVII. Print.

Heidegger, Martin, *Sein und Zeit.* Tübingen: Niemeyer, 2006. Print.

Kenny, Anthony. *Achinas on Mind.* New York: Routledge, 1993. Print.

Kierkegaard, Søren. *Las obras del amor.* Spanish Trans. Demetrio García Rivero and Victoria Alonso. Salamanca: Sígueme, 2006. Print.

Moreno Báez, Enrique. "Perfil ideológico de Cervantes." *Suma Cervantina.* Ed. J. B. Avalle-Arce and E. C. Riley. London: Tamesis, 1973. 233-73. Print.

Morón Arroyo, Ciriaco. "El prólogo del *Quijote* de 1605." *Studi in Memoria di Giovanni Allegra.* Ed. G. Mastrangelo Latini et al. Pisa: 1992. 125-44. Print.

---. *Para entender* El Quijote. Madrid: Rialp, 2005. Print.

Muñoz Iglesias, Salvador. *Lo religioso en* El Quijote. Toledo: Estudio Teológico de San Ildefonso, 1989. Print.

Palmer, Alan. *Fictional Minds.* Lincoln, NE: University of Nebraska Press, 2004. Print.

Ryan, Marie-Laurie. *Possible Worlds, Artificial Intelligence. Narrative Theory.* Bloomington, IN: Indiana University Press, 1991. Print.

Scott, Walter. *Old Mortality.* New York: Everyman's Library, 1968. Print.

Searle, John R. *The Rediscovery of Mind.* Cambridge, MA: MIT Press, 1992. Print.

Williamson, Edwin. "El juego de la verdad en *El Casamiento Engañoso* y *El Coloquio de los perros.*" *Actas del II Coloquio Internacional de la Asociación de Cervantistas.* Madrid: Anthropos, 1989. 183-200. Print.

Contributors

Robert S. Astur, PhD, is the director of the Virtual Reality Laboratory, Olin Neuropsychiatry Research Center in Hartford, Connecticut, and assistant professor adjunct in the Department of Psychiatry of Yale University School of Medicine. His current projects include: the application of virtual spatial memory tests to psychiatric groups with specific brain abnormalities; examining the effects of abused drugs on memory processes and brain activity; and deciphering the effects of gender and aging on memory processes.

José Barroso Castro received his PhD from Cornell University. He is currently Director of Editorial Mendaur, a Spanish press that publishes books on literature, humanism, religion, and the history of Spain and Europe. He is the author of two books on the theory of reading and textual criticism: *Sobre la comprensión poética* (Madrid: Visor-Antonio Machado Libros, 2001); and *Memorias da morte: A cultura clerical do pasamento* (Pobra do Caramiñal: Editorial Mendaur, 2009). Among his recent articles are: "Las Meninas y Don Quijote: dos modos para la identificación en mundos ética y poéticamente posibles," *Critica del testo* 9 (2006), 2-19; and "Conciencia en acto: autoextrañamiento y reminiscencias clásicas en "Adolescencia" de Vicente Aleixandre," *Iberoromania* 63 (2006), 27-51.

Ineke Bockting holds doctoral degrees from the Universities of Amsterdam, The Netherlands, and Montpellier, France. She has taught at universities in The Netherlands, Norway, and France, and she is now a full professor at the University of Paris, France. Her publications include articles on various aspects of the American South, ethnic literatures, travel-narrative, autobiography, and literary stylistics and pragmatics, as well as a book-length study of the novels of William Faulkner, entitled *Character and Personality in the Novels of William Faulkner: A Study in Psychostylistics* (Lanham: University Press of America, 1995).

Fritz Breithaupt received his PhD from Johns Hopkins University in 1997. He was the Distinguished Remak Scholar (2009-10) at Indiana University, where he teaches as associate professor of Germanic Studies and adjunct professor of Comparative Literature and Cognitive Science. He is the author of *Kulturen der Empathie* (Frankfurt: Suhrkamp, 2009); *Der Ich-Effekt des Geldes: Zur Geschichte einer Legitimationsfigur* (Frankfurt: Fischer, 2008); and a book on Johann Wolfgang Goethe entitled *Jenseits der Bilder: Goethes Politik der Wahrnehmung* (Rombach: Freiburg, 2000). At Indiana University he has served as director of West European Studies and the official EU Center of Excellence. He also writes a column on academia for the magazine *Zeit Campus*.

Diana Calderazzo is a PhD candidate in Theatre Arts at the University of Pittsburgh, currently living in Manhattan and writing her dissertation on cognitive-based approaches to experiencing and understanding the work of Stephen Sondheim. Her writing on related topics has appeared in *Theatre Journal*, *Theatre Symposium*, and *The Sondheim Review*. She teaches for Fordham University College of Liberal Studies in Westchester, New York.

Vince D. Calhoun, PhD, is the Director of Image Analysis of MR Research at The Mind Research Network in Albuquerque, New Mexico, where he develops techniques for making sense of complex brain imaging data. Because each imaging modality has limitations, the integration of these data is needed to understand the healthy and especially the disordered human brain. Calhoun has created algorithms that map dynamic networks of brain function, structure, and genetics, and how these are impacted while being stimulated by various tasks or in individuals with mental illness such as schizophrenia. He is associate professor within the Department of Electrical and Computer Engineering, Neurosciences, and Computer Science, at the University of New Mexico, and associate professor, adjunct, in the Department of Psychiatry at Yale University

Mikko Keskinen is Professor of Comparative Literature at the University of Jyväskylä, Finland. He is the author of *Response, Resistance, Deconstruction: Reading and Writing in / of Three Novels by John Updike* (Jyväskylä: Jyväskylä University Press, 1998) and *Audio Book: Essays on Sound Technologies in Narrative Fiction* (Lanham: Lexington Books, 2008). He has published numerous articles on literary theory and contemporary American, British, and French literature in journals such as *Critique*, *Journal of International Women's Studies*, *PsyArt*, *The Romanic Review*, and *Imaginaires*. His recent chapter-length contributions to edited volumes on criticism have appeared in *Novels of the Contemporary Extreme* (London: Continuum, 2006) and *Terrorism, Media, and the Ethics of Fiction: Transatlantic Perspectives on Don DeLillo* (London: Continuum, 2010).

Seth Knox received his PhD from the Department of Germanic and Slavic Languages at Wayne State University. He is currently Assistant Professor of German at Adrian College in Adrian, Michigan. Knox is the author of *Weimar Germany between Two Worlds:*

The American and Russian Travels of Kisch, Toller, Holitscher, Goldschmidt, and Rundt (New York: Lang, 2006). He is also the author of several entries in *The Greenwood Encyclopedia of Folktales and Fairy Tales* (Westport, CT: Greenwood, 2008) and "A Political Tourist Visits the Future: Ernst Toller's American and Russian Travels near the End of the Weimar Republic" in *Cross Cultural Travel: Papers from the Royal Irish Academy Modern Languages Symposium on Literature and Travel, National University of Ireland, Galway, November 2002* (New York: Lang, 2003).

Paula Leverage is Associate Professor of French and Medieval Studies, and Director of the Center for Cognitive Literary Studies, at Purdue University. She is a graduate of Cambridge University and Toronto University, where she first discovered cognitive theory as a doctoral student and Commonwealth Scholar. She is the author of *Memory and Reception: A Cognitive Approach to the Chansons de Geste* (Amsterdam: Rodopi, 2010) and has also published extensively on memory and literature in journals such as *Romania, Romance Notes, Dalhousie French Studies, Olifant*, and book collections.

Dan Lloyd is the Thomas C. Brownell Professor of Philosophy at Trinity College, Connecticut. He is the author of *Radiant Cool: A Novel Theory of Consciousness* (Cambridge: MIT Press, 2004), a book joining noir fiction with a theory of consciousness, and *Simple Minds* (Cambridge: MIT Press, 1989). His current projects include *Ghosts in the Machine* (Rowan and Littlefield, forthcoming), a philosophical dialogue about minds, brains, and computers, and *Subjective Time* (MIT Press, forthcoming), an anthology on the philosophy, psychology, and neuroscience of experienced temporality. He is the editor of the journal *Frontiers in Theoretical and Philosophical Psychology*, and in his spare time he likes to convert brain scan data into music.

Orley K. Marron teaches at Bar Ilan University, Israel, from which she received her PhD in English Literature. She has a MSc degree in Computer Science from Marist College as well as a BSc in biology from the University of Houston, where she worked for several years in neurobiology research. Her dissertation explored the function of animated man-made objects in the literature of Nathaniel Hawthorne and Lewis Carroll, and how such objects are used to convey algorithmic problem solving or moral dilemma resolution. Her current work explores Theories of Mind in science fiction, visual art in fantastic literature, and fantastic models for dealing with trauma.

Howard Mancing is Professor of Spanish at Purdue University. He is the author of *The Chivalric World of Don Quijote: Style, Structure, and Narrative Technique* (Columbia: University of Missouri Press, 1982); *Text, Theory, and Performance: Golden Age Comedia Studies*, co-edited with Charles Ganelin (West Lafayette: Purdue University Press, 1994); *The Cervantes Encyclopedia*, 2 vols. (Westport, CT: Greenwood, 2004); and *Miguel de Cervantes' "Don Quixote": A Reference Guide* (Westport, CT: Greenwood, 2006). In addition, he has published over forty articles and essays on Cervantes, Unamuno, *Lazarillo de Tormes*, and the picaresque novel, narrative theory, comparative literature, the canon, the teaching of literature, academic administration, cognitive approaches to the study of literature, and other subjects, in a variety of books and in journals such as *Anales Cervantinos*, *Cervantes*, *Estudios Públicos*, *Forum for Modern Language Studies*, *Hispania*, *Hispanic Review*, *Modern Language Notes*, *Modern Fiction Studies*, *Publications of the Modern Language Association of America*, and *Semiotica*. He is currently the President of the Cervantes Society of America. At the present time he is working on a book on cognitive science and literary theory tentatively titled *Voices in Everything: Restoring the Human Context to Literary Theory*.

Keith Oatley is Professor Emeritus of Cognitive Psychology at the University of Toronto, a Fellow of the Royal Society of Canada, and a Fellow of the British Psychological Society. His research focuses on the psychology of emotions and the psychology of fiction. He is the author or co-author of some 150 journal articles and chapters, and six books on psychology, including: *Best Laid Schemes: The Psychology of Emotions* (Cambridge, New York: Cambridge University Press, 1992) and *Selves in Relation: An Introduction to Psychotherapy and Groups* (London: Methuen, 1984). He has also written two novels, one of which, *The Case of Emily V.* (London: Secker and Warburg, 1993), won the 1994 Commonwealth Writers Prize for Best First Novel. He also edits and writes for *OnFiction: An Online Magazine on the Psychology of Fiction*.

Alan Palmer is an independent scholar living in London. He is the author of *Social Minds in the Novel* (Columbus: Ohio State University Press, 2010), and *Fictional Minds* (Lincoln: University of Nebraska Press, 2004). *Fictional Minds* was a co-winner of the Modern Language Association Prize for Independent Scholars and also a co-winner of the Perkins Prize (awarded by the International Society for the Study of Narrative). His articles have been published in the journals *Narrative*, *Semiotica*, and *Style*, and he has contributed chapters to several edited volumes. He is an honorary research fellow at the Department of Linguistics and English Language, Lancaster University.

Godfrey Pearlson, MD, is the director of the Olin Neuropsychiatry Research Center, a state-of-the-art fMRI facility in Hartford, Connecticut, and Professor of Psychiatry at the Yale University School of Medicine. His research projects include: identifying the structural and functional cerebral correlates of normal aging and of major neurodevelopmental and neurodegenerative psychiatric disorders; determining the functional cerebral actions of abused drugs; and exploring the interactions between genetics, neuroimaging, and pre-symptomatic expression of brain-based disorders in at-risk persons.

Natalie Phillips is a PhD candidate in English at Stanford University, where she is currently an American Council of Learned Societies / Mellon Fellow. Her current project, *Distraction: Problems of Attention in Eighteenth-Century Literature*, argues that the emergence of competing theories of attention in the Enlightenment transformed both how writers portrayed the fictional mind and how they sought to capture readers' focus.

She has received fellowships from the Stanford Humanities Center, the Mabelle McLeod Lewis Fund, and the Society for the History of Authorship, Reading, and Publishing. Her most recent article, "'Tis Tris': *Tristram Shandy* and the Literary History of a Cognitive Slip," has been solicited by *Modern Philology*, and her manuscript, "Economies of Attention: Readers and the Eighteenth-Century Essay," is forthcoming as a chapter in *The History of Reading* (New York: Palgrave Macmillan, 2011).

Klarina Priborkin received her PhD from Bar Ilan University, Israel. Her thesis, *Ghostly Bridges: Cross-Cultural Mother / Daughter Storytelling in Postmodern Texts by Ethnic American Women Writers*, focuses on problems of cross-cultural communication between ethnic mothers and their American-born daughters. Priborkin currently teaches English and American literature at Givat Washington College of Education. Her article "Mother's Dreams, Father's Stories: Family and Identity Construction in Chitra Banerjee Divakaruni's 'Queen of Dreams'" has been published in *South Asian Review* 29 (2009), 199-219. She has also published "Cross-Cultural Mind-Reading or Coming to Terms with the Ethnic Mother in Maxine Hong Kingston's *The Woman Warrior*" in *Toward a Cognitive Theory of Narrative Acts*, ed. Frederick Luis Aldama (Austin: University of Texas Press, 2010).

Richard Schweickert is Professor of Psychological Sciences at Purdue University. He developed an interest in dreams while working on his bachelor's degree in mathematics at Santa Clara University. After working as a statistician at Bellevue Psychiatric Hospital, he received his master's degree in mathematics from Indiana University and his PhD in mathematical psychology from the University of Michigan. His research is on network models of human information processing, short-term memory, and dreams. He has served as Associate Editor of *Psychonomic Bulletin & Review* and Editor of the *Journal of Mathematical Psychology*. He is a fellow of the American Association for the Advancement of Science and of the Association for Scientific Psychology.

Mark Turner is Institute Professor and Professor of Cognitive Science at Case Western Reserve University. He is the founding director of the Cognitive Science Network. His most recent book publication is an edited volume, *The Artful Mind: Cognitive Science and the Riddle of Human Creativity* (New York: Oxford University Press, 2006). His other books and articles include: *Cognitive Dimensions of Social Science: The Way We Think about Politics, Economics, Law, and Society* (New York: Oxford University Press, 2001); *The Literary Mind: The Origins of Thought and Language* (New York: Oxford University Press, 1996); *Reading Minds: The Study of English in the Age of Cognitive Science* (Princeton: Princeton University Press, 1991); and *Death is the Mother of Beauty: Mind, Metaphor, Criticism* (Chicago: University of Chicago Press, 1987). He has been a fellow of the Institute for Advanced Study, the John Simon Guggenheim Memorial Foundation, the Center for Advanced Study in the Behavioral Sciences, the National Humanities Center, the National Endowment for the Humanities, and the Institute of Advanced Study of Durham University. He is a fellow of the Institute for the Science of Origins, external research professor at the Krasnow Institute for Advanced Study in Cognitive Neuroscience, and distinguished fellow at the New England Institute for Cognitive Science and Evolutionary Psychology. In 1996, the Académie française awarded him the Prix du Rayonnement de la langue et de la littérature françaises.

Jennifer Marston William is Associate Professor and Chair of German at Purdue University. She has published a book on German literature, *Killing Time: Waiting Hierarchies in the Twentieth-Century German Novel* (Lewisburg: Bucknell University Press, 2010), in which she examines how cognitive metaphors have been used by German and Austrian novelists to reveal and criticize social hierarchical patterns. She has co-edited a critical edition of Anna Seghers's novella *Aufstand der Fischer von St. Barbara* (Berlin: Aufbau Verlag, 2002) and has published articles on German literature and film in such journals as *German Studies Review*, *The Germanic Review*, and the *Journal of the Kafka Society of America*. Her current projects include serving as co-editor for entries on German literature in *The Literary Encyclopedia* and a book on cognitive approaches to historical film.

Allen Wood, Professor of French, has been at Purdue University since 1984. He received his PhD from the University of Michigan in Comparative Literature. He has published *Literary Satire and Theory: A Study of Horace, Boileau, and Pope* (New York: Garland, 1985) and *Le Mythe de Phèdre: Les Hippolyte français du dix-septième siècle* (Paris: Honoré Champion, 1996), an edition of three seventeenth-century French tragedies treating the Phaedra plot. He has written some thirty articles on various aspects of seventeenth-century French literature, including the more recent "Racine's *Esther* and the Biblical / Modern Jew" in *Papers in Seventeenth Century French Literature* 36 (2009), 209-18, and a forthcoming study, "Molière's Miser, Old Age, and Potency" for *Age on Stage*, ed. Leni Marshall and Valerie Lipscomb (New York: Palgrave Macmillan, forthcoming). Professor Wood is also co-editor of the journal *Global Business Languages* and Editor in French for the Purdue Studies in Romance Literatures series.

Zhuangzhuang Xi is a graduate student in the Department of Psychological Sciences at Purdue University. She has a BS in Psychology and a BA in Economics, both from Peking University. She is a member of The Society for Mathematical Psychology and of The International Association for the Study of Dreams.

Lisa Zunshine is the Bush-Holbrook Professor of English at the University of Kentucky, Lexington. Her interests include eighteenth-century British literature, narrative theory, and cognitive cultural studies. She is the author of the first monograph on Theory of Mind and literature: *Why We Read Fiction: Theory of Mind and the Novel* (Columbus: Ohio State University Press, 2006), and the following books: *Bastards and Foundlings: Illegitimacy in Eighteenth-Century England* (Columbus: Ohio State University Press, 2005); *Strange Concepts and the Stories They Make Possible: Cognition, Culture, Narrative* (Baltimore: The Johns Hopkins University Press, 2008). She is co-editor (with Jocelyn

Harris) of *Approaches to Teaching the Novels of Samuel Richardson* (New York: Modern Language Association, 2006), and editor of *Introduction to Cognitive Cultural Studies* (Baltimore: The Johns Hopkins University Press, 2010).

Index

www.ingramcontent.com/pod-product-compliance
Lightning Source LLC
Chambersburg PA
CBHW071157100726
47908CB00002B/410